Antique Tra

Oriental

An
Identification
and Value
Guide

Antiques & Art

2ND EDITION

edited by
Mark F. Moran

© 2003 by Krause Publications

All rights reserved. No portion of this publication may be reproduced or transmitted in any form or by any means, electronic or mechanical, including photocopy, recording, or any information storage and retrieval system, without permission in writing from the publisher, except by a reviewer who may quote brief passages in a critical article or review to be printed in a magazine or newspaper, or electronically transmitted on radio or television.

Published by

krause publications
An F&W Publications Company

700 East State Street • Iola, WI 54990-0001
715-445-2214 • 888-457-2873
www.krause.com

Please call or write for our free catalog of publications. Our toll-free number to place an order or obtain a free catalog is 800-258-0929 or please use our regular business telephone 715-445-2214.

Library of Congress Catalog Number: 2003107995
ISBN: 0-87349-698-1

Printed in United States

Acknowledgments

Articles
Some of the articles contained in this volume have been reprinted with permission from the *Orientalia* journal.

Line Art (including Marks)
Carl Andacht

Photography
Mark Moran, Daniel Stone Studios, Floral Park, New York, and Tom Edson (photographs of the Edson and Luhn collections)

A special thanks to the following for their contributions and support: Leon and Toni Andors, Richard A. Bowser, Lee Chinalai, Leonard Davenport, Tom and Kay Edson, Arthur Field, Liz Fletcher, Mark Fogel, Paul Fogelberg, Richard and Karen Goodman, Harold Jaffe, Howard and Florence Kastriner, Charles Kelly, Virginia Keresey, Larry Kiss, Dr. Michael B. Krassner, Richard Lambert, Steve Leonard, Ina Levy, David Migden, Carol Mohlenhoff, Raymond Nickel, Gardner Pond, Dr. and Mrs. Bernard Rosett, Mrs. Florence Simon, and Dr. and Mrs. Sam Sokolov.

The authors' appreciation is also expressed to the press and Oriental departments of Christie's and Christie's East, New York City.

Contents

Introduction

Art and antiques from China, Japan, Korea, the Pacific Rim, and Southeast Asia have fascinated collectors for centuries. The study of treasures from even one of these areas has been a life's work for many devotees, but for the beginning collector, the main obstacle has always been the language.

Who are the Ainu? What is the origin of Banko pottery? How was a cha wan used? Why is the figure of Daruma so distinctive? How long did the Edo Period last? Are Guan Yin and Kuan Yin the same? What is the chief attribute of Jurojin? Would you want to drink from a kapala? Is the Manchu Dynasty known by other names? How did Mu Wang often travel? Should you be afraid of an oni? What's another name for paulownia? How did Rimpa painting get its name? What is the composition of sentoku? When did T'ien Chi rule China? How is an uchiwa different from other fans? Where was a yatate usually attached? When was Zeshin active?

The answers to all these questions may be found in the 4,000-word glossary that has been exhaustively researched to take some of the mystery out of collecting antiques and art from the Far East.

For instance, here's part of a sample description you might find in an antique shop, reference book, auction list, or price guide:

"Document box and cover, gold hiramakie, nashiji, takamakie, and hirame on roironuri ground with pine, grasses, and flowers in a continuous pattern ..."

Pretty confusing for the beginner, isn't it?

Here's what the detailed listings and glossary in *Antique Trader's Far East Antiques & Art* will tell you:

"Document box (called a 'bunko' in Japan) and cover, gold **hiramakie** (a Japanese lacquer technique, known as low relief, this technique was introduced in the Kamakura period [sources differ: either 1186 or 1192 to 1333]; a single layer of lacquer is applied to the ground, sprinkled with gold or silver powders, and allowed to dry; a coat of thin lacquer is then applied to fix the particles, and given a final polish), **nashiji** (irregularly shaped flakes of gold suspended in clear or yellowish lacquer; also called "pear ground," gold, silver, or gold-silver alloys of reddish-yellow coloration used on lacquer, principally as a ground), **takamakie** (high relief; this technique involves building up a design using two or more layers of lacquer or lacquer compounds; the final surface is usually decorated), and **hirame** (large, irregular flakes of gold roughly sprinkled on a black lacquer ground, also fat gold flakes used in lacquer decoration, named for their resemblance to a flounder) on **roironuri** ground (a waxy black or mirror-black finish; a brilliant and highly reflective black lacquer) with pine, grasses, and flowers in a continuous pattern …"

And that's just a tiny fraction of what you'll find. By tapping this wealth of information provided in *Antique Trader's Far East Antiques & Art*, the better equipped you'll be to start acquiring treasures of your own.

The gathering of information for this book was greatly assisted by appraiser James E. Billings of Minneapolis, who also served as a consulting editor; Richard K. Spence of Circle of the Moon Antiques in Cherry Hill, New Jersey; and Edgar L. Owen, Ltd. of Lake Hopatcong, New Jersey. Detailed contact information for each of these can be found in our "Resources" section.

Apparel and Textiles

CHINESE APPAREL

Early Chinese apparel was characterized by upturned slippers, flowing robes, full sleeves, unshaped shoulders, and a center front opening. With the beginning of the Manchu Dynasty, many fashion changes took effect: The shaved head and queue (long, hanging braid worn at the back of the head) replaced the Chinese topknot, for instance. The Manchu also redefined the style of clothing worn by both government and court officials, introducing slim belted trousers, boots, tight sleeves, close-fitting bodices (which overlapped on the front from left to right), horseshoe cuffs, and slits in the robes. The dragon robe, a semiformal court coat, was reserved for members of the Imperial family and for other nobles and officials. The five-clawed dragon was worn exclusively by the Emperor and his family.

In the mid-17th century, the Manchu rulers adopted the use of mandarin squares, badges worn to indicate rank. Civil officials wore various bird insignia, and animal insignia designated military officials (see accompanying table). A solid square was used for the back of an outer jacket, and a split square (two halves) was worn across the open front. The badges were

Mandarin Square Insignia (Listed by Rank)

RANK	CIVIL OFFICIALS	MILITARY OFFICIALS
First Order	Phoenix	Kylin (a mythical animal)
Second	Gold Bird (unidentified type)	Lion
Third	Peacock	Panther
Fourth	Crane	Tiger
Fifth	Pheasant	Bear
Sixth	Stork	Small Tiger
Seventh	Mandarin Duck	Rhinoceros
Eighth	Quail	Stork
Ninth	Paradise Flycatcher (similar to a sparrow)	Seahorse

appliqued in place and could be easily removed or changed as the wearer's rank was upgraded.

During the 19th century, wives of officials also wore mandarin squares. Their badges were mirror images of the ones worn by their spouses. For example, if an illustration shows a red sun disc on the upper right side of a mandarin square, then the square was worn by the wife of an official, since the husband's badge would show the disc at upper left.

JAPANESE APPAREL

During the 16th through 19th centuries, Japan's economic growth stimulated the rise of urban centers, a wealthy merchant class, and a sophisticated bourgeois culture. The decorative and applied arts flourished, and textile design was among the supreme arts. Clothes featuring dazzling designs and made with fabric that demonstrated innovative weaving techniques indicated status and wealth for the men and women of the shogunal and imperial courts, as well as those of the wealthy merchant class.

One particular Japanese garment that has become well known is the kimono. Originally a kosode (ladies' inner robe), it has evolved into a beautiful, elaborately decorated outer garment. This is how modern usage defines kimono, although the word is actually Japanese for clothing.

Obi (the cummerbund and back tie of the Japanese kimono) are just as collectible as the kimono. Often made of silk brocades with intricate patterns, they are used as wall hangings (panels) or converted into pillow covers.

Traditional Japanese Clothing Types

Traditional Japanese clothing can be divided into the following categories:

CLOTHING ACCESSORIES–obi (belt), shoes, socks, etc.
HAKAMA–Japanese pants
HAORI–short silk jackets
KIMONO–meaning clothing or things to wear–the basic Japanese clothing
MICHIYUKI–overcoats
NAGAJUGAN–undergarments
SHIRO-MAKU–wedding kimono
UCHIKAKE–most formal kimono
YUKATA–summer kimono

Apparel and Textile Values

Altar frontal, red silk ground worked in shades of blue, green, and white with gold couching and peacock feather filaments; writhing dragon amidst clouds and secondary dragons above a wave band; cloud and lishui stripe (from the name of the town of this style's origin in Guangdong Province, China); pleated short blue silk panels with peony roundels at the bottom; Chinese, late 19th century, 72 in. by 42 in. **$1,000-$1,500**

Altar frontal, blue silk brocade, woven-in gilt braid, primarily pale oranges, greens, and blues, four-toed dragon above waves, narrow border of meandering lotus (below a fringe) woven with a pair of dragons, Chinese, late 18th century, 36 in. by 33 in. **$2,000-$3,000**

Chinese altar table hanging made from iridescent red silk, decorated with embroidery designs of cranes, flowers, and pine trees, dating to the mid-19th century. With fine hand embroidery in designs that represent happiness and long life. The hanging is made in two pieces of silk. The overall fabric measures 38 in. by 38 in., with a 7 in. red cotton attachment at the top with tie strings. **$350**

Apron, green silk, front and back panels with couched gold dragons between phoenix and dragons on narrow pleats, Chinese, circa 1900, 36 1/2 in. long. **$600-$800**

Appliqué picture, framed, hand-painted silk, the kites with real feathers, Japanese, Meiji period, frame size 11 in. by 15 3/4 in. **$550-$750**

Banner, silk worked in colors; phoenix, cranes, lions, rock-work, flowers, fruit, and foliage on a red ground with green peacock feather filaments, all with a foliate gold-trimmed border; Chinese, circa 1900, 134 in. by 40 in. **$1,500-$2,500**

Coat, pink brocade (Benares), long flaring form with gold meandering flowers on a ground of pink floral sprigs, quilted lining, Indian, circa 1920, 54 in. long. **$300-$500**

Coat, blue broadcloth (Ainu) with lighter blue stitched pattern on the edges, Japanese, late 19th century. **$2,000-$3,000**

Coat, fireman's, canvas, measuring 51 in. by 28 in., Japanese, dating to the early 20th century. The coat is woven in traditional indigo blue with red and white highlights. The kanji on the back reads: Ohira. The collars show the name of the fire company as Matsubi Street Fire Fighting, 21 Public. The coat has some wear and some patches. The color has faded some from wear. **$150**

Kimono jacket or coat, silk, measuring approximately 50 in. from shoulder to shoulder, 30 in. in length from the collar and approximately 40 in. in circumference, Japanese, dating from the mid-20th century. The coat has an overall stenciled design of pine branches in green on a pale green silk fabric. Jackets such as this were often worn over the kimono as an outer coat. Fine and original condition. **$75**

Dragon robe, silk, burgundy with gold couched dragons and Shou medallions, frayed cuffs, Chinese, circa 1900, 53 in. long. **$450-$650**

Dragon robe, silk, gold couched dragons amidst clouds, bats, 100 Antiques, peaches; hem with rolling waves satin-stitched over the lishui in blue, peach, white, and yellow, Chinese, late 18th/early 19th century, 56 in. long. **$1,000-$1,500**

Dragon robe, silk, light blue with couched gold dragons and clouds, bats, and peonies detailed in Peking knots, wide lishui stripe with waves, Chinese, late 19th century, 52 in. long. **$500-$700**

Embroidered silk brocade seat cover, gold ground with colors, the motif featuring five cranes and tortoise diapers (repetitive patterns), the tassels in the form of long-tailed tortoises, Japanese, early Meiji period, 24 1/2 in. by 28 in. **$1,800-$2,200**

Dragon robe, silk, sienna with Peking knotted motif of 100 Antiques and gold couched dragons with blue, satin-stitch clouds; Chinese, circa 1900, 50 in. long. **$700-$900**

Elbow cushion covers, silk brocade worked in peach, yellow, and red-orange stylized lotus on a gray ground; Chinese, early 20th century, 8 1/2 in. by 9 in., pair. **$300-$400**

Embroidered silk fan case embellished with glass beads, Chinese, circa 1910. **$100-$125**

Embroidered silk scissors case embellished with glass beads, Chinese, circa 1910. **$100-$125**

Furoshiki, or giftwrapping cloth, cotton, silk-screened with a Clifton Karhu design that bears the artist's name. (Karhu is one of the few Westerners who is acknowledged as a master of Japanese woodblock print techniques. This cloth is modeled after one of his works.) Japanese. The furoshiki measures approximately 3 feet square. The origin of furoshiki, which originally meant bathroom cloth, dates to the 14th century. When Ashikaga Yoshimitsu built his elaborate Muromachi Palace in Kyoto, he had a large, second-floor bath used by guests. Since their wet feet left tracks on the wooden floors, bathers got into the habit of bundling their clothing in easily recognizable cloth squares, or furoshiki, to protect their belongings. Over time, the cloths came to be used for gift giving. **$150**

Jacket, silk, pink with red and white painted flowers, Japanese, early 20th century, 42 in. long. **$100-$125**

Jacket, silk, ivory with autumnal painted flowers and embroidered leaves, Japanese, early 20th century, 38 in. long. **$185-$225**

Jacket, silk, black with red lining and a white mon, Japanese, early 20th century, 40 in. long. **$200-$250**

Framed embroidery, silk on metallic thread, showing scholar's tools, circa 17th century, overall 51 in. by 21 in. **$3,500**

Handbag, silk (possibly made from sleeve bands) with stitched designs of coins, flowers, and squared scrolls, clasp also decorated with applied coins, with woven strap, Chinese, overall 24 in. by 6 3/4 in. **$1,200**

Jacket, silk, blue ground embroidered with gold couched floral medallions above couched gold and silver waves and lishui stripe, Chinese, 19th century, 39 in. long. **$1,000-$1,500**

Jacket, silk, black with gold and silver couched double gourds and Shou medallions, Chinese, late 19th/early 20th century, 44 in. long. **$1,000-$1300**

Jacket, summer gauze, yellow with white sleeve bands and cloud collar embroidered with figures and flowers, Chinese, mid-to-late 19th century, 39 in. long. **$1,700-$2,000**

Kimono jacket of woven violet/purple silk with floral patterns in green, yellow and red, measuring approximately 52 in. across the sleeves and 30 in. in length. Japanese. The inside is lined with white satin/silk decorated with woven abstract landscape designs in red. **$85**

Kimono, silk summer-weight, measuring 46 in. by 52 in., Japanese, dating to the first half of the 20th century. The kimono is dyed with wavy lines of flowers in pale orange, deep orange, and violet. It is lined with white silk. A few small spots can be seen only on close inspection. **$100**

Uchikake, or wedding kimono, silk, measuring 52 in. across the sleeves and 68 in. in length, Japanese, dating to around 1950. The silk background is decorated with dyed and embroidered red, green, black, and orange fans and flowers. It is in fine original condition. It comes with a narrow yellow obi to secure the front. **$300**

Tomesode, or formal kimono, made of pale sea-green silk with painted, dyed, and embroidered designs of flowers, Japanese dating to the early to mid-20th century. The kimono has a white silk lining that has some stains, which are not visible from the outside. It is 51 1/8 in. wide and 65 in. in length. Fine original condition. **$125**

Furisode, or informal kimono, made of pale peach silk with painted, dyed, and embroidered designs of cherry blossoms, Japanese, dating to the early to mid- 20th century. The kimono has a white silk lining that has some stains, which are not visible from the outside. The kimono is 51 1/8 in. wide and 63 in. in length. Fine original condition. **$125**

Tomesode, or formal kimono, made of black silk with a dyed and embroidered design of birds of paradise along the hem, Japanese, dating to the early to mid- 20th century. The kimono has three mon, or family crests, on the back and sleeves. Fine original condition. **$225**

Kimono, silk, pale purple with irises, early 20th century. **$350-$450**

Kimono, silk crepe, black with red lining, white chrysanthemums overall, early 20th century. **$150-$250**

Kimono (wedding), silk, white with embroidered silver and gold cranes with prunus flowers, 20th century, 6 ft., 4 in. long. **$1,500-$2,500**

Kimono, silk crepe, pink chrysanthemums embroidered on a light blue ground, fringe on sleeves, early 20th century. **$400-$600**

Kimono, silk, embroidered gold dragon and clouds overall, silk lining, black ground, early 20th century. **$700-$900**

Kimono, silk, burgundy with embroidered wisterias and foliage, early 20th century. **$500-$700**

Mandarin square, gold satin stitches and Peking knots, quail on rock-work, Chinese, late 19th century, 12 in. by 12 in. **$275-$325**

Mandarin square, gold couching and Peking knots with satin stitches in colors, peacock, Chinese, circa 1900, 11 in. by 12 in. **$225-$275**

Mandarin square, Peking knots and gold couching on a black ground, lion, Chinese, late 19th century, framed size 15 in. by 15 in. **$250-$300**

Mandarin square, satin stitches and couching in white and gold, crane, framed within a carved rosewood-handled tray, Chinese, late 19th century, tray size 12 in. by 16 in. **$300-$375**

"Fukuro" (double-fold) rokutsu (60% patterned) obi, Japanese, made in the early 20th century for use with the kimono. Its design is woven in nishiki brocade using metallic threads in a mon, or family crest, and spring pavilion design. Colors are soft oranges, yellows, browns, and reds. The obi measures 80 in. in length and is 13 in. wide. There are 2 small fold stains (approximately 1/2 in.). **$250**

Obi, silk, gold needlework with phoenix and pines in colors on a green ground, early 20th century. **$200-$300**

Obi, silk, fans (all forms, including single stick) in colors on a gold ground, early 20th century. **$250-$375**

Obi, silk, cranes and flowers in colors on a white ground, early 20th century. **$300-$400**

Obi, silk brocade, gold and silver threads, floral motif with baskets of flowers, gold ground, circa 1900. **$450-$600**

Obi, silk brocade, Three Friends (pine, plum, and bamboo) motif in greens, blues, and browns on an ecru ground, Meiji period. **$700-$900**

Obi, silk brocade, black ground, cranes and fans in gold and colors, circa 1900. **$350-$450**

Obi, silk brocade, riverscape in colors and gold, late 19th century. **$350-$450**

Obi, woven of brick red/orange silk with hexagonal designs of multicolored flowers similar to Imari porcelains, Japanese, dating to the early to mid- 20th century. The Imari designs are highlighted with gold thread. The obi measures 14 ft. in length and 12 in. across. The entire front is decorated as is three-quarters of the reverse. **$250**

"Fukuro" or double-fold obi was made in the early 20th century for use with the kimono. Its design is woven in nishiki brocade using metallic threads in a design of flowers and birds in shades of purple, green, and gold. The obi measures 12 ft. in length and is 13 in. wide. Japanese. **$300**

Panel embroidered in silk threads, figures playing blind man's bluff, Japanese, circa 1910, framed size 9 in. by 12 in. **$300-$400**

Panel embroidered in metallic silver and gold threads, peony blossoms, and foliage on a tan ground, Japanese Edo period, early 19th century, framed size 36 in. by 36 in., poor condition. **$300-$400**

Panel, silk-stitched tapestry (colors), 100 Children motif, red ground, Chinese, late 19th century, framed size 90 in. by 56 in. **$1,500-$2,200**

Japanese silk maru (formal) obi with celebratory patterns of imperial carriage, pine trees, and fans, circa 1930s, 13 ft. 2 in. by 12 1/2 in. **$250**

Japanese silk obi with crane pattern in brown, taupe, and black, hand woven, circa 1920, 12 ft. 7 in. by 12 1/2 in. **$450**

Picture, framed, embroidery on silk, satin-stitched in autumnal hues, Japanese, circa 1910, framed size 20 in. by 16 in. **$550-$775**

Panel, silk kesi (tapestry weaving) worked with figures in a scenic motif including a garden and pavilion on a blue ground, frayed borders, Chinese, 19th century, framed size 25 in. by 70 in. **$2,000-$3,000**

Panel, silk kesi, the Immortals wandering about the Hills of Longevity; red, green, pale peach, and blue; Chinese, first half of the 19th century, framed size 72 in. by 45 in. **$5,000-$7,000**

Panel, silk kesi woven with phoenix, flowers, streams, attendants, and four guardian patches with flowers and phoenix on a red-orange ground; frayed, new backing, Japanese, late Meiji period, framed size 72 in. by 40 in. **$1,200-$1,700**

Panel, silk kesi, figures, and pavilion in a garden on a blue ground, frayed borders, Chinese, 19th century, framed size 26 in. by 78 in. **$2,500-$3,500**

Panel (door), silk squares with figures of the Immortals, 100 Antiques in black satin borders, Chinese, 19th century, 82 in. by 80 in. **$2,800-$3,300**

Panel, silk with embroidered standing cranes in shades of gray, white, ivory, and silver in a marsh scene, Japanese, Meiji period, framed size 72 in. by 86 in. **$3,500-$4,500**

Panel, cotton, gold leaf appliqué, central panel with applied flowering plants in gold leaf on a navy ground, border with profuse meandering floral designs, cotton lining, Indian, late 18th/early 19th century, 50 in. by 60 in. **$1,500-$2,000**

Pillow, silk brocade, Imperial yellow, metallic gold dragon in center with a floral diapered (repetitive pattern) ground worked in peach, blue, and green; Ch'ien Lung (Qianlong), 18th century, 26 in. high. **$2,000-$3,000**

Priest's robe woven with motifs of phoenix, Shishi (usually a mythical lion or dog), and peony blossoms with dragons, Japanese, late Edo period, circa 1800, 45 in. by 78 in. $1,200-$1,800

Priest's robe, floral pattern with applied brocade, Japanese, late 18th/early 19th century, 45 in. by 80 in. **$2,000-$3,000**

Priest's robe, silk brocade, gilt thread with Buddhist wheels and trellis pattern, six applied square patches woven with floral roundels, Japanese, late 18th/early 19th century, 82 in. by 46 in. **$1,200-$1,600**

Priest's robe, silk brocade, gilt and colors with bird and flower motif, Japanese, early 19th century, 51 in. by 52 in. **$1,000-$1,600**

Robe, silk, blue with stitched irises, skirt tapering outward, cuffed sleeves, Chinese, late 19th century, 54 in. long. **$1,200-$1,500**

Robe, silk, dark blue with satin-stitched motif of circular medallions featuring a pair of dragons, sleeves, and hem embroidered with peony and plum blossoms, Chinese, late 19th/early 20th century, 54 in. long. **$1,200-$1,500**

Robe, silk, embroidered with couched gold and knotted motifs of stylized flowers on a patterned red ground filled with satin-stitched butterflies, Chinese, circa 1900, 41 in. long. **$700-$900**

Robe, silk, fur lining, red ground with pale blue, lavender, and salmon butterflies with black borders, separate collar piece, Chinese, late 19th century, 50 in. long. **$1,000-$1,500**

Robe, silk, informal, satin-stitched with flowers in colors on a red ground, Chinese, late 19th century, 55 in. long. **$700-$1,000**

Robe, silk, red with satin-stitched roundels of 1000 Flowers motif, sleeves embroidered with birds and butterflies, Chinese, circa 1920, 54 in. long, needs some work. **$800-$1,200**

Robe, silk, couched dragons in gold on a pale orange ground (the dragons worked on deep blue medallions), Chinese, late 19th century, 55 in. long, some fading. **$1,000-$1,500**

Robe, silk, informal, quilted red with scattered floral sprays and black borders embroidered with flowers, Chinese, late 19th century, 55 in. long. **$1,500-$2,100**

Robe, silk gauze (summer garment) satin-stitched with large floral medallions on a red ground, wide sleeves in deep blue worked with floral roundels, Chinese, circa 1900, 53 in. long. **$1,500-$2,000**

Robe, silk gauze, red couched gold dragons and clouds, Chinese, late 19th century, 55 in. long. **$900-$1,500**

Robe, wool/felt, red ground worked with a pattern of white cranes in flight, wide cuffs worked in butterflies, Chinese, late 19th century, 52 in. long. **$900-$1,250**

Silk hanging, red with multicolored embroidery in the satin stitch, trimmed, border not original, Chinese, circa 1900, 100 in. by 65 1/2 in. **$1,200-$1,800**

Saddle cover, ivory ground with a pair of scalloped floral medallions and scattered floral sprays surrounded by an ivory primary border and two navy blue guard borders, Tibetan, late 19th/early 20th century, 4 ft., 7 in. by 2 ft., 7 in. **$800-$1,200**

Scroll, satin ground embroidered with three laughing figures; orange, blue, and yellow; Chinese, 17th century, 58 in. by 24 in. **$1,750-$2,500**

Scroll embroidered in satin stitches with a motif of peonies and rock-work in blues, ivory, and yellow; Chinese, late 17th/early 18th century, 30 in. by 15 in. **$1,700-$2,500**

Seat cover embroidered on the front in gold and colored threads with three cranes and foliage, four gold kame ("turtle" in Japanese) tassels, Japanese, Meiji period, 20 in. by 21 in. **$1,200-$1,500**

Seat cover, Imperial yellow, silk with satin-stitched lotus, Chinese, 18th century, Ch'ien Lung (Qianlong), 21 in. wide. **$1,200-$1,500**

Shawl, rectangular, foliate boteh (a leaf-shape design, like a paisley) projecting from each corner, numerous stylized plants forming border, two rectangular panels of botehs flanking the red field, numerous floral motifs on grounds of green, blue, mustard, and red, Indian, late 19th century, 11 in. by 4 1/2 in. **$600-$800**

Shawl, embroidered silk crêpe, rose with large peony at each corner, smaller flowers overall, some fringe remaining but otherwise good condition, Chinese, circa 1925, 64 in. by 64 in. **$1,500-$1,800**

Shawl, silk crêpe, black with embroidered flowers, butterflies, and Shou symbols overall, no fringe, Chinese, circa 1925, 60 in. by 60 in. **$700-$900**

Shawl, silk, white with varied red roses overall, Chinese, circa 1930, 30 in. by 30 in. **$200-$300**

Skirt, woman's, red silk panels with extensive gold thread floral decorations, bordered by blue and black floral silk ribbons, topped by a cotton waistband, measuring 40 in. in length and 43 in. in the waist, Chinese, dating to the late Ching Dynasty, or the end of the 19th century. There is only minimal wear to the garment. The gold and red panels are iridescent. The amount of gold in the panels indicates that this was made for and worn by the wealthy class. **$450**

Skirt, red silk, front and back panels decorated with foo (mythical) dogs and Precious emblems, side pleats with dragon heads, Chinese, circa 1900, 36 in. long. **$700-$900**

Chinese iridescent black silk table cover, woven with lotus floral designs using heavy gold and silver thread embroidery, dating to the late 19th century. The cloth measures approximately 22 in. square. There is some loss of the metallic thread from pulls and wear over time but this does not affect the overall design. This fabric was brought back from China at the time of the Boxer Rebellion (1900-1901). **$200**

Theater costume, red silk, gold couching and satin-stitched florets, sleeves embroidered with lotus and lions, bats on waist, Chinese, 18th century, 50 in. long. **$3,500-$4,500**

Wall hanging, blue cloth, dyed motif of Three Friends with mon, or family crests, Japanese, 19th century, 60 in. long. **$300-$500**

Canton Enamel

(Chinese Enamel on Copper)

Painted enamels in China are also called Canton enamels, after the city that was the principal manufacturing location. This technique is directly influenced by Western art, and a great part of Canton enamels was produced for export. The Chinese called the painted enamel "Western porcelain" (yangci), the decoration "Western colors" (yangcai)—it is very different from the traditional Chinese motifs and colors. Painted enamels are made by laying a ground of opaque enamel, generally white, and on this the main colors are superimposed and fired.

Canton Enamel Values

Ashtray with green jade handle, hexagonal bowl with floral panels on a white ground, green interior, marked China, circa 1930. **$100-$150**

Bottle/vase painted with the dragon and cloud pattern, late 19th century, 16 1/2 in. high. **$600-$800**

Box and cover, circular, the lid painted with three dignitaries on a pavilion terrace, the sides with fruiting vines, star cracks, 18th century, 3 in. diameter. **$700-$900**

Boxes and covers, boats and a mountainscape, both forming a continuous pattern, light and dark blue, light blue interiors, the bases with a four-character Ch'ien Lung mark (and of the period), 3 in. diameter, pair. **$1,500-$2,500**

Censer and cover, tripod, painted with panels of European scenes including landscapes and seascapes, famille rose (rose family), flaking and star cracks, Ch'ien Lung (Qianlong) four-character mark, but early 19th century, 5 1/2 in. high. **$1,500-$2,500**

Figure of a rabbit, pink eyes, blue and white fur, circa 1900, 3 in. long. **$600-$800**

Jardinières, famille jaune (yellow family), rectangular, canted corners, painted with two panels of flowers on a busy floral ground, filled with trees and branches having hardstone leaves and berries, old damages, circa 1900, 14 in. high, pair. **$600-$800**

Napkin rings, white ground with floral motifs, early 20th century, set of 4. **$80-$100**

Saucer dish, famille rose, painted with European gentlemen and attendants near a riverbank, the border with dragons and foliage, the reverse with flower heads on a blue cracked-ice ground, surface chips restored, 18th century, 5 in. diameter. **$1,200-$1,800**

Saucer dishes, famille rose, yellow ground painted with five dragons, lotus borders, restored, 18th century, 8 1/2 in. diameter, pair. **$1,800-$2,500**

Smoking set: cylindrical cigarette container, round ashtray, and matchbox holder, each with a scenic reserve, pale green interiors, marked Made in China, circa 1930. **$100-$125**

Snuff box, famille rose, the cover painted with two European gentlemen and a lady in a picnic scene, the sides and bottom covered with puce floral sprays, restored, 18th century, 3 in. wide. **$2,000-$3,000**

Sweetmeat set, 8 fan-shaped trays radiating from a central dish, each painted with romantic scenes based on Chinese legends, famille rose with black and turquoise borders, early 19th century, 18 in. diameter, set. **$200-$300**

Tray (circular) with 6 sections around a circular dish, each with motif of figures in landscapes, scratched and chipped, early 20th century, 16 in. diameter. **$200-$300**

Vase, famille rose, baluster form, a panel on each side painted with birds perched on peony branches, lime green ground with pink lotus and scrolls, early 19th century, 9 in. high. **$800-$1,200**

Vase, 1000 Flowers pattern overall, early 20th century, 6 in. high. **$100-$125**

Vase, a panel on each side painted with sages in a landscape, overall yellow floral ground, minor restoration, 19th century, 10 in. high. **$2,500-$3,500**

Celluloid (Japanese)

Celluloid is a tough, flammable thermoplastic. Japanese celluloid figures—some depicting the Seven Luck Gods, geisha and peasants—were popular tourist items from the 1930s to the 1950s.

Japanese celluloid showing the Seven Lucky Gods (one missing) and dragon boat, in the form of an open clamshell with dragon on top, 2 3/4 in. by 3 1/4 in. by 2 7/8 in. $50

Japanese celluloid showing a man carrying two covered buckets on a pole balanced on his shoulder, 2 3/4 in. by 3 1/8 in. by 1 1/2 in. **$55**

Japanese celluloid showing woman and child carrying sticks on their heads, leading an ox carrying four covered buckets, 4 1/2 in. by 3 1/8 in. by 2 1/2 in. **$90**

Japanese celluloid showing a geisha holding a parasol, riding on a bamboo raft that is being guided by a man holding a long pole, 5 1/4 in. by 2 7/8 in. by 1 3/4 in. **$60**

Japanese celluloid showing the Seven Lucky Gods and dragon boat, in the form of an open clamshell with landscape showing Mount Fuji on top, hand painted, 2 5/8 in. by 3 1/8 in. by 2 3/4 in. **$60**

Japanese celluloid showing a warrior god (?), marked on the bottom No. 4, 3 1/4 in. by 1 3/4 in. by 1 1/4 in. **$60**

Japanese celluloid match holder showing a chimpanzee seated next to a tree stump; he has the index finger of his left hand held to his mouth and a jar in his right hand, 5 5/8 in. by 4 1/8 in. by 3 in. **$150**

Japanese celluloid showing the Seven Lucky Gods riding in a boat with a bird in the prow, and the sail bears the image of a dragon, on a black base that is signed, excellent condition, 5 7/8 in. by 6 in. by 2 3/8 in. **$90**

Japanese celluloid of a fisherman with pole in his hand, and a creel containing a fish on his back, hand painted, excellent condition, 3 3/8 in. by 2 1/8 in. by 2 in. **$50**

Japanese celluloid of a geisha holding a parasol and lantern, hand painted, 2 1/4 in. by 2 3/4 in. by 2 1/2 in. **$45**

Japanese celluloid showing a geisha riding in a covered cart being pulled by an ox that is led by a man in a broad hat, 6 1/4 in. by 3 3/8 in. by 2 1/8 in. **$100**

Champleve and Cloisonné

Champlevé is a style of enamel decoration in which the enamel is applied and fired in cells depressed (as by incising) into a metal background. Cloisonné is enamel decoration in which the enamel is applied and fired in raised cells (as of soldered wires) usually on a metal background.

Champlevé

Cox and cover, enameled, hammered copper, the flowers and foliage in pastel hues in low relief, signed Ando, Japanese, Meiji period, circa 1905, 6 1/2 in. by 4 1/2 in. **$2,000-$3,000**

Candleholders, each with 15 upturned branches terminating in a pricket sconce, the bases round and flat, some enamel losses, Chinese, circa 1900, 28 in. high, pair. **$1,200-$1,500**

Censer, Shishi (usually a mythical lion or dog), finial, loose ring handles, large peony motif in primary colors, Japanese, early 20th century, 6 1/2 in. high. **$100-$200**

Censer and cover, two looped handles, three masked feet, Buddhistic lion finial, the reticulated cover with lappets (a fold or flap), the body with alternating panels of longevity characters, Chinese, impressed Ming mark, but late 19th century, 16 in. high. **$750-$950**

Censer in the form of a Buddhistic lion, squat body, standing four square, the head forming the lid, Chinese, late 19th century, 13 in. high. **$500-$700**

Censers modeled as standing geese, detachable wings forming the covers, yellow ground with polychrome feathers, Chinese, early 20th century, 15 1/2 in. high, pair. **$900-$1,200**

Figure of Kuan Yin, flowing robes with a lotus scroll pattern, Chinese, 19th century, 6 1/2 in. high. **$300-$400**

Figure of a seated Lohan, his green robes decorated with flowers, birds, and dragons, Chinese, late 19th/early 20th century, 18 in. high. **$800-$1,200**

Figure of a phoenix with colorful feathers, primary hues, Chinese, early 20th century, 11 3/4 in. high. **$600-$800**

Figure of a Samurai (on horseback) wearing a suit of armor, his pole arm missing, losses to the enamel, circa 1915, 15 in. high. **$600-$850**

Figure of a water buffalo standing four square, Chinese, late 19th century, 6 1/2 in. long. **$275-$350**

Lamp, archaic motif, the enamels in primary colors, losses to the enamels, circa 1905, 5 in. high. **$1,200-$1,500**

Lamp (floor), bronze body with archaic motifs, electrified, no shape, losses to the enamels, Japanese, circa 1900, 63 in. high. **$1,000-$1,500**

Lantern, globular, entirely pierced with chrysanthemums and leaves, the top with a loose ring, Japanese, circa 1885, 16 in. high. **$700-$900**

Lantern, open-barrel form with flowers and vines, Japanese, late 19th century, 12 1/2 in. high. **$285-$400**

Planters decorated with flowers, vines and squared scrolls, one measuring 14 in. by 10 1/2 in., second 15 1/2 in. by 10 1/2 in. **$500 each**

Urn, lobed, elaborately decorated with flowers, vines and animals, 9 3/4 in. by 11 3/4 in. **$1,800**

Ruyi sceptre, the center and ends with gilt bats around Shou characters, Chinese, late 19th/early 20th century, 17 1/2 in. long. **$500-$700**

Vase, gourd form, peony motif in primary hues, marked *Made in Japan*, circa 1930, 8 in. high. **$100-$150**

Vase, pear-shaped, two elephant-head handles, a peony band around the center in primary hues, early Showa period, 7 in. high. **$100-$125**

Vase, baluster form, bronze body with a peony motif, Japanese, early 20th century, 8 in. high. **$85-$125**

Weight, Shishi (usually a mythical lion or dog), with brocade ball, Japanese, early 20th century, 6 1/2 in. long. **$100-$125**

Cloisonné

The name cloisonné is derived from the French word *cloison*, meaning cell. Basic cloisonné is a metal body with designs made of wire cells that have been filled with enamels.

Creation of a cloisonné object begins with bending and hammering a sheet of metal into the desired shape. The artist then paints the design onto the metal sheet. Once the wires are bent into shapes and placed against the metal to form the partitions, or cells, a layer of enamel (powdered glass) is sifted over them and gently fired to secure the wires in place. (On ceramic bodies, or Japanese Totai, vegetable glue was used.)

Before firing begins, the cells must be packed with enamel in powdered form. The colors of the fused enamel depend on the mixture of natural minerals, and in turn, the temperatures at which the object is fired depend on the colors being used. Those needing the highest heat are fired first, after which the cells are packed again and refired until they are even with the height of the wires. Finally, the piece is polished—with stones of various coarseness, followed by charcoal, and then with powdered horn mixed with oil—until the proper finish is obtained.

Chinese Cloisonné

Chinese cloisonné, called Ch'ing tai-lan after the period of the Ming Dynasty during which it was developed (1450-56), can have gold, bronze, brass, or copper bodies. Designs usually include a primary motif with a background diaper (repetitive pattern) such as clouds, double T, bats, and so on. These background patterns were used to strengthen the pattern as well as to enhance its aesthetic quality. The motifs, which are somewhat stylized, include popular themes such as the dragon in pursuit of the flaming pearl (the pearl representing truth), the lotus and scroll, Buddhistic symbols, masks, and 1,000 Flowers. Objects, both ornamental and occasional as well as functional, include animals, figures, water pipes, snuff bottles, censers, and vases.

For the most part, Chinese cloisonné marks are reign marks (see the markings listed in the "Prices on Chinese Porcelain and Pottery" section).

Japanese Cloisonné

Japanese cloisonné is called *Shippoyaki. Yaki* means ware. *Shippo* has two definitions: beauty or goodness, and Seven Precious jewels (which can be combinations of pearl, shell, agate, gold, silver, lapis lazuli, coral, and amber).

Japanese cloisonné is a bit more complicated than its Chinese counterpart. The body may be silver, copper, papier-mache, lacquer, pottery, porcelain, or brass. Unlike Chinese cloisonné, which usually has a reign mark if marked, Japanese cloisonné can have factory marks and/or artists' signatures/seals. The enamels can be opaque, translucent, or transparent. Designs featured on Japanese cloisonné are naturalistic and may encompass large or small areas, geometric borders, designs in reserves, or some combination of the two were also used. Scenic and floral motifs were popular. Objects include standard occasional and decorative pieces as well as netsuke, inro, ojime, buttons, pins, tsuba, pipes, and so on.

Japanese cloisonné features a technique known as *counter-enameling*, used to prevent large areas from warping. In these objects, the unworked and undecorated reverse is covered with counter-enameling, as are interiors and bases.

See the figures on the following page for examples of Japanese cloisonné marks.

Types of Japanese Cloisonné

Akasuke (pigeon blood). Transparent red enamel over a copper body. The term is also used to describe yellow, green, blue, and lavender created in the same manner.

Ginbari. Silver foil wrapped around a metal body, applied with translucent or transparent enamel.

Moriage (Cameo). The motif has enamel piled above the surface of the piece, forming a pattern in mild relief. A certain area may have been embossed, and enamels added, layer by layer, before firing.

Musen shippo. Wireless cloisonné.

Shotai shippo (pliqué à jour). Transparent enamel, the body etched away with acid to create a stained-glass effect.

Totai shippo. Ceramic-bodied cloisonné.

Yu-musen shippo. A combination of wired and wireless motifs.

Yusen shippo. Wired enamel.

Japanese Cloisonné Marks

Ando Jubei

Gonda Hirosuke

Gonda Hirosuke

Hayashi Kihyoe

Hayashi Kodenji

Inaba Cloisonné Company

Hayashi Tanigoro

Kawaguchi

Namikawa Sosuke

Kawade Shibataro

Namikawa Yasuyuki

Ota

Takeuchi Chubei (totai maker)

Cloisonné Values

Basin, flat rim, black ground with a yellow dragon, the well with four more dragons on the exterior, blue counterenameled base with large Ming mark (but early 20th century), Chinese, 13 in. diameter. *$350-$450*

Basin, hexafoil, gilt interior and turquoise ground, the decoration including dragons and Shou characters, some losses in the enamel, Chinese, 17th century, 5 1/2 in. diameter. **$600-$900**

Bottle/vase, cylindrical, long neck, turquoise ground with formal lotus meander, Chinese, late 19th century, 15 in. high. **$400-$600**

Bulb bowl, Millefleurs, brightly colored, the counterenameling a bluegreen, copper rim and base, marked *China*, circa 1930, 10 in. diameter. **$250-$325**

Ashtray, blue ground with T-pattern, white flowers, green foliage, blue counterenameling on interior, Chinese, marked China, circa 1930, 4 in. diameter. **$25-$45**

Box, Japanese, the ground shaded in pale blue, dove on maple branch, wire and wireless, the base with a Namikawa Sosuke silver-wire mark, restored, circa 1900, 4 in. by 5 in. **$2,000-$3,000**

Box and cover, black ground, overall floral motif in colors, the interior lined with wood, base with Inaba mark in silver wire, motif in silver wire, marked *Japan*, circa 1925, 5 in. by 4 in. **$500-$700**

Box and cover, black ground with large pastel flower heads, Japanese, early 20th century, 2 1/2 in. square. **$275-$375**

Box and cover, brass wire, phoenix and leaf motif on lid, floral roundels on sides, black ground, Japanese, circa 1915, 5 in. wide. **$200-$300**

Box and cover, circular, black ground, the lid with a yellow dragon, the sides with cloud patterns, marked *China*, circa 1935, 4 in. diameter. **$150-$225**

Box and cover, circular, phoenix and flowers on a green and goldstone ground, Japanese, late 19th century, 4 in. diameter. **$250-$350**

Box and domed cover, circular, overall large lotus meandering between gilt rims, turquoise ground, Chinese, 18th century, 2 1/2 in. diameter. **$600-$750**

Candlesticks in a floral pattern, late Ming Dynasty, with large drip pans having a Greek key border that is repeated around base, minor damage to one base, 14 1/2 in. by 6 1/4 in., **pair.** **$1,800**

Box, cylindrical, decorated with a yellow five-toed dragon, bottom and interior covered in turquoise blue enamel, excellent condition, 6 1/8 in. by 2 1/2 in. **$300**

Box and cover, flattened ovoid form, silver wires, three butterflies on the lid within a brocade border, some damage, a plaque is missing from the base, the work is similar to that attributed to Namikawa Yasuyuki, Japanese, Meiji period, 3 1/2 in. diameter. **$500-$600**

Box and cover, flattened circular form, silver wire and enamels worked in a motif of three cranes within a brocade border, the base with a silver plaque marked *Namikawa Yasuyuki,* some damage, Japanese, Meiji period, 3 1/4 in. diameter. **$2,000-$3,000** (*Note:* Correct attribution by means of a maker's seal or mark raises values.)

Box and cover, kiku (chrysanthemum) shape, silver wire, black ground with colorful motif of butterflies, a few minor cracks, Japanese, late Meiji period, 6 in. diameter. **$1,500-$2,500**

Box and cover, lobed, motif of a phoenix in colors on an aventurine (goldstone) ground, Japanese, late 19th century, 3 in. diameter. **$250-$350**

Box and cover, lozenge-shaped, foliage on the sides, blue T-pattern forming squares around the top, Chinese, late 19th/early 20th century, 4 1/2 in. wide. **$200-$300**

Box and cover, rectangular, the cover with two fans, both decorated with cranes, the yellow ground with scattered floral roundels, the sides with scrolls, crack on the base, Japanese, Taisho period, 4 in. by 7 in. **$300-$400**

Box and cover, silver wire and enamels worked with a bird perched on a cherry branch, pale blue ground, Japanese, circa 1930, 4 in. wide. **$300-$500**

Box and cover, silver wire, the cover with a carp on a shaded light blue ground, Namikawa Sosuke seal in silver wire on the base, Japanese, Meiji period, 5 1/2 in. wide. **$20,000+**

Box and cover, yellow dragon and flaming pearl motif on a black ground with cloud patterns, Japanese, early Showa period, 3 1/2 in. by 2 1/2 in. **$275-$375**

Box and cover, yellow ground, the lid inset with a pierced, pale celadon jade panel carved with a long life emblem, overall lotus and scrolls and Shou characters, Chinese, late 19th century, 13 1/2 in. wide. **$800-$1,200**

Boxes and covers, yellow ground with T-pattern wire work, the covers with a central Shou character roundel surrounded by five hard-stone bats, the interiors with blue counterenameling, Chinese, late 19th century, 10 in. wide, pair. **$1,500-$2,000**

Box and cover enameled in primary colors with a phoenix on a rectangular panel, the ground profusely decorated with fans and flowers, brass mounts, brass interior carved with birds in flight above grasses, Japanese, Meiji period, 5 3/4 in. by 4 3/4 in. by 3 1/2 in. **$500-$700**

Censer with cover, tripod feet, decorated with t'ao-t'ieh (monster masks) in turquoise and green on a dark blue ground, the cover surmounted with a gilt Buddhistic lion, Chinese, marked Lao T'ien Li, 9 1/2 in. high. **$1,500-$2,000**

COURTESY OF THE EDSON COLLECTION

Bowl, plique-a-jour, enameled with peony, lilies, and chrysanthemums on a pale green ground, silver rim and foot, cracked, Japanese, Taisho period, 5 1/2 in. diameter. **$700-$900**

Bowl, plique-a-jour, maple and prunus on a pale green ground, chrome mounts, Japanese, Showa period, 4 in. diameter. **$500-$700**

Bowl, silver wire with butterflies on a deep blue ground, cracked, Japanese, circa 1900, 3 in. diameter. **$100-$125**

Bowl, the center of the interior decorated with a lotus pond on a blue ground beneath a red ground band of Precious Things, the exterior with scattered flower-head roundels on a turquoise ground, Chinese, 19th century, 15 1/2 in. diameter. **$2,500-$3,500**

Candleholders modeled as standing ducks looking to the left and to the right, turquoise bodies with dense dragon scrolls, their heads set with jade sconces, triangular bases, Chinese, late 19th/early 20th century, 11 in. high. **$900-$1,200**

Censer, tripod, three bulbous feet, overall lotus and scroll pattern on a medium blue ground, severely damaged, Chinese, 17th century, 9 1/4 in. high. **$900-$1,200**

Censer, three rounded feet, brass wire worked in numerous mon symbols, the cover with a missing finial, Japanese, circa 1910, 3 1/2 in. high. **$100-$125**

Censer, tripod, decorated with three white phoenix in flight amidst scrolling chrysanthemums on a turquoise ground, the dragon handles replaced, Chinese, 17th century, 4 1/2 in. wide. **$300-$500**

Censer, tripod, flat bottom, flaring rim, three stub legs and two Buddhistic lion mask handles, turquoise ground with a motif of lotus meander, old damages, Chinese, 17th century, 4 3/4 in. diameter. **$900-$1,200**

Censer and cover, tripod masked legs, chih lung (hornless dragons) handles, lotus finial, flowering and fruiting peach branches overall in red, blue, and green on a turquoise ground, Chinese, 18th century, 7 in. high. **$1,500-$2,000**

Censers, modeled as long-tailed birds looking to the left and to the right, the bodies turquoise, the wings polychrome, gilt beaks and legs, damages to the legs, Chinese, 18th century, 7 in. wide, pair. **$3,000-$4,000**

Cup, small, with bump-out base, possibly for matches, decorated with stylized floral motifs, 2 3/8 in. by 2 1/8 in. $245

Chamber candlesticks, wide, shallow drip pans, apricot ground decorated with clusters of flowering branches, the sides set with twig handles, Chinese, last half of the 19th century, 5 1/2 in. wide. **$500-$800**

Charger, butterfly, and flowers against a medium blue ground, darker blue counterenameling, pitting overall, two cracks, Japanese, late 19th century, 12 in. diameter. **$300-$500**

Charger, three standing cranes amongst bamboo, blue ground, the rim with a floral border, copper body, Japanese, circa 1915, 26 in. diameter. **$800-$1,200**

Charger, blue ground with a motif of birds in flight above foliage and flowers, intricate diapered (repetitive pattern) border around the rim, Japanese, circa 1900, 11 in. diameter. **$700-$950**

Charger, foliate form, brass wire and colored enamels worked in a motif of coiled dragons on a goldstone ground, Japanese, late 19th century, 12 in. diameter. **$350-$550**

Charger, silver wire and enamels worked in a motif of pheasants and chrysanthemums on a blue ground, narrow diapered (repetitive pattern) border around the rim, some chipping and loss of enamel, Japanese, circa 1900. **$800-$1,200**

Charger, the rim with a band of floral lappets, pale blue ground with a hawk in flight above flowering peony branches, surface with minor flaws, Japanese, circa 1885, 15 in. diameter. **$1,500-$1,800**

Cigarette box, hinged cover, black ground with colored kiku (chrysanthemum), gilt metal interior in katakiribori (chiseling that imitates a paint brush's stroke) with birds and bamboo, Japanese, early Showa period, 5 in. wide. **$325-$500**

Dish, oval, everted rim, phoenix on a diapered (repetitive pattern) floral and foliate ground, blue-green counterenameling, Japanese, circa 1870, 13 1/2 in. wide. **$700-$900**

Dish, shallow with flat, everted rim, the center with two confronting five-toed dragons facing the flaming pearl amidst cloud scrolls, the rim with flower-head meanders, the exterior with lotus scrolls, losses to enamel filled in with wax, Chinese, 16th century, 9 1/2 in. diameter. **$900-$1,200**

Flask, cylindrical, long neck, two gilt dragon handles, spreading foot, scenic motif above fish and breaking waves, Chinese, late 19th century, 16 in. high. **$1,200-$1,600**

Jar and cover, small, with stylized floral motifs, numbered on the bottom "1722," excellent condition, 4 3/8 in. by 3 1/2 in. **$600**

Flask, circular, flattened form, the front and back with scenic motifs including deer, pine, and cranes, the neck with overlapping green leaves, Chinese, circa 1900, 12 1/2 in. high. **$900-$1,200**

Figures of cockerels standing on rock-work bases, mirror image, open beaks, green ground with colored feathers and tails, restoration to one, Chinese, 20th century, 9 1/2 in. high, pair. **$1,500-$2,500**

Figures of cranes, each standing on flat, circular base, white bodies with polychrome feathers and tail feathers, candle sconces missing, Chinese, 18th century, 18 in. high, pair. **$5,000-$6,000**

Figures of ducks, crouching position, dark blue ground, thick and thin wires, colorful feathers, gilt beaks and gilt webbed feet, Chinese, early 20th century, 9 in. wide, pair. **$900-$1,200**

Figures of standing ducks, heads raised, turquoise ground with polychrome feathers, Chinese, 20th century, 6 1/2 in. high, pair. **$400-$700**

Figures of elephants, each with a vase on its back, blue ground, floral scroll motifs overall, one badly bruised, Chinese, early 20th century, 16 in. high, pair. **$1,800-$2,400**

Figures of elephants, 13 in. tall and 7 in. across, dating to the mid-to-late 19th century. The bodies appear to have been made of a copper alloy as seen in the tusks and the ends of the trunks and tails. The bodies have the typical multicolor enamel on turquoise blue of these pieces. There is some mild pitting of the pink enamel that looks like it has been present since manufacture. The exposed copper surfaces have darkened and patinated with age. Fine original condition. **$400**

Figures of kylin (a mythical animal), deep blue-green, scaly bodies, blue faces, gilt horns, manes, tail, and hoofed feet, Chinese, late 19th century, 12 in. wide, pair. **$1,500-$2,500**

Figures of pheasants perched on grassy rock-work, pierced bases interspersed with flower heads, the feathers predominately Indian red and turquoise, Chinese, early 20th century, 9 1/2 in. high, pair. **$1,000-$1,500**

Figures of quails looking to the left and to the right, detachable backs, gilt legs and beaks, deep blue and white breasts and polychrome feathers, Chinese, early 20th century, 4 1/2 in. high, pair. **$900-$1,500**

Matchbox holder, openwork brass holder designed to take a standard box of small wood matches and ornamented with finely detailed imperial dragons against cloud backgrounds with waves below and encircling the blue pill (pearl) representing the elixir of immortality, identical cloisonné scene both sides, Chinese, circa 1920s, 1 5/8 in. by 2 5/8 in. **$250-$350**

Jar and cover, Millefleurs on a medium blue ground, bruise on one with loss of enamel, Chinese, circa 1930. **$70-$125**

Jar and cover, three legs, globular form, red ground with large phoenix and tail plumage in yellow, blue, and green, the cover with spider mums, silver mounts, minor nicks and dents, marked *Kumeno Teitaro*, Japanese, Meiji period, 6 3/4 in. high, pair. **$2,500-$3,500**

Jar and cover, blue exterior with continuous leafy lotus amidst fan and circular shaped panels of flowers, turquoise counterenameling, Japanese, first quarter of the 20th century, 12 in. high. **$200-$300**

Jar and cover decorated with floral roundels on a black ground, Japanese, Meiji period, 3 in. high. **$300-$500**

Jar and cover, floral geometric panels on a muddy turquoise ground, some loss of enamel, Japanese, circa 1865, 12 1/2 in. high. **$700-$900**

Jar and cover, overall design of cherry blossoms on a medium blue ground, the rim of the cover with a black dragon-scale band, marked *China,* circa 1935, 8 in. high. **$100-$175**

Jar and cover, overall florals in an overlapping pattern on a black ground, marked *China*, circa 1935, 6 1/2 in. high. **$100-$175**

Jar and cover, overall T-pattern with large-petaled chrysanthemums scattered on a medium green ground, base marked *China,* circa 1935, 6 in. high. **$75-$125**

Jar and cover, ovoid, silver wire worked with two fish and lilies on a blue-gray ground, Japanese, Meiji period, 5 in. high. **$600-$900**

Jardinières, circular, turquoise ground, lotus and scroll pattern overall, the jardinières contain hard-stone trees, spinach jade leaves, agate flowers, and carnelian berries, old damages to both, Chinese, early 20th century, 24 in. high (to top of trees), pair. **$600-$900**

Chinese cloisonné model of a phoenix perched upon a branch of flowering hydrangea mounted as a lamp, the phoenix dated circa 1900, the mounts dated circa 1922, the phoenix 14 in. high, the lamp overall 27 in. high. **$2,500-$3,500**

Pipe, silver with silver chasings and an agate mouthpiece, dating to the early 20th century. The pipe measures 22 in. in length and is 1/2 inch in diameter, Chinese, fine original condition. **$300**

Plaque, concentric green and blue bands of scrolling polychrome flowers, minor surface repair, Chinese, late Ming Dynasty, 7 in. diameter. **$800-$1,200**

Platters, round, showing birds and flowers on a turquoise background, excellent condition, 12 in. by 1 1/2 in., pair. $1,300

Planter, pink lotus meander and leafy vines overall on a turquoise frond, the foot decorated with florets, Chinese, 18th century, 6 in. wide. **$1,200-$1,500**

Pricket candlesticks, the shafts set into flaring sconces and standing on domed, knobbed bases, turquoise ground with lotus scrolls, Chinese, late 19th/early 20th century, 19 in. high. **$1,500-$2,500**

Ruyi (scepter), long shaft cast with three panels of peach sprays in relief at the head, center and base of the shaft: turquoise ground with key pattern, Chinese, early 20th century, 22 in. long. **$700-$1,000**

Ruyi (scepter), oval head set with four enamel-on-copper peaches, additional peaches on the center of the shaft and the terminal, the turquoise ground with lotus meander, Chinese, early 20th century, 20 in. long. **$1,200-$1,800**

Smoking set: ashtray, matchbox holder, and cigarette jar mounted on a footed tray, all black with a brass-wire T-pattern, Chinese, circa 1925. **$100-$200**

Smoking set: cigarette jar, ashtray, and matchbox holder, floral pattern on a black ground interspersed with T-patterns, marked *China*, circa 1930. **$50-$75**

Smoking set: tray with two compartments for cigarettes and cigars, a compartment for ashtrays, and a compartment for the matchbox holder, deep blue ground with a T-pattern in brass wire, marked *China*, circa 1937. **$200-$300**

Sake bottle (tokkuri), pale blue with a motif of ju characters in orange, white, and green, Japanese, circa 1925, 6 in. high. **$300-$400**

Spittoon, turquoise ground with red and yellow lotus and scrolls, red and blue floral reserves, Chinese, 5 in. high. $900-$1,200
COURTESY OF THE EDSON COLLECTION

Teapot, miniature, decorated with flowers and butterflies, excellent condition, 3 3/8 in. by 2 1/2 in. by 2 in. $400

Specimen set, six round dishes, each decorated with two butterflies within a formal border and exhibiting the various stages of cloisonné manufacture, Japanese, circa 1890, 5 in. diameter. **$450-$650**

Table, a cloisonné plaque of pale blue with a motif of plants, fruit, and scholar's utensils set in a brass table with a lower shelf, the panel Chinese, 19th century, 16 1/2 in. square. **$700-$1,000**

Teapot, measuring 6 in. tall and 7 in. from handle to spout. The overall multicolor design is typical of Japanese period cloisonné work. It is coated on the interior with turquoise enamel. Japanese Golden Era (circa 1885-1900). Fine original condition. **$250**

Teapot, dark blue lotus leaves on a yellow ground, eight Sacred Emblems (see "trigrams") and clouds encircling the body, the spout issuing from a makara head (mythical sea creature with an elephant head), dragon-form handle, domed lid, Chinese, 19th century, 11 in. high. **$800-$1,200**

Teapot, pear-shaped, curved spout, domed lid with knobbed bud finial, green ground with brightly enameled flower heads, Japanese, early 20th century, 6 in. high. **$150-$200**

Tea set, green ground with blue leaf motif, Japanese, early 20th century. **$175-$225**

Tea set, blue ground with small flower heads overall, covered teapot, covered sugar and open creamer, Japanese, early 20th century. **$250-$350**

Tray, approximately 8 in. square, dating to the 1950s. The tray shows a bamboo design in green on a metallic ivory background, with original box and paperwork. The tray has a 2 mm chip along one edge. Japanese. **$75**

Tray, three-toed dragon in the center with overall geometric designs, a medium green ground, Japanese, late 19th century, 12 in. wide. **$400-$600**

Tray, a fruiting vine with two birds flying above, blue ground, formal border, Japanese, late Meiji period, 13 in. square. **$600-$800**

Vase, Japanese, deep blue ground, silver wire, motif of birds and flowers, marked Inaba Nanaho, Meiji period, 5 in. high. **$3,000-$4,000**
COURTESY OF THE EDSON COLLECTION

Tray, pale blue shaded ground with motif of cock, hens, and chicks, hairlines, cracks, and bruising, signed *Namikawa Sosuke*, Japanese, Meiji period, 12 1/2 in. square. **$500-$750**

Tray, rectangular, green ground with Mt. Fuji and scenic motif, Japanese, circa 1920, 10 in. long. **$300-$450**

Vase in an urn form, decorated with vivid and elaborate floral motif in shaded enamels, excellent condition, 8 1/2 in. by 4 3/4 in. **$1,250**

Tray, upturned edges, dating to the mid-20th century. It has a large orange-yellow chrysanthemum on a green background. The tray was produced by the Inaba Cloisonné Co. There is a 1/8 in. chip out of one rim that has been repaired. Japanese, 7 in. square. **$75**

Vase, archaic form, scrolls forming stiff long leaves between ruyi-head borders at the foot and mouth, red, yellow, green, and blue enamel on a turquoise ground, Ch'ien Lung (Qianlong), Chinese, 18th century, 13 in. high. **$1,800-$2,500**

Vase in an urn form with flaring mouth, decorated with vivid stylized floral motifs in lapis blue and iridescent greens, excellent condition, 7 1/4 in. by 3 1/8 in. **$695**

Vase, four-lobed with alternating cranes and butterflies in shaped panels against a red ground, bent lip, dent in base and minor cracks, Chinese, 19th century, 6 in. high. **$100-$200**

Vase, black ground with scattered white flowers, Chinese, early 20th century, 4 1/2 in. high. **$100-$200**

Vase, akasuke (pigeon blood), white chrysanthemums against a red ground, Japanese, early Showa period, 8 in. high. **$150-$225**

Vase, motif of dense chrysanthemums on a dark green ground, Japanese, late 19th/early 20th century, 5 7/8 in. high. **$250-$350**

Vase, large yellow flowers scattered on a dark blue ground with overall brasswire cloud patterns, Chinese, early 20th century, 4 in. high. **$150-$200**

Vase, open work with vines and flowers in primary colors, some loss of enamel, Chinese, 6 in. high. **$150-$225**

Vase, white flowers and green foliage on a black ground, marked *China*, 4 1/2 in. high, circa 1925. **$100-$125**

Vase, a vertical cylinder between two slender cylinders, parcel gilt base, Chinese, 17th century, 4 1/2 in. high. **$800-$1,200**

Vase, baluster form, red ground with brass wire worked in a T-pattern with scattered lotus scroll, marked *China*, circa 1930, 10 in. high. **$100-$125**

Vases, Japanese, mirror image, blue ground, silver wire, rims, and bases, diapered (repetitive pattern) band around the base and rim, the motif with numerous flowers, birds, and branches, bases marked Hayashi Kiyoe, 10 in. high. **$5,000-$7,000/pair**
COURTESY OF THE EDSON COLLECTION

Vase, decorated with flying cranes, silver body, late 19th century, Japanese, 3 5/8 in. by 2 7/8 in. **$400**

Vase, with silver wire, rim, and base, motif of life-like hydrangeas and sawtooth foliage, Japanese, marked Hayashi Kodenji on the base, Meiji period, 9 3/4 in. high. **$6,000-$8,000**

Vase, baluster form, short, everted neck, silver wire and colored enamels worked in flowering plum branches on a deep blue ground, copper foot and rim, Tadashi workshop seal, Japanese, Meiji period, 3 1/2 in. high. **$375-$450**

Vase, baluster form, silver wire and enamels worked with cranes in flight, silver mounts, Ando workshop seal, Japanese, Taisho period, 13 in. high. **$3,500-$4,500**

Vase, baluster form, yellow, orange, and purple flowers on a deep blue ground, copper mounts, Japanese, circa 1900. **$300-$500**

Vase, baluster form, everted rim, copper wire and pastel enamels worked in a wreath of mums around the shoulder, midnight blue ground, similar pattern on neck, silver foot and rim, Ando mark on base, 14 in. high, Taisho period. **$3,500-$4,500**

Vase, baluster form, tall, trumpet neck, copper wire and colored enamels worked in cherry blossoms on branches against a light blue ground, Japanese, circa 1900, 28 in. high. **$2,000-$3,000**

Floor vase, decorated with finely enameled hawk and sparrows on one side, pheasants on the other, the two sides portraying autumn and spring with the appropriate flowers in bloom, a white and a gray dragon around the neck, Japanese, circa early 20th century, 36 in. tall, rare this large. **$4,500-$4,750**

Vase, baluster form, everted rim, dark blue ground, silver wire and colored enamels worked in flowers and butterflies, Tadashi seal, Japanese, Meiji period, 4 3/4 in. high. **$250-$375**

Vase, birds and flowers on a goldstone ground, shaped panels filled with flowers around the shoulder and foot, Japanese, late Meiji period, 10 1/2 in. high. **$300-$500**

Vase, black with silver wire worked in a motif of cranes in flight, silver foot and rim, base with Ando mark, circa 1930, 10 1/2 in. high. **$1,600-$2,400**

Vase, bold white and lavender irises and green leaves on a bright turquoise ground, Japanese, early Showa period, 6 1/2 in. high. **$300-$400**

Vase, with a midnight blue ground, the motif with autumnal leaves and a bird perched upon a branch, diaper (repetitive pattern) border at neck and foot, silver and gold wire, the base with a Hayashi Kodenji mark, Japanese, 10 in. high. **$5,500-$7,500**

COURTESY OF THE EDSON COLLECTION

Vase with pale blue-green ground, silver wire, floral motif in pale shades of pink with green foliage, the base with an Ando mark, minor ding on back, Japanese, early 20th century. **$500-$700**

Vase, cabinet, in ginbari style of red enamel over hammered silver, measuring 2 1/2 in. by 2 1/2 in., dating to the Meiji-Taisho periods (1868-1926). The silver has a dragon in the clouds decoration and a starburst, which may be a manufacturing flaw. The enamel is a deep, rich red typical of wares of this type. The vase bears the seal of the Ando studio on the base. Japanese. Excellent original condition. **$150**

Vase, ginbari, lavender ground with two writhing chartreuse dragons in confrontation, Japanese, early 20th century, 6 1/2 in. high. **$185-$275**

Vase, ginbari, pale lavender ground with brightly enameled writhing dragon in primary colors, silver wire, Japanese, early 20th century, 7 in. high. **$200-$300**

Vase in modified mei ping form, the neck with a diapered (repetitive pattern) band in pastel hues, motif of cranes and flowers with silver wire, silver rim and base, minor hairlines in the gray ground, Japanese, late 19th century. **$700-$900**

Vase, mei ping form, green ground with pink and white plum blossoms, T-pattern, lappet border at the foot, Chinese, signed Lao T'ien Li, 11 1/2 in. high. **$900-$1,200**

COURTESY OF THE EDSON COLLECTION

Vase, ginbari, shaded green to gold orange, the foil with aquatic plants, the body with orange bulgy-eyed goldfish, signed *Hayashi Kodenji*, Japanese, 10 in. high. **$3,500-$4,500**

Vase, ginbari, stippled blue ground with pink hibiscus and foliage, Japanese, Taisho period, 14 in. high. **$900-$1,285**

Vase, ginbari with incised foil ground, a kingfisher flying among large flowering lotus, bruised, Japanese, Taisho period, 12 in. high. **$700-$900**

Vase, ginbari, cylindrical form. The brass body is covered with silver foil followed by a rich, red glass enamel. The artist included a branch of bamboo in green. The rims are silver mounted. The vase has a 1 in. bruise at the right, lower base of the bamboo that has been filled. Unsigned, but typical of pieces from the Ando workshop. Japanese, dating to the early 20th century, 8 1/2 in. high, 3 in. at the base, and 2 in. at the mouth. **$150**

Chinese cloisonné vase, black ground, cloud pattern, white flowers and shaded green foliage, brass wires, copper body marked China, circa 1934, 8 in. high. **$75-$125**

Vase, silver rim and base, wireless, muted gray ground and pink and white flowers, modified pear shape, Japanese, late Meiji period, 6 in. high. **$900-$1,200**

Vase, green-flecked ground (goldstone) with a pink hen and three chicks among flowers and foliage, dented, Japanese, circa 1900, 8 in. high. **$100-$200**

Vase, green-flecked ground (goldstone) with flowering vines in pastel hues, copper rim and foot, Japanese, circa 1910, 5 in. high. **$150-$185**

Vase, green ground with pale green clouds, yu-musen, chrome mounts, Japanese, Showa period, 7 in. high. **$100-$175**

Vase, light blue ground with scattered flowers, diaper (repetitive pattern) band around the neck, copper rim and foot, Japanese, 5 1/2 in. high, circa 1920. **$100-$175**

Vase, long neck, bulbous body, butterflies in colored enamels on a deep blue ground, copper rim and foot, Japanese, late 19th century, 9 1/2 in. high. **$900-$1,200**

Vase, long neck, bulbous body, silver wire and enamels worked in a motif of hen and chicks, silver foot and rim, Japanese, 8 3/4 in. high. **$1,000-$1,500**

Vase, mei ping form (lobes, and floral scrolls carved and incised under the glaze), the yellow ground with a key pattern, ruyi band at the neck, lappet band at the foot, Chinese, circa 1925, 14 in. high. **$200-$300**

Vase, mei ping form, overall Millefleurs on a black ground, Chinese, circa 1935, 12 in. high. **$200-$300**

Vase, moriage, worked in silver wire with branches of pink and white flowers and deep green leaves on a pale blue ground, hairlines, Japanese, early 20th century, 7 in. high. **$800-$1,200**

Vase, moriage, a naturalistic motif of trailing vines on a gray ground, hairlines, base with Ando mark, 9 in. high. **$2,000-$3,000**

Vase, overall swirling patterns divided by a ruyi band at the shoulder, the foot with a dragon-scale pattern, marked *China*, circa 1930, 10 in. high. **$100-$175**

Vase, ovoid form, the pale blue ground with goldfish and aquatic plants, silver rim and foot, yu-musen, Japanese, circa 1930, 9 in. high. **$2,200-$3,500**

Vase, ovoid form, two medallions of butterflies above flowers worked in silver wire and colors on a cream ground above and below lappet bands, Japanese, late 19th century, 6 in. high. **$300-$400**

Vase, ovoid form, yellow ground decorated with pink roses and green foliage, chrome mounts, Japanese, Showa period, 6 in. high. **$150-$185**

Vase, ovoid form, akasuke (pigeon blood) with white roses and green foliage, chrome foot and rim, Japanese, Showa period, 4 in. high. **$100-$175**

Vase, ovoid form, silver wire worked in hanging blade panels of phoenix and floral panels between gadroon-inlaid borders, silver foot and rim, Ando seal on base, minor chips, 10 3/4 in. high. **$800-$1,200**

Vase, ovoid form, silver wire worked in a band of peony and foliage on a gray ground, Japanese, circa 1915, 4 1/2 in. high. **$300-$375**

Vase, ovoid with wide mouth and waisted neck, flaring foot, a mountainscape in pale green and gray on a pale pink ground, chrome mounts, Japanese, early Showa period, 10 in. high. **$300-$500**

Vase, ovoid with a tall neck, worked in silver wires with a motif of butterflies above irises, black ground, formal borders on neck and foot, cracked and chipped, base signed *Kyoto Shibata*, Meiji period, 8 in. high. **$1,500-$2,200**

Vase, ovoid body worked in silver wire with a bridge spanning a river, the banks with pine trees, pale brown ground, badly cracked on the back (where there is no motif), base marked *Kyoto Namikawa*, Japanese, circa 1910, 4 1/2 in. high. **$1,500-$2,000**

Vase, pear-shaped with short neck, gray ground with hen and chicks worked in silver wire and enamels, minor hairlines, Japanese, late 19th century, 6 in. high. **$900-$1,200**

Vase, pear-shaped, a fierce dragon in gray, white, and red on a midnight blue ground, Japanese, late Meiji period, 4 1/2 in. high. **$200-$300**

Vase, plique-a-jour, plum blossoms on a blue ground, 5 in. high. **$900-$1,200**

Vase, akasuke (pigeon blood) with wisteria motif, Japanese, Showa period, 7 in. high. **$175-$225**

Vase, red ground with overall brass-wire T-pattern, marked *China*, circa 1930, 12 in. high. **$100-$175**

Vase, red, pink, and purple flowers on a silver blue-gray ground, the base marked *Adachi*, Japanese, 7 1/2 in. high. **$500-$700**

Vase, rust ground with scattered yellow blossoms and green foliage, copper rim and foot, marked *China*, circa 1925, 12 in. high. **$125-$175**

Vase, silver wire and blue and violet enamels worked in hydrangea on a deep blue ground, silver rim and foot, base with Hayashi Kodenji lozenge mark, Japanese, Meiji period, 3 1/2 in. high. **$5,000-$6,000**

Vase, silver wire and enamels worked in a continuous iris pattern on a pale blue ground, lappet band around the shoulders, diaper (repetitive pattern) on rim and foot, repaired, Japanese, late 19th century, 5 1/2 in. high. **$500-$700**

Vase, silver wire, rosebuds and one open rose with foliage on green ground, chrome neck and rim, marked *Japan*, 9 in. high. **$100-$175**

Vase, silver wire with birds in flight among wisteria on a deep blue ground, the foot with a diapered (repetitive pattern) band, Japanese, circa 1910, 9 1/2 in. high. **$500-$700**

Vase, silver wire with a bird perched on a flowering branch, pale blue ground, silver rim and foot, chipped, Japanese, circa 1910, 4 in. high. **$100-$150**

Vase, silver wire of a celadon green/blue ground color with roses on stems in subdued pastels of green, brown, and yellow on a graduated cylindrical body, measuring 12 in. in height and 4 in. across at its widest point, dating to the Meiji Era. Although unsigned, the style and quality of workmanship are consistent with the work of Ando Jubei or Namikawa Sosuke, Japanese. **$1,200**

Vase, squat body, silver wire worked in a band of peony on a yellow ground, Japanese, circa 1920, 3 1/2 in. high. **$250-$350**

Vase, tapering hexagonal form, silver wire worked in wisteria in shades of lilac on a light green ground, silver rim and foot, base marked *Namikawa Yasuyuki*, Japanese, Meiji period, 9 1/2 in. high. **$5,000-$6,500**

Vase, wisteria, drilled for a lamp base, late 19th century, 17 1/2 in. by 7 in. $2,950

Vases, black ground with silver wire and enamels worked in a bird and bamboo pattern, diapered (repetitive pattern) rims, copper mounts, Japanese, circa 1910, 8 1/2 in. high. **$800-$1,200**

Vases, beaker form decorated with panels of flowers above stiff leaves and bats at the bases, bases poorly restored, Chinese, circa 1900, 16 in. high, pair. **$800-$1,200**

Vases, blue ground worked in silver wire and enamels with numerous flowers, stamped *Ota* on the base, Japanese, Meiji period, 3 1/2 in. high, pair. **$700-$950**

Vases, double gourd, Millefleurs tied with ribbons in relief at the waist, Chinese, mid-Ch'ing (Qing) Dynasty, 12 1/2 in. high, pair. **$5,000-$7,000**

Vases, midnight blue with wisteria and foliage, one cracked, Japanese, Meiji period, 12 in. high, pair. **$450-$650**

Vases, modified mei ping form, turquoise ground with Millefleurs pattern, a lappet band at the base, marked *China*, early 20th century, 14 in. high, pair. **$300-$500**

Vases, globular form, overall floral and leafy scroll motif in colors on a violet blue ground, some enamel loss, Japanese, circa 1900, 14 in. high, pair. **$450-$650**

Vases, rouleau form (sometimes called a club shape), the green ground with an overall T-pattern, the necks with scrolling lotus, the bodies with large flowers above lappet bands, mounted and pierced as lamps, Chinese, early 20th century, 12 1/2 in. high, pair. **$400-$600**

Vases, salmon ground with blue dragons, mirror image, damages on both, Japanese, late 19th century, 8 3/4 in. high, pair. **$275-$375**

Vases, short necks, dark blue ground, irises and foliage in a continuous motif, both dented, Japanese, circa 1910, 12 in. high, pair. **$450-$650**

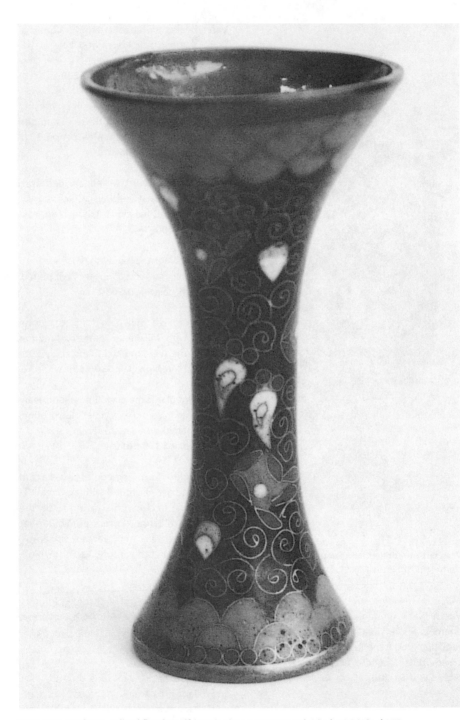

Vase, trumpet form, stylized floral motif, interior has green enamel, 2 in. by 3 3/4 in. $145

Vases, blue "Celeste," showing birds in a leafy, floral setting with stylized floral motifs around top of necks, circa late 1800s, 10 in. by 5 1/2 in., **pair. $975**

Vases, silver wire and enamels worked in chrysanthemums and foliage on a pale green ground, Japanese, circa 1900, 6 in. high, pair. **$700-$900**

Vases, slender pear-shaped bodies with black grounds and motifs of egrets above a stream and aquatic plants, copper mounts, Japanese, circa 1910, 7 in. high, pair. **$1,200-$1,800**

Vases, yen-yen (or baluster) shape, each decorated with pine, plum, prunus, and bamboo amidst rock-work, tappet borders, trumpet necks with lotus scrolls, Chinese, circa 1900, 17 in. high, pair. **$700-$1,200**

Vases, yen-yen shape, overall scrolling lotus above stiff leaves at the base, poorly restored bases, Chinese, 19th century, 19 in. high, pair. **$1,000-$1,500**

Totai (cloisonné on porcelain)

Box and cover, porcelain body, blue ground with motif of a hen and two chicks, diapered (repetitive pattern) border, signed *Takeuchi Chubei*, Japanese, late 19th century, 4 1/4 in. by 3 1/4 in. **$900-$1,200**

Bowl, porcelain body, the interior with a floral center medallion, the exterior with a yellow ground and scattered floral mon in colors, marked *Owari*, circa 1880, 7 in. diameter. **$900-$1,200**

Candlestick, panels of butterflies and flowers, autumnal hues, base marked *Noritake*, 8 in. high. **$300-$400**

Flowerpot, bucket form, porcelain, blue ground with motif of blossoming peony branches, circa 1880, 6 in. high. **$500-$700**

Flowerpot, porcelain body, blue ground with continuous motif of nesting birds, base marked *Chubei*, circa 1885, 7 1/2 in. diameter. **$1,200-$1,800**

Ginger jar, tree bark, porcelain body, bamboo motif in autumnal hues, circa 1910, 5 in. high. **$300-$450**

Jar and cover, porcelain body, the black ground with a motif of birds perched on branches, markings on base indicating this was one of a pair, 15 1/4 in. high. **$2,000-$3,000**

Mug, porcelain body, orange plum blossoms on a bark ground, base marked *Noritake*, 7 in. high. **$300-$450**

Natsume (tea caddy), the lid with a dragon, the body with a motif of floral mon, the base with a blue and white band, late 19th century. **$900-$1,200**

Left: Vase, cloisonné on porcelain, blue ground with floral motifs, modified pear shape, Japanese, circa 1875, 9 in. high. $500-$700. Right: Vase, cloisonné on porcelain, a blue ground and delicate floral motif with insects, the rim and base with diapers and mon, the base marked Takeuchi Chubel, Japanese, circa 1875, 5 in. high. $700-$900

Tea set, teapot, sugar, creamer, and six cups and saucers with six cake plates, tree bark with a bamboo pattern, each piece signed *Tashiro*, circa 1910. **$700-$1,000**

Vase, pottery body, moriage, motif of wisteria and foliage in bright red, blue, and violet predominating, silver wires, 8 in. high. **$2,000-$3,000**

Vase, pottery body, moriage, motif of blossoming peony branches, silver wires, 9 1/2 in. high. **$2,500-$3,500**

Vase, serpent handles, motif of irises and butterflies, autumnal hues, base marked *Noritake*, 8 in. high. **$350-$575**

Vase, tree-bark cloisonné, ceramic body with a long, narrow neck and bulbous body, showing a bird on a flowering branch, excellent condition, 11 in. by 4 5/8 in. **$400**

Vase, tree-bark cloisonné, ceramic body in tapering oval form with short wide neck, showing a bird clinging to a leafy branch, excellent condition, 9 7/8 in. by 6 in. **$2,750**

Tree bark, silver wires and autumnal shades with flowers, foliage, and birds, a diaper (repetitive pattern) band at the rim, Japanese, Meiji period, late 19th century, 15 in. diameter. **$900-$1,200**

Cloisonné on pottery, bean-shaped cloisons, white ground in the center with floral motif, pale blue and deep blue outer bands, Japanese, signed Kinkozan, circa 1875, 7 in. diameter. **$500-$600**

Vase, tree-bark cloisonné, ceramic body in urn form, showing a four-toed dragon, signed on the bottom, excellent condition, 4 1/2 in. by 2 1/4 in. **$150**

Vase, tree-bark cloisonné, ceramic body in an ovoid form, showing a quail in a leafy setting, excellent condition, 9 7/8 in. by 6 3/4 in. **$2,950**

Vase, tree-bark cloisonné, ceramic body in an urn form, showing a bird flying above a leafy, floral set-ting, excellent condition, 6 in. by 3 1/4 in. **$400**

Chinese cloisonné wine set, peach form with red lotus and blue dragons on a turquoise ground, tray 9 1/2 in. diamete. **$1,000-$1,500**
COURTESY OF THE EDSON COLLECTION

Vase, tree-bark cloisonné, ceramic body with a long narrow neck, bulbous body and flaring mouth, showing a bird in a leafy, floral setting, excellent condition, 14 1/2 in. by 6 1/2 in. **$2,900**

Vase, porcelain body, tree bark with a writhing dragon around the body, autumnal hues, Meiji period, 14 in. high. **$1,000-$1,500**

Vase, pottery body, shaded red ground with bird perched on a flowering branch, realistically detailed, circa 1890, 15 in. high. **$1,000-$1,600**

Vase, pottery body, blue ground with bean-shaped cloisonné forming geometric motifs and floral mon, signed *Kinkozan*, circa 1885, 5 in. high. **$300-$475**

Vase, brown, corrugated earthenware body decorated with cloisonné glaze lanterns of red and green leaves, measuring 10 1/2 in. by 7 in., dating to the early 20th century. The vase has some minor losses to the surface of the leaves. It has an impressed *Made in Japan* on the base, probably pre- World War II. **$100**

Vase, porcelain body, bulbous with short neck, red-orange leaves and vines on a tree bark ground, marked *Noritake*, 4 in. high. **$300-$400**

Vase, pottery body, blue ground with scattered floral mon, base marked *Kinkozan*, circa 1880, 8 1/2 in. high. **$600-$800**

Vases, porcelain bodies, pear-shaped with flaring foot, the neck and foot with underglaze blue and white diapers (repetitive pattern), the bodies with flowers and foliage on a light blue ground, signed *Takeuchi Chubei*, circa 1885, 12 in. high, pair. **$2,000-$3,000**

Chinese Mud Figurines

These small figurines, usually with two- or three-color glazes, were popular (and once inexpensive) tourist items, and are still being made today. The larger, more elaborate examples have seen dramatic price increases.

Elder, white beard and hair, brown and green attire, marked China, circa 1910, 1 in. high. **$10-$15**

Elder, green glazed attire, holding a bowl, marked China, circa 1905, 1 in. high. ....**$10-$15**

Elder, green glazed attire, holding a fan, marked China, circa 1925, 3 in. high. ....**$25-$35**

Elder with coin and peach (long life), marked China, circa 1925, 5 in. high. **$45-$65**

Elder with beard, blue glazed attire, holding a book, marked China, circa 1925, 3 1/2 in. high. **$20-$30**

Elder, fisherman, pole missing, marked China, circa 1930, 4 1/2 in. high. **$30-$40**

Elder, coin carrier, marked China, circa 1935, 6 in. high. **$45-$60**

Elder seated on rock-work, yellow and green glazed attire, marked China, circa 1935, 6 in. high. **$50-$75**

Elder with a fan, marked China, circa 1930, 5 in. high. **$45-$65**

Elder with yellow and blue attire, large yellow hat at the back, marked China, circa 1930, 7 in. high. **$75-$85**

Vase, brown, green, and blue glazes with figures of elders in various poses, marked China, circa 1920, 8 in. high. **$100-$150**

Mud figure, large, of a sage regarding a monkey with a peach, polychrome glazing, signed, Chinese, 20th century, 12 in. by 9 1/2 in. by 8.5 in., larger than usual for these pieces. **$550-$650**

Mud figure, large wild man or forest spirit seated on a rock, every detail, from his movable bracelets to his horns and individual claw-like fingernails and toenails, rendered in lifelike detail, Chinese, circa mid-20th century, 12 1/2 in. by 15 in. by 19 in., weight 29 lbs., excellent condition, signed on reverse. **$2,500-$3,500**

Mud figure showing a woman and leper(?), glazed in yellow, green and brown, Chinese, 3 3/4 in. by 2 3/8 in. by 1 3/4 in. **$70**

Wall pocket, blue and green glazing with flowers, marked China, circa 1925, 6 in. wide. **$75-$100**

Woman with basket of flowers, marked China, circa 1930, 6 in. high. **$50-$75**

Woman holding a bowl, green and yellow attire, her hair with a high topknot, marked China, circa 1920, 4 in. high. **$40-$55**

Chinese Porcelain & Pottery

BLANC DE CHINE

Blanc de Chine, or "white of China," is a 19th century French term used to describe creamy white glazed wares exported to Europe during the 16th and 17th centuries. The Chinese term for these ceramics is bai ci, but the blanc de chine term is used commonly today. Since the majority of these wares were made in Dehua, the capital of Fujian Province, "Dehua ware" is a more accurate term and helps to distinguish the Chinese ceramics from European ceramics that fall into the blanc de chine category.

Dehua ware can be divided into three basic types based on body style and intended use. Figures are the most common and include a variety of representations of animals; Buddhist and Daoist personages such as Guanyin (a Buddhist deity also called Avalokitesvara); and legendary Chinese characters. Western figures were also made for export. Items such as bowls, dishes, plates, and cups manufactured for everyday use make up the second type. Scholar's table items, such as mold-formed seals, brush washers, and water droppers make up the third type.

The most desirable characteristics of Dehua ware are a thick, creamy glaze, a dense clay body, a sugary texture, and fissures in the base created during firing of the dry clay. Glaze shades range from pure white to light green to light pink or rose. The Chinese prefer pieces with an ivory white glaze while those with a pinkish rose tint were highly prized by Europeans.

Sixteenth and 17th century Dehua ware figures were refined and well-sculpted but less decorated than 18th and 19th century pieces. The latter often have technically difficult additions of ribbons, jewelry, and hand-held objects that draw the eye away from the comparatively poorer sculptural quality. Several famous artists are known, including He Chaozong (1522-

1612?), Lin Chaojing (17th century), and others. These artists stamped their works on the reverse using four character archaic script in square or gourd-shaped surrounds.

The value of Dehua ware is somewhat subjective and is based on individual tastes. Genuine Ming and early Qing Dynasty pieces sell for thousands of dollars. Unfortunately, Dehua porcelain has been imitated using modern molds. The presence of a seal is not a guarantee of authenticity. The buyer should be careful also of European and Japanese white porcelains that can be mistaken for genuine Chinese Dehua.

Blanc de Chine values:

Bodhisattva seated upon a Buddhistic lion, early 19th century, 16 in. high. **$3,500-$4,500**

Box and cover, circular, molded peony blossom on lid, K'ang Hsi, 6 in. diameter. **$1,000-$1,350**

Brush holder, cylindrical, reticulated with leaf and lotus motif, K'ang Hsi, 5 in. high. **$800-$1,200**

Brush washer, Chinese melon-ribbed blanc de chine, measuring 2 1/2 in. by 3 in., dating to late 18th or early 19th century. This type of foot rim and glaze can be found on Kang Hsi wares, and the piece probably dates to that era. The brush washer comes with its own stand that appears to be a later addition. **$150**

Buddhistic lion seated with paw on brocade ball, mane braided down the back, taper sticks at the side, damage to taper sticks, early 18th century, 14 in. high. **$600-$900**

Buddhistic lions seated on tall rectangular bases, each with brocade ball under one paw, bells on collars, damages, 18th century, 11 1/2 in. high, pair. **$900-$1,200**

Candle holder, column upon waves, two dragons encircling the column, chips and hairlines, 18th century, 6 in. high. **$800-$950**

Censer, cylindrical with banded rim, three ruyi-shaped feet, incised geometric pattern, 17th century, 5 in. by 4 in. **$1,200-$1,500**

Cup, branch handle, late 19th century, 3 1/4 in. wide. **$65-$75**

A large blanc de chine figure of Kuan Yin (Guanyin), standing in jeweled flowing robes, wearing a high diadem with a miniature figure of Amitabha, and holding a small pot, the right hand in vitarka mudra, on a lotus base, mounted as a lamp, 21 in. high. Realized price (including the 10 percent buyer's premium), Christie's East, New York City. **$2,860**

Dish, Kuan Yin (or Guanyin) seated on rocky outcrop above a swirl of breaking waves and lotus plants, a small acolyte standing at the left, 18th century, restored, 10 in. high. **$500-$650**

Kuan Yin (or Guanyin) seated on oval base; long, flowing robes and pendant jewelry; firing cracks; extremities chipped; impressed four-character mark, 18th century, 13 in. high. **$4,000-$6,000**

Kuan Yin (or Guanyin) standing on domed base of molded waves; long robes, jeweled necklace and pendant, a long cowl across the high topknot; 19th century, 15 in. high. **$650-$950**

Kuan Yin (or Guanyin), long, flowing robes, a flower in one hand, marked *China*, 10 in. high. **$75-$100**

Kuan Yin (or Guanyin), long, flowing robes, a peach in one hand, marked *China*, 12 in. high. **$100-$125**

Libation cup, oval form, three small feet, exterior with branches and prunus in relief, early 18th century, 3 1/2 in. diameter. **$600-$900**

Vase, flattened baluster form, hexafoil panels of branches and prunus with birds molded in relief, 19th century, 5 1/2 in. high. **$200-$300**

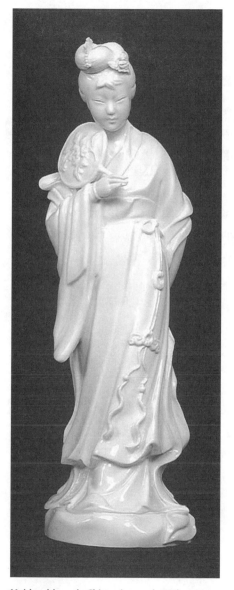

Maiden, blanc de Chine, circa early 20th century, finely modeled maiden, perhaps a concubine wearing long robes bound with silk and jade ties, and holding a fan, her long hair reaching down over her hips on the reverse, her head lowered in respect, 9 in. tall, the number "46" and a single character inscribed in the interior, excellent condition. **$950-$1,350**

Vase, pear-shaped, long neck, flared rim, applied dragon, 19th century, 14 in. high. **$400-$600**

Vase and cover, applied dragon's-head handles, Buddhistic lion finial, late 18th century, 7 in. high. **$900-$1,200**

Water dropper, lotus leaf form, tripod foot, 18th century, 3 in. diameter. **$700-$900**

Wine pot molded with prunus branches, upright handle, three bracket feet, flat cover, flower finial, early 18th century, rim chips, 8 in. high. **$3,000-$4,000**

CHINESE EXPORT PORCELAIN

In the West, the introduction of wares known as *Chinese export porcelain* dates from the late 17th century, during the K'ang Hsi (Kangxi) period (1662-1722). The Portuguese were the first to bring this porcelain to Europe, and Dutch traders successfully followed their example. In 1784, the China Empress landed in Macao near Canton (where the porcelain was decorated after its manufacture at Ching te chen). Shortly afterward, blue and white porcelain was shipped to America, where demand for these wares matched the high levels already reached in Europe.

Chinese export wine or teacup measuring 2 1/2 in. by 1 1/4 in., dating to the mid- 19th century. The cup has a scalloped edge with brown dressing. It is decorated in a typical period design in overglaze enamels of peaches and yellow flowers. There are alternating lotus panels of fruits encircling the base. A two-character mark on the base in Zhuanshu script reads: *Da Qinq*, or Great Ching. **$75**

Chinese export shallow bowl, possibly Lowestaff, decorated with scenes of acrobats and musicians performing before a royal (?) household, with a floral-decorated rim, 8 3/4 in. by 1 5/8 in., minor paint chipping. **$225**

Chinese export dragon platter, heavily potted, measuring 12 in. by 1 3/4 in. deep, dating to the early 20th century. This charger has an underglaze of red, five-toed dragon in the center surrounded by overall floral and dragon designs. These designs are executed in heavy overglaze enamels and are both impressed and outlined with black. The platter's overall color is rich mustard yellow. The rim is highlighted in gold that has some wear. The reverse has a fully decorated border of happiness characters and floral designs. The platter has a spurious Qianlong reign mark and the dragon and enamel work are in a later style. Fine original condition. **$100**

Chinese blue and white yuhuchun or bottle vase, in lotus and vine design measuring 10 in. in height, dating to the late 19th/early 20th century. The vase has a brown/orange tint to the shiny crackle glaze in some areas. The underglaze vines are done in a deep blue. The straw-colored foot shows some fritting. There is iron pitting in the glaze around the top rim and a few bubbles in the blue double ring on the base. Fine original condition. **$165**

Chinese blue and white prunus storage jar measuring 9 in. tall and approximately 7 in. at the waist, dating to the late 19th century. The jar has a false, four-character, Kang Hsi Chinese reign mark on the base typical of pieces from this period. The prunus design depicts early spring flowers breaking through the river ice. The lid and the body have surface hairline fractures that have been stabilized. **$150**

Chinese export birds and flowers plate or shallow bowl, measuring 10 in. by 1 3/4 in., dating to the late 19th/early 20th century. This charger has an underglaze blue design of birds and flowers in the center. These designs are highlighted in heavy overglaze enamels of yellow, green, and brown. The border shows three bird medallions alternating with trailing vines and flowers. The reverse has an unusual fully decorated border of landscape and floral designs. The bowl has a spurious Ming reign mark. Fine original condition. **$85**

CANTON BLUE AND WHITE

The term Canton blue and white ware refers to porcelain produced during the 18th and 19th centuries specifically for export to Europe or the United States.

The amount of porcelain produced and exported fluctuated with the political climate in China. Canton porcelain takes its name from the port of Canton, where porcelain blanks made in Qingdezhen were decorated in large warehouses and owned by foreign merchants.

Since this porcelain was intended entirely for export to the West, it was made in shapes that were foreign to the Chinese taste. Decorations were often created on demand from specific patterns provided by the customers of the shipping agents in England, continental Europe and the United States. The quality of the clay used in production and the attention paid to kiln placement and firing varied, making the porcelain body appear pure white at its best and speckled from grit or ash particles at its worst. Most wares were painted or stenciled in underglaze blue using Western patterns. The blue color varies from pale blue to black depending on the intensity of the pigment and the heat of the kiln fire. Each piece was covered with a translucent glaze that gave it a final blue-white appearance. Most have a glazed base and unglazed foot rim.

The motifs found on these wares incorporate some or all of the following elements in various combinations: island, bridge or bridges, river, trees, birds, mountains, rocks, figures, clouds, and boats.

The value of Canton export porcelain depends on many factors, including the clay used, the quality of the blue pigment, the skill of the artist and the fineness of overall work. Condition is paramount since much Canton ware was shipped as ballast in the holds of clipper ships. Rim chips and hairline cracks, which are commonplace, decrease overall value. Prices increase in general from basic Canton blue and white to Nanking to Fitzhugh to armorial porcelain. The rarer the design—for example, an armorial dinner service plate produced for George Washington—the greater the asking price.

Fitzhugh porcelain in colors other than blue brings high prices. High-quality wares typically sell in the thousands of dollars. Values can be found through online auctions with prices ranging between $50 for a Canton plate with minor chips to $250-$500 for larger pieces with no damage. Beware of modern imitations and English blue and white produced in Canton patterns.

Bowl, underglaze blue and white, lotus and scroll motif in Ming style, Chinese, mid-19th century, 4 1/2 in. diameter. **$200-$300**

Basket with under-plate, reticulated, 10 in. long. **$600-$800**

Bidet with stand and wood cover, 15 in. long. **$1,800-$2,500**

Bottle, water, 8 1/2 in. high. **$450-$600**

Bowl, cut corners, 10 1/2 in. diameter. **$625-$825**

Bowl, scalloped, 8 1/2 in. diameter. **$400-$600**

Box with cover, 5 3/4 in. square, 6 1/2 in. high. **$700-$1,050**

Cider pitcher and cover, Buddhistic lion finial, 8 in. wide. **$1,000-$1,500**

Creamer, 3 1/2 in. high. **$130-$165**

Creamer, 3 in. high. **$125-$150**

Dish, diamond shape, 9 1/2 in. by 6 in. **$250-$400**

Dish (vegetable), open, 9 in. by 7 in. **$225-$450**

Dish, oval, 11 in. by 8 1/4 in. **$300-$425**

Dish (shrimp), 10 in. by 9 1/2 in. **$450-$700**

Dish (vegetable), 11 in. long. **$300-$475**

Ginger jar, 6 in. high. **$150-$200**

Gravy boat, 5 1/2 in. long. **$150-$300**

Gravy boat, two-ended, with liner, 8 in. long. **$900-$1,200**

Hot-water plate, 9 1/2 in. diameter. **$300-$450**

Hot-water plate; open, two-piece vegetable server with vented insert; 10 1/2 in. long. **$450-$750**

Jar, oil storage, 10 in. high. **$300-$450**

Mug, twisted handle, 4 in. high. **$300-$450**

Mug, twisted handle, 3 1/2 in. high. **$300-$400**

Jar, covered storage, Chinese blue and white, circa 1890, rim chips, 8 1/2 in. by 7 1/2 in. $425

Platter, 13 1/2 in. diameter. $300-$450

Platter, oval, 13 in. by 10 in. **$225-$400**

Platter, 15 in. by 12 in. **$285-$450**

Platter, well and tree, 18 in. by 15 in. **$600-$900**

Rice bowl, cover and stand, 4 1/2 in. diameter. **$100-$175**

Soup bowl, 8 1/2 in. diameter. **$75-$125**

Scepter case, late 18th or early 19th century, showing deer in a landscape and tendril/dragon decoration, 14 in. by 2 1/2 in. by 4 1/2 in. **$300**

Sugar bowl, twisted handle, 4 1/2 in. high. **$375-$500**

Sweetmeat tray and cover, 6 in. long. **$600-$800**

Syllabub and cover. **$125-$200**

Teapot with cover, drum form, 5 1/2 in. high. **$450-$600**

Teapot with domed cover. **$600-$800**

Tile, round, 6 in. diameter. **$300-$400**

Tile, 6 in. square. **$300-$400**

Trencher (salt). **$400-$500**

Tureen, oval with strap handles, 8 1/2 in. diameter. **$750-$1,000**

Umbrella stand, 24 in. high. **$1,000-$1,500**

Urn, baluster form, 13 in. high. **$650-$950**

Vase, baluster, underglaze blue and white, the body on a tall, flaring foot and painted with a scene of eccentric Immortals amongst pine, lingzhi fungus, and rock-work between molded bands of geometric devices, the neck further painted with a bird on a gnarled pine among bamboo, lingzhi, and pierced rocks, star crack and small gold lacquer rim repair, Yung Cheng (Yongzheng) mark (and of the period), 8 7/8 in. high. Realized price (including the 10-percent buyer's premium), Christie's East, New York City. **$715**

FAMILLE ROSE

The term *famille rose* was introduced by the French to describe Chinese porcelain decorated in overglaze enamels with a predominant rose or red color. This palette, known as *fan cai* to the Chinese, developed in the later years of the reign of the Kangxi emperor as an outgrowth of earlier *famille verte*, or green palette wares. Initially, foreign red pigment was used to paint flower petals over a glassy, opaque white base. The introduction of more pigments gave the porcelain artist a wide range of softer and gentler colors. This style of decoration reached its zenith in the Yongzheng (1723-1735) and Qianlong (1736-1796) reigns.

Toward the end of the 18th century, export wares in the famille rose palette became increasingly popular in the West. The wares made for export were styled after the European mode of the times, with many of the patterns containing western or European figures. Other patterns contained Chinese and Mandarin figures; animals and fowl of all kinds were prominent in the designs. Shapes included animal form tureens and garniture sets comprised of two beaker-shaped vases and three to five covered jars.

Most of the patterned wares date from the end of the Chia Ch'ing period (1796-1820) and were developed in the early 19th century.

Chinese baluster vase in famille rose floral colors and decorations, measuring approximately 12 in. high. The body of the vase is made in a square tapered shape. The base bears a red-orange six character Xian Feng reign mark that would date it to between 1851 and 1861, but most likely a later copy. Mint original condition. **$100**

Chinese baluster vase in famille rose floral colors and decorations, measuring approximately 12 in. high. The body of the vase is made in a square tapered shape. The base bears a red-orange six character Xian Feng reign mark that would date it to between 1851 and 1861, but most likely a later copy. Mint original condition. **$100**

Chinese Famille rose bowl with wooden lid, Guangxu reign mark (1875-1908) in underglaze red, measuring 4 in. tall by 5 in. across and 17 in. circumference. The painting is of a procession around the bowl with a man riding a dragon and others carrying flags and banners. There is minor rubbing of colors, but otherwise the bowl is in very good original condition with no damage or repairs. It is set on a new wooden stand. **$150**

ROSE MEDALLION

Rose Medallion is a pattern that contains alternating reserves of birds and/or flowers and figures around a central floral medallion. Most pieces are decorated with four reserves. The space between the reserves is filled with pink peony blossoms and green tendrils on a gilt ground. Better quality porcelains have gold highlights in the hair of the woman. Because the gold is unfired and was added last, it wears away rapidly with use. The same is true of the softer enamel colors. Pristine wares are rare.

Bowl, Chinese export rose medallion, measuring 9 in. by 4 in., dating to the mid- to-late 19th century. The bowl has four alternating interior panels of roses and people. The exterior is treated in the same way. The enamels are bright and thick, showing minimal wear. The base is covered with a clear glaze that shows the white porcelain body. It is unmarked, which dates it to the mid 1800s. The bowl has had a small rim chip, repaired. **$150**

Bowl, Chinese export rose medallion, measuring 7 in. across and 2 7/8 in. high. Its interior is hand-painted in the typical rose medallion style with two floral/bird panels alternating with two figural panels surrounding a central medallion of butterflies. The outside of the bowl is painted in a similar fashion. There are two 1/8 in. professionally repaired chips on the rim that are visible only with very close inspection. There is minor rim fritting as expected. The base is unmarked and has the characteristic appearance of an early to mid-19th century piece. **$100**

Dish, Chinese rose medallion, measuring 8 1/2 in. across by 1 in. deep. The "orange peel" base, the heavy potting, the style/coloration, and red *CHINA* mark all date this to the late 19th or early 20th century. **$175**

Pendant made from a curved fragment or shard of a 19th century rose medallion vase, measuring approximately 2 in. by 1 1/2 in. in a silver surround. **$50**

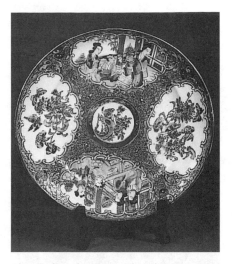

.Plate, early 19th century, gilt and green ground with butterflies and bats, 10 1/4 in. diameter. **$165-$225**

Soup bowl, circa 1885, 9 in. diameter. **$200-$225**

Platter, ovoid, Chinese export rose medallion, measuring 10 1/4 in. in length, 8 in. across and 1 in. in depth. One filled rim chip and minor fritting. It is marked *CHINA* on the base in red, dating this to the late 1890s. **$185**

The following objects are taken from a complete dinner service dating from the late 19th century. All the pieces are perfect unless noted otherwise.

Basin, 15 in. diameter. **$1,500-$2,000**

Basket, reticulated, and under-plate, 10 1/2 in. diameter. **$900-$1,200**

Bowl, 4 1/2 in. diameter. **$300-$600**

Bowl, 8 1/2 in. diameter. **$700-$950**

Box with cover, 6 in. square. **$475-$600**

Candlestick, 6 in. high. **$600-$800**

Candlestick, 8 in. high. **$900-$1,200**

Creamer, helmet shape. **$225-$400**

Garden seat, hexagonal, with open-work cash symbols, 19 in. high. **$3,500-$4,500**

Garden seat, barrel form, with double open-work cash symbols, 19 1/2 in. high. **$2,500-$3,500**

Pitcher, 6 in. long. **$300-$450**

Plate, 8 in. diameter. **$200-$275**

Plate, 12 in. diameter. **$285-$475**

Plate, 14 in. diameter. **$450-$600**

Platter, 16 in. diameter. **$700-$1,150**

Platter, 9 in. by 12 in. **$600-$800**

Punch bowl, 14 in. diameter. **$1,800-$2,200**

Punch bowl, 15 1/2 in. diameter. **$2,000-$2,800**

Punch bowl, chips on rim, rubbing, 16 in. diameter. **$1,400-$1,600**

Punch bowl, 16 in. diameter. **$2,500-$3,500**

Punch bowl, 18 in. diameter. **$3,200-$4,500**

Sugar bowl and cover, 6 in. long. **$300-$450**

Teapot, helmet shape. **$475-$650**

Vase, 6 in. high. **$125-$185**

Vase, 8 in. high. **$275-$350**

Vase, oviform, two fixed Buddhistic lion and ring handles, mid to late 19th century, 24 in. high. **$2,000-$2,500**

Vase, oviform, panels of ladies divided by bands of flowers, foliage, and medallions, scalloped rim, circa 1885, 24 in. high. **$1,800-$2,400**

Vases, pear-shaped, with cup-shaped rims and elephant-head handles, one damaged, late 19th century, pair. **$1,400-$2,500**

Vases, oviform, applied gilt dragons around long neck, late 19th century, 26 in. high, pair. **$3,500-$4,500**

Vases, one of a pair, mid-19th century, each decorated with panels of court ladies and alternating panels of figures in interiors with birds and fruiting, flowering boughs on a gilt and green ground, the neck flanked with Buddhistic lion-form handles, the shoulder with applied kylins, one heavily restored, chips to both, 35 1/2 in. high. Realized price (including the 10 percent buyer's premium), Christie's East, New York City. (There are many reproductions of this kind of vase, which look great "from a distance of about eight feet," according to one appraiser. These sell on the decorative market for between **$650 and $850.**) **$3,520**

ROSE CANTON

Rose Canton is the same as Rose Medallion, with the exception of the figures. Rose Canton contains absolutely no figures. The pattern has alternating panels or reserves of butterflies and flowers.

Additional Patterns

Famille rose porcelain was produced in a wide variety of patterns depending on the buyer's request. Designs that appear strange to Western eyes do so because Chinese artists often were given only a general idea or a poor drawing of what was desired. Their interpretations resulted in unusual appearing people and backgrounds. For the most part, however, patterns such as those following were well established. In some dinner services, a central pattern might be used but the rim or border decorations would vary.

Patterns in the famille rose palette include the following:

100 Golden Butterflies: A colorful pattern produced in the late 19th century, typically in dinner services.

Auspicious Figures: Four figures alternate with clusters of symbols taken from the 100 Antiques pattern. This includes Buddhist and Taoist symbols and the attributes of the Eight Immortals. The symbols radiate like the spokes of a wheel around the center figure.

Bouquet: A center motif of a floral bouquet with or without trailing ribbons and bows, surrounded by open space.

Cabbage Leaf Pattern or Butterfly and Cabbage: This pattern was produced throughout the latter 18th and the 19th centuries. The cabbage leaves are usually a deep green. The pattern may be accented with butterflies or coins.

Dragon and Chrysanthemum: This pattern, dating from the Kuang Hsu period, contains orange dragons and white chrysanthemums on either a turquoise or yellow ground.

Garden: In the center, a segment of garden; there is also a great deal of open space.

Imari: The earliest Chinese Imari dates from the 18th century. For the most part, the glaze has a gray, greenish, or bluish green tint, and there is usually a brown or reddish brown foot rim (where the glaze stops). The red in Chinese Imari is a coral hue; the blue never runs, and it is always crisp and lighter than its Japanese counterparts. This Imari bears no evidence of spur marks.

Millefleur or 1000 Flowers Pattern: This pattern was produced throughout the 18th and 19th century both for domestic use and for export. Pieces may have reign marks on the base. They represent some of the finest artistry in the use of the famille rose palette.

Rooster Pattern: A late 19th or early 20th century pattern produced in dinner sets. It features multiple black and red roosters in landscape scenes.

Rose and Long Life: One large peony with a bird perched on a branch.

Rose Mandarin: This is among the most expensive of all the rose palette export patterns. The pattern contains Mandarin figures in various poses (scenic landscapes and river scenes are also included). The borders of the objects usually contain some combination of fruit, flowers, butterflies, and foliage (but all of those elements are not necessarily present).

Tobacco Leaf: Tobacco leaf pattern export porcelain is among the rarest of designs since much less of this type was manufactured than Rose Medallion. Individual plates can sell for more than **$2,000** if in fine condition.

Example of Auspicious Figures Pattern:
Chinese export washbasin done in famille rose palette, measuring 15 1/2 in. by 5 1/2 in., dating to the late 19th century. The construction by hand from rings of clay is evident in the body shape. The central panel bears a peacock. It is surrounded by multiple auspicious Buddhist symbols in overglaze enamel. The exterior has three abstract orange designs. The base has an orange peel texture consistent with this period. There is minor fritting of the rim to the touch. The bowl has an accompanying wooden base. **$300**

Examples of Dragon and Chrysanthemum Pattern:
Dish, turquoise ground, orange dragons, white flowers, gilt border, late 19th century, 8 in. diameter. **$250-$350**

Fishbowl, turquoise ground, orange dragons, white flowers, fitted wood stand, late 19th century, 8 in. by 16 in. **$2,500-$3,500**

Garden seat, turquoise ground, orange dragons, white flowers, late 19th century, 19 1/2 in. high. **$2,800-$3,600**

Bowl with scalloped rim, four panels of floral motifs and a central floral spray, late Ch'ien Lung, 18th century, 8 1/2 in. diameter. **$600-$900**
COURTESY OF THE LUHN COLLECTION

Plate, dinner, with a central motif of a basket filled with flowers, the border highlighted with gilt, circa 1770, 9 1/4 in. diameter. **$700-$925**
COURTESY OF THE LUHN COLLECTION

Jardiniere, yellow ground, dragons, white flowers, key-fret border, late 19th century, 9 1/2 in. by 15 in. **$800-$1,200**

Tile, turquoise ground, orange dragons, white flowers, key-pattern border, late 19th century, 25 in. square. **$1,200-$1,500**

Vase and cover, yellow ground, two writhing orange dragons, white flowers, the cover with a gilt Buddhistic lion finial, a turquoise floral band on the cover and at the foot, late 19th century, 28 in. high. **$2,200-$2,800**

Examples of Chinese Imari Pattern:

Barber's bowl, peony sprays with cell pattern, foliage scrolls on border, reverse with peony sprays, fritting, early 18th century, 10 1/4 in. diameter. **$1,500-$1,800**

Pot, covered, with handle, floral motif and trellis around the center with fighting cocks, mid-18th century, 4 1/2 in. high. **$2,000**
COURTESY OF THE LUHN COLLECTION

Bowl, exterior motif of pavilions and willow, the interior border with trellis ground and floral cartouches, mid-18th century, 10 1/2 in. diameter. **$500-$700**

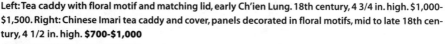

Left: Tea caddy with floral motif and matching lid, early Ch'ien Lung. 18th century, 4 3/4 in. high. $1,000-$1,500. Right: Chinese Imari tea caddy and cover, panels decorated in floral motifs, mid to late 18th century, 4 1/2 in. high. $700-$1,000
COURTESY OF THE LUHN COLLECTION

Dish, oval, motif of pagodas and riverscape, chips on rim, Ch'ien Lung, 15 1/2 in. wide. **$500-$700**

Dish, central motif of flowers and basket, early 18th century, 8 in. diameter. **$600-$700**

Jardiniére, large clusters of scrolling lotus-head foliage and long fronds of curly leaves, a band of chevron at the rim, base drilled, 18th century, 16 in. diameter. **$2,500-$3,500**

Jars, baluster form with domed covers, knob finials, pheasant on rock-work with dense floral patterns, the necks with a band of flowers, riverscapes on the covers, one jar restored, early 18th century, 24 1/2 in. high, pair. **$3,500-$4,500**

Jars, baluster form with domed covers and biscuit Buddhistic lion finials, motif of birds on rock-work, peony lappets on shoulders and above foot, 18th century, 29 in. high, pair. **$9,000-$12,000**

Plate, pagodas amongst peony and prunus, early 18th century, 9 in. diameter. **$400-$500**

Tankard, cylindrical, scenic motif with dense florals, circa 1800, 3 1/2 in. high. **$300-$500**

Teapot and cover, globular, decorated with birds perched on branches, peony, and rock-work, late 18th century, 6 in. wide. **$350-$450**

Tureen and cover, oval, floral handles, fruit finial, mid-18th century, 6 1/2 in. wide. **$900-$1,200**

Bouillon, small size, twisted branch-and-leaf handles, first quarter of the 19th century. **$100-$150**

Lid with gilt finial, early 19th century. **$200-$250**

Box, barrel-form, with cover, circa 1875, damaged, 6 in. high. **$200-$300**

Vases, beaker form, waisted, painted with pheasants on rock-work, cell pattern lappets at the trumpet neck, riveted, early 18th century, 15 in. high, pair. $1,500-$2,200

Examples of Rose Mandarin Pattern:
Beaker vases, flaring neck, spreading foot, early 19th century, 15 in. high, pair. **$3,500-$4,500**

Beaker vases, flaring neck, spreading foot, late 19th century, 15 in. high, pair. **$1,500-$2,200**

Bough vases, octagonal, faceted sides, removable tops, first half of the 19th century, 10 in., pair. **$3,500-$5,000**

Bowl; panels of figures, trees, and pavilions, gilt scroll ground, 19th century, 11 in. diameter. **$350-$500**

Coffeepot and cover, ladies and pavilions, hairline, late 18th century. **$450-$600**

Dish, oval, dignitaries, scholars, and ladies on a terrace with tables and awning, the border with butterflies and flowers, early 19th century, 16 in. wide. **$2,200-$3,100**

Garden seat, hexagonal shape, a seated dignitary addressing an audience, double-pierced cash symbols on two sides; all between bands of fruit, foliage, and raised bosses; early 19th century. **$4,500-$6,000**

Garden seat, barrel form, a dignitary addressing an audience, pierced cash symbols, bands of fruit and flowers, upper and lower bands of raised bosses, early 19th century, 19 1/2 in. high. **$3,500-$4,500**

Jardiniére, hexagonal (with stand), continuous scene of dignitaries, scholars, and ladies; flat rim with bird cartouches and floral ground; early 19th century, 9 1/2 in. diameter. **$2,500-$5,500**

Mug, cylindrical, Y-pattern ground in iron red, floral edge, panels of standing figures in landscapes, late 18th century, 4 3/4 in. high. **$450-$600**

Punch bowl, butterflies, flowers, and foliage borders, key-pattern bands, early 19th century, 18 in. diameter. **$6,000-$8,000**

Punch bowl, the border with flowers, butterflies, and foliage, early 19th century, 16 1/2 in. diameter. **$4,500-$5,000**

Punch bowl, flowers, foliage, and fruit borders, key-pattern band, early 19th century, 14 in. diameter. **$3,500-$4,500**

Snuff box, gilt mounts, ladies, pavilions, and trees on lid and exterior, rubbed, 18th century, 3 in. diameter. **$1,500-$2,500**

Teacup and saucer, puce landscapes, red and black cell patterns, 19th century. **$175-$225**

Teapot and cover, landscapes with ladies and attendants, late 19th century. **$300-$400**

Tureen and cover, dignitaries and children with seascape in the background, gilt scroll border, Buddhistic lion finial, late 18th century, chips and crack, 15 in. wide. **$1,500-$2,000**

Vase, baluster form, painted on both sides with panels of ladies and dignitaries, bands of fruit and flowers dividing the panels, gilt Buddhistic lion cubs applied on either side of the neck, first half of the 19th century, 25 in. high. **$5,000-$6,000**

Vases and covers, groups of ladies in two panels, the panels divided by two smaller panes of figures within gilt key-pattern borders edged with scattered fruit and floral sprays, early 19th century, 26 in. high. **$10,000-$12,000**

Examples of Tobacco Leaf Pattern:
Basin, late 18th century, 12 in. diameter. **$2,000-$3,000**

Bowl, famille rose, flowers and large-veined leaves, two bamboo-form loop handles, rim in need of restoration, 18th century, 6 in. wide. **$475-$675**

Dish, mid-18th century, 15 in. wide. $2,500-$3,500

Dish, cushion-shaped, early 19th century, 7 in. diameter. **$900-$1,300**

Plate, lobed, 18th century, 8 1/2 in. diameter. **$800-$1,200**

Salt (domed), famille rose, scalloped rim, the top painted with peony sprays, overlapping large serrated leaves in underglaze blue, turquoise, pink, and light green, 18th century, 4 in. wide. **$700-$900**

Sauce tureen and cover with stand (red Tobacco Leaf), underglaze blue and red, hare-head handles, floral finial, exotic flowers and serrated leaves, floral roundels, 18th century, 8 in. wide. **$1,500-$1,800**

NANKING BLUE AND WHITE

Nanking blue and white has motifs similar to those used in Canton blue and white; the difference between the two wares is found in the border. Canton blue and white has a blue lattice or network outer border, sometimes overworked with a primitive star pattern and an inner pattern of wavy lines. These wavy lines, called *clouds*, enclose a diagonal lined pattern called *rain*. Thus, the Canton border is referred to as *rain and clouds*.

The Nanking border, on the other hand, is diapered on the outer edge, sometimes with a geometric, diamond-based pattern, and contains an inner border of spearheads.

Note, too, that the term Nanking was used by the English in the 18th century to denote better-quality Canton blue and white.

Bowl, scalloped, 9 in. diameter. **$450-$600**

Box and cover, 7 in. long, 3 1/2 in. wide, 2 1/2 in. diameter. **$1,000-$1,500**

Dish, leaf-shaped, twig handle, 6 in. long. **$175-$275**

Dish, leaf-shaped, no handle, 7 1/2 in. long. **$200-$300**

Dish (vegetable), oval, 11 in. long. **$400-$500**

Flagon, Buddhistic lion finial, orange-peel glaze, 11 1/2 in. high. **$1,500-$2,500**

Flagon, Buddhistic lion finial, orange-peel glaze, 11 1/2 in. high. **$900-$1,500**

Gravy boat, twisted handle, gilt trim, 7 1/2 in. long. **$275-$300**

Platter, 14 in. by 11 in. **$345-$500**

Platter, oval, 19 in. by 16 in. **$450-$675**

Pot (chocolate), pear-shaped, Buddhistic lion finial, 9 in. high. **$750-$1,000**

Saucer and cup, no handle, gilt trim. **$200-$300**

Syllabub and cover. **$150-$250**

Tea caddy, 5 1/2 in. high. **$225-$350**

Tea caddy, gilt trim, 5 in. high. **$600-$800**

Trencher (salt). **$450-$600**

Tureen with cover and under-plate, gilt-flower finial, twisted handles, 7 1/2 in. diameter. **$600-$725**

Umbrella stand, 24 in. high. **$1,200-$1,600**

FITZHUGH

Fitzhugh is a pattern that may be found in red, sepia, blue, orange, green, and black, but basic Fitzhugh is blue and white. It was produced at the same time as Canton and Nanking, as well as in the same place. Sometimes its pattern elements are gilt outlined or trimmed with gilt borders. Blue and white wares of this period with gold highlights are referred to as "clobbered" porcelain. The gold highlights may have been added in China at the time of production or in Europe at a later date.

A circular medallion adorns the center of the Fitzhugh pattern (from time to time, the medallion was replaced, by special order, with an eagle or monogram). While the border is generally post and spear, it can also be varied.

Other characteristics of this porcelain include four panels of floral designs, and a wide border broken in several areas and filled with diaper patterns. One Fitzhugh border contains a trellis with four split pomegranates showing fruit inside. Some of the diapered symbols are shaped like butterflies with their wings spread.

Oval sauce tureen and cover; brown; entwined, berried branch handles; gilt flower finial; early 19th century, 8 in. wide. **$1,200-$1,500**

Oval serving dish, bright green over black, outlined pattern, gilt border, circa 1810, 18 in. wide. **$1,000-$1,500**

Tazza, blue and white, shallow, quatrefoil bowl on waisted and domed foot, rectangular medallion of pomegranates surrounded by Fitzhugh-pattern bands, late 18th century, 12 in. wide. **$1,500-$2,200**

Tea bowl and saucer, sepia and gilt with fruiting vine border, early 19th century. **$200-$300**

Teapot, blue and white, short, grooved spout, intertwined, berried handle, oval floral medallion enclosing gilt monogram, Fitzhugh-pattern bands on the shoulder and cover, small crack in body, late 18th century, 6 1/2 in. high. **$600-$800**

Warming dish, green, circular, circa 1810, 9 1/2 in. diameter. **$1,000-$1,500**

Animal Tureens

Note: There are many contemporary reproductions of the following antique pieces being sold, often claimed as "authentic." Buyer beware!

Carp tureen, fin as the loop handle to the cover, iron red and gilt, repair to the tail, 19th century, 12 in. wide. **$2,000-$2,500**

Crab tureen and cover, pincers curled to the front, eight legs around the sides, late 19th century, 7 in. wide. **$700-$900**

Duck tureen, head, features, and tail in shades of brown, grisaille, and black, yellow webbed feet, repair to cover, 19th century, 11 1/4 in. wide. $**2,500-$3,700**

Goose tureen, the cover formed as the upper part of the body, yellow beak, pink crest, puce head feathers, brown body feathers, feet tucked beneath a white breast, old restoration, Ch'ien Lung, 13 1/2 in. long. **$18,000-$25,000**

Barber's bowl, famille verte, centrally painted shield-shaped coat of arms and coronets above a scroll with peony sprays, the upward-curving border reserved with animal cartouches on a blue cell-pattern ground, early 18th century, 9 1/4 in. diameter. **$2,500-$3,500**

ARMORIAL

Armorial (or heraldic) pattern export wares date from the end of the K'ang Hsi period, circa 1695. Armorial designs were specially ordered: scenes replicated from European prints, ship motifs, figurines, animals, birds, and so on. Border patterns also vary. The East India Company processed orders in Ching te chen, and the porcelain blanks were sent to be decorated at Canton.

Barber's bowl, famille verte, centrally painted shield-shaped coat of arms and coronets above a scroll with peony sprays, the upward-curving border reserved with animal cartouches on a blue cell-pattern ground; rubbed—little of the pattern remains, early 18th century, 9 1/4 in. diameter. **$800-$1,200**

Coffeepot and cover, famille rose, pear-shaped, large coats of arms and crests, shades of blue on a gilt foliage ground, puce (dark red) landscapes, early 18th century, hairline in lid, crack in body, 8 3/4 in. high. **$800-$1,200**

Meat dish, oval, a falcon crest in the center (below the motto *Vraye Foy* and above the molded tree-of-life strainer), circa 1800, 19 1/2 in. wide. **$600-$900**

Oval serving platter, Van Rensselear pattern, central butterfly medallion, gilt and puce floral bands, late 18th century, 20 in. diameter. **$600-$900**

Plate painted with coat of arms and elaborate mantling below the crest within a scroll and dot band, the border decorated *en grisaille* with elaborate cartouches and figures, Ch'ien Lung, 14 in. diameter. **$1,675-$2,300**

Plate, famille rose, central gilt shield-shaped coat of arms showing three nude female bust lengths below a larger crest, bamboo and flower-head borders, Ch'ien Lung, 15 in. diameter. **$1,500-$2,000**

Plate, central shield-shaped coat of arms with leafy swags below coronet, all set on a rock-and-tree vignette below a red, blue, and gilt spear-head-and-scroll border, Ch'ien Lung, 9 1/2 in. diameter. **$900-$1,200**

Plate, coat of arms within feathery mantle beneath a seated lion crest, all within spear-heads, four grisaille landscape scrolls at the border, Ch'ien Lung, two hairlines, 9 1/2 in. diameter. **$500-$600**

"En grisaille" refers to a style of monochromatic painting in shades of gray, used especially for the representation of relief sculpture, or to simulate one. It may also refer to a gray underpainting, laid for subsequent color glazing. Also, a kind of paint that can be fired onto glass.

Plate, famille rose, molded and scalloped rim, centrally painted coat of arms and crest amongst floral sprays, the well with a gilt dentel band below with underglaze blue cell pattern, late 18th century, rim chips, 9 1/2 in. diameter. **$300-$400**

Punch bowl, plain interior, the exterior with two coats of arms, the shield supporting a gilt coronet and falcon crest, dividing a grisaille and peacock band, cracks, mid-18th century, 11 1/2 in. diameter. **$500-$600**

Soup plate, famille rose, central shield-shaped coat of arms beneath the crest and within floral mantling, the well with gilt scrolling band, the border with an underglaze blue band of prong and cell cartouches, a shaped rim, late Ch'ien Lung, 9 1/2 in. diameter. **$350-$500**

Tankard, famille rose, cylindrical, loop handles, shield-shaped coat of arms, blank scroll, crest, and mantling beneath a band of chain-link, restored crack, mid-18th century, 4 1/2 in. high. **$375-$500**

Teapot and cover, angular spout with foliate strap handle, small flower heads enclosing coat of arms, foliate finial, minor rim chips, Ch'ien Lung, 10 in. wide. **$400-$600**

Tureen with hare-head handles, coats of arms on both sides and supporters beneath a floral swag, dentil band at rim, no cover, Ch'ien Lung, 12 1/2 in. wide. **$500-$600**

Tureen and cover, famille rose, coat of arms and lion mask pad feet, loop handles at ends, lotus bud finial dividing two stag crests at the rim, Ch'ien Lung, restored handles, 11 1/2 in. diameter. **$1,800-$2,500**

NOTES ON CH'ING (QING) DYNASTY PORCELAINS

The K'ang Hsi (Kangxi) Period: 1666-1723

Among the popular wares introduced during the K'ang Hsi period were those classified as famille verte, famille noire, and famille jaune (green, black, and yellow families, respectively). Famille verte can be found in combination with a powder blue (also known as soufflé blue), which was blown onto the porcelain through a tube–likely one with a piece of gauze stretched over the end. Famille noire is marked by dark green over a black slip ground, while famille jaune has a yellow ground. The yellow enamels are always light and transparent; the transparency of the green hues is similar. Both yellow and green enamels produced toward the end of the period have varying shades.

Also during this period, the use of overglaze blue was instituted. Previously, porcelain had been subjected to the time-consuming process of double firing: once for overglaze enamels, and another time for underglaze blue. The new glaze, evident in five-color Chinese porcelain (wu ts'ai) and in famille verte wares, is thin with a lustered finish.

Three-color ware on biscuit–san ts'ai–is synonymous with the reign of Emperor K'ang Hsi. San ts'ai enamels were fired directly on the biscuit, mainly in hues of green and yellow with aubergine (eggplant purple).

From 1677, the use of the Imperial K'ang Hsi mark on porcelain was forbidden. This rule was not always observed, however, so there were pieces made toward the end of the period that in fact have reign marks.

Finally, it was during this reign that Canton and Nanking blue and white wares were introduced.

The Yung Cheng (Yongzheng) Period: 1723-1736

From 1723, the pink color palette referred to as famille rose was used to decorate Chinese porcelains, including the export wares. Famille rose pink is opaque, as are the accompanying greens and yellows, which are never-theless similar to the shades of the preceding period. The use of bright turquoise, on the other hand, is similar to that of the Chia Ching period of the Ming Dynasty.

Designs from this period are less crowded than in previous wares, and are done in Chinese taste, incorporating an abundance of florals and birds. Individual pieces tend to have a less pronounced foot, but a sharper rim.

The paste of Yung Cheng porcelains is smooth, white, and quite fine. Enamels of the period have a shiny quality and are very clear, and the translucent glaze is whiter than that used during the K'ang Hsi period.

Marks include four or six characters, sometimes in a double square with canted corners. These marks were reproduced during the 1920s and 1930s on eggshell porcelains.

The Ch'ien Lung (Qianlong) Period: 1736-1796

It is often difficult to distinguish Yung Cheng wares from early Ch'ien Lung wares. The palette for this reign did, however, include several innovations such as the introduction of pale lime green, painting in sepia, and imitations in porcelain of wood grains (bamboo), lacquer, bronze, and silver.

An especially popular new color was European green, used throughout the remainder of the Ch'ing Dynasty. Look for this green (which may be a turquoise or blue-green hue) on the interior, inside rim, or foot of a piece.

Another innovation of the Ch'ien Lung period was the moving picture, which involved an outer section—a vase—rotating around a stationary, inner core. The inner core was painted with reserves of a continuous motif, visible through open panels in the outer vase. Thus, when the vase revolved around the core, it created the illusion that the picture inside was actually moving.

Ku Yueh Hsuan (Ancient Moon Terrace), an opaque white porcelain resembling milk glass, is associated with the reign of Ch'ien Lung, even though it dates back to the reign of K'ang Hsi. Ku Yueh Hsuan was made at Ching te chen and sent to the Imperial Palace Workshops in Peking (Beijing) for decoration.

Ch'ien Lung porcelain features a pure white paste with a smooth base rim. Colors are vivid and brilliant, not washed out. The glaze is translucent white. In the latter part of the period, orange-peel glaze (which has a rippled effect) came into use and was produced throughout the Ch'ing Dynasty.

Marks of the period consist of either four or six characters within a double square having canted corners. Like the marks of previous periods and dynasties, they have been copied extensively.

The Chia Ch'ing (Jiaqing) Period: 1796-1820

Among the distinguishing characteristics of this reign is the sand grit that is sometimes found embedded in the glaze (in and around the foot rim). In addition, the porcelain, for the most part, became more thick-walled. Copies of the preceding Ch'ing Dynasty reigns were also produced.

The Chia Ch'ing period initiated the production of Canton Rose patterned wares, which continued throughout the 19th and early 20th centuries. These wares are currently made available in reproductions, as well.

Priced examples of Chinese porcelain and pottery (traditional):

Monochromes

Apple green bottle/vases, finely crackled, late 19th century, 6 1/2 in. high. **$300-$500**

Apple green bottle/vase, large crackle, brown foot, late 18th/early 19th century, 8 1/2 in. high. **$500-$700**

Apple green bottle/vase, crackled glaze, early 19th century, 5 1/2 in. high. **$150-$225**

Apple green bowl, incised chrysanthemum and leafy scroll, 18th century, 5 1/2 in. diameter. **$600-$800**

Apple green vase, body with dog-head handles, tall garlic neck, late 18th century, 8 1/4 in. high. **$1,000-$2,000**

Blue bottle/vase, bulbous body, wide, long neck, white rim, base, and interior, Ch'ien Lung six-character mark (and of the period), 21 in. high. **$4,000-$6,000**

Blue bowl, everted rim (chipped), white interior, Kuang Hsü six-character mark (and of the period), 4 in. diameter. **$200-$300**

Blue bulb bowl, everted rim, white rim and interior, late 18th/early 19th century, 7 1/2 in. diameter. **$350-$450**

Blue jardinières, square, molded with bamboo borders, circular panels on sides, pierced, early 20th century, 11 1/2 in. high, pair. **$375-$475**

Blue kendi (a device for smoking), powder blue, pear-shaped spout, traces of gilt decoration, flaring neck, Ch'ien Lung, 8 1/2 in. high. **$700-$1,000**

Blue kendi (powder blue), onion-shaped spout, traces of gilt floral decorations, landscape panel, 18th century, 9 1/2 in. high. **$450-$700**

Blue sauce dish incised with five-toed dragon and flaming pearl—the exterior, with lotus meander, Kuang Hsü six-character mark (and of the period), 13 in. diameter. **$400-$650**

Blue sauce dish, plain interior, deep blue glaze stopping neatly around the foot, early 18th century, 8 1/2 in. diameter. **$700-$900**

Blue vase (powder blue), yen-yen shape, traces of gilt decoration, 18th century, 16 in. high. **$1,000-$1,500**

Blue vases, slender necks, globular bodies, gilt dragons and flaming pearls, Kuang Hsü six-character mark (and of the period), 15 in. high, pair. **$1,200-$1,500**

Blue vase (powder blue), square form, elephant head handles, gilt sprays of grasses, landscape panels, T'ung Chih six-character mark (and of the period), 11 1/2 in. high. **$600-$800**

Blue vase (powder blue), beaker form, four central, serrated vertical flanges, late 18th/early 19th century, 9 in. high. **$600-$800**

Blue vases (powder blue), rouleau (rolled) form, gilt-enriched landscape, pierced and mounted as lamps, late 18th/ early 19th century, 18 in. high. **$800-$1,000**

Blue vase (powder blue), baluster form, gilt chrysanthemums, late 18th century, 6 1/2 in. high. **$300-$400**

Blue vase (powder blue), even glaze, white interior, late 18th/early 19th century, 8 in. high. **$500-$750**

Robin's egg blue brush washer, applied chih lung at rim, late 19th century, 3 in. diameter. **$350-$450**

Robin's egg blue vase, flared foot, trumpet mouth, glaze shading to white on the interior; Ch'ien Lung mark, but late 19th century; 13 in. high. **$2,500-$3,500**

Robin's egg blue vase, baluster form, late 19th century, pierced and mounted as a lamp, 15 1/2 in. high. **$250-$350**

Café au lait bottle/vase, pear-shaped, mask and ring handles, flared neck, 19th century, 9 1/2 in. high. **$600-$800**

Café au lait bowl, iridescent brown interior, pale brown exterior, white rim and base, K'ang Hsi six-character mark (and of the period), 4 3/4 in. diameter. **$2,000-$3,000**

Café au lait bowl; everted rim; the exterior, a pale washed brown; plain interior; 18th century, 7 in. diameter. **$600-$800**

Café au lait bowl, everted rim, molded with two thin ribs on the exterior, Ch'ien Lung six-character mark (and of the period), 7 in. diameter. **$2,000-$3,000**

Cherry red box and cover, turquoise interior and base, late 19th century, 4 in. diameter. **$175-$225**

Cherry red (also termed Lang Yao) bottle/vase; even, rich red glaze pooling neatly around the foot; late 18th/early 19th century, 12 1/4 in. high. **$1,000-$1,500**

Cherry red saucer dish, white interior, dark red glaze, Yung Cheng six-character mark (and of the period), rim chips, 8 in. diameter. **$500-$700**

Cherry red vase, baluster, rib at the neck, 19th century, 14 in. high. **$700-$900**

Cherry red vase, baluster form, one rib at neck, chips on the foot, 18th century, 13 in. high. **$2,000-$2,500**

Claire de lune bottle, double gourd, even glaze stopping neatly around the foot, Ch'ien Lung six-character mark, but late 18th/early 19th century, 12 in. high. **$1,500-$2,200**

Claire de lune brush washer, translucent glaze pooling at the foot, fret chips on interior, K'ang Hsi six-character mark (and of the period), 4 3/4 in. diameter. **$900-$1,200**

Claire de lune bowl, incised motif of crane and clouds in a roundel on the interior, the exterior with a floral meander, 19th century, 9 1/2 in. diameter. **$600-$900**

Claire de lune vase, molded elephant head and ringed ears, pierced and mounted as a lamp, early 20th century, 14 in. high. **$200-$275**

Claire de lune vase, square form, molded with Buddhist trigrams (the eight possible combinations of three whole or broken lines used especially in Chinese divination) on the angles, short neck, spreading foot, crackled glaze, Ch'ien Lung six-character mark (and of the period), 11 in. high. **$9,000-$12,000**

Copper red bowl, deep, rich, colored glaze thinning near the rim, white interior, Yung Cheng six-character mark (and of the period), 4 1/4 in. diameter. **$3,500-$4,500**

Copper red bowl, plain interior, 18th century, 6 in. diameter. **$500-$700**

Copper red jarlet, globular with wide mouth, white interior, glaze stopping neatly around the foot, K'ang Hsi six-character mark (and of the period), 3 1/4 in. diameter. **$1,050-$1,450**

Copper red saucer dish, glaze thinning around the rim and darkening at the center, 18th century, 6 1/2 in. diameter. **$700-$900**

Copper red stem bowl, ribbed foot, deep, rich glaze thinning at the ribs, plain interior, Yung Cheng six-character mark (and of the period). **$5,500-$7,500**

Coral dish, the coral ground decorated with flowering chrysanthemums painted in a central roundel below a fluted well, damaged, 18th century, 7 in. diameter. **$600-$900**

Coral vase, oviform body with tall slender neck, dragon applied at the neck, base and interior glazed in European green, early 19th century, 12 in. high. **$900-$1,200**

Flambé bottle/vase, tapered cylindrical body, inverted trumpet-shaped neck, red glaze with lavender splashes, circa 1900, 9 3/4 in. high. **$250-$350**

Flambé bottle/vase, globular, tall flaring neck, streaked glaze, violet blue in some areas around the foot and neck, late 19th century, 13 in. high. **$300-$500**

Flambé bottle/vase, late 19th century, 5 in. high. **$75-$100**

Flambé figures, Buddhistic lions glazed red with purple and white streaks, early 20th century, 10 in. high, pair. **$300-$400**

Flambé jar, oviform, ribbed shoulder, animal mask handles, streaked olive and purple glaze stopping around a shallow-cut foot, glazed base, 18th century, 13 1/2 in. high. **$650-$850**

Flambé vase, pear-shaped, cup rim, rib at shoulder, streaked with cherry red and purple glazes, 19th century, 12 1/2 in. high. **$400-$500**

Flambé vases, rectangular with two molded, tubular handles, red glaze streaked with purple and gray, 10 1/2 in. high, early 20th century, pair. **$300-$500**

Gold bowl, short foot, exterior covered with an even gilt, Yung Cheng six-character mark (and of the period), 3 1/2 in. diameter. **$1,500-$2,500**

Iron rust bottle/vase, pear-shaped with a reddish/brown, mottled gray glaze, 18th century, 4 in. high. **$400-$600**

Iron rust bottle/vase, gray-flecked reddish brown glaze, globular body, slender neck, concave base, 18th century, 4 1/2 in. high. **$600-$700**

Iron rust censer, tripod; globular body, short, everted rim, mottled glaze stopping around the neck of the interior, late 19th century, 6 in. wide. **$300-$450**

Iron rust vase, mei ping form, pink-brown glaze with metallic gray, thinning to white around the rim, trimmed foot; concave base, 18th century, 3 1/2 in. high. **$600-$800**

Lavender vase, baluster form, short neck, rib halfway up the neck, large crackled glaze, K'ang Hsi, 8 1/2 in. high. **$1,600-$2,200**

Lavender vase, broad, ovoid body, tall neck, animal mask handles, Yung Lo mark, but late 19th/early 20th century, 5 in. high. **$200-$300**

Lavender bowl, glaze thinning and pooling at the foot, plain interior, Hsien Feng six-character mark (and of the period), 6 1/2 in. diameter. **$1,200-$1,800**

Liver red saucer dish, white everted rim, even glaze, Tao Kuang six-character mark (and of the period), 8 in. diameter. **$700-$1,000**

Liver red vase, mei ping form, tapered waist, pale glaze thinning to white around the lip and base, Ch'ien Lung seal mark (and of the period), rim fretting, 7 1/2 in. high. **$1,200-$1,500**

Mirror black bottle/vase, globular body, cylindrical neck, garlic mouth, 14 in. high, 19th century. **$500-$750**

Mirror black teapot, globular with domed lid, traces of gilt birds and plants, 18th century, 5 in. high. **$500-$700**

Mirror black vase, mallet shape, cylindrical neck, late 19th/early 20th century, 6 in. high. **$100-$175**

Mirror black vases, ovoid bodies, open S-shaped handles, pierced and mounted as lamps, early 20th century, 12 3/4 in. high, pair. **$350-$500**

Mirror black vase, rouleau form, traces of gilt floral motif, K'ang Hsi, old damages, 12 1/2 in. high. **$600-$800**

Mirror black vase, rib at the flaring neck, spreading foot, glaze thinning to brown at the rim, late 19th century, 18 1/2 in. high. **$500-$750**

Peach-bloom amphora, double white rib at the base of the neck, mottled copper red with greenish flecks, K'ang Hsi six-character mark, but 19th century, 8 1/2 in. high. **$1,000-$1,500**

Peach-bloom amphora, large patches of white and mushroom, K'ang Hsi six-character mark, but 19th century; 10 in. high. **$400-$700**

Peach-bloom amphora, soft mottled copper red with olive green flecks, late 19th/early 20th century, 6 1/2 in. high. **$600-$800**

Peach-bloom box and cover, a rich red glaze paling in some areas and having green spots, shallow concave foot, plain interior, K'ang Hsi six-character mark (and of the period), 2 3/4 in. diameter. **$3,500-$4,500**

Peach-bloom box and cover, the glaze flecked with green, K'ang Hsi six-character mark (and of the period), 2 3/4 in. diameter. **$6,000-$8,000**

Peach-bloom saucer dish, ashes of roses, 19th century, 12 in. diameter. **$400-$600**

Peach-bloom vase, slender tapering form, narrow shoulder, tall flaring neck, mottled glaze with green flecks, glaze thickening around the base, deeply recessed base glazed in white; K'ang Hsi six-character mark, but late 19th century; 6 1/2 in. high. **$500-$700**

Peach-bloom water pot, three incised archaic dragons, roundels with clouds and scrolls, glaze in liver red to gray, K'ang Hsi six-character mark (and of the period), minor restoration at the foot, 5 in. wide. **$1,500-$2,500**

Purple libation cup, oval shape, broad rim, angled strap handle, K'ang Hsi, 4 in. diameter. **$1,500-$2,500**

Purple saucer dish, everted rim, interior incised with five-toed dragon, flaming pearl, and cloud scrolls, rim fretting, K'ang Hsi six-character mark (and of the period), 10 in. diameter. **$2,000-$3,000**

Sang de boeuf bowl, shallow with raised rim, base and interior glaze pate blue, Hsuan Te mark, but 18th century, 10 in. diameter. **$600-$900**

Sang de boeuf vase, baluster form, red glaze thinning at the bulbous neck and pooling in a double rib at the shoulder, late 19th century, 21 in. high. **$600-$900**

Sang de boeuf vase, baluster form, slender body, trumpet mouth, glaze thinning to white at the rim, 19th century, 21 in. high. **$800-$1,000**

Sang de boeuf vase, double gourd, the glaze with purple streaks at the neck, late 19th/early 20th century, 13 in. high. **$600-$800**

Sang de boeuf vase, pear-shaped, spreading neck, band at shoulder, two elephant-head handles with fixed rings, early to mid-19th century, 8 in. high. **$600-$800**

Sang de boeuf vase, pear-shaped, white interior and base, Ch'ien Lung six-character mark (and of the period), 10 3/4 in. high. **$900-$1,500**

Sang de boeuf vase, pear-shaped, translucent red glaze with areas of Flambé, first half of the 19th century, 10 in. high. **$300-$600**

Tea-dust bottle/vase, even matte glaze, 19th century, 10 in. high. **$300-$500**

Tea-dust censer, tripod, oval form with rounded sides, green-powdered brown glaze stopping short of the feet, 18th century, 4 in. long. **$600-$800**

Turquoise bottle/vase, early 19th century, 4 3/4 in. high. **$200-$275**

Turquoise bottle/vase, three ribs on the lower portion of the tall slender neck, evenly glazed, 18th century, 10 1/4 in. high. **$1,000-$1,500**

Turquoise figures, the Eight Immortals, incised details, early 20th century, 6 1/2 in. high. **$300-$400**

Turquoise figures, Buddhistic lions, mirror image, rectangular bases, fierce expressions, early 20th century, 12 in. high, pair. **$300-$500**

Turquoise figure, lady seated upon an elephant, crackled glaze, early 20th century, 10 3/4 in. high. **$250-$300**

Turquoise figures, Pu Tai seated on flat, oval base, loosely draped robes open at the front revealing a large stomach, late 19th/early 20th century, 3 in. high, pair. **$250-$400**

Turquoise garden seat, barrel-shaped, two rows of raised bosses, a center band of incised floral motifs, early 20th century, 19 1/2 in. high. **$800-$1,000**

Turquoise jar, speckled glaze, neck shaved, pierced-wood lid, 17th century, 5 in. high. **$400-$600**

Turquoise water dropper, a Buddhistic lion, 18th century, 2 in. high. **$475-$550**

Turquoise vase, globular; tall, cylindrical neck, four incised four-toed dragons, flaming pearls, flame scrolls, glaze partially covering the foot, biscuit base, late 19th century, 14 1/2 in. high. **$400-$600**

Yellow bottle/vase (lemon yellow), finely crackled, bulbous with long neck, early 19th century, 17 1/2 in. high. **$1,050-$1,400**

Yellow bowl (Imperial yellow), incised decoration—under the glaze—with two five-toed dragons pursuing flaming pearls amongst clouds and stylized waves, Ch'ien Lung six-character mark (and of the period), 5 3/4 in. diameter. **$3,000-$5,000**

Yellow bowl incised on exterior with dragons, flames, rocks, and waves, white interior and base, damaged, Tao Kuang seal (and of the period), 4 1/2 in. diameter. **$800-$1,200**

Yellow dish, flared rim, glaze thinning at base, base glazed white, Ming Dynasty, Chia Ching mark (and of the period), 6 in. diameter. **$15,000-$20,000**

Yellow figures, the Eight Immortals, incised details, early 20th century, 5 1/2 in. high. **$200-$300**

Yellow moon flask, elephant-head ears, eight trigrams (the eight possible combinations of three whole or broken lines used especially in Chinese divination) in relief, late 19th century, 9 1/2 in. high. **$400-$600**

Yellow sauce dish, two five-toed dragons on interior, the exterior motif with cranes in flight, Kuang Hsü six-character mark (and of the period), 5 in. diameter. **$600-$800**

Yellow sauce dish (Imperial yellow), mottled, restored, Ming Dynasty, 6 in. diameter. **$1,000-$1,600**

Yellow saucer dish (Imperial yellow/deep lemon), damaged, Ming Dynasty, Hung Chih six-character mark (and of the period), 8 1/2 in. diameter. **$1,500-$1,800**

Yellow saucer dish (Imperial yellow), incised decorations of dragon and lotus meander over entire surface, plain interior, damaged, Ming Dynasty, Chia Ching, 8 in. diameter. **$1,500-$2,200**

Yellow vase, pear-shaped, high, hollow foot, applied elephant mask handles, flared, upturned mouth, the body carved with lotus and peony, 19th century, 8 1/2 in. high. **$900-$1,200**

Ming Dynasty Pottery and Porcelain Marks

年
洪
製
武

Hung Wu
1368-1398

Hung Wu (seal form)
1368-1398

年
永
製
樂

Yung Lo
1403-1424

Yung Lo (archaic form)
1403-1424

Hsuan Te
1426-1435

Hsuan Te (seal form)
1426-1435

化
大
年
明
製
成

Ch'eng Hua
1465-1487

Ch'eng Hua (seat form)
1465-1487

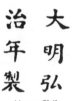

Hung Chih
1488-1505

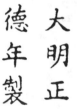

Ch'eng Te
1506-1521

靖
大
年
明
製
嘉

Chia Ching
1522-1566

Lung Ch'ing
1567-1572

Wan Li
1573-1619

Wan Li (archaic form)
1573-1619

啟
大
年
明
製
天

T'ien Ch'i
1621-1627

Ch'ung Cheng
1628-1643

Blue and White

Bottle, double gourd, motif of eight trigrams (the eight possible combinations of three whole or broken lines used especially in Chinese divination) and fire scrolls, Ming Dynasty, 16th century, fritting, 4 in. high. **$600-$900**

Bottle, motif of arrow vases on tripod tables between borders of foliage, plantain leaves on neck, meandering lotus on flared rim, K'ang Hsi, 9 in. high. **$1,800-$2,400**

Bottle, motif of alternating panels with ladies holding fans and seated beside tripod censers, lotus lappets around neck and hatched pattern on everted rim, K'ang Hsi, 9 in. high. **$2,000-$3,000**

Bottle, pear-shaped, panels of riverscapes alternating with scholars, floral sprays at shoulder, body crack, K'ang Hsi, 10 1/2 in. high. **$500-$700**

Bottles painted with scrolling foliage between bands of lappets, the necks with applied dragons (mirror image), late 19th century, 14 in. high, pair. **$700-$900**

Bowl, pheasant in flight, peony and bamboo on exterior, chips, Ming Dynasty, early 17th century, 8 in. diameter. **$300-$400**

Bowl, key-pattern panels on exterior with roundels of Arabic calligraphy, interior band of Arabic, made for the Islamic market, chipped, Ming Dynasty, late 16th/early 17th century, 8 in. diameter. **$2,000-$3,000**

Bowl, foliate rim, interior motif of a bird standing on a rock below peach spray panels, similar motif on exterior, Ming Dynasty, Wan Li, 5 1/2 in. diameter. **$450-$700**

Bowl, interior motif of pagoda and rock with fisherman and boats, riverscape exterior, Ming Dynasty, Wan Li, 4 1/2 in. diameter. **$500-$750**

Bowl, exterior painted with carp, horse, dragon, and other animals above breaking waves, top and bottom with key-pattern and tooth-pattern bands, six-character Hsuan T'ung mark (and of the period), 8 in. diameter. **$2,000-$3,000**

Bowl, everted rim, motif of official and monk with pavilion and fence, the interior with an elder in a roundel below pine branches, K'ang Hsi, 7 3/4 in. diameter. **$800-$1,200**

Bowl, everted rim, globular, painted with dragons and flaming pearls, mid-17th century, transitional, 9 1/2 in. diameter. **$475-$750**

Bowl, globular tripod, four roundels of cranes, the base with Yung Cheng mark, but 19th century, 9 1/4 in. diameter. **$400-$600**

Bowl and cover, domed lid, flower-head finial, overall motif of foliage and horses, crack in body, Ming Dynasty, early 17th century, 5 in. high. **$600-$800**

Bowl and cover, shallow bowl, bud finial, scrolling foliage, Ming Dynasty, late 16th/early 17th century, 6 in. diameter. **$600-$800**

Box and cover, four lion mask feet, motif of carp and waves, peony sprays and vines at trim, repaired, Ming Dynasty, late 16th/early 17th century, 4 in. square. **$750-$1,000**

Box and cover, ingot-shaped, cover painted with phoenix and lotus within a key-pattern rim, the lower part painted with lappets of cell and dot pattern, the interior divided into two compartments, Ming Dynasty, 16th century, 4 1/2 in. diameter. **$3,000-$4,000**

Box and cover, scenic motif on lid within double bands, early 20th century, 3 in. diameter. **$50-$75**

Box and cover, lady and attendant with pine branch on lid, four-character Ch'ien Lung mark on base, but early 20th century, 3 1/2 in. diameter. **$45-$65**

Brush pot, cylindrical, motif of the immortals and officials, fritting, K'ang Hsi, 7 in. diameter. **$1,000-$1,500**

Brush pot, cylindrical, motif of fisherman and lake with landscape, K'ang Hsi, 5 in. high. **$1,200-$1,500**

Brush pot, cylindrical, figures and landscape, 19th century, 5 1/4 in. high. **$250-$350**

Brush pot, cylindrical, two panels of figures on horseback, four-character Ch'eng Hua mark on base, but late 19th century, 5 1/2 in. high. **$125-$225**

Dish, porcelain, the center motif of flowers and foliage surrounded by a diaper divided by floral reserves, the border containing flowers and emblems, damaged, Ch'ien Lung, 18th century, 11 1/2 in. diameter. $300-$400

Candlesticks, tall and square, formed in two parts (as a large bell supporting a slender conical upper section), overall lotus and scroll divided by key-pattern borders, early 19th century, 21 in. high. **$3,000-$4,000**

Candlesticks, one with chips, ribbed stems, wide flanges, domed feet with radiating Shou characters, mid to late 19th century, 11 1/2 in. high. **$1,000-$1,500**

Dish, seated lady watching a boy chasing a butterfly, the border with four panels of tulips dividing larger, fan-shaped panels, Ming Dynasty, T'ien Ch'i/Ch'ung Cheng, 14 in. diameter. **$1,800-$2,500**

Dish, aster pattern, leaf mark on base, chipping, K'ang Hsi, 13 in. diameter. **$700-$900**

Left: Underglaze deep dish, the recessed well decorated with stylized fruit and Power-head medallion within a border containing the eight Taoist Emblems, the exterior with scrolling foliage above ruyi spearhead border, Ch'ien Lung mark (and of the period), 8 in. diameter. Realized price (including the 10-percent buyer's premium), Christie's East, New York City. **$605**

Dish, motif of central basket of peony, trellis-pattern border, 18th century, 12 in. diameter. **$400-$600**

Dish, scrolling peony on interior, exterior with branches, fritting, K'ang Hsi, 14 in. diameter. **$400-$600**

Dish, central spray of finger citrus and peach branches, 18th century, 7 1/2 in. diameter. **$300-$400**

Dish, rocky riverscape with bird in flight, chips, Ch'ien Lung, 12 1/2 in. diameter. $400-**$600**

Ewer, animal handle with face peering over rim, three leaping horses among Precious Things emblems, minor fritting, early 17th century, 7 1/4 in. diameter. **$500-$8,000**

Ewer, pear-shaped, serpentine spout, scrolling lotus and bands of ruyi heads with plantain leaves on the neck, Ming Dynasty, Wan Li, 5 3/4 in. high. **$500-$750**

Ewer, serpentine spout, scrolling lotus on body, ruyi heads on foot, floral sprays on neck, garlic top, damaged (metal mounts, rim, chain, and stretcher), Ming Dynasty, first half of the 16th century, 11 in. high. **$1,500-$2,000**

Ewer and cover, hexagonal, bulbous spout, arched handle, painted with landscapes and a procession of dignitaries, damages, mid-19th century, 8 1/2 in. wide. **$300-$350**

Ewer, serpentine spout, globular body, motif of peony, chrysanthemum, and lotus in molded, petal-shaped panels, trellis pattern on the conical neck, rim chips, K'ang Hsi, 8 in. high. **$600-$900**

Garden seat, barrel-shaped, lion mask handles, brocade balls and lotus on top, peacocks and peony at the center between borders of raised studs, waves, and lappets at the base, restored, Ming Dynasty, 16th century, 14 1/2 in. high. **$800-$1,200**

Garden seat, hexagonal, painted with flowering shrubs between two bands of raised studs, late 19th century, 19 in. high. **$550-$700**

Garden seat, blue ground with white sprays of blossoms and two pierced coin symbols, hairlines, circa 1900, 18 in. high. **$300-$500**

Jar, soft paste, oviform, village scene and riverscape, the neck shaved, 18th century, 12 1/2 in. high. **$600-$800**

Jar, oviform, motif of scrolling chrysanthemum between bands of lotus, tooth pattern around the shoulder, chipped, circa 1755, Transitional, 8 in. high. **$350-$500**

Jar, square form, two panels of figures and pavilion with riverscape, two panels of calligraphy, second half of the 19th century, 11 in. high. **$150-$225**

Jar and cover, Hawthorne pattern, circa 1900, 8 in. high. **$125-$175**

Jar and cover, bird finial, motif of 100 Antiques, cracked, 18th century, 6 in. high. **$400-$600**

Jar and wood cover, five boys playing in a garden, 18th century, 6 1/2 in. high. **$750-$950**

Jars and wood covers, Hawthorne pattern, early 19th century, 5 in. high, pair. **$200-$300**

Jardinière, four large panels of hunters and game birds between ruyi lappets, 19th century, 18 in. diameter. **$2,500-$3,500**

Jardinières and underplates, square form tapering to base, continuous scenic motif, mid to late 19th century, 9 1/2 in. wide, pair. **$900-$1,200**

Jardinières, everted rim, continuous mountainous riverscape with pavilions, three bracket feet with floral sprays, pierced bases, late 19th century, 19 1/2 in. high, pair. **$1,200-$1,600**

Jardinières, continuous motif of children, lappets at the foot and ruyi shape lappets at the top, 19th century, 14 1/2 in. high, pair. **$1,500-$2,500**

Jardinières, tapering cylindrical form painted with fish and water plants, bases pierced, 20th century, 10 in. diameter, pair. **$700-$900**

Jardinières, octagonal with everted rims, stylized lotus and scroll above lappets, the foot reticulated and painted with cloud scrolls, one with restoration on rim, 19th century, 14 1/2 in. diameter, pair. **$1,200-$1,500**

Jardinières, rectangular with four bracket feet, a band of lotus and scroll between gadrooned and cloud-scroll borders beneath flange and key-pattern rim, 19th century, 16 in. long, pair. **$1,500-$2,000**

Jardinières, circular, painted with four-toed dragons and flaming pearls above wave border, one damaged, early 19th century, 13 1/2 in. diameter, pair. **$1,500-$2,000**

Kendi, roundels of flower heads and breaking waves at center, lotus on mammiform (breast-shaped) spout, lappets around foot, repair to spout, Ming Dynasty, early 16th century, 7 1/2 in. high. $**1,200-$1,800**

Kendi painted with meandering budding flowers, lozenge symbols at the shoulder, hairlines, Ming Dynasty, late 16th century, 7 in. high. **$750-$1,000**

Left: Covered oval tureen, Chinese export blue and white, ribbed body, domed lid, applied leaf-and-peach handle, floral sprigs and key fret border at the cusped rim, the sides flanked by lion mask handles, a flaring foot, Ch'ien Lung, 18th century, 13 in. long (over handles). Realized price, Christie's East, New York City: **$1,045.** Right: Covered oval tureen, Chinese export famille rose, the domed cover with a pomegranate finial, the body enameled with peacocks perched on rock-work surrounded by leafy peonies within scrolling foliate border, the sides similarly decorated and flanked by iron red hare's head handles, 18th century, 11 3/4 in. long. Realized price (including the 10-percent buyer's premium), Christie's East, New York City. **$1,760**

Kendi, panels of leaves and peach sprays overall, leaves on neck, mammiform (breast-shaped) spout, damaged, Wan Li, 7 in. high. **$300-$500**

Kendi, meandering hibiscus motif and scrolling foliage, mammiform (breast-shaped) spout, restored and chipped, Wan Li, 7 1/2 in. high. **$600-$950**

Kendi, cranes and clouds on hexagonal scale pattern, emblems at shoulder, crack on spout, Wan Li, 5 in. high. **$500-$700**

Kendi, meandering chih lung and flower sprays, foliage at waist, mammiform (breast-shaped) spout (chipped), 17th century, 7 in. high. **$600-$800**

Kendi, panels of riverscapes, lotus sprays on body, onion-shaped spout, ruyi lappets at shoulder, plantain leaves on neck, flared rim, Ch'ien Lung, 9 in. high. **$950-$1,500**

Stem cup, two fruiting vines on exterior, roundel of vine at center of interior, key-pattern band on foot, Ming Dynasty, 17th century, 5 in. diameter. **$1,500-$2,000**

Stem cup, leaping carp and waves in center of interior below a trellis-pattern border, 17th century, 5 in. diameter. **$600-$900**

Vase, mei ping form, motif of stylized lotus at the center, lappets and key pattern around foot, lappets around shoulder, Ming Dynasty, 16th century, 8 1/2 in. high. **$800-$1,200**

Vase, double gourd, Buddhistic lions and ribboned balls around center of upper and lower lobes, borders of interlocking foliage and lappet band around foot, damages, Ming Dynasty, 16th century, 15 1/2 in. high. **$2,500-$3,500**

Teapot, porcelain, K'ang Hsi period, some roughness under the lid. **$500-$700**

Vase, pear-shaped, meandering lotus and chrysanthemums with chevron borders, plantain leaves on neck, lappets around foot, badly damaged, 14th century, 9 in. high. **$250-$350**

Vase, baluster form, loop handles, meandering lotus overall, plantain leaves on neck, fritting, 15th century, 7 in. high. **$1,500-$2,500**

Vase, pear-shaped, dragon handles, two panels of scholars crossing a bridge with riverscape, divided by scholar's utensils and censers, prunus branches and cell pattern around rim, chips on base, K'ang Hsi, 15 in. high. **$2,700-$3,800**

Vase, baluster form, pheasant in flight (and other flying birds) with rock-work, hatch pattern around shoulder, camellia and rock-work around neck, minor chips, K'ang Hsi, 18 in. high. **$3,500-$5,000**

Vase, beaker form, panels of archaic vessels and scholar's utensils within floral lozenge borders, damaged, K'ang Hsi, 10 1/4 in. high. **$600-$800**

Vase, baluster form with domed cover, lion mask ears, peony above lappets, ruyi lappets around shoulder, foliage on neck, a body crack painted over—poor restoration, 19th century, 26 1/2 in. high. **$650-$1,000**

Vase, blue with white slip relief motif of plum tree and bamboo, mid-19th century, 9 in. high. **$400-$500**

Vase, baluster form, dense scrolling peony above band of lotus petals, the shoulder with hatch pattern, tooth pattern around neck, Ch'ien Lung, 15 1/2 in. high. **$1,500-$2,000**

Vase, baluster form, scrolling peony between bands of lappets, the shoulder with ruyi lappets, late 18th century, 14 3/4 in. high. **$1,200-$1,800**

Vase, double gourd; five-toed dragons, flaming pearls, and cloud scrolls; lappets on neck; cell pattern around foot; late 19th century, 16 in. high. **$700-$900**

Vases, hexagonal, overall lotus meander between ruyi lappets, circa 1900, 24 in. high, pair. **$2,000-$3,000**

Vase, yen-yen shape, painted with zodiac animals, late 19th century, 16 1/2 in. high. **$650-$825**

Vase, dappled blue overall, early 20th century, 9 1/2 in. high. **$100-$150**

Vase, yen-yen shape, panels of the Immortals in landscapes, flaring neck, drilled and mounted as a lamp, 18th century, 18 1/2 in. high. **$1,200-$1,500**

Vases, baluster form, overall chrysanthemum and vines motif, pierced wood covers, pierced and mounted as lamps, circa 1900, 14 in. high, pair. **$700-$950**

Blue and Yellow

Bowl, two yellow dragons above two overlapping petals, plain interiors, each with tiny rim chips, Ch'ien Lung (Qianlong) six-character mark (and of the period), 5 in. diameter. **$1,000-$1,500**

Dish, everted rim, centrally painted with five-toed dragon and flaming pearl amongst fire scrolls with a border of two dragons and flaming pearl, repeated on exterior, Tao Kuang (Daoguang) six-character mark (and of the period), 9 3/4 in. diameter. **$2,000-$3,000**

Dish, everted rim, centrally painted with five-toed dragon and flaming pearl amongst fire scrolls with a border of two dragons and flaming pearl, repeated on exterior, rim chips, Tao Kuang (Daoguang) six-character mark (and of the period). **$1,000-$1,500**

Dish, everted rim, centrally painted with five-toed dragon and flaming pearl amongst fire scrolls with a border of two dragons and flaming pearl, repeated on the exterior, Ch'ien Lung (QianLong) six-character mark (and of the period), 9 1/2 in. diameter. **$3,000-$4,000**

Dish, everted rim, centrally painted with five-toed dragon and flaming pearl amongst fire scrolls with a border of two dragons and flaming pearl, repeated on the exterior, rim chips, Ch'ien Lung (Qianlong) six-character mark (and of the period). **$2,800-$3,500**

CELADON

In Chinese, the name "qingci" means "greenish porcelain." So why is this known as "celadon"? Celadon was the hero of the French writer Honore d'Urfe's romance, "L'Astrée" (1610), the lover of the heroine Astrée. He was presented as a young man in green and his dress became fashionable in Europe. It was about this time that the Chinese qingci made its debut in Paris. People compared its color to Celadon's suit and started to call the porcelain "celadon."

Bowl, Chinese, measuring 6 1/2 in. by 2 3/4 in., dating to the late Sung Dynasty (960-1280 AD). It has an olive green celadon glaze over a heavily potted, porcelaneous body that has turned to reddish-brown with firing. The pale green glaze covers the piece evenly, creating a smooth surface. It has inscribed free-form designs on the interior and is molded into a melon or ribbed shape on the exterior. This bowl has characteristics of early Northern Sung Chinese Yaozhou wares. **$180**

Bowl, Chinese, thinly potted, measuring 5 in. by 2 1/2 in., dating to the late Sung Dynasty (960-1280 AD). It has a pale green celadon glaze over a porcelaneous body that has turned to pale brown with firing. The rim is unglazed and has marks of an old metal protective covering. The interior has impressed designs of flowers and plants. Fine original condition with some minor chipping and roughness of the rim as expected. This bowl comes with a silk-lined protective box of later date. Scholars attribute these wares to the Ying Ching productions of the Sung Dynasty. The glaze of Ying Ching porcelains has been described as "misty blue," which fits this bowl. The potters of the Northern Sung often stacked bowls together in the kiln to increase production. The rims were left unfired to prevent sticking to the kiln or other wares. As a result, they had rough rims that were often covered with gold or silver. This bowl has evidence of such treatment. The impressed design is typical of those found in the Northern Chinese Yaozhou and Ying Ching kilns. It is finely done, which is another characteristic of later Song wares. **$350**

Bowl, Chinese, thinly potted, measuring 7 in. by 2 3/4 in., dating to the late Sung Dynasty (960-1280 AD). It has a pale green celadon glaze over a porcelaneous body that has turned to pale brown with firing. The rim is unglazed and has marks of an old metal protective covering. The interior has impressed designs of smiling boys and plants. Fine original condition with some roughness of the rim as expected. Scholars attribute these wares to the Ying Ching productions of the Sung Dynasty. The glaze of Ying Ching porcelains has been described as "misty blue," which fits this bowl. The potters of the Northern Sung often stacked bowls together in the kiln to increase production. The rims were left unfired to prevent sticking to the kiln or other wares. As a result, they had rough rims that were often covered with gold or silver. This bowl has evidence of such treatment. The impressed design is typical of those found in the Northern Chinese Yaozhou and Ying Ching kilns. It is finely done, which is another characteristic of later Song wares. **$500**

Bowl, Chinese, measuring 5 1/2 in. by 2 1/2 in., dating to the 14th or 15th century Ming Dynasty. The simple, heavily potted clay body has turned to reddish-brown with firing. The body rests on a glazed, straight foot rim and curves upward to a reversed, rolled lip. The thick, olive green glaze has some bubbles near the foot. The center interior is unglazed, as is the foot, indicating that this bowl was fired with another one stacked inside. Fine original condition. **$150**

Basin, stylized floral medallion and fretted border, flat, everted rim, brown foot rim, early Ming Dynasty, 14 in. diameter. **$1,500-$2,000**

Bottle/vase molded and carved with archaic dragons and tree peony between bands of lotus and stiff leaves, a key fret on the rim; Ch'ien Lung mark, but 19th century, 20 1/2 in. high. **$1,200-$1,500**

Bowl carved with a single open flower on a peony spray on the interior, translucent olive green glaze, paler on the base, Northern Sung (Song) Dynasty, 8 1/2 in. diameter. **$3,000-$5,000**

Bowl molded and carved on the exterior with sprays of lotus, tree peony, and fruits, with clouds and scrolls, plain interior, Yung Cheng six-character mark (and of the period), 13 in. diameter. **$10,000-$20,000**

Bowl, exterior carved with foliage meander, the interior with six ribs rising to the everted rim, the glaze with a large crackle, damage to the rim, Northern Sung (Song) Dynasty, 4 3/4 in. diameter. **$500-$750**

Bowl, pale glaze with incised emblems and vases on the exterior, plain interior, late 19th century, 5 1/2 in. diameter. **$200-$300**

Bowl, short foot, inward-curving rim, pale olive green glaze, Northern Sung (Song) Dynasty, 4 1/2 in. diameter. **$500-$700**

Bowl, square with canted corners, relief motif of phoenix outlined in gilt, Tao Kuang seal, but late 19th century, 5 in. square. **$300-$500**

Bowl, flat rim, small, molded floral medallion, exterior molded with petals and meander, Ming Dynasty, 15th century, 6 1/2 in. diameter. **$2,000-$3,000**

Bowl, flat, everted rim, the interior with molded radiating petal flutes, the exterior with molded-in relief petals, recessed base, 18th century, 10 in. diameter. **$600-$900**

Bowl, shallow, flattened rim, deep, semi-translucent, olive green glaze, gray biscuit foot, kiln adhesions on base, Northern Sung (Song) Dynasty, 6 1/4 in. diameter. **$1,000-$1,500**

Bulb bowl (also called a Narcissus bowl), squat, three short feet, floral motif, flattened rim, Ming Dynasty, 12 in. diameter. **$800-$1,000**

Bulb bowl, tripod, bombe body, trellis pattern with clouds on the exterior, the interior a burnt, reddish brown, Ming Dynasty, 9 in. diameter. **$700-$900**

Dish, even glaze on exterior and interior, short foot, late 18th century, 6 in. diameter. **$200-$300**

Dish (Lung Ch'uan, a county of Chekiang province), flaring rim carved with lotus heads and scroll around a central flower head, blue-green glaze, chips on foot, Yüan Dynasty, 8 3/4 in. diameter. **$600-$750**

Dish, hexafoil, shallow well, orange-fired foot, pale blue glaze, large crackle, Southern Sung (Song) Dynasty, 6 in. diameter. **$2,000-$3,000**

Dish, the incised interior motif of flowering lotus and four fruiting branches filling the well, Ming Dynasty, 14th/15th century, 13 1/4 in. diameter. **$900-$1,200**

Figure of Pu Tai (the Laughing Buddha, also known as Hotei in Japan) seated and leaning on bag of happiness, his face, feet, body, and hands glazed brown, early 20th century, 7 in. high. **$85-$125**

Figure of Pu Tai seated on rock-work with one arm resting on bag of happiness; his hands, feet, face, and body all orange-fired gray biscuit, Ming Dynasty, 17th century, 8 in. high. **$2,500-$3,500**

Figure of Shou Lao (the God of Longevity), early 20th century, 11 in. high. **$150-$200**

Garden seat, barrel form, plain exterior with two bands of bosses, early 20th century, 18 1/2 in. high. **$350-$450**

Garden seat, barrel-shaped, molded lion mask and ring handles (four), Ming Dynasty, 18 in. high. **$3,500-$4,500**

Jardinière, globular, everted rim, incised peony and foliage with cloud scrolls, plain interior, late 18th/early 19th century, 10 1/2 in. high. **$800-$1,000**

Moon flask, each side with carved lotus sprays and leaves, long narrow neck, chih lung handles, Yung Cheng six-character mark (and of the period), chipped, 11 1/2 in. high. **$4,500-$6,500**

Vase, pear-shaped, glaze slightly crackled, damaged, Yüan Dynasty, 6 1/2 in. high. **$400-$600**

Vase, ribbed body, short cylindrical neck, everted rim, ivory glaze on interior, olive green glaze on exterior, shallow-cut foot, crack in body, Yüan Dynasty, 8 in. high. **$600-$800**

Vase, two molded dragons around the neck and shoulder, mounted as a lamp, early 20th century, 16 1/2 in. high. **$250-$325**

Vase, yen-yen form, trumpet neck, incised design of prunus and peony, crackled glaze, 16th century, 15 in. high. **$1,200-$1,500**

Vase, baluster form, molded with scrolling lotus and foliage, elephant-head fixed ring handles, Ch'ien Lung mark, but 19th century, 17 in. high. **$600-$900**

Vase, pear-shaped, molded with tassels of scrolls, pierced handles, Ch'eng Hua six-character mark, but late 19th century, 15 in. high. **$500-$700**

Vase, pear-shaped, motif of scrolling foliage, loop and wide ring handles, pierced and mounted as a lamp, Ming Dynasty, 12 in. high. **$1,000-$1,500**

Water dropper (Lung Ch'uan) modeled as a cockerel, olive green glaze, chipped, Yüan/Ming Dynasty, 2 3/4 high. **$300-$450**

Chien Yao (Hare's Fur)
Bowl, Chinese Song Dynasty (960-1234), from the Jian kilns. Such deep brown bowls were valued by Song scholars because they contrasted well with the frothy, white tea used in those days. These bowls are highly prized by the Japanese, who call them temmoku. The body is of brown clay that is covered to just above the foot rim with a thick and lustrous iron glaze. The glaze has fired to a deep brown-black with streaking and spots, creating a desired hare's fur pattern on both the interior and the exterior. The bowl measures approximately 5 in. by 3 in. and is in fine original condition. **$500**

Bowl, mottled and streaked glaze thinning at the foot, restored, Sung (Song) Dynasty, 5 in. diameter. **$700-$900**

Bowl, conical, streaked and splashed on the interior in a pale olive brown on a chocolate ground, shallow-cut stoneware foot, damaged, Southern Sung (Song) Dynasty, 4 3/4 in. diameter. **$400-$550**

Bowl, cylindrical rim streaked with lavender and cream on a deep brown glaze, shallow-cut buff stoneware foot, Sung (Song) Dynasty, 4 3/4 in. diameter. **$700-$900**

Bowl, conical, everted rim, dark olive brown translucent glaze thinning to brown at the rim, gray stoneware with shallow-cut foot, misfired glaze, Southern Sung (Song) Dynasty, 5 1/2 in. diameter. **$600-$800**

Bowl, the interior streaked coffee brown over a crackled darker brown ground, glaze degradation, 4 1/2 in. diameter. **$600-$900**

Chün Yao
Bud vases, pear-shaped, cylindrical handles, blue glaze mottled and splashed with lavender, a band of bosses (raised ornamentation) below the neck, 18th century, 3 3/4 in. high, pair. **$500-$700**

Dish, flat, everted rim, pale lavender glaze with large crackled, reddish splash across the interior, minor chips on foot, Yüan Dynasty, 4 1/4 in. diameter. **$1,500-$2,500**

Vase, broad, tapering body, short, trumpet neck, air bubbling in the glaze, deep lavender, reddish brown biscuit foot, Yüan Dynasty, 11 3/4 in. high. **$600-$900**

Copper Red

Bottle, pear-shaped with elongated neck, Buddhistic lion in underglaze copper red around the body, 18th century, 8 in. high. **$800-$1,200**

Bowl, three carp on exterior in underglaze copper red, plain interior, scratches on interior, Yung Cheng (Yongzheng) six-character mark (and of the period), 9 in. diameter. **$5,000-$7,000**

Bowl, three carp in underglaze copper red on the exterior; plain interior; Yung Cheng (Yongzheng) six-character mark on base, but 19th century; 8 3/4 in. diameter. **$300-$500**

Chinese porcelain water container (brush washer) with a copper red glaze, fire crack in rim, 18th century, 4 in. diameter. $500-$750
(IF REIGN MARK IS PRESENT)

A large water container (brush washer for larger size brushes) with copper red glaze, 18th century, 8 in. diameter. (Note: The large-sized containers generally have nicks or chips to the rim because of the beating they received from the large-sized brushes.). **$800-$1,200**

Copper Red and Blue

Bowl painted with four copper red dragons amongst clouds above waves, with a central dragon roundel, Ch'ien Lung (Qianlong) mark on base, but 19th century; 7 in. diameter. **$300-$500**

Bowl, the rim mounted in silver, Eight Immortals on the exterior, the interior with Shou Lao in a medallion; Hsuan Te (Xuande) mark on the base, but 18th century; 7 3/4 in. diameter. **$600-$800**

Dish, the center and exterior with red dragon and blue waves, the exterior with a cash-pattern band, Chia Ch'ing (Jiaqing) seal (and of the period), 7 in. diameter. **$2,200-$3,500**

Dishes, the well decorated with a red dragon and blue breaking waves, the exterior with dragons and waves, Ch'ien Lung (Qianlong) seal (and of the period), 7 in. diameter, pair. **$3,500-$5,500**

Dishes, the well decorated with a red dragon and blue breaking waves, the exterior with dragons and waves, one damaged, Ch'ien Lung (Qianlong) seal (and of the period), 7 in. diameter, pair. **$1,700-$3,000**

Jardinière, plain interior, exterior with dragon and breaking waves, hairlines, 18th century. **$1,000-$1,500**

Vase, beaker form, painted in underglaze blue and copper red with small areas of celadon glaze, the upper part with fishing boats and pines, the center with two chih lung and ruyi sprays, the spreading foot with a pine grove and fisherman, crack on base, rim chips, K'ang Hsi (Kangxi), 17 1/2 in. high. **$900-$1,300**

Vase, sloping shoulders with panels of flowers on a cell-pattern ground, the body with pine and prunus, the neck with blue bamboo, cup-shaped lip, 18th century, 16 1/2 in. high. **$1,200-$1,600**

Vase, yen-yen beaker form, flying cranes and pines repeated on the neck, 18th century, 18 in. high. **$1,000-$1,500**

Crackled (Oatmeal Hue) Glaze

Large Chinese Imperial dragon vase with oatmeal crackle glaze in a modified beaker shape with raised, dark brown decorations of Imperial, five-toed dragons chasing a flaming pearl and a crane, bearing a false Cheng Hua, Ming Dynasty mark, but dating to the early 20th century. The vase measures 18 in. in height, 27 in. in circumference and 6 1/2 in. across the rim. Excellent condition with no evidence of damage or repairs. **$250**

Vase, fluted mouth banded in brown, the body with famille rose floral decoration, brown band at the base, early 20th century, 12 in. high. **$100-$155**

Vase, blue and white decoration of scholar's utensils, mid-19th century, 12 in. high. **$500-$700**

Vase, famille verte, a continuous motif of warriors on horseback, Ch'eng Hua seal, but late 19th century, 10 in. high. **$125-$185**

Vase, Buddhistic lion mask and ring handles, molded key-pattern bands in deep brown around the shoulder and base, late 19th century, 14 in. high. **$250-$350**

Vase, pear-shaped, underglaze blue birds above brown bands, neck shaved (reduced), early 20th century, 11 in. high. **$75-$100**

Egg and Spinach

Bowls, bodies splashed with leaf green, yellow-ochre, and aubergine over white slip, hairlines, 18th century, 7 in. diameter, pair. **$600-$800**

Bowls, flaring rims, damages to each, K'ang Hsi (Kangxi), 7 1/2 in. diameter, pair. **$800-$1,200**

Buddhistic lion joss (Incense) stick holder, rectangular base, paw on brocade ball, damaged, late 19th century. **$300-$400**

Buddhistic lion joss (incense) stick holder, rectangular open-work base, paw resting on cub's head, K'ang Hsi (Kangxi), 14 1/2 in. high. **$3,500-$5,500**

Parrot perched on rock-work base, iron red beak, 18th century. **$400-$600**

Jar, broad baluster form, monster mask handles applied at the shoulders, interior partially glazed green, late 19th/early 20th century, 11 in. high. **$550-$750**

Vase, double gourd, 18th century, 7 in. high. **$1,500-$2,500**

Fa Hua

Bowl, exterior glazed turquoise with white and green flowering sprays in relief, interior glazed dark turquoise, flaking and chips, Ming Dynasty, 7 3/4 in. diameter. **$500-$700**

Censer, tripod with two turquoise dragons in relief on an aubergine ground, 17th century, 6 in. high. **$600-$800**

Censer, tripod, streaked deep aubergine with turquoise splashed, repair on rim, 17th century, 7 3/4 in. high. **$700-$900**

Jar, oviform, three lotus heads and foliage in relief, lappets in relief at the shoulders; turquoise, cream, and aubergine glazes; chip on foot; 15th/16th century. **$2,000-$3,000**

Jarlet, aubergine with a turquoise interior, 17th century, 3 in. high. **$375-$475**

Famille Jaune

Ewer in the form of Buddhistic lion crouching on a brocade ball and clasping one side of a hexagonal baluster, decorated with panels of prunus and trellis, rectangular base, K'ang Hsi (Kangxi) style, circa 1900, 7 in. high. **$375-$500**

Parrots, pierced rock-work bases, mirror image, incised and molded markings indicating feathers, late 19th/early 20th century, 3 in. high, pair. **$100-$150**

Left: Chinese porcelain Buddhistic-lion-form wine pot, circa 1900, 7 in. high. $100-$175. Right: Chinese Buddhistic lion with brocade ball, marked China, circa 1930, 4 in. high. $35-$50

Teapot, hexagonal, six bracket feet, each panel painted with a standing lady, spout and handle with geometric pattern, Buddhistic lion finial, K'ang Hsi (Kangxi), 7 in. high. **$6,000-$8,000**

Vase, pear-shaped, painted with scholars and dignitaries holding fans and scepters, K'ang Hsi (Kangxi) mark, but late 19th century, 12 1/2 in. high. **$500-$700**

Vase, baluster form, continuous motif of pairs of birds perched on tree peony, late 19th century, 15 3/4 in. high. **$600-$800**

Vase, tapering square form, tall flaring neck, each side with a warrior, late 19th/early 20th century, 15 in. high. **$700-$900**

Vase, baluster form; panels of lotus, camellia, and other flowers surrounded by birds, K'ang Hsi (Kangxi) mark, but late 19th century, 20 1/2 in. high. **$700-$900**

Vase, square form, each side painted with terraces and buildings, late 19th century, 20 in. high. **$900-$1,200**

Famille Noire

Fish bowl, exterior painted with continuous floral sprays, key and chevron border, interior with carp and water weeds, early 20th century, 19 1/4 in. diameter. **$1,500-$2,500**

Immortals, each seated with an attribute, early 20th century, 6 1/2 in. high, set of 8. **$600-$900**

Jardinière, flattened rim, continuous scene of birds perched on gnarled branches of flowering prunus in shades of green, yellow, white, and aubergine on a black ground, late 19th century, 14 1/4 in. high. **$1,200-$1,600**

Vase, yen-yen form, painted with a pair of pheasants on rock-work, late 19th century, 17 in. high. **$500-$700**

Vase, baluster form, warrior on horseback brandishing his spear, late 19th century, 16 in. high. **$700-$1,000**

Vase, baluster form, overall continuous motif of flowers, mounted as a lamp, circa 1900, 15 in. high. **$300-$500**

Vases, square form, each side painted with tall, upright, flowering peony and green, pierced rock-work, late 19th century, 14 1/2 in. high, pair. **$1,500-$2,200**

Vases and covers, Buddhistic lion finials, overall motif of flowers and scrolling vines, one restored, one damaged, late 19th century, 20 in. high, pair. **$1,500-$2,000**

Vases, square form, mirror image, each side painted with prunus and branches, trumpet necks, late 19th century, 27 in. high, pair. **$2,000-$3,000**

Famille Rose

Bowl, shallow, motif in Chinese taste, a rose-colored flowering plum and two colored bamboo on the exterior, plain interior, Ch'ien Lung (Qianlong) six-character mark (and of the period), 4 1/2 in. diameter. **$3,500-$5,500**

Bowl, yellow ground, everted rim, densely painted with flowers and foliage, five red bats on the interior, Tao Kuang (Daouguang) six-character mark (and of the period), 7 in. diameter. **$2,000-$3,000**

Bowl, two roundels of standing ladies, ruby ground with lotus scrolls, plain interior, Kuang Hsü (Guangxu) seal (and of the period), 5 1/2 in. diameter. **$500-$700**

Bowls, exteriors painted with a cockerel, hen, and chicks between daisy, peony and rock-work borders; Yung Cheng (Yongzheng) six-character mark on bases, but early 20th century; 4 1/2 in. diameter, pair. **$600-$800**

Brush pot, continuous motif of warriors engaged in battle, late 18th/early 19th century, 4 in. high. **$350-$500**

Dish, insects and rock-work with flowering peony, tufts of grass and foliage, 18th century, 6 in. diameter. **$700-$900**

Dish painted with a lady and Immortal between deer and male attendant, peony sprays forming the border, cracked, 18th century, 15 in. diameter. **$800-$1,000**

Figure, standing boy (one of the Hoho Erxian twins) wearing attire enameled with lotus, holding a blue vase in both hands, early 19th century, 11 in. high. **$900-$1,200**

Figure, dragon, red, spiky fins and fangs on a pink, swirling cloud base, late 19th century, 10 in. diameter. **$1,200-$1,500**

Figures, Eight Immortals, each on a rectangular base, some with minor chips, early 19th century, 10 in. high. **$2,500-$3,500**

Figure, phoenix perched on a rockwork base, mounted as a lamp, silk shade with fringes intact, early 20th century, 9 1/2 in. high. **$275-$350**

Figure, Shou Lao, open mouth, holding staff and peach, early 20th century, 24 in. high. **$400-$600**

Fish bowl, massive, densely painted with groups of pavilions, groves of willow and pine, scholars relaxing, sages fishing, and geese flying, all below a key-pattern border, the rim with iron red flower heads, early 20th century, 27 in. diameter. **$3,000-$5,000**

Fish bowls, relief motif of warriors on horse-back in landscapes, 19th century, 21 in. diameter, pair. **$6,000-$8,000**

Fruit, gourd, early 20th century, 3 in. diameter. **$50-$75**

Fruit, three peaches joined by a molded leafy branch, pinkish glaze, early 20th century, 2 1/2 in. wide. **$100-$125**

Fruit, peach, early 20th century, 4 1/2 in. diameter. **$75-$100**

Fruit, pomegranate, early 20th century, 4 in. diameter. **$50-$85**

Garden seat, miniature, two landscape panels, two pierced cash symbols between raised bosses (ornamentation)and foliate ground, Chia Ch'ing (Jiaqing), circa 1800, 9 in. high. **$1,250-$1,800**

Garden seat, barrel-shaped, pierced on two sides with double cash symbols, the central band of birds and peony between bands of stylized lappets and lower band of cell pattern, late 19th/early 20th century, 19 in. high. **$1,200-$1,600**

Garden seats, hexagonal, two sides pierced with cash symbols, upper and lower border with pink ground and raised bosses, the body with scrolling pink flowers and celadon vines, lappet border at the base, late 19th/early 20th century, 19 in. high, pair. **$3,500-$4,500**

Garden seats, Millefleurs, quatrefoil section, black ground, one with major restoration, circa 1900, 19 in. high. **$2,500-$3,500**

Garden seats, top with pierced cash symbols, upper and lower borders with raised bosses (ornamentation) and pink lotus, green scrolling foliage, a center band with scene of wooded mountain landscape, late 19th/early 20th century, 19 in. high, pair. **$2,500-$3,500**

Garniture set, pair of vases mounted as lamps and a censer with a wood cover; panels of Precious Things reserved on a floral diaper ground; the censer with four monster mask feet; late 19th century; the censer, 11 1/2 in. high; the lamps, 12 in. high. **$1,000-$1,500**

Garniture set, two beaker-form vases on domed bases, tripod censer and cover with Buddhistic lion finial and two joss (incense) stick holders; each decorated with Precious Things, blue interiors, and key-pattern border; mid to late 19th century, 9 in. high. **$3,000-$4,000**

Jar, baluster form, a continuous scene of children playing within a fenced terrace, late 19th century, 12 1/2 in. high. **$700-$900**

Jar and cover, baluster form, the celadon body painted with a large band of dragons between bands of flower heads and blue key pattern—all on a gold ground, early 20th century, 22 in. high. **$1,100-$1,700**

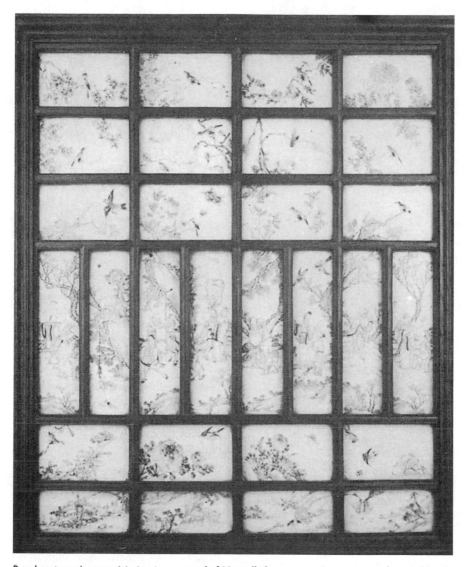

Panel, rectangular, porcelain-inset, composed of 28 small plaques, a continuous scene of court elders at leisure in a rock-work landscape with pine, prunus, and fruiting boughs, the upper and lower sections with peony and birds, circa 1900, 26 1/2 in. by 32 in. Realized price (including the 10-percent buyer's premium), Christie's East, New York City. **$495**

Vase, Chinese porcelain, with a turquoise ground and children, elephant head and ring ears, Kuang Hsü four-character mark (and of the period), circa 1900, 2 1/2 in. high. **$100-$150**

Chinese porcelain spoon, turquoise ground with famille rose motifs of butterflies and flowers, Kuang Hsü period, late 19th century, 7 in. long. **$150-$250**

Jardinière, narrow foot, everted rim, overall motif of tables, scholar's utensils, and Shou characters between painted and gilt bands of Buddhistic emblems, early 20th century, 19 1/2 in. high. **$1,000-$1,500**

Jardinière, globular, motif of immortals and attendants by a lakeside between pink and turquoise brocade bands, the lip with Precious Things, early, 16 in. diameter, 14 in. high. **$800-$1,200**

Jardinière, interlocked cash and peach sprays within lappet borders, late 19th century, 14 in. diameter. **$1,000-$1,500**

Jardinières, iron red dragons confronting the flaming pearl amidst clouds and above breaking waves, Kuang Hsü (Guangxu) period, 16 in. diameter, pair. **$1,800-$2,500**

Jardinières with stands, exteriors with four circular reserves of vases filled with flowers, lappet border under rim, overall motif of floral sprays, Kuang Hsü (Guangxu) period, 15 in. diameter, pair. **$2,000-$3,000**

Vase, one of a pair, Chinese eggshell-porcelain, mirror image, early 20th century, 9 in. high. **$700-$900**

COURTESY OF HOWARD AND FLORENCE KASTRINER

Footed box with cover, Chinese porcelain, motif of confronting dragons on two sides, the short sides having vases in various sizes and shapes (part of the 100 Antiques motif), a hard-wood replacement lid with matching stand, both of which were produced in the late 19th/early 20th century (when it was fashionable to add lids and stands even if they were not needed), restoration to one leg, K'ang Hsi, 6 in. high. **$1,200-$1,800**

Panel, a central pink dragon on a blue ground with scrolling foliage and key-pattern borders, late 19th century, 26 in. square. **$1,500-$2,500**

Plaque, two birds perched on flowering branches, hardwood frame, early 20th century, framed size 22 in. by 18 in. **$400-$600**

Plaque, a dragon and rock-work, wood frame, early 20th century, framed size 21 in. by 16 in. **$350-$500**

Plaque, scholar seated beside a table on a terrace, hardwood frame, late 18th/early 19th century, framed size 19 in. by 14 in. **$2,500-$3,500**

Plaques, figures and riverscape, hardwood frame, late 18th/early 19th century, framed size 7 in. by 4 in., pair. **$1,200-$1,600**

Plates, ruby ground, painted with green dia-pered scroll unfurled to reveal a black cockerel perched beside flowering peony, rim chips, Ch'ien Lung (Qianlong) six-character mark (and of the period), 8 3/4 in. diameter, pair. **$4,000-$6,000**

Ruyi sceptre painted to simulate cloisonné, foliage motif overall, three pierced inset plaques with pink Shou characters, Ch'ien Lung (Qianlong) six-character mark (and of the period), 20 1/2 in. long. **$7,500-$10,000**

Saucer dish, eggshell, painted with the eight horses of MuWang on a terrace beneath a willow, their bodies pink, white, brown, or gray; Yung Cheng (Yongzheng) mark, but early 20th century; 7 1/2 in. diameter. **$250-$400**

Saucer dish, eggshell, two birds seated on pierced rock-work below peony sprays and above daisies, early 20th century, 10 in. diameter. **$300-$500**

Saucer dishes, ruby-glazed, bright pink/crimson, white exteriors, late 18th/early 19th century, 7 1/2 in. diameter, pair. **$1,500-$2,000**

Sweetmeat dish and cover, mottled pink exterior with green vines and leaves, green interior divided into four key-pattern compartments, late 19th century, 10 in. wide. **$300-$475**

Teapot, fluted body painted with panels of flowering trees, early 19th century, 10 in. wide. **$275-$375**

Trays, oval, lobed, with an iron red inscription in the center surrounded by lime green bands with pink foliage carried over to the exterior; four short, gilt feet; gilt rims; iron red Chia Ch'ing (Jiaqing) seal on a lime green ground (and of the period), 6 1/2 in. wide, pair. **$3,000-$5,000**

Vase, beaker form, gilt and painted with colored peony-laden censers beneath ruyi-shaped lappets, all between puce diapered bands, 18th century, 7 1/4 in. high. **$600-$800**

Vase, bulbous with long neck, continuous motif of pheasants and peony and other blossoms issuing from rockwork, 18th century, 15 1/2 in. high. **$4,000-$6,000**

Vase, Chinese eggshell-porcelain, in the style of Ch'ien Lung, the base with a four-character commendation mark, early 20th century, 4 in. high. **$400-$650**

Vase, pear-shaped, Millefleurs on a black ground, loose ring handles; Ch'ien Lung (Qianlong) mark, but early 20th century; 15 in. high. **$500-$700**

Vase, pear-shaped, Millefleurs pattern on a gilt ground, loose ring handles; Ch'ien Lung (Qianlong) mark, but late 19th century; 14 in. high. $**1,000-$1,500**

Vase, pear-shaped, 100 Deer motif, Ch'ien Lung (Qianlong) seal (and of the period), mounted as a lamp. **$5,000-$7,000**

Vase, ruby glaze, short-waisted neck, circa 1800, 7 in. high. **$1,000-$1,500**

Vase, hexagonal, pomegranate handles, pairs of birds on rock-work in one band and herons and lotus in another divided by bands of diapers and scholar's utensils, late 19th/early 20th century, 23 in. high. **$1,500-$2,500**

Figure, gray pottery horse, Han Dynasty, 207 BC-220 AD; massive horse powerfully modeled with erect posture, the rounded neck with "hogged" mane reaching up between the alert ears, the head strongly detailed with flared nostrils and open mouth revealing the teeth, 25 in. by 30 in., weight 40 lbs., remains of white slip under ancient soil. Separately made head inserts into body. Han tomb figures of large size have been found in human figures, chickens, pigs, and dogs, but horses are rare. **$8,500-$9,500**

Vases, square baluster bodies with blue ground and four rectangular reserves (two calligraphic and two with lotus and cranes), the blue ground with pink dragons, bats and flowers, key pattern around neck and foot, European green interiors and bases, Chia Ch'ing seal (and of the period), 10 in. high, pair. **$8,000-$12,000**

Vases, ovoid, painted with 100 Antiques motif on a celadon ground, Buddhistic lion handles, early 20th century, 37 in. high, pair. **$4,000-$6,000**

Vases, celadon ground, enameled with birds and flower sprays, mounted as lamps, late 19th century, 16 in. high. **$700-$950**

Famille Verte

Bowl, high cylindrical foot, the motif of Precious Things on an ochre-yellow ground, K'ang Hsi (Kangxi), 4 1/2 in. diameter. **$600-$800**

Bowl, exterior with four panels of flowers and vases, reserved on a ground of scrolling peony, rim chips, K'ang Hsi (Kangxi), 11 in. high. **$900-$1,200**

Brush pot, motif of a Taoist figure on a terrace, restored rim, K'ang Hsi (Kangxi), 5 in. high. **$500-$700**

Charger, round, Chinese, done in Famille Verte colors with a central painting of maidens and children in a garden scene, bordered by a wide, multicolor overglaze enamel diaper, measuring 13 1/4 in. in diameter, dating to the mid to late 19th century. The reverse shows a speckled white glaze on a white porcelain body, gray foot rim and pontil marks characteristic of late Ching Dynasty porcelain. Some of the colors of the robes have faded from use over time but there is no other structural damage. **$300**

Charger, iron red chrysanthemums within a striped and diapered border—all enclosed by a wide border of iron red, aubergine, and yellow flower heads, Ch'eng Hua mark, but late 17th century, 14 in. diameter. **$1,500-$2,000**

Figures, Buddhistic lions, each figure with loose eyes, rectangular bases decorated with fan-shaped panels of lotus, enameled on biscuit in yellow, green, aubergine, and black, K'ang Hsi (Kangxi), 12 in. high, pair. **$6,000-$8,000**

Figure, Han Dynasty mythical beast, 207 BC-220 AD; gray earthenware two-horned lion, one foot missing, 9 in. long. **$200-$275**

Figure, dignitary with a long beard and impassive expression, the head reserved in biscuit, seated on an aubergine throne, his robe with yellow dragons and aubergine flaming pearls and clouds, K'ang Hsi style, late 19th century, 25 in. high. **$2,500-$3,500**

Figure, one of the Erxian twins (deities) standing on a square base wearing an apron jacket and holding a vase, chipped, early 18th century, 11 in. high. **$750-$900**

Figure, Kuan Yin, hair piled high and coiled beneath a cowl, robes in yellow, green, and aubergine, 18th century, 9 in. high. **$1,200-$1,500**

Figures, the Eight Immortals, each seated and each with an attribute, one with a beard and mustache, circa 1900, 5 in. high. **$1,000-$1,500**

Figures, parrots, green feathers, black and white beaks, peach-colored rock-work base, late 19th/early 20th century, 7 in. high, pair. **$600-$800**

Figure, Han Dynasty female attendant, Western Han, 206-5 BC, large earthenware figure wearing long robe painted with white, dark red, black, and vermilion pigments, 26 in. tall, rare in this size. **$3,500-$3,750**

Figure, Han Dynasty male attendant, Western Han, 206-5 BC, large earthenware figure in long robe painted with white, pale blue, and black pigments, 18 3/8 in. tall, rare. **$1,500-$1,750**

Figure, Han Dynasty female attendant, Western Han, 206-5 BC, large earthenware figure in long robe painted with white, dark red, and black pigments, 18 in. tall, rare. **$1,500-$1,750**

Figure, large Han Dynasty head of a girl, Western Han, 206-5 BC, earthenware head with ornate hairstyle painted with dark violet pigment, 7 1/2 in. by 7 7/8 in., rare. **$2,500-$2,750**

Figure, large Han Dynasty female head, Western Han, 206-5 BC, earthenware head with ornate hairstyle, remains of white pigment, 8 1/2 in. tall, rare. **$2,500-$2,750**

Figure, large Han Dynasty female head, Western Han, 206-5 BC, earthenware head with ornate hairstyle, remains of white and black pigments, 8 in. tall, rare. **$2,500-$2,750**

Figure, large Han Dynasty musician, 207 BC- 220 AD, kneeling drummer with remains of pigment, 15 1/2 in. **$1,000-$1,250**

Figure, Han Dynasty drummer, 207 BC- 220 AD, with highly animated features and outstretched leg, considerable remains of polychrome under ancient soil, 15 1/2 in. tall, rare this large. **$3,500-$3,750**

Jar, storage, Chinese, measuring 10 in. in height, dating to the late Ming or early Qing Dynasty. The jar is decorated in black-outlined scrolls and flowers using red and green enamel, freely applied washes over an off-white orange peel glaze. There is a border of alternating panels around the neck and a lappet diaper around the base. The base is glazed and unmarked. This may have had a top in the past. The glaze, style of painting, and foot all date this to the 17th or early 18th century Qing Dynasty. Fine original condition. **$450**

Jar, globular, bands of court ladies and flowered jardinières on a diapered ground, the shoulders with medallions of Precious Things emblems, crack in base, K'ang Hsi (Kangxi), 9 in. high. **$500-$700**

Figure, Han Dynasty musician, 207 BC- 220 AD, kneeling zither player with remains of pigment, 14 1/3 in. tall. **$350-$450**

Figure, Han Dynasty earth spirit, 207 BC-220 AD, seated fantastic beast with wings and a large central horn, 12 in. tall, one ear reattached. **$1,000-$1,250**

Jar, baluster form, continuous scene of noblemen receiving military figures, K'ang Hsi (Kangxi), 13 in. high. **$1,000-$1,500**

Jardinière, cylindrical, the body decorated with butterflies above peony and chrysanthemum growing among pierced rock-work, the flat, everted rim with a band of scrolling lotus heads, the base pierced, rim chips, K'ang Hsi (Kangxi), 9 1/2 in. high. **$1,500-$2,500**

Joss (incense) stick holders, mirror image, Buddhistic lions seated on rectangular bases, front paws raised, one with a cub and one with brocade (pierced) ball, bulging eyes, hexagonal holders issuing from their backs, green, ochre, aubergine/brown; minor damages, K'ang Hsi (Kangxi), 8 in. high, pair. **$1,200-$1,600**

Joss (incense) stick holders, Buddhistic lions standing on leaf-shaped stands, deep green, yellow, and aubergine, mounted on ormolu stands, K'ang Hsi (Kangxi), 5 1/4 in. high. **$1,200-$1,600**

Joss (incense) stick holders, Buddhistic lions standing on rectangular bases, green, yellow, and aubergine, late 19th century, 6 in. high. **$400-$600**

Kendi, body molded with vertical ribs, motif of continuous landscape, neck with silver mount, restored spout, K'ang Hsi (Kangxi), 9 in. high. **$1,500-$2,000**

Planter, three bands of various diapers, four bracket feet, 19th century, 9 in. long. **$900-$1,200**

Figure, Han Dynasty mythical beast, late Eastern Han, circa 100-220 AD, gray earthenware traces of slip, in the form of bronze weights used to hold down the edges of seating mats, the function of the hole is uncertain, perhaps a holder, 8 in. long. **$650-$750**

Plate, flowers growing from a pierced rock-work rim with iron red flower heads on a white ground, damaged, K'ang Hsi (Kangxi), 9 1/2 in. diameter. **$300-$600**

Saucer dish painted with a seated lady resting against rock-work with two butterflies at her side, damaged, K'ang Hsi (Kangxi), 7 1/2 in. diameter. **$1,500-$2,000**

Vase, rouleau shape, boys playing games above a green and orange lappet border, trellis design of birds, fruit, and flowers below the shoulders, the rim with a formal border, late 19th century, 16 1/2 in. high. **$900-$1,200**

Vase and cover, continuous riverscape, the cover with leaf-shaped panels of riverscapes and florals, rim and cover restored, K'ang Hsi (Kangxi), 22 in. high. **$1,200-$1,500**

Water dropper, long-tailed bird perched on a peach, old damages, spout chipped, K'ang Hsi (Kangxi), 3 3/4 in. wide. **$300-$500**

Figure, Sui Dynasty tomb figure, 581-618 AD, standing warrior with considerable red, white, and black paint, 14 in. tall, professional repair at waist and upper mold seams. **$650-$1,250**

Figures, Tang Dynasty (618-907 AD) clay tomb figures in the form of dancers, traces of original paint, arm of left figure repaired, otherwise very good condition, taller figure with base, 11 3/4 in. by 5 1/4 in. by 3 in., **pair. $975**

Funerary Objects, Assorted Vessels

Amphïora, straw-glazed, two handles springing from the shoulder and forming dragon heads biting the cup-shaped rim, damages, small piece of rim missing, Tang Dynasty, 17 in. high. **$600-$800**

Figure, an attendant wearing coat and trousers and a cap, the pottery with traces of red pigment, Northern Wei Dynasty, 6 1/2 in. high. **$1,200-$1,600**

Figure, an attendant, head bowed, hands clasped and pierced to hold a standard, loose coat and high boots, Sui Dynasty, 10 in. high. **$1,200-$1,500**

Figure, a camel standing on four squares on a rectangular base, white-painted red pottery, legs restored, Tang Dynasty, 11 1/2 in. high. **$1,000-$1,600**

Figure, a court lady wearing a high-waisted, pleated gown, the gray pottery with traces of pigment, restored, Northern Wei Dynasty, 6 1/2 in. high. **$300-$400**

Figure, a dog, ears erect, collar on neck, the glaze a silvery green iridescence, Han Dynasty, 9 1/2 in. long. **$2,500-$3,500**

Figure, a dog, recumbent position, drooping ears, arched backbone, ochre glaze, Tang Dynasty, 3 1/2 in. long. **$2,500-$3,500**

Figure, an equestrian, the rider's hands raised as if holding reins, the horse's head tucked, yellow glaze, minor restoration, Sui Dynasty, 10 1/2 in. high. **$3,500-$4,500**

Figure, an equestrian, glazed green and buff, the horse—head turned to the left—standing on four squares on a rectangular base, rider and horse restored, Tang Dynasty, 12 1/2 in. high. **$6,000-$8,000**

Figure, a lady equestrian, hair tied in a topknot, the horse with an open mouth and looking to the left, the tail, ears, and legs restored, Tang Dynasty, 14 3/4 in. high. **$3,000-$5,000**

Figure, a horse looking to the left, high ridged saddle and short saddle cloth, some red and black pigment visible, pink buff body, restored, Tang Dynasty, 11 in. high. **$4,000-$6,000**

Figure, Lokapalo wearing helmet and armor, left arm raised with clenched fist, standing on a crouching lion, legs cracked, no pigment remaining, Tang Dynasty. **$1,500-$2,500**

Figure, Chinese, grandmother, traces of red pigment on dress, Tang Dynasty, 11 3/4 in. high. **$1,000-$1,500**

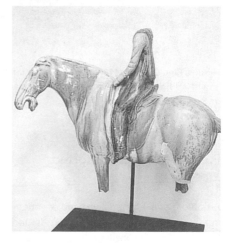

Figure, Tang Dynasty (618-907 AD) sancai (polychrome glaze) pottery horse and rider tomb figure, with flowing glaze in green, ocher, and rust, rider's head missing and damage to horse's legs, on custom metal stand, measurements without stand, 13 3/4 in. by 10 1/2 in. by 4 1/2 in., collection of James E. Billings. **$1,000-$1,400**

Figure, Han Dynasty court lady, 207 BC-220 AD, wearing long robes standing in a graceful pose with hair drawn up into a knot on the left side of the head, her hands clasped over her upper abdomen, 17 in. tall, the head reattached, remains of paint. **$1,750-$2,500**

Figure, large Han Dynasty court figure, 207 BC-220 AD, male attendant standing respectfully with arms crossed and wearing long robes and a peaked hat, remains of polychrome, 24 1/2 in. tall, crack at neck in need of stabilization. **$1,450-$1,750**

Figure, large Han Dynasty dancer, 207 BC-220 AD, female dancer wearing a long-sleeved robe and high hat with one hand raised, 10 in. by 17 1/2 in., some wear. **$950-$1,350**

Figure, large Han Dynasty performer, 207 BC-220 AD, male figure wearing a long-sleeved robe and high hat with hands on his hips, head tilted back in song, 14 1/2 in. tall, some wear and age cracks to base. **$650-$950**

Figure, Han Dynasty musician, 207 BC-220 AD, figure kneeling and playing a long upturned pipe, 7 1/2 in. tall. **$450-$750**

Figure, a soldier wearing breastplate and tunic, the hand socketed as if to hold a spear; gray pottery with traces of red, black, and white pigment; Northern Wei Dynasty, 7 in. high. **$1,500-$2,000**

Figure, a soldier wearing a tunic, hands clasped at his chest, restoration to the face, Tang Dynasty, 14 in. high. **$700-$900**

Figure, a standing lady, straw glaze, long robe, hair in a high loop, neck and base restored, Tang Dynasty. **$1,000-$1,500**

Figure, a standing lady, hands clasped, long flowing robe (white and orange with red borders) flaring at the base, pink pigment on face, damaged, Han Dynasty, 12 3/4 in. high. **$1,200-$1,800**

Figure, Han Dynasty groom, 207 BC-220 AD, bearded male attendant, probably a foreigner judging by his large nose and tunic, standing with right hand against his chest, the left along his side, 6 1/4 in. tall, considerable detail and white slip under ancient soil, a rare type. **$450-$750**

Figure, Han Dynasty warrior, 207 BC-220 AD, warrior standing erect with peaked hat and armor, remains of polychrome, 13 1/2 in. tall, back and front reattached along molding seam. **$400-$750**

Figure, a standing lady, her robe with traces of white pigment, her hair knotted and having traces of black pigment, restored, Tang Dynasty, 12 1/2 in. high. **$3,000-$5,000**

Jar, modified pear shape, the body with bands of wave patterns, glazed green and brown on the red body, damaged, Han Dynasty, 12 1/4 in. high. **$900-$1,200**

Hearth model, Han Dynasty, 207 BC-220 AD, olive glazed terra cotta hearth stove model with fire hole, two cooking pots, molded fish, food, tongs, pots, 8 in. by 7 in., excellent condition. **$1,250-$1,500**

Jar, granary, Han Dynasty, Eastern Han, 25-220 AD, green-glazed earthenware with some iridescence, 11 5/8 in. tall. **$950-$1,250**

Jar, textured, Eastern Han, circa 1-220 AD, hard-fired gray-ware jar with finely textured textile-like design around the body, 5 in. by 8 1/4 in., excellent example. **$650-$750**

Han Dynasty "rooster" jar, Eastern Han, 25-220 AD, green-glazed rooster from earthenware, 9 in. tall, some areas of glaze flakes on reverse, rare form. **$350-$450**

Jar, textured, Eastern Han, circa 1-220 AD, hard-fired gray-ware jar with finely textured textile-like design around the body, 4 3/4 in. by 8 in., excellent example. **$500-$650**

Pottery head fragments, origin unknown, possibly India, terracotta with remnants of original pigment, mounted on stand, height of head on right without stand, 2 1/2 in., **pair. $135**

Chinese neolithic vessel, Gansu Yangshao Culture, Northwest China, circa 2500 BC, two-handled pot with black cross within circle designs on red background, small loop handles low on the sides, 12 in. by 12 in., rim chip. **$450-$650**

Chinese neolithic vessel, Gansu Yangshao Culture, Northwest China, circa 2500 BC, with cross within circle designs on the upper half, paint generally better quality than usual and a large example, 13 In. by 15 in. **$950-$1,250**

Chinese neolithic vessel, Gansu Yangshao Culture, Northwest China, circa 2500 BC, with rectangular designs on the upper half, paint fading, 15 in. by 16 in. $600-$850

Chinese neolithic vessel, Gansu Yangshao Culture, Northwest China, circa 2500 BC, with red and black rhomboid designs on the upper half, paint faded on reverse, 10 1/2 in. by 12 in. $500-$750

Chinese neolithic vessel, Gansu Yangshao Culture, Northwest China, circa 2500 BC, with zigzag and cross within circle designs on the upper half, repaired, 12 in. by 13 in. $450-$650

Chinese neolithic vessel, Gansu Yangshao Culture, Northwest China, circa 2500 BC, two-handled pot with black geometric zoomorphic and net designs on the upper half, paint generally better quality than usual and a scarce example with zoomorphic motifs, 14 in. by 14 in. $1,000-$1,250

Chinese neolithic vessel, Gansu Yangshao Culture, Northwest China, circa 2500 BC, two-handled pot with black circular net motifs on the upper half, small loop handles low on the sides, 10 in. by 11 in., intact. **$750-$950**

Chinese neolithic vessel, Gansu Yangshao Culture, Northwest China, circa 2500 BC, two-handled pot with black circular net motifs on the upper half, unusual ridged handles, 4 1/2 in. by 5 in. **$250-$350**

Chinese neolithic vessel, Gansu Yangshao Culture, Northwest China, circa 2500 BC, two-handled pot with rhomboid motifs on the upper half, a small zoomorphic head projecting with painted eyes and mouth, 4 in. by 4 1/2 in., rare type. **$250-$350**

Chinese neolithic vessel, Gansu Yangshao Culture, Northwest China, circa 2500 BC, two-handled pot with lentoid motifs on the upper half, 3 3/4 in. by 4 1/4 in. **$250-$350**

Chinese neolithic vessel, Gansu Yangshao Culture, Northwest China, circa 2500 BC, single-handled pot with rhomboid motifs on the upper half and net pattern on the neck, 3 1/2 in. by 3 7/8 in. **$250-$350**

Well-head, Han Dynasty, Eastern Han, 25-220 AD, gray earthenware with twin dragonheads, 9 in. tall, rare. **$350-$450**

Jar, one handle, painted with a band of chocolate brown lozenge that is repeated on the neck, chipped, Neolithic (second/third millennium BC), 5 3/4 diameter. **$650-$960**

Jar, broad, globular body painted dark brown and reddish brown with lozenges divided by panels of triple lines, chipped, Neolithic (second/third millennium BC), 5 in. diameter. **$800-$1,200**

Jar, black splashed glaze, two small, looped handles, restored rim and handles, Tang Dynasty, 6 1/2 in. high. **$1,500-$2,000**

Jar, red pottery with overlapping square panels of vertical and horizontal lines, chipped, Neolithic (first millennium BC), 14 in. diameter. **$1,800-$2,500**

Jar, globular, gray pottery, overlapping trellis pattern on the body, plain band at the shoulder, chipped, Neolithic (first millennium BC). **$2,500-$3,500**

Jarlet, green- and straw-glazed in a double gourd form, chips on foot, Tang Dynasty, 3 1/2 in. high. **$1,000-$1,500**

Pillow, buff pottery with a green glaze, fan-shaped foliate headrest on a grid with interlocking circles, ochre edge with incised wave patterns, waisted body, flanged foot, chip on foot, Ch'in (Qin) Dynasty, 11 in. wide. **$1,000-$1,500**

Pillow, red pottery with a green and yellow glaze, the pillow formed as a recumbent lion with fierce expression, unglazed base, minor restoration, Ch'in (Qin) Dynasty, 13 in. long. **$2,000-$3,000**

Vase, globular, high, flat foot, spinach green and silver glaze, pierced and mounted as a lamp, Han Dynasty, 16 in. high. **$800-$1,200**

Green and Aubergine

Bowls, everted rims, exterior with aubergine five-toed dragons pursuing the flaming pearl above breaking waves, damages to one, K'ang Hsi (Kangxi), 4 1/2 in. diameter, **pair. $1,000-$1,500**

Bowls, everted rims, incised with two five-toed dragons and flaming pearls and fire scrolls above waves, plain interiors, hairlines on both, 18th century, 4 1/2 in. diameter, pair. **$1,000-$1,500**

Architectural tiles, Chinese, circa 18th-19th century, 12 green glazed pedestals 5 1/2 in. by 5 1/2 in. by 19 1/2 in., and 16 square openwork tiles also green glazed, measuring 12 3/4 in. by 12 3/4 in. by 1 1/2 in. (some with corner breaks), some removable cement still adhering, one of each type is shown. $1,500-$2,750 for all

Green and Blue

Chinese porcelain figures of two of the Eight Immortals, bisque faces and hands, deep green and blue painted attire, black beards, marked Made in China, circa 1930, 6 1/2 in. high, each. $50-$75

Vase, baluster form, painted in green enamel, outlined in underglaze blue, five four-toed dragons pursuing flaming pearls above waves, Ch'eng Hua mark, but 19th century, 7 1/2 in. high. **$300-$400**

Yellow and Green

Bowl, exterior with incised and enameled five-toed dragons and flaming pearls with phoenix above a petal lappet band, the center of the interior with a longevity symbol, K'ang Hsi (Kangxi) six-character mark (and of the period), 4 1/2 in. diameter. **$5,000-$7,000**

Dishes, exterior with two five-toed scaly dragons chasing flaming pearls amidst clouds on a yellow ground, white interior, Kuang Hsü (Guangxu) six-character mark (and of the period), 7 in. diameter, pair. **$1,200-$1,500**

Saucer dish incised and painted with a green dragon pursuing the flaming pearl on the interior, Kuang Hsü (Guangxu) six-character mark (and of the period), 5 3/4 in. diameter. **$750-$1,000**

Honan

Bowl, Chinese Song Dynasty-style (960-1234), from the Jian kilns, measures approximately 6 1/4 in. by 2 1/2 in. The thinly potted body is of yellow-buff clay that is covered to just above the foot rim with a thick and lustrous iron glaze. The shallow, unglazed, hand-cut foot is burnt red from firing. The brown-black glaze has amber spots scattered both inside and out. The different glaze parabolas suggest the bowl was dipped several times in glaze. The exact way in which these glazes were produced is unknown. The placement of the amber areas suggests that this bowl was splashed with ash glaze after an initial immersion. All three layers show through in small areas where the amber glaze has worn off, producing a three-dimensional quality of white to tan to brown-black. There is an overall crackle most noticeable on the interior. Such deep brown bowls were valued by Song scholars because they contrasted well with the frothy, white tea used in those days. These bowls are highly prized by the Japanese, who call them temmoku. This has all the characteristics of a fine, 14th/15th century Southern Song Dynasty-style iron glazed bowl. Copies of these bowl were made in the 17th/18th centuries. Fine original condition. **$300**

Jar, globular with 27 ribs, unglazed rim, the body with a black glaze stopping short of the cut buff stoneware foot, Sung (Song) Dynasty, 5 in. high. **$2,500-$3,500**

Jar, globular with 27 ribs, unglazed rim, the body with a black glaze stopping short of the cut buff stoneware foot, Sung (Song) Dynasty, 8 in. high, cracked and chipped. **$400-$600**

Vase, double gourd, the sections joined by rope-twist handles, neck reduced, damaged, Sung (Song) Dynasty, 10 1/2 in. high. **$400-$600**

Jar, glazed, Song Dynasty, 960-1259, with molded domed lid (not original but of the period), a fine transparent glaze over the white clay body, 3 3/8 in. by 3 3/4 in., hairlines from rim. **$125-$150**

Jar, glazed, Song Dynasty, 960-1259, with molded lid in the form of a tiled roof, a fine transparent glaze over the white clay body, 3 1/4 in. by 3 3/4 in., excellent condition. **$175-$250**

Jar, glazed, Song Dynasty, 960-1259, with molded lid in the form of a tiled roof, a fine transparent glaze over the white clay body, 3 in. by 3 3/8 in., excellent condition. **$175-$250**

Jar, glazed, Song Dynasty, 960-1259, with molded lid in the form of a tiled roof with ornate ridge ornamentation, a fine transparent glaze over the white clay body, 3 3/4 in. by 4 3/4 in., excellent condition. **$350-$450**

Song Dynasty glazed jar, 960-1259, with molded lid in the form of a tiled roof with ornate ridge ornamentation, a fine transparent glaze over the white clay body, 4 in. by 6 1/2 in., excellent condition. **$350-$450**

Ming and Ch'ing (Qing) Dynasty Pottery

Figures, Buddhistic lions, one with paw on cub, one with paw on brocade (pierced) ball, green and blue glazes streaked with white, Shekwan ware, early 20th century, 9 in. high, pair. **$225-$375**

Figure, Buddhistic lion, glazed black with blue and white streaks and mottling, paw on brocade ball, Shekwan ware, circa 1900, 7 in. high. **$100-$150**

Figure, Buddhistic lion seated on a brown-glazed, waisted, rectangular stand, her paw on a cub, open mouth, collar with descending tassels, extremities chipped, Shekwan ware, circa 1900, 30 in. high. **$900-$1,200**

Figure of Chen Wu seated on a rock-work throne, glazed turquoise, green, and ochre, hands and face unglazed, 17th century, 12 in. high. **$600-$900**

Figure of Chen Wu seated on a high-backed throne, his loose-fitting attire glazed purple and ochre, roof tile, mounted as a lamp, Ming Dynasty, 14 in. high. **$1,000-$1,500**

Figure of a crab, green glaze with white on pincers, Shekwan ware, early 20th century, 6 3/4 in. wide. **$75-$120**

Altar, large house, Ming Dynasty, 1368-1644, exceptionally large and heavy terra cotta altar with bench in the interior (note that back wall does not show in image), the exterior green and brown glazed, 15 in. by 16 in. by 8 in., 35 lbs., minor inconsequential chips and good iridescence and adhered ancient soil, rare this large. **$2,500-$2,750**

Bowl, ceramic tripod, late Ming Dynasty, decorated with three-toed dragons flanking a flaming pearl, on a carved wooden stand, with a spurious 15th century mark on bottom, measurements with stand, 9 3/4 in. by 6 1/2 in. **$1,200**

Chest, glazed, Ming Dynasty, 1368-1644, larger example with molded hasp and handles, 6 1/3 in. tall, with removable lime deposits. **$250-$350**

Dish, blue and white with motifs of gourds, slightly scalloped rim, Ming Dynasty, Wan Li, 6 in. diameter. **$90 -$1,200**

Figure, large Ming Dynasty horse, 1368-1644, an especially large and fine example, 13 in. by 13. 3/4 in. **$1,500-$1,750**

Figure, life-size head of Kwan Yin (also spelled Guan Yin, Quan Yin, and Kuan Yin), Ming or Ching Dynasties, large molded pottery head of the goddess of compassion in accomplished style with traces of yellow and red pigment, possibly somewhat older, 6 1/2 in. by 8 1/2 in. by 12 in., free standing, intact. **$2,000-$2,750**

Figure, Ming Dynasty polychrome horse, 1368-1644, green, yellow and black glaze, 11 1/2 in. long. **$750-$850**

Figures, mirror image, scholars with hands clasped, their faces and extremities unglazed, one restored, mounted as lamps, Ming Dynasty, 15 in. high, pair. **$2,500-$3,500**

Figure, Ming Dynasty tomb figure (14/15th century), glazed in vibrant red and green with black highlighted facial features, 16 1/2 in. high and in excellent condition with no evidence of damage. **$800**

Figure of a mythological dog, red, green, and blue glazes streaked with white on high points, Shekwan ware, early 20th century, 7 1/2 in. wide. **$100-$125**

Figure, Shou Lao seated on a high-backed throne, his robes glazed purple and turquoise, roof tile, mounted as a lamp, 12 1/2 in. high, Ming Dynasty. **$1,200-$1,500**

Jar, storage, glazed black, the neck with a band of bosses (ornamentation)and two small loop handles, Ming Dynasty, 24 in. high. **$1,000-$1,500**

Tile maker's figure of a Bodhisattva seated beside books on a lotus base above pierced rock-work, glazed green, very old damages, 17th century, 12 1/4 in. high. **$700-$900**

Figure, Ming Dynasty horse, 1368-1644, with the rare turquoise, black, brown, green and pale yellow glaze, insertion hole for tail at rear, 10 in. by 11 in., very rare coloration. **$1,100-$1,500**

Figure, large Ming Dynasty horse, 1368-1644, with the rare turquoise, black, and green glaze on cream, 12 in. by 13 1/2 in., rare. **$1,100-$1,500**

Jar, lidded ginger, blue and white, Ching Dynasty, circa 17th/19th century, decorated with floral pattern, a small molded foo lion serving as the knob of the lid, four small handles on body, 8 in. by 8 1/2 in. **$200-$350**

Jar, large glazed, Ming or Ching Dynasties, brown glazed jar with five small pierced handles in the form of Tao Tieh heads, the body with incised floral motifs, 18 in. by 23 in. **$1,450-$2,250**

Tile maker's figure of a demon (standing over a cloud) on a cylindrical base, glazed green, ochre, and brown, chipped, 17th/18th century, 14 1/4 in. high. **$1,200-$1,600**

Tile maker's figure of a dragon standing on clouds, glazed yellow, green, and aubergine, 18th century, 23 in. long. **$1,500-$2,500**

Tile maker's figure of a standing guardian wearing elaborate armor, glazed green and ochre, mounted on a wood base, chips to the surface, late Ming Dynasty, 22 in. high. **$1,500-$2,500**

Tile maker's figure of an equestrian, glazed green and brown, late 19th century, 9 1/2 in. high. **$200-$300**

Tile maker's figure of an equestrian, the dignitary wearing his armor, the horse in galloping position, glazed green, amber, and mustard yellow, chips to the surface, 18th century, 13 1/2 in. high. **$1,000-$1,500**

Roof tiles, seated Kylin, green glaze, damaged, Ming Dynasty, 11 1/4 in. high, pair. **$1,200-$1,800**

Roof tiles, standing male figures wearing green-, amber-, and cream-glazed attire; Ming Dynasty, 16 in. high, pair. **$2,500-$4,000**

Vase, mallet shape, two handles, mottled and streaked with a blue-black glaze, Shekwan ware, late 19th century, 7 in. high. **$200-$285**

Vase, baluster form, thick blue-black glaze, Shekwan ware, 18th century, 12 1/2 in. high. **$200-$275**

Miscellaneous

Bowls, Chinese porcelain, the first is pure white porcelain covered on the exterior in a yellow glaze enhanced with inscribed and overglaze enameled designs of vines and flowers with four roundels of dragons and birds with flaming pearls, dating to the mid-20th century. The bowl has a multicolor Greek key upper border. It measures 6 3/4 in. by 2 3/4 in. The inner glaze has a few black specks but is otherwise in perfect condition. The base bears a four-character Ch'ien Lung reign mark in overglaze red enamel, but the bowl does not date from this era. Its characteristics are more of those found in a fine turn-of-the-century copy. The second is a conical bowl with black underglaze and multicolor overglaze enamels in a flower and vine design on a pure white porcelain body, measuring 7 in. by 3 in. The bowl has a 20th century Jingdezhen (known as the "porcelain city" since the Song Dynasty, with a 1,700-year history of porcelain-making) mark on the base. Excellent original condition; pair. **$125**

Chinese porcelain bowl, underglaze blue and white with motifs of dragons and diapers, late 18th century. **$1,500-$1,800.**
COURTESY OF THE VIRGINIA KERESEY COLLECTION

Bowl, octagonal, Chinese, decorated with multicolor overglaze enamel, measuring approximately 8 in. across, dating to the early 20th century. The bowl is decorated on the cavetto (a concave molding having a curve that approximates a quarter circle) with floral designs around a central medallion of two ducks in the water. The exterior is done in multicolor enamel with carved or pressed accents of flowers and vines on a yellow background. It is heavily potted and has an overall orange peel effect to the white glaze. There is rubbing and enamel loss on one edge of the bowl. The base bears a false Qian Long six-character reign mark. **$200**

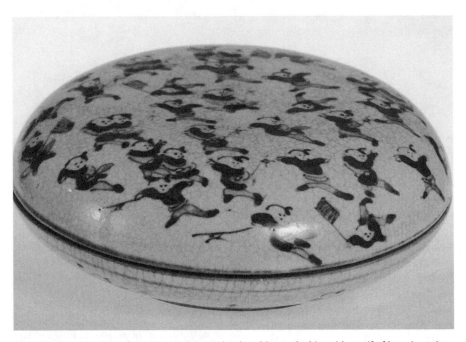

Box and cover, circular, soft-paste porcelain, underglaze blue and white with motif of boys in various poses, K'ang Hsi mark (and of the period), 6 in. diameter. **$1,000-$1,500**
COURTESY OF THE VIRGINIA KERESEY COLLECTION

Bowl, white porcelain with a peacock and flame design in overglaze enamels on the exterior, Chinese, measuring 5 3/4 in. by 3 in., dating to the late 19th century, or Kuang Hsu reign (1875-1908). The bowl bears a hallmark on its base. There is an old, sealed, hairline crack. **$75**

Bowls, pink and white glaze, Chinese, measuring 4 in. by 2 1/2 in., dating to the 20th century. Each bowl has impressed or hidden outer designs of auspicious Buddhist symbols under a lustrous pink glaze. The inner surface of the white porcelain body is covered with a pure white glaze. The bases bear the factory marks and the words "Made in China," pair. **$75**

Bowl, blue and white bowl, Chinese, measuring 7 in. by 2 3/4 in., dating to the 17th century. The bowl is decorated with underglaze blue that has a distinctly purple color. Flowers are painted on the cavetto and center; landscape scenes are painted on the exterior. The bowl has a typical orange peel feel and the foot rim shows an orange clay. The rim shows "mushikui," or a moth-eaten appearance. This is typical of ko-sometsuke, or old Chinese blue and white wares shipped to Japan as well as better quality Chinese domestic wares made in the Ming Tiangi period (1621-27). There is one old 1/4 in. rim chip. Fine original condition. **$300**

Brush pot dating from the Tang Dynasty, 3 1/2 in. diameter. **$900–$1,200**

Bowl, porcelain, Chinese, designed with four roundels of stylized dragons chasing flaming pearls and a central inner medallion of a flaming pearl in overglaze green, orange, and white enamels, dating to the late 19th or early 20th century. The bowl has a four-character hallmark on the base in orange. It is smudged and hard to read. The bottom left character looks like Chinese for prosperity. The bowl is in fine and original condition with one firing defect in the center that shows the underlying orange-brown clay body. There is some pitting of the white glaze. **$75**

Brush holder, Chinese, hand-potted on the wheel then incised to resemble bamboo stalks, decorated with a bird and floral design in enamels of aubergine, blue, red, and brown, measuring 10 3/4 in. in height and 4 1/2 in. across. The potting style and multicolor glaze are reminiscent of earlier Yüan and Ming Dynasty pieces, but this is not of that period. Probably mid to late 19th century. Excellent and original condition with no evidence of cracks, chips, or repairs. **$500**

Brush washer, earthenware, large, Chinese, covered with a tea dust glaze, measuring 9 in. in diameter and 2 in. high, dating to the late 19th or early 20th century. The brush washer has an accession number in India ink on the base as well as a red "CHINA" mark, the latter dating this to the late Ching Dynasty. **$150**

Dish, underglaze blue and white with circular motifs of dragons and flames, Chinese K'ang Hsi style, circa 1800, 5 1/2 in. diameter. **$250-$375**

Brush washer, porcelain, Chinese, measuring 5 in. by 1 1/2 in., with a bluish-white crackle glaze, decorated with an interior landscape scene and exterior scenes of a procession, dating to the late 19th century. The figures on the outside are repetitive and appear to have been applied under the glaze as transfers. The inner rim is covered with a brown glaze. The foot rim is off-white and contains black specks. The base bears a six-character, false K'ang Hsi reign mark in a double-blue circle done by a master calligrapher. The style of potting, absence of hollow line, the use of transfer printing, and type of clay all date this to the late 19th century, before the Kuang Hsü reign. **$100**

Figure, large Chinese porcelain goddess, circa early 20th century, polychrome smiling goddess standing with a dragon and goldfish at her feet, her hand raised in a blessing, 17 in. by 38 1/2 in., one small flaked area. **$4,500-$4,750**

Coffee pot with top, underglaze blue on white porcelain, Chinese, measuring 4 3/4 in. in height by 3 1/2 in. at its widest, bearing a Guangxu reign mark (1875-1908) in overglaze red. The design is of a three-toed dragon. The spout and rim areas have been "clobbered," or enhanced with gold. Possibly part of a child's set. The coffeepot is in original excellent condition with no evidence of damage or repairs. **$125**

Left: Chinese porcelain plate with floral motif in shades of pink, green, and orange, overglaze orange Ch'ien Lung mark on base, circa 1930, 6 in. diameter. $25-$40. Right: Chinese porcelain plate with motif in orange, green, and pink, overglaze orange mark on base indicating Ch'ien Lung, circa 1925, 9 in. diameter. **$65-$95**

Dish, Chinese, dating from 1862 to 1874, the reign of the Tongzhi emperor. It is lobulated in design and measures 4 in. across and is 2 in. high. The porcelain is of high quality and has a bluish tinge with few imperfections. The dish is decorated around three-quarters of the circumference with a family scene in the famille rose palette. There is a four-character Tongzhi mark in seal script on the base. The period before Tongzhi's reign was marked by civil war in China that led to the destruction of the Imperial kilns in Jingdezhen in the 1850s. Most porcelain produced from this time until that of the Guangzu emperor at the end of the century was of poor quality. This piece is the exception that proves the rule. It is not Imperial but represents the fine porcelain pieces done after the kiln was rebuilt or by remaining artisans. Porcelain of this quality with this reign mark is hard to find. **$125**

Dishes or plates, cafe au lait, Chinese, measuring 6 in. by 1 1/4 in., dating to the 19th century. The dishes have an overall cafe au lait surface glaze. They are decorated in rich, multicolor overglaze enamels with auspicious fungus and plant designs. They have apocryphal Ming Dynasty six-character reign marks on the reverse, each one from a different calligrapher. However, the body, style, and execution are all consistent with a later, 19th century date. Fine original condition; pair. **$600**

Teapot in orange and gold with two reserves, porcelain, Chinese, circa 1925. $65-$95

Serving dish, large porcelain, Chinese, measuring 8 in. in diameter by 4 in. in height, dating to the second half of the 20th century. The bowl has painted enamel figures of a boy and a sage as well as calligraphy that gives the artist's name and seal. The reverse has characters that translate to "Delicious food puts a smile on your face." Fine original condition. **$85**

Figure of a girl holding a peony, Chinese export, circa 1850, girl is finely modeled and decorated in overglaze enamel of pale blues, reds, and greens, stands 10 1/2 in. high, and measures 3 1/2 in. across the base. The base is unmarked and unsigned, which is characteristic of pre-1890 ceramic exports. **$100**

Seal, Chinese blue and white porcelain, measuring 2 3/4 in. high, dating to the 19th century or earlier. One side shows the typical Chinese landscape, the other side is Chinese poetry. Fine original condition. **$100**

Teapot, Chinese, I Hsing, measuring 7 1/2 in. by 5 in., dating to the mid-20th century. This teapot is formed in the shape of a tree trunk. The base shows the typical impressed seal of the I Hsing potters. Fine original condition. .. **$115**

Vase, porcelain with a mirror black glaze, Chinese, six-character K'ang Hsi mark (and of the period), 7 in. high. **$1,800-$2,500**

Left: Chinese porcelain Flambé-glazed globular vase, heavily potted with a thick, everted rim, the shoulders flanked by molded mask and ring handles, covered in a rich, streaked burgundy and lavender-purple glaze stopping short of the foot, the interior thinning to a grayish crackled glaze, 18th century, 9 in. high. Realized price (including the 10-percent buyer's premium), Christie's East, New York City. **$1,540**. Right: Chinese 1 Hsing (Yixing) teapot with a robin's egg glaze, faintly impressed mark on the base, 9 1/2 in. high. Realized price (including the 10-percent buyer's premium), Christie's East, New York City. **$1,100**

Vase, Chinese monochrome, measuring 9 in. high and 4 1/2 in. at its widest. The vase is made of white porcelain and has a low foot rim. It rises gently from the foot to a rounded shape, then cuts back in to be joined by three rings of clay at the neck that rise into a flared mouth. The interior is covered with a fine clear glaze that shows the white body. The overall glaze is a copper-based matte red that fits into the general category of peach bloom or ox-blood red. The base is glazed and has a six-character archaic script Qianlong mark. However, the mark has the 3-point trident in the zhi character that is incorrect for the period. The overall style of the vase, the foot rim, and the apocryphal reign mark all date this vase to the late 19th or early 20th century at the latest. **$200**

Vase, Chinese prunus (the botanical name for a large group of deciduous and evergreen trees and shrubs), in underglaze blue over white, dating to the late Ching Dynasty, measuring 12 in. tall. The vase has one small rim depression under the glaze from the time of firing. It bears a six-character, false K'ang Hsi reign mark in underglaze blue on the base. Late 19th or early 20th century. **$200**

Vase, porcelain, Chinese, measuring 12 1/2 in. high, with paintings of three figures, calligraphy, and borders in multicolor overglaze enamels, dating to the early 20th century. The vase is painted on the front with three historical figures, one of which is dressed like a judge. The back bears a message in Chinese characters of congratulations, good luck, and long life. The base has a four-character, red enamel seal of Jingdezhen, the famous center of Chinese porcelain manufacture. Probably a gift or reward for a special occasion. Excellent original condition. **$200**

Baluster vase, Chinese blue and white Yen-Yen, with a fine, white porcelaneous body decorated in an underglaze blue landscape painting of deer, trees, and cranes. The vase is accented with an elongated cloud diaper around the base and simple, double blue lines at the waist. It measures 18 in. high with a 5 in. base and an 8 in. flared mouth. There is a firing dimple with two small glaze defects on one side. The grayish white, tapered foot, the glaze color, the absence of hollow line and glaze bursts in the blue, and the shape all date this vase to the mid to late 19th century. **$900**

Bud vase, garlic, Chinese, with a fine, white porcelain body decorated in wucai, or underglaze blue, and overglaze multicolor enamels, of pairs of birds, with floral diapers at rim and midsection, and clouds at the base. Some figures are outlined in blue while others are outlined in black, typical of wucai porcelain. There is a Ming Dynasty, Wan Li (1573-1619) mark in underglaze blue around upper rim, probably a false mark, with the vase dating to the 20th century. The vase stands approximately 10 in. high. Probably made for a wedding present, given the decoration. **$125**

Vase, porcelain, with gilt motifs, Chinese, Ch'ien Lung (Qianlong) six-character mark (and of the period), small wax repair on the foot, 4 in. high. **$700-$900**

Square mallet vase, Chinese San Ts'ai, measuring 8 1/4 in. high and 2 1/2 in. across at its widest, dating to the late 17th or early 18th century. The vase is finely potted of thin clay slabs that taper to a square foot with a hand-cut rim. It has an overall, runny, egg-yolk glaze with decoration of birds and flowers in overglaze green and aubergine purple. The spiky plantain leaf border on the neck is in the Kangxi style. The colors are applied in washes over the finely drawn, black-outlined designs. The interior of the mouth has a white glaze. The vase bears a four-character mark that reads: Shi jin tang zhi, or "Hall for a rich and colorful tapestry of generations." Fine original condition. **$800**

Swatow

Box and cover, blue and white with large lotus flowers, rim chips on the inside, 15th century, 4 in. diameter. **$200-$300**

Dish, a circular panel of buildings on the well with quatrefoil panels enclosing figures and boats, red and turquoise, 16th century, 15 in. diameter. **$600-$800**

Dish, blue and white, painted with a phoenix, peony, and bamboo, panels of peach and foliage on the border, cracked, 17th century, 14 in. diameter. **$400-$600**

Dish, blue and white with motif of pheasant and peony within a diaper border, cracked, 17th century, 18 1/2 in. diameter. **$400-$600**

Dish, incised peony in green, red, and turquoise between flower heads radiating from a central peony roundel, 17th century, 14 in. diameter. **$550-$750**

Jar, blue and white, four loop handles at the shoulders, stylized peony motif, cracked, 1/th century, 9 1/2 in. high. **$200-$300**

Ting Wares

Bowl, rounded sides, exterior with carved lotus and leaves, Northern Sung (Song) Dynasty, 4 in. diameter. **$1,200-$1,800**

Dish molded on the interior with Buddhistic lions with a key-pattern border, ivory glaze, copper rim, crack on base, Sung (Song)/Yüan Dynasty, 5 1/2 in. diameter. **$2,000-$3,000**

Dish, circular, carved with a stylized flower under a creamy white glaze, rim in the biscuit, Sung (Song) Dynasty, 4 1/2 in. diameter. **$1,500-$2,500**

Dish carved with a central roundel of two fish and waves, plain exterior, glaze stopping neatly around the shallow-cut foot, rim in the biscuit, unglazed base, Sung (Song) Dynasty, 6 3/4 in. diameter. **$800-$1,200**

Tou ts'ai (Doucai)

Bowl painted on the exterior with six lotus blossoms and a foliage meander above ruyi lappets around the foot, plain interior, Tao Kuang (Daoguang) seal (and of the period), 5 3/4 in. diameter. **$1,800-$2,600**

Bowl, a central, full-faced dragon surrounded by six phoenix medallions, the exterior with Shou characters, Hsuan Te mark, but 18th century. **$900-$1,200**

Bowl, conical, painted with groups of flowers on the exterior and a central lotus on the interior, Tao Kuang (Daoguang) six-character mark (and of the period), 5 in. diameter. **$1,800-$2,500**

Dish, the well decorated with lotus heads and scrolling stems around a central flower head, the everted rim decorated with eight flower heads and vines, the exterior painted with bats, 18th century, 9 1/2 in. diameter. **$800-$1,000**

Dish, everted rim painted with a flower head and fine, interlinked pearls; the reverse with five iron red bats; 19th century, 6 1/4 in. diameter. **$275-$400**

Dish, a centrally painted duck and flowering lotus plants below a narrow border, the exterior with wading duck and lotus, 19th century, 6 1/2 in. diameter. **$300-$500**

Dishes, the interiors painted with a full-faced, five-toed dragon and fire scroll, the borders with a wave pattern; Hsuan Te mark, but 19th century; 7 1/2 in. diameter, pair. **$300-$500**

Dishes, the interiors with dragon and clouds bordered by carp and waves, breaking waves on the reverse, hairlines on one, Ch'eng Hua mark, but 18th century, 6 1/2 in. diameter, pair. **$1,200-$1,600**

Saucer dish painted with a large flower head on a lotus pod, the exterior with similar motifs, 19th century. **$350-$500**

Saucer dishes painted with a central Shou roundel within eight Shou characters and bands of scrolls, the exteriors with scrolls and stylized foliage, Ch'ien Lung (Qianlong) six-character mark (and of the period), 8 1/2 in. diameter, pair. **$3,500-$5,000**

Vase, everted rim, slender body, painted with birds in flight and flowering branches; Ch'eng Hua mark, but 18th century; 7 1/2 in. high. **$1,000-$1,500**

Tz'u Chou (Cizhou)

Bowl, the exterior with calligraphy and foliage, Ming Dynasty, 6 1/2 in. diameter. **$400-$500**

Figure of an Immortal seated on a lotus base, ivory with brown cloud scrolls, 20th century, 8 in. high. **$200-$300**

Figure of Chen Wu seated on a rock-work base, his hands resting on his knees, 17th century, 8 1/2 in. high. **$800-$1,200**

Figure of a recumbent tiger painted deep brown over cream slip, minor cracks, Yüan Dynasty, 3 1/2 in. wide. **$700-$900**

Jar, baluster form, continuous scene of noblemen on horseback in a landscape, damaged, transitional, circa 1650, 11 in. high. **$500-$700**

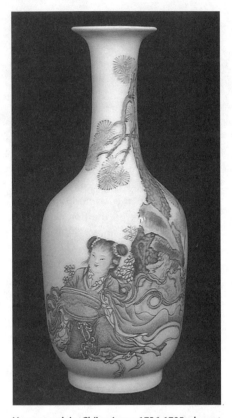

Vase, porcelain, Ch'ien Lung, 1736-1795, elegant form painted with a court maiden under a pine tree opening a box to reveal her lucky pet bat inside, four Chinese characters in black on the reverse, 3 1/2 in. by 8 1/2 in., fine painting with vibrant color and choice condition, Ch'ien Lung seal on base in red. **$750-$1,250**

Jar painted with cranes in flight above an iron red band of wave pattern, the shoulders with a band of prunus, pine, and scrolls, damage to the neck, 18th century, 5 1/4 in. high. **$350-$450**

Jar, globular, painted with alternating panels of five-toed dragons and flaming pearls above crested waves, Wan Li mark (and of the period), cracked and badly scratched, 6 in. diameter. **$2,200-$3,300**

Box and cover, porcelain, Wu ts'ai, dragon-and-cloud and phoenix-and-cloud motifs, Chinese, Ming Dynasty, 1 3/4 in. by 1 1/4 in. **$600-$900**

Jar, ovoid with painted calligraphy on the upper border, the center with large floral motifs and key pattern, imperfections in the glaze, Yüan Dynasty, 12 in. high. **$1,500-$2,200**

Pillow, concave, rectangular, sloping surface with a barbed medallion enclosing a mountainscape, the front painted with a flower, the back with calligraphy, leaf and scroll borders, cracked, Yüan Dynasty, 12 1/4 in. high. **$1,200-$1,800**

Pillow incised through the white slip with a crane in flight above clouds, a flower head border, old cracks and damages, Yüan Dynasty, 8 1/2 in. long. **$1,500-$2,200**

Vase, pear-shaped, trumpet neck, three bands of stylized flowers painted over cream slip, the slip and clear glaze stopping irregularly above the deeply cut foot, glaze fret to rim and foot, small hairlines, Sung (Song) Dynasty, 10 in. high. **$2,000-$3,000**

Vase, pear-shaped with a wide band at the mouth, translucent brown splashes on a deep brown opaque ground, damaged, Sung (Song) Dynasty, 5 1/4 in. high. **$500-$800**

Vase, pear-shaped with a trumpet mouth, cream slip under a translucent glaze, shallow-cut buff stoneware foot, neck chipped, Sung (Song)/Yüan Dynasty, 10 in. high. **$700-$950**

Wu ts'ai (Wucai)

Dish, centrally painted with birds in flight, fruiting peach tree, and rock-work, four floral cartouches divided by the cell pattern on the border, late Ming Dynasty, 8 in. diameter. **$300-$500**

Saucer dish painted with two boats and islands, hairlines, Ming Dynasty, 6 in. diameter. **$185-$250**

Saucer dish painted at the center with a panel of a bird on a berry branch, wide cell ground, borders reserved with fruit panels, restored, Wan Li six-character mark (and of the period), 6 1/4 in. diameter. **$350-$550**

Sweetmeat box, the interior with seven compartments, each decorated with birds and flowering branches, matching exterior, chips on base and rim, Wan Li six-character mark (and of the period), 9 in. diameter. **$2,000-$3,000**

Tea caddy and cover, octagonal, painted with lappets of flowering branches, rim chip on cover, frittings, 18th century, 4 1/2 in. high. **$400-$600**

Vase decorated with horses and a floral ground, Transitional, 12 1/2 in. high. **$2,000-$3,000**

Teapot, I Hsing (Yixing), with a blue glaze, square form, faintly impressed mark on base, first half of the 19th century, 6 in. high. **$800-$1,200**

Teapot, I Hsing (Yixing), in double-tree-trunk form, terra cotta, blue, and cream with branch-form finish, bamboo-form spout, branch-form handle, early 19th century, 3 in. high. **$250-$350**

Vase; globular, with two panels of dragons on a lotus ground below stiff leaves, the flaring neck with lotus scrolls below a chevron pattern, Wan Li mark, but 19th century, 9 in. high. **$400-$600**

Vase, double gourd, the lower half with birds in a wooded landscape below three bands of ruyi heads, the upper part with two phoenixes in flight, Wan Li six-character mark (and of the period), 10 in. high. **$1,200-$1,600**

Left: I Hsing (Yixing) water dropper of a boy upon a buffalo, late Ch'ing Dynasty. $200-$300. Right: I Hsing water dropper of a monk reading and seated beside a pig, late Ch'ing Dynasty. $275-$375

Vases, beaker form, flaring upper section painted with a dignitary beside a bridge, with ladies and attendants within clouds, camellia sprays and rock-work in the central section, peach sprays on the lower sections, the interiors of the necks with scrolling peony, damaged, 17th century, 20 1/2 in. high, pair. **$2,000-$3,000**

I Hsing (Yixing)

Box and cover, peach form, yellow with brown splashes, 18th century. **$700-$1,000**

Brush washer, peach form, yellow with brown splashes, supported on three feet formed by walnut, lychee, and peanut, 18th century, 3 3/4 in. wide. **$1,500-$2,200**

Bulb bowl with enameled flowers and three stub feet, marked China, circa 1930, 9 in. diameter. **$100-$145**

Figure of a seated Lohan wearing flowing robes folding at the base, 18th century, 5 1/2 in. high. **$2,000-$3,000**

Flower pot in the form of a tree stump, marked China, circa 1930, 5 in. high, 6 in. diameter. **$150-$220**

Teapot, Chinese, I Hsing, in the shape of a cluster of bamboo, measuring 7 in. high and 11 1/2 in. from spout to handle. The base has an impressed mark typical of this type of ware, early 20th century. There is a 1 mm chip on the handle grasp. **$150**

Teapot, rare blue glaze, rectangular with flat cover, early 19th century, 6 in. high. **$800-$1,000**

Teapot, compressed globular form, a single molded band at the widest point, loop handle, curved spout, 18th century, 7 1/4 in. wide. **$1,000-$1,500**

Teapot, compressed globular form, loop handle, short spout, olive brown with gritty texture, signed Qu Hua, 20th century. **$900-$1,200**

Teapot, globular with mushroom-shaped lid, the body with applied fruits and nuts of lighter-colored clay, bamboo-stem-form spout, 19th century, 4 1/2 in. high. **$600-$800**

Teapot, green glaze, melon ribbed with leaves and vine around the body, drooping loop handle, short, bent spout, 19th century, 4 in. high. **$650-$850**

Teapot, lozenge shape, square handle and spout, bracket feet, circa 1800, 7 1/2 in. wide. **$1,000-$1,500**

Teapot, robin's egg blue, C handle, S-curved spout, domed lid, 18th century, 6 in. high. **$2,500-$3,500**

Teapot, robin's egg blue, simulated bamboo handle, spout, and finial, interior of cover chipped, early 19th century, 5 3/4 in. high. **$1,200-$1,500**

Teapot, rounded rectangular form, spout and handle molded as a branch and enameled yellow, applied yellow and green grape leaves, early 20th century, 4 1/2 in. high. **$100-$150**

Teapot, tree trunk form, body with applied branches, leaves, and berries, flat cover, 19th century, 5 1/2 in. high. **$600-$800**

Tea set, teapot and six cups, all in the form of tree stumps, marked China, circa 1925. **$100-$150**

Tea set, teapot, sugar, creamer, and tray, all with applied pewter embellishment, dragon motif, marked Shanghai, China, circa 1935. **$275-$375**

Vase, tree stump form, marked China, circa 1935, 7 in. high. **$100-$175**

Vase, beaker form, applied plum blossoms and branches, the flowers in a cream-colored clay, early 20th century, 9 in. high. **$300-$500**

Water pot molded as a miniature teapot, short spout, looped handle, bud finial, 19th century. **$400-$600**

Ch'ing Dynasty

Shun Chih
1644-1661

Shun Chih (seal form)
1644-1661

K'ang Hsi
1662-1722

K'ang Hsi (seal form)
1662-1722

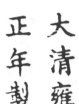

Yung Cheng
1723-1735

Yung Cheng (seal form)
1723-1735

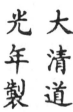

Ch'ien Lung
1736-1795

Ch'ien Lung (seal form)
1736-1795

Chia Ch'ing
1796-1820

Chia Ch'ing (seal form)
1796-1820

Tao Kuang
1821-1850

Tao Kuang (seal form)
1821-1850

Hsien Feng
1851-1861

Hsien Feng (seal form)
1851-1861

T'ung Chih
1862-1874

T'ung Chih (seal form)
1862-1874

Kuang Hsü
1875-1908

Kuang Hsü (seal form)
1875-1908

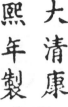

Hsüan T'ung
1909-1912

Hsüan T'ung
1909-1912

Dolls, Games & Toys

The Japanese celebrate two yearly doll festivals, the Girls' Festival on March 3 and the Boys' Festival on May 5. During these celebrations, families display dolls that have been handed down for generations. Dolls for the Girls' Festival represent Japan's emperor and empress and members of their court. Dolls for the Boys' Festival include figures of heroes and warriors. Through the dolls, the children learn about their country's culture, history, and outstanding men and women.

Japanese toy timeline, in brief:

1945 to 1949: Exports of Japanese-made toys such as celluloid figures and spring-driven toys started, and friction toy cars were put on the market.

1950 to 1959: The manufacturing of plastic toys started in Japan. The first electric toys, a sedan car and airplane, were put on sale. A radio-controlled toy car made its first appearance. The first Japanese-made plastic models were put on the market. The sale of Japanese-made miniature cars started.

1960 to 1969: A vinyl doll, "Winky" (Dakko-Chan), came into fashion. The first Japan International Toy Fair (now called the Tokyo Toy Show) was held. Walking dolls and dress-up dolls were put on sale. Toy racing cars appeared on the market. Character toys such as Astro Boy were introduced. A talking doll made its first appearance. Space-related toys were widely sold, influenced by the Apollo missions.

Dolls

Bijin (Japanese beauty), cloth face and hands, red silk kimono, flowers in her hair, wood base, post-World War II, 18 in. high. **$75-$100**

Boy on horseback, dressed in suit of armor, encased in glass, Japanese, early Showa period, 16 3/4 in. high. **$185-$275**

Boy and girl, silk garments, used as needle cases, Chinese, circa 1925, 2 1/2 in. high. **$125-$185**

Boy and girl, porcelain heads, movable arms and legs, Japanese, circa 1925, 6 in. high. **$125-$175**

Left: Hakata doll of the lion dancer, the costume in red and gilt. $150-$250. Right: Hakata doll of the wisteria maiden, removable hat, red and lavender robes with gilt trim, 8 in. high. **$175-$275**

Elderly man and woman, silk garments, movable arms, legs, and heads, garments removable, Chinese, circa 1930, 11 1/2 in. high. **$200-$300**

Eight Immortals, silk padded with cotton and mounted on a strip of paper, Chinese, circa 1920, 9 in. high. **$100-$200**

Eight Immortals, silk padded with cotton and mounted on a strip of paper, Chinese, circa 1920, 11 1/2 in. high. **$125-$225**

Eight Immortals, silk padded with cotton and mounted on a strip of paper, Chinese, circa 1920, 13 in. high. **$140-$240**

Eight Immortals, silk padded with cotton and mounted on a strip of paper, Chinese, circa 1920, 15 3/8 in. high. **$250-$350**

Eight Immortals, silk padded with cotton and mounted on a strip of paper, Chinese, circa 1920, 18 in. high. **$350-$500**

Eight Immortals, silk padded with cotton and mounted on a strip of paper, Chinese, circa 1920, 22 in. high. **$500-$700**

Emperor and Empress Japanese Hina dolls, in the seated or "suwari-bina" position for Girls' Day. The long, refined faces, padded seven-layer garments ("itsutsuginu") on the Empress, the Empress's coronet, and the layered, brocade robe with bib on the Emperor all date these to the Edo period, pre-1868, and are of the Kyoho style. The faces are covered with "gofun" or white paste made from ground shells. The dolls were given on "jomi," the third day of the third month, or March 3, at the "hina matsuri," or Hina Doll Festival. This style of doll dates from the mid-15th century. The bases measure 8 in. by 5 in., and the dolls measure 5 1/2 in. to the top of the head. Excellent condition with only minimal wear. **$500**

Emperor and Empress, both seated on tatami mats, lacquer and oyster-shell faces, elaborate red and gold silk brocade attire, Japanese, late Meiji/early Taisho period, 12 in. high. **$400-$600**

Geisha doll, Japanese, measuring approximately 12 1/2 in. high, dating to the 1950s. The doll stands on a lacquered wood base. The face appears to be made of gofun, a white paste made from ground shells. She is dressed in silk garments. **$75**

Geisha wearing a silk kimono and holding an umbrella, lacquer and oyster-shell face, Japanese, early Showa period, 18 1/2 in. high. **$125-$200**

Hakata, geisha with black and gold kimono, Japanese, 20th century, 8 3/8 in. high. **$125-$175**

Hakata, girl holding fan, marked Made in Japan, 20th century, 10 in. high. **$65-$96**

Lama (priest), flexible body, movable arms and legs, silk attire, Chinese, circa 1900, 10 in. high. **$200-$300**

Lacquer palanquin, or chair with poles, Japanese, measuring approximately 10 in. in length and 5 in. high, dating to around 1950. The chair was part of a set of lacquer items that accompanied a girl's Hina doll received on Girls' Day. The body of the palanquin is decorated in floral scroll patterns with gold lacquer. It comes with its own storage box. Fine original condition. **$150**

Pin-cushion doll, silk crepe with floral motif, Japanese, circa 1915. **$75-$125**

Samurai, lacquer face and hands, Japanese, Showa period, 16 in. high. **$150-$175**

Samurai seated on a folding chair and wearing helmet, armor, and sword, Japanese, Meiji period. **$400-$650**

Tanikaze, Japanese sumo wrestler, porcelain, measuring 9 in. in height and 5 in. across at his widest, dating to the mid-20th century. Tanikaze Kajinosuke was the fourth of the sumo champions known as "yokozuna," appearing on the ranking lists for the sport in 1789. He is wearing the hemp rope decorated with paper cuttings that is the official garb of the yokozuna. The doll comes in his own box with his name and that of the artist on the front. Fine original condition. **$150**

Young girl wearing flowered silk kimono, Japanese, early Showa period, 14 1/2 in. high. **$200-$275**

Woman holding a flowering branch, lacquer and silk, Japanese, Showa period, 14 1/4 in. high. **$100-$175**

Woman with four interchangeable wigs, original box, Japanese, circa 1930, 6 in. high. **$75-$125**

Games

Bank, wood inlaid with various colored woods forming a motif of Hotei, Japanese, circa 1925, 2 1/2 in. by 4 in. by 4 3/4 in. **$50-$85**

Battledore, court lady in brightly colored silk brocade attire, Japanese, early Showa period, 12 1/2 in. high. **$200-$300**

Battledore (or hagoita, similar to the paddle used in badminton) showing a Samurai in appliqued silk brocade, orange, purple, gold, and colors, the reverse with painted flowering branches, Japanese, circa 1935, 24 in. high. **$300-$500**

Battledore (hagoita) with silk brocade karako (children) on one side, painted plum blossoms on the reverse, Japanese, circa 1925, 17 in. long. **$300-$400**

Chess set, ivory, carved as officials and warriors upon puzzle balls and lotus bases, Chinese, circa 1900. **$500-$700**

Chess set, emperor and empress and attendants, stained in red and white, Chinese, early 20th century. **$600-$800**

Chess set, ivory, red, and white, carved as officials and warriors, oval bases, Chinese, early 20th century. **$400-$600**

Chess set painted in colors and gilt, warriors riding horses, camels, and elephants, each piece with lotus bases, Indian, 20th century. **$1,800-$2,500**

Child's tea set, tray, cups and saucers, covered creamer and sugar, and teapot, yellow Awaji ware, Japanese, circa 1925. **$100-$125**

Child's tea set, tray, cups and saucers, covered creamer and sugar, and teapot, green Awaji ware, Japanese, circa 1925. **$100-$125**

Game box containing five small covered boxes, black and gilt lacquer, rectangular with rounded corners, overall decoration of floral sprigs, Chinese, 19th century, 11 1/2 in. by 10 in. by 3 in. **$900-$1,200**

Game box, octagonal, painted with panels of figures on terraces, elaborate foliate borders, the interior with boxes and small trays with card counters, some missing, Chinese, 19th century, 15 in. long. **$400-$600**

Game box, red and black lacquer, octagonal, containing six covered boxes and 12 trays, exterior decorated with fruit and flower borders, the details in red, the interior with garden scenes, Chinese, early 19th century, 11 3/4 in. by 13 1/4 in. by 4 1/2 in. **$1,000-$1,500**

Pair of Chinese gambling or game chips made of mother of pearl, measuring 2 1/4 in. by 1/2 in., dating to the turn of the century. They are surface carved with birds and flowers in cartouches. Fine original condition. **$75**

Cribbage board, inlaid wood, Japanese, early Showa period, 10 1/2 in. by 3 in. by 2 1/2 in. **$50-$75**

Furniture (toy), inlaid wood, two benches, two chairs, and a table, Japanese, circa 1920, 4 1/2 in. high. **$150-$250**

Household set (living room with three folding sections) furnished in Japanese style, toy dresser and mirror, wood tea set, and boy and girl dolls, Japanese, circa 1925, largest piece 5 1/2 in. high. **$300-$500**

Mah-jongg set, wood container, rectangular, two drawers, ivory counters, Chinese, circa 1920. **$150-$200**

Mah-jongg set, bamboo and bone tiles, bone counters and dice, flat wooden box with gold Shou character on lid, Chinese, circa 1925. **$125-$175**

Early Japanese toy (circa 1920), double-clock-work biplanes with the original box. $3,000-$4,000

COURTESY OF STEPHEN LEONARD

Pin box, ivory, hinged lid, overall relief carving of floral medallions flanked by leaves, the border with a foliate chain and saw-edge banding, silver hinges, the interior divided into two compartments, Indian, 19th century, 9 1/2 in. by 2 3/4 in. by 2 in. **$400-$600**

Toilet set, comb, brush, mirror, and clothes brush; antimony embossed with a scenic motif; Japanese, circa 1920, 3 in. by 1 in. **$100-$125**

Toys

Battery-operated artist (draws nine different pictures), circa 1965, Japanese. **$450-$650**

Equestrian, hand-painted celluloid, Japanese, circa 1930. **$275-$400**

Fred Astaire tap dancer, Japanese. **$400-$500**

Kobe toy (named for the city where they were made in the late 19th and early 20th centuries), a boat with two animated figures, Japanese. **$700-$900**

Kobe, double figures depicting a thief running with a sake bottle, the other figure beating him upon the head, Japanese. **$800-$1,200**

Kobe, a figure reading, Japanese. **$350-$500**

Kobe, a figure eating, Japanese. **$300-$400**

Kobe, a figure plucking a musical instrument, Japanese. **$350-$475**

Kobe, a rabbit and a monkey with musical instruments, Japanese. **$700-$900**

Kobe, the Three Wise Monkeys, Japanese. **$3,000-$3,700**

Kobe toy, largest known, with 12 animations, early 20th century, Japanese, 6 1/2 in. long. **$2,500-$3,000**
COURTESY OF STEPHEN LEONARD

Kobe toys. Left: Watermelon eater with head, mouth, and both arms in animation. $200-$300. Right: Meatball eater with head, mouth, and right arm in animation. **$400-$500.**
COURTESY OF STEPHEN LEONARD

Louie Armstrong (Satchmo), Japanese. **$400-$550**

Popeye with lantern, Japanese. **$265-$300**

Sparky, all-tin robot, Japanese. **$225-$300**

Windup clown on stilts, Japanese. **$300-$450**

Windup duck, hand-painted, circa 1935, Japanese. **$125-$200**

Windup roadster with hand-painted figure, Occupied Japan. **$150-$225**

Rare clockwork Kobe toy, wound by rotating the head in front, Japanese, early 20th century. **$4,000-$5,000**
COURTESY OF STEPHEN LEONARD

Ephemera

Ephemera is usually defined as collectibles not intended to have lasting value. These items include anything meant to be discarded after use, including paper, containers, posters, tickets, broadsides, etc.

Editions of Nippon magazine from 1939 and 1940, in English, approximately 60 pages each, minor handling wear, 14 1/2 in. by 10 1/2 in. **$15-$20 each**

Photo albums, late-19th century albums with hand-colored gravures averaging approximately 8 in. by 10 in., can retail at **$300-$500**. Early 20th century albums have values as low as $150 for a group of 20-30 photos.

Postcard albums with lacquer covers, dating circa 1900, approximately 30-50 postcards, including hand-colored collotype; photo postcards can retail at **$350-$900**, depending upon condition and type/style of the cards.

Souvenir book from Japan's N.Y.K. Line, printed in Spanish, dated 1932, with information about the line's ships, and brief histories on ports of call, including fold-out color map, 94 pages, moderate handling wear, 7 1/2 in. by 5 in. **$30**

Japanese child's schoolbook, circa 1930s, reading from right to left, soft cover, near mint, 8 1/4 in. by 5 7/8 in. **$18**

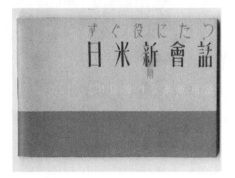

Fold-out tourist map of Kyoto, full color, circa 1930s, showing a geisha on the front, with text in Japanese and English, map folds out to 38 in. by 10 1/2 in., minor handling wear. **$18**

Japanese-English text translation book, with hand-written note in front cover saying that it was purchased at a Japanese department store on the Ginza on Nov. 6, 1945, 74 pages, near mint, 3 1/2 in. by 5 in. **$15**

Erotica

An album of 12 erotic paintings in ink and color on paper, including various domestic scenes such as a lady embracing a scholar drinking wine; a scholar at his window approaching a lady on her bed; a lady with a gentleman seated in a bath; a lady and gentleman and her servant; a lady and gentleman on a broad chair; a lady and gentleman on a yellow carpet; each painting 5 3/4 in. by 7 3/4 in., Chinese, late Ch'ing (Qing) Dynasty. **$3,500-$4,500**

Chest tied with tasseled rope, the lid removable to reveal two lovers lying on a tatami mat, boxwood and ivory, circa 1900. **$1,000-$1,500**

Hand warmer, porcelain, the top and sides pierced, the front and back with scenes featuring groups of men and women engaged in amorous pursuits, Chinese, early 19th century, 8 1/4 in. long. **$1,800-$2,200**

Illustrated book of wood-block prints, a parody of erotic sumo wrestling scenes, Meiji period. **$350-$550**

Illustrated book of wood-block prints, a manual attributed to Kunichika, late 19th century. **$500-$700**

Ivory carving of a pair of lovers, Japanese, late 19th century. **$2,000-$3,000**

Boxes from the late 1930s or early 1940s, which contained Japanese marital aids/aphrodisiacs, with applied paper labels, and containing instructions in Japanese and English, excellent condition, each measuring approximately 2 3/8 in. by 3 5/8 in. by 1 1/2 in. **$20 each**

Ivory carving of a reclining nude, two loose bracelets on her left hand, her hair stained black; she wears shoes for bound feet; Chinese, circa 1930, 10 in. long. **$500-$700**

Ivory figure of a reclining nude, her left arm across her waist, her hair painted black; surface cracks, circa 1900, 11 in. long. **$250-$400**

Ivory reclining nude, Chinese, circa 1920, 9 in. long. **$600-$800**

Marble sculpture of Okame, a phallic symbol which, when inverted, reveals Okame engaged in erotic pursuits, 19th century, 5 in. high. **$1,000-$1,500**

(Note: Although traditionally known as doctors' dolls or medicine ladies, reclining nudes were never intended as a medical tool, but rather, to have a titillating effect on the owner.)

Netsuke, Okame, the base unscrewing to reveal her innermost secrets, Japanese, late 19th century. **$600-$900**

Netsuke, a couple lying upon a brocade kimono, Japanese, early Showa period. **$200-$300**

Netsuke, manju, kagamibuta, Okame laughing as she realizes the erotic significance of the long-nosed Tengu mask on the reverse, ivory with red and black tints, Japanese, late 19th century. **$600-$900**

Netsuke, walrus ivory, Okame carrying a large mushroom (which has erotic significance), signed Shugetsu. **$1,000-$1,500**

Painting, gouache with gold on paper, a prince and a lady on a canopied couch set on a veranda, Indian, Guler, circa 1820, 10 in. by 8 in. **$2,500-$3,500**

Painting, hand scroll with 12 erotic scenes in sumi, color, and gofun on silk, Japanese, early Showa period. **$1,500-$2,000**

Japanese wood-block print, a young man and a beauty seated on a bench, Utamaro, oban tate-e, good impression and condition, slightly faded. Realized price (including the 10-percent buyer's premium), Christie's, New York City. **$1,980**

Painting, hand scroll, ink and color on paper, a series of erotic scenes, Chinese, circa 1900, 5 1/2 in. by 78 in. **$800-$1,200**

Pipe, bamboo with silver terminals, a sliding saya hiding an engraved shunga design of two lovers, Japanese, Meiji period. **$900-$1,200**

Punch bowl (Rose Mandarin), two panels, one with a young woman in the arms of an older man, the other with a lady in converse with a young man, the base with a couple engaged in amorous embrace, mirrored by dogs in a doorway; early 19th century, restored, 9 1/2 in. diameter. **$1,800-$2,500**

Screen, ink and colors on paper, Maidens Bathing in a Mountain Stream, the right panel opens to reveal an erotic scene of two lovers, panel size 55 1/2 in. by 30 1/2 in. **$5,500-$7,500**

Snuff bottle, famille rose, a nude beauty bathing before her lover, Chinese, early 20th century. **$300-$500**

Snuff bottle, famille rose, molded in relief with a ménage à trois on one side and a couple on the reverse, early 19th century. **$1,875-$2,500**

Snuff bottle, a reclining nude on both sides, the stopper in the form of a shoe for bound feet, Chinese, circa 1925. **$300-$550**

Wood-block print, a young man and a housemaid, Koryusai, chuban yoko-e, good impression, color, slightly soiled. **$900-$1,200**

Wood-block print, a couple regarded by a cat, two mice beside them, from Ehon Tsuhi no Hinagata (Models for Loving Couples), Hokusai, good color and impression, center fold, soiled and slightly rubbed, nicked edges, oban yoko-e, 1812. $1,800-$2,200

Fans

Early Japanese fans were of two types, the tuan shan "round fan" and the bian mian "screen fan." The latter was any rigid fan that could be conveniently held in the hand. It was traditionally made of feathers or silk stretched over a round or oval frame. The ceremonial fan differed essentially in that it was of a larger size, and was mounted on a long pole and used by attendants in the ceremonial entourage of high officials at important functions or processions.

Chinese or Japanese bamboo and paper fan with calligraphy designs, measuring approximately 9 in. in length, dating to the 1950s. **$35**

Ivory/Shibayama, a motif of cranes and flowers in mother-of-pearl, coral, aogai, and lacquer, Japanese, Meiji period, 12 in. long. **$4,000-$6,000**

Ivory/Shibayama with a motif of leaves, grasses, insects, and butterflies, the reverse with cranes, Japanese, Meiji period, 10 in. long. $2,**500-$3,500**

Black and gilt lacquer, spatulating blades connected by interlaced white ribbon, painted on both sides with gardens and figures, Chinese, circa 1850, 14 3/4 in. wide. **$700-$900**

Japanese fan, ivory with Shibayama inlay in designs of flowers, foliage, and insects, the fan with painted scenes of courtesans, ivory ojime in the form of a rabbit with inlaid coral eyes, silk tassel acts as the netsuke, Meiji period, late 19th century. **$1,000-$1,500**

Painted gouache landscape, the figures with silk bodies and painted ivory heads, carved sandalwood sticks, Chinese, circa 1875, 11 1/2 in. high. **$600-$800**

Chinese fan, bone and feathers, the feathers painted with Chinese beauties and flowers, early 20th century. **$200-$300**

Embroidered fan in a floral motif with birds and insects, also simulated Chinese coins, with original box showing figures in a landscape, late 19th century, fan (open) measures 21 in. by 11 1/2 in. **$600**

Bright colors on paper, the front with three oval panels depicting the harbor of Hong Kong, the reverse with birds perched in a bouquet of flowering peony, mounted in a gold and black lacquered wood frame, Chinese, late 19th century, 25 in. wide. **$1,000-$1,500**

Gilt and colors on paper, both sides with audience scenes and court figures within pavilions, their faces in applied painted ivory, Chinese, 19th century, 20 in. wide. **$500-$750**

Painted paper, a landscape scene on both sides, ivory mounts, Chinese, late 19th century. **$300-$425**

Paper painted with a landscape scene, ivory mounts, Chinese, late 19th century. **$275-$400**

Peacock feathers, sand-carved-bone sticks, silk tassels, Chinese, circa 1900, 13 1/2 in. long. **$175-$200**

Carved sandalwood with repetitive geometric motifs, silk cord and tassel, Chinese, circa 1915, 7 1/2 in. long. **$125-$175**

Cut silk and painted ivory on paper leaf, one side with a continuous landscape, the other with figures in a courtyard, carved ivory sticks, fitted lacquer box, Chinese, circa 1830, 10 in. high. **$500-$700**

Silk painted with maple leaves, lacquer sticks, silk cord with ivory ojime and tassel, Japanese, late Meiji period, circa 1900. **$800-$1,200**

Watercolors and cut silk on paper, ivory details, carved sandalwood sticks, silk tassels and feathers, Chinese, mid-19th century, 11 1/2 in. high. **$400-$600**

White feathers, bone handle, silk tassels, the feathers painted with flowers near the top, Chinese, circa 1910, 9 in. by 13 1/4 in. **$125-$250**

Folk Art: Japanese

Mingei describes "arts of the people." It was coined in 1925 by the scholar, Dr. Soetsu Yanagi (1889-1961), by combining the Japanese words for people (min) and art (gei).

Set of Japanese wood trays and a box, decorated with lacquer and surface carvings, dating to the 1950s. The set includes a large, fish-shaped tray with surface carvings of scenery and the artist's seal in red lacquer, measuring 13 in. by 10 3/4 in. by 3/4 in., two smaller fish-shaped trays measuring 9 1/2 in. by 7 1/4 in. by 1/2 in., a box measuring 5 1/2 in. by 4 in. by 2 in., and two square trays measuring 7 in. by 5 1/2 in. The backs of the fish trays are carved to represent scales. **$75**

Japanese wood and brass "sumitsubo," or inkpot, used by the carpenter to measure and draw straight lines, measuring approximately 10 in. in length, dating to the mid-20th century. This piece has been made by a master craftsman, who has signed it on the back of the bowl. It looks like zelkova wood, which is preferred by the Kyoto craftsmen for its fine grain and durability. The end hole is encircled with brass. It is missing the string. The bowl is accented with a kame, or tortoise, carving. This sumitsubo has obviously been used. **$150**

Japanese Mingei folk art well assembled from bamboo, wood, raffia, and driftwood. This piece has two woven bamboo and wood buckets suspended on a woven bamboo wheel, fastened to a wooden well house roof, which is fastened in turn to a driftwood assemblage. The piece stands approximately 26 in. high and 15 in. square at the base. **$250**

Japanese "kanban," or shop sign made of bamboo using three nodes, measuring 25 1/2 in. by 6 in., dating to the early to mid-20th century. The bamboo is carved with blossoms and three Kanji characters. The first two read: Fuku To, the last is a kakihan. The characters translate into: good fortune and rice plant. The sign may represent a brand name, a specific store for rice, or a type of rice used at the New Year. The bamboo has a rich patina from age, the carving is crisp, and the colors are vibrant. **$250**

Furniture

KOREAN

Korean furniture is simple, making classic use of straight lines. Constructed from woods such as pine, pagoda, paulownia, pear, persimmon, and combinations, this furniture is also marked by distinctive hardware (mostly iron) accents. The pieces that were originally more expensive—those made for the aristocracy—can have white or yellow brass hardware; silver was used occasionally.

During the Yi Dynasty (1392-1910), furnishings included carved, lacquered, or inlaid storage chests, tables, and folding screens. Among the chests, which are of particular interest to collectors of Korean furniture, are bin-shaped storage containers or utility boxes used for the storage of household goods and grain such as rice. Also of interest are the medicine chests with their many drawers. Sometimes the names of the medicines are painted on or carved into the drawers.

CHINESE

Chinese furniture has simple, gently curved lines. (Most of the elaborately carved pieces are lacquer furniture or were made specifically for export to the West.) Cutting, joining, and finishing were carefully done.

Chinese furniture employs a variety of woods. Hua-li rosewood (also known as Burmese or East Indian rosewood) has shades ranging from dark to blonde, and is characterized by a translucent, satiny finish. Hung-mu redwood, a cousin of rosewood, is a much darker wood used extensively in the 19th and 20th centuries. It is like American mahogany, but the grain is much finer. Hua-mu burl, displaying the curly patterns of the roots from which it is taken, often appears in inlaid pieces. Chests are often made of camphor wood. Extremely popular among these are the chests with high-relief carving, produced during the 1920s and 1930s.

Note that teak is an Indian wood used exclusively for Indian furniture.

JAPANESE

Among the Japanese furniture pieces of interest to collectors are clothing stands, cabinets, trays, desks, tables, and tansu (chests of drawers). The Japanese tansu with the finest woods, made for the daimyo (ruling families) and the samurai (warriors), had four large drawers, sometimes lacquered in part. The plainer tansu were produced for the poorer classes.

In addition to tansu, export furniture of the late Meiji and Taisho periods (1868-1926), as well as that of the early Showa period (1926-1989), is attracting a growing interest, especially those pieces with elaborate carving and/or lacquered motifs.

Also, the "shodana"—a shallow tea cabinet—is uniquely Japanese. It has sliding and hinged doors, drawers, and usually is asymmetrical in shape.

GENERAL INFORMATION

When trying to determine whether an ornately carved piece of furniture is Chinese or Japanese, remember the following: Japanese furniture made for Western markets follows the change in styles from Victorian to art nouveau to art deco.

Collectible Asian furniture does appreciate in value, although the appreciation is low (unless the pieces are proven to be important or of significant provenance). Unfortunately, the same cannot be said for the value of new furniture.

For information on the care and upkeep of Oriental furniture, see "Guidelines for Care of Oriental Antiques and Art" found near the back of this book.

Furniture Values

Altar table, hardwood, paneled top and rounded ends, the apron pierced with scrollwork and terminating as fungus, rectangular legs waisted in two places with foliage in low relief, Chinese, 19th century, 87 in. long, 42 in. high, 21 in. deep. **$1,650-$2,700**

Altar table, hardwood, rectangular, four square legs with scroll feet, the frieze with archaistic scroll brackets and carved on the long side with three bat-shaped scrolling motifs, Chinese, early 19th century, 69 in. long, 37 1/2 in. wide, 21 in. deep. **$3,700-$5,250**

Altar table, hardwood, rectangular top over a pierced and carved foliate scrolling apron, four square legs and scroll toes, Indonesian, 39 in. long. **$600-$900**

Armchair, hardwood, the back pierced and carved with confronting dragons, dragon armrest, ivory eyes, the serpentine seat with a centrally carved Tokugawa mon, cabriole legs, Japanese, Taisho period. **$600-$900**

Armchair, red lacquer, yoke-shaped back, gilt splat, folding leather seat, trestle supports and hinged footrest, gilt metal mounts with foliate scrolls, Japanese, late Edo period, 43 1/2 in. high. **$1,500-$2,500**

Armchairs, low with rectangular backs, carved paneled splats and seats, carved arm supports, legs joined by simple stretchers, one leg broken, Chinese, early 20th century, 40 in. long, pair. **$600-$800**

Armchair carved in the form of bamboo, back carved as shoots and leaves, late 19th century, original finish with noticeable shrinkage to seat board, 21 3/4 in. by 19 1/2 in. by 41 in. **$2,500**

Armchairs, hung-mu, the crest rail above an S-scrolled splat, oval marble panel inset on the backs, circular legs, box stretcher on frontal bracket support, Chinese, 19th century, pair. **$2,500-$3,500**

Armchairs, hung-mu, each with rectangular paneled seat, aprons at front and sides with carved foliage, the front apron extending to the footrail and the stretchers at the bottom with narrow skirts, stepped arms, yoke-shaped backs edged with pierced fretwork, the central splat carved with foliage on the front and back, Chinese, 19th century, 42 in. high, pair. **$2,500-$3,500**

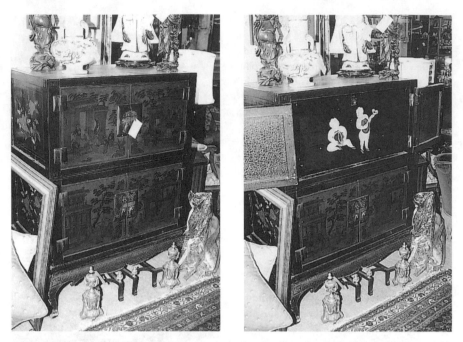

Cabinet/desk, lacquered, Chinese, with painted exterior showing a landscape on double doors, with cast bronze latches and hinges, and drop-front writing surface behind upper doors, interior decorated with figures of two musicians, mid-18th century, 35 in. by 21 in. by 48 3/4 in. **$3,750**

Basin stand (folding), six rectangular legs with block finials, joined by upper and lower hexagonal bar stretchers, Chinese, 19th century, 26 1/2 in. high. **$1,000-$1,500**

Bed (hardwood opium bed), rectangular, detachable sides and back, the base with scrolled apron carved with two dragons, four carved Buddhistic lion-mask feet, the back with three scenic panels flanked by side panels of pine and prunus, in need of restoration, Chinese, 19th century, 77 in. by 36 in. by 38 in. **$900-$1,200**

Bed, hardwood, rectangular canopy carved with panels of birds, vessels, and dragons above a fretwork ceiling, the upholstered mattress above four drawers, all supported on wide scroll feet; needs some restoration/repair, Chinese, circa 1900, 93 1/2 in. by 129 in. by 33 1/2 in. **$1,000-$1,500**

Bed (canopied marriage bed), red- and gilt-lacquered wood, pierced and carved birds and leafy scrolls in high relief on a red ground, Chinese, late 19th century, outside frame 66 in. wide, overall 90 in. long. **$2,800-$4,000**

Bench, back carved with two lacquer panels depicting bamboo and birds surmounted by two confronting dragons beneath Mt. Fuji, arms with carved dragons, seat with hinged lid, some minor cracking, Japanese, Meiji period, 50 in. by 59 in. by 22 in. **$1,400-$1,900**

Bench, the back with two lacquer panels of birds and bamboo carved in high relief, below, a view of Mt. Fuji; the arms carved with dragons; the seat carved with three Tokugawa mon within a key-pattern border, in need of some repair, Japanese, late Meiji period, 50 in. by 60 in. by 24 in. **$1,800-$2,400**

Bench, hardwood, the back carved with open-work trees flanked by two acanthus finials, the arms as sprouting branches, the rectangular seat with scroll-pattern border, floral apron, four back supports, Japanese, late Meiji period, 50 in. by 26 in. by 52 in. **$900-$1,200**

Cabinet, pine, two parts (three sets of sliding doors and five drawers), Japanese, Meiji period, 60 in. high. **$900-$1,200**

Cabinet on stand, rectangular, stepped shelving, two pairs of sliding doors, four hinged doors, brown lacquer ground with gold and black hiramakie (low relief) and hirame (large, irregular flakes of gold roughly sprinkled on a black lacquer ground, also fat gold flakes used in lacquer decoration, named for their resemblance to a flounder), motifs of birds and insects among flowers, old damages and wear, Japanese, late 19th century, 31 in. by 48 in. **$5,500-$7,500**

Cabinet (chandana/tea cabinet), burl keyaki wood, four sliding paneled doors above two glass doors that enclose a cased and sectioned interior, the lower case with a bowed door and a glass door, Japanese, late Meiji period, 30 in. by 50 in. **$1,700-$2,500**

Cabinet, carved red (cinnabar) lacquer, two square hinged doors above two larger doors enclosing a shelf and two drawers, all above a shallow drawer, bracket feet, the front carved with ladies and attendants with children beside pavilions in landscapes, all within borders of key pattern, the top and sides with cell pattern, brass hinges and locks, some old damages, Chinese, 18th century, 14 1/4 in. by 26 in. **$2,500-$3,500**

Cabinet, hung-mu (redwood), two narrow central doors with low-relief carvings of cloud scrolls between upper and lower doors enclosing a shelf and two drawers, metal hinges and lock plates with Shou characters and Shou character pulls, Chinese, early 19th century, 79 in. high. **$2,800-$4,000**

Cabinet, fruitwood, asymmetrical arrangement of drawers, doors, and shelves joined by a bridge, overall motifs of birds, flowers, and foliage inlaid in bone, ivory, and mother-of-pearl, some inlay missing, Japanese, Meiji period, 86 in. high. **$2,200-$3,500**

Cabinet, black lacquer, two doors, the front decorated in low relief with mother-of-pearl, hard stone, and gilt in a motif of children playing on a grassy terrace watched by ladies at the sides, all within borders of mother-of-pearl dragons, crackle to the surface, Chinese, circa 1900, 34 in. by 52 in. **$1,000-$1,500**

Armchairs, one of a pair, hung-mu (redwood) marble-inset, stepped backrest carved with cloud scrolls and set with marble plaque below a burl panel, angular scroll arms, the rectangular seat over a simple scroll-carved apron and square straight legs joined by stretchers, Chinese, 19th century. Realized price (including the 10-percent buyer's premium), Christie's, New York City. **$935**

Armchairs, one of a pair, Chinese elm wood horseshoe-back, each with curved, rounded crest rail, rounded stiles, a curved, solid splat shallowly carved with lobed ruyi-head medallion above a sunken, paneled seat, square straight legs with pierced key fret brackets and joined by a footrest and stretchers, 18th century. Realized price (including the 10-percent buyer's premium), Christie's East, New York City. **$1,045**

Cabinet, two parts, two large doors and four drawers in the lower section, two large and four small doors in the upper section, with one drawer and one cupboard, iron mounts, Japanese, early Meiji period, 68 in. high. **$1,500-$2,200**

Cabinet, hardwood, rectangular, a long upper compartment with sliding panels above open shelves and carved with peony blossoms and Shishi, the frame simulating bamboo edged with carved flowers, Japanese, late Meiji period, 16 in. by 54 in. **$1,200-$1,800**

Cabinet, black and gilt lacquer, two doors enclosing an interior of shelves and columns fitted with variously sized drawers above two larger drawers, overall motifs of riverbanks and pavilions on a gilt-lacquered, pierced stand, brass bail handles, some damages, Japanese, Meiji period, 57 1/2 in. high. **$1,200-$1,800**

Cabinet, hardwood, glass-encased, extensively carved with irises, four interior shelves, rectangular plinth, four shaped legs, Japanese, late 19th century, 68 in. high. **$2,500-$3,500**

Chair, rosewood, reclining, cylindrical head-rest above a curved paneled splat back connected to the frame, curved arms with another set of curved arms flanking the paneled seat, a draw front nesting leg support, Chinese, 19th century, 32 in. high. **$900-$1,200**

Chest, pine, supported on low legs, the hinged front with plain iron mounts and an iron lock, Korean, Yi Dynasty, 19th century, 37 in. by 13 1/4 in. by 24 1/2 in. **$600-$800**

Chest, burl and elm wood, plain top, brass-mounted corners, front with four paneled sliding drawers above two paneled doors mounted with circular brass mounts, shaped apron, short cabriole legs joined by stretchers at the sides, Korean, Yi Dynasty, 19th century, 37 in. by 37 in. by 20 in. **$900-$1,200**

Chest, black and gilt lacquer, the hinged cover decorated with pairs of confronting dragons and phoenix within a band of red key scrolls on a gilt ground, sides similarly decorated, bronze loop handles, circular lock plate, with matching low table stand, Chinese, circa 1900, 18 in. by 37 in. by 24 in. **$1,000-$1,500**

Chest of drawers, hardwood, the front with mock drawers, paneled pull-out drawers and small doors all inlaid in mother-of-pearl with Buddhist emblems, short cabriole feet, Korean, Yi Dynasty, 41 in. by 39 in. by 14 in. **$1,000-$1,500**

Chest, red lacquer, rectangular with two long drawers above a pair of short drawers, iron hardware and side handles, Japanese, early 20th century, 26 1/2 in. wide. **$450-$600**

Chest, camphor wood, high-relief carving of warriors, some on horseback, overall brass mounts and lock plate, Chinese, circa 1925, 21 in. by 36 in. by 24 in. **$800-$1,200**

Chest, storate, honey-toned camphor and elm wood, the rectangular top with two removable lids and brass latches revealing slide compartments above a pair of small cupboard doors opening to a plain interior, sunken paneled sides, bracket feet, Chinese, 19th century, 36 in. high, 34 1/2 in. wide. Realized price (including the 10-percent buyer's premium), Christie's East, New York City. **$935**

Cupboard, hinged drop front revealing three small drawers, the sides with large carrying handles, brass mounts pierced with swastika, shaped apron, Korean, Yi Dynasty, 19th century, 37 1/2 in. by 34 1/2 in. by 18 in. **$800-$1,200**

Cupboard, huang hua-li, rectangular, floating paneled top and sides, rounded stiles extending to form feet and joined by curved aprons, doors reveal trays and drawers, Paktong pulls, legs cut down, Chinese, early Ch'ing (Qing) Dynasty, 56 in. by 28 in. **$2,000-$3,000**

Chest, carved camphor wood, motif of prunus overall, brass mounts and brass label (The Wing On Co Ltd., Shanghai), Chinese, circa 1920, 25 in. long, 10 1/2 in. deep, 15 in. wide. **$300-$400**

Desk, hardwood, carved with a dragon coiled around Mt. Fuji above stepped shelving, a cupboard section (beside the shelving) carved with phoenix and foliage, the lower part with two drawers above cabriole legs, Japanese, circa 1900, 40 in. by 36 in. **$1,200-$1,800**

Desk, hung-mu (redwood), the detachable, paneled top rests upon two pedestals with two pairs of drawers, straight legs joined by rectangular box stretchers having interlocking, flattened struts, brass bail handles, Chinese, early 20th century, 30 in. by 62 in. **$1,000-$1,500**

Desk, lacquered wood, hinged top section set on detachable cabinets that are set on a low rectangular support, the two doors reveal shelves and drawers, overall motif of gilt-lacquered birds and flowers on a black ground, brass mounts, warped, nicks around the bottom, Japanese, early Showa period, 62 1/2 in. high. **$800-$1,200**

Desk and chair, the upper part surmounted by pierced and carved irises and foliage above two side doors revealing shelves, the apron with pierced and carved foliage, cabriole legs, matching chair, Japanese, late Meiji period, desk 50 in. high. **$1,000-$1,500**

Dresser and mirror, keyaki wood, four drawers and beveled, rectangular mirror, Japanese, 20th century, 19 in. by 37 in. **$350-$450**

Game table, floating paneled top, stepped sides, each with a small drawer, four square legs terminating in hoof feet (inward-curving), Chinese, early 20th century, 30 in. by 33 in. **$800-$1,000**

Garden stools, hardwood, barrel form, open sides with four intersecting medallions between rows of bosses, marble circular plaque set in the tops, Chinese, first half of the 20th century, 20 1/2 in. high. **$1,100-$1,600**

Garden stool, lacquer over wood with mother of pearl inlay in the form of a geisha, with stylized floral decorations, Japanese, 17 3/4 in. by 15 in. **$375**

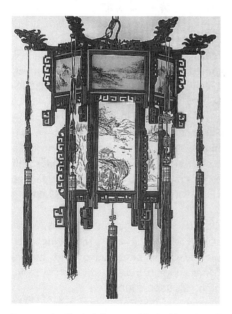

Lantern, hardwood frame with inside-painted glass panels, silk tassels, original hook, one of a pair, electrified, Chinese, early 20th century, the frame measuring 28 in. high (not including the length of the tassels), **pair. $2,000-$3,000**

Ice chest, a two-panel cover fitting over a tapered, square case, brass bail handles, painted red, Chinese, late 19th century, 19 3/8 in. wide. **$650-$750**

Mirror, rectangular, banded with ivory mosaic work, gilt bronze support, Chinese, 15 in. by 20 in. **$500-$700**

Mirror, the gilt wood frame with panels carved with the Eight Immortals on a band of floral scrolls, Chinese, circa 1800, 27 1/2 in. by 38 3/4 in. **$500-$800**

Mirror, octagonal, the gilt wood frame carved with scrolls, Chinese, early 19th century, 26 1/2 in. by 37 in. **$400-$600**

Money chest, hinged cover, iron pattern of raised bosses around the sides, Japanese, 19th century, 16 in. by 10 in. **$300-$500**

Screen, four panels of embroidered ecru silk, each with varied flowers, foliage, and birds in flight worked in gold thread, black-lacquered frames, Japanese, Taisho period, leaf size 19 in. by 6 in. **$2,000-$3,000**

Screen, Shibayama, two panels, each decorated in gold and silver lacquer and inlaid with mother-of-pearl and coral songbirds and butterflies in a mountainous landscape with a river and waterfalls, the back with songbirds perched on flowering prunus branches, Japanese, late Meiji period, 35 in. by 73 in. **$3,500-$5,000**

Screen, six-leaf, inlaid on one side with hard stones, ivory, and mother-of-pearl within cell-pattern bands above a border of kylin (mythical animal), the motif a continuous battle scene with warriors on horseback, losses to inlay, some surface damage, Chinese, late Ch'ing (Qing) Dynasty, each leaf 15 in. by 68 in. **$1,800-$2,800**

Screen, Coromandel, from a Buddhist temple, with pierced and polychrome base, titled "Rest the Spirit Villa," showing the temple grounds and buildings in lacquer on wood, 59 in. by 23 1/2 in. by 55 in. **$1,450**

Screen, eight-panel Coromandel, a flock of geese amongst reeds and rock-work on a gilt ground, Chinese, late Ch'ing (Qing) Dynasty; each leaf 68 1/2 in. high, 16 1/2 in. wide. **$1,500-$2,500**

Screen, hardwood, four panels, each inset with three porcelain plaques (famille rose with the 100 Antiques motif), the reverse with red lacquer floral motifs, Chinese, late 19th century; each panel 70 in. high, 20 in. wide. **$2,000-$3,000**

Screen, hardwood, four panels, each leaf carved in shallow relief with Immortals and attendants in a mountainous landscape, the reverse with bats and Shou characters, the square feet with archaistic scroll brackets, Chinese, circa 1900, each panel 74 1/2 in. high, 17 1/2 in. wide. **$2,000-$3,000**

Screen, hardwood, four panels carved with numerous pierced geometric and foliate designs, each panel with two knob finials, Indian, circa 1900, each panel 78 in. high, 21 in. wide. **$650-$900**

Settee, hung-mu (redwood), rectangular backrest with three oval rings above spindle supports, flanked by armrests with single rings and spindles, the paneled seat above a frieze of rectangles on rounded, straight legs joined by side stretchers and footrest, Chinese, circa 1900, 42 in. long. **$2,500-$3,500**

Shodana, an open upper part above two hinged doors, each with an inlaid figure of a dancer in ivory and sheet, the interior with three drawers, wood refinished, Japanese, circa 1900, 41 in. by 44 in. **$2,000-$3,000**

Side chairs, hardwood, finely pierced, circular scroll backs with drop-in, serpentine seats, pierced apron on pad legs with animal heads and feet, Indian, 19th century, 35 in. high, pair. **$600-$800**

Side chairs, round top rail supported by a curved, rectangular back-splat, the straight, square legs joined by a tow footrest and stretchers, Ming style, Chinese, 19th century, 21 in. by 16 1/2 in. by 43 in., pair. **$850-$1,250**

Side chairs, carved red (cinnabar) lacquer, open rectangular back, center splat carved with flowering trees, straight legs joined by stretchers, overall carving of vines and flower heads, one in need of restoration, Chinese, 19th century, 30 in. high, pair. **$1,800-$2,400**

Stand (for kimono), black and gold lacquer decorated with flowering clematis growing upon a trellis, copper mounts, badly chipped and cracked, Japanese, Meiji period, 21 1/2 in. wide. **$700-$900**

Stool and storage box made of bamboo with painted panels of leaves and birds, front opens to reveal storage area, original tacked leather upholstery, Japanese, late 1800s, 21 in. by 19 1/2 in. by 14 1/2 in. $750

Stands, hardwood with inset marble tops, five legs joined by a pentagonal stretcher, the legs and rim carved with prunus, Chinese, circa 1925, 33 in. high, pair. **$900-$1,200**

Stand, hardwood, inset marble top, four legs, the apron carved with foliage, Chinese, circa 1925, 20 in. high. **$325-$475**

Stand, wood, carved and pierced with irises and foliage, four cabriole legs, the top with a red lacquer dragon, Japanese, Taisho period, 28 in. high. **$475-$675**

Stool, hardwood, rounded frame forming two side legs, Chinese, circa 1930, 15 1/2 in. high. **$500-$700**

Table, hardwood, the rim carved with a lappet border, a pierced apron carved with daisy-like flowers, the top set with pink marble, supported on a tripod pedestal base with stylized paw feet, Japanese, late Meiji/early Taisho period, 36 in. high. $**900-$1,200**

Table, hardwood console, rectangular, paneled top above a pierced and carved apron frieze of curvilinear foliage, four square, tapered legs, Indonesian, 19th century. **$1,200-$1,800**

Table, oval form standing on four elephant legs joined by a crossbar, profusely carved overall, 54 in. diameter by 30 in. high. **$700-$1,000**

Table, carved red (cinnabar) lacquer, the top with a flower head and dense checker pattern, the sides with dragons and flaming pearls among dense cloud whorls, the latter design repeated on the apron, four rectangular feet, minor repairs, Chinese, late 19th century, 36 in. long. **$2,000-$3,000**

Table, polychromed and lacquered, octagonal form, eight open-work, folding legs, each with a flowering plant, profusely decorated and outlined in black and gilt lacquer, Indian, circa 1900, 28 in. diameter. **$900-$1,500**

Table (side table), hung-mu (redwood), rectangular top, the narrow sides carved with key fret, four slender cabriole legs terminating in hoof feet (inward-curving), scroll-shaped apron, plain stretcher front, Chinese, early 19th century, 36 in. high. **$700-$1,000**

Table, low, black lacquer, rectangular section with open frame, interstices carved to resemble lotus panels, bronze mounts, cracked, Japanese, late 19th century. **$1,200-$1,500**

Table, hardwood, circular drum form on five inward-curving legs joined by a bottom stretcher, a frieze around the top with fruiting vine, Chinese, circa 1900, 20 1/2 in. wide. **$600-$900**

Table, hardwood, low with inserted burl wood top section, the four inward-curving legs joined by a frieze pierced with dragons, Chinese, circa 1935, 37 in. wide. **$600-$900**

Table, black-lacquered wood, the top inlaid with mother-of-pearl, coral, jade, and painted figures of ladies in a garden, inward-curving legs, glass top, Chinese, circa 1935, 42 in. long, 28 in. high. **$800-$1,200**

Tables, nest of four, hardwood, rectangular and low, the plain tops with mock bamboo surrounds and legs, joined by friezes pierced with fruiting vines, Chinese, late 19th century, 18 in. high to 28 in. high. **$1,200-$1,600**

Chinese table, mid-19th century, original red stain finish with shallow scroll decoration to skirt and leg brackets, 33 1/2 in. by 34 1/4 in. by 11 5/8 in. **$3,000**

Tansu (chest of drawers), double-sided kaidan (stepped) with nine steps, keyaki wood, iron mounts, each side with sliding doors, one hinged door, three vertical doors, Japanese, mid-19th century, 85 in. high. **$3,000-$4,500**

Tansu (chest of drawers) kuruma-wheeled, two sliding lattice doors; one cabinet and two drawers with locking bar front; iron mounts, late Edo/early Meiji period, 40 in. high. **$2,500-$3,500**

Tansu (chest of drawers) (Issho), kiri wood, four drawers with iron mounts and pulls, Japanese, early 20th century, 36 in. by 42 in. **$500-$700**

Tansu (chest of drawers), oak and kiri wood, three drawers and two sliding doors in the upper section, two doors in the center, two drawers in the base, Japanese, late 19th century, 58 1/4 in. high. **$1,000-$1,500**

Glass

PEKING (BEIJING) GLASS

The first Peking glass factory was built in the Forbidden City within the palace walls in 1696. It was overseen by a German priest, who brought many Western techniques of glass and enamel work to the Chinese. The first Peking glass items produced were made with single-colored or clear glass that was either carved or faceted. Overlay glass was developed later, which involved dipping a glass item into a vat of molten glass of a contrasting color. After cooling, the second color was carved away to reveal the color underneath. As this technique developed, more colors and multiple layers were used. Peking glass items are still being produced today.

Bottle, blue, translucent, pear-shaped, rim chips, Chinese, 19th century, 5 in. high. **$200-$400**

Bottle, yellow, opaque, rim chips, incised Ch'ien Lung (Qianlong) mark, but 19th century, 4 3/4 in. high. **$200-$300**

Bottle/vase, red, the body and neck joined with a molded ring, Ch'ien Lung (Qianlong) mark, but 19th century, 10 in. high. **$700-$1,000**

Bowl, amber yellow, relief motif of flowers and figures, Chinese, 19th century, 6 1/2 in. diameter. **$600-$900**

Bowl, deep blue, Chinese, 18th century, 8 in. diameter. **$700-$1,100**

Bowl, green overlay carved through to the milk glass on the exterior with birds perched on blossoming branches, Chinese, circa 1910, 6 3/4 in. diameter. **$200-$325**

Bowl, green overlay carved through to the milk glass on the exterior with four panels of foliage, Chinese, circa 1922, 7 in. diameter. **$200-$300**

Bowl, red, four panels featuring carved Buddhistic lions, Chinese, 19th century, 5 1/2 in. diameter. **$700-$1,000**

Glass, ruby red, lotus form, Chinese, 19th century, 6 1/2 in. diameter. **$325-$450**

Bowl, white with cobalt blue overlay carved with birds on flowering branches, Chinese, 19th century, 6 in. diameter. **$700-$1,000**

Bowls, circular, each with short foot and everted rim, carved with a lake, lotus, and carp through red overlay to a milk white ground, Chinese, 19th century, 10 1/2 in. diameter, pair. **$1,800-$2,500**

Candlesticks, green clouded glass, square base, Chinese, circa 1920, 4 in. diameter, 2 1/2 in. high, pair. **$125-$285**

Dish, oval, snowflake glass with etched leaf pattern in blue overlay, Chinese, circa 1925, 5 3/4 in. diameter. **$300-$475**

Ice cream dish and underplate, hexagonal, clear blue, Chinese, circa 1930, the dish 4 3/4 in. diameter, the plate 6 1/2 in. diameter. **$100-$175**

Finger bowl, purple with fluted edge, marked China, circa 1930, 2 in. high, 4 3/4 in. diameter. **$100-$150**

Jar and cover, magenta-red overlay carved through to the snowflake glass with a large dragon, Chinese, 19th century, 4 3/4 in. high. **$900-$1,500**

Jars and covers, blue overlay carved through to a milk-glass ground with prunus sprays and birds, each marked China, circa 1930, 6 3/4 in. high, pair. **$575-$685**

Plates, blue glass recessed at the center, minute rim chips on three, each marked China, circa 1950, 7 in. diameter, set of 6. **$300-$400**

Figure of an oxen in pale watermelon pink and white, excellent condition, 4 3/4 in. by 2 7/8 in. by 1 3/4 in. **$150**

Vase, milk glass with green-overlay motifs of birds, flowers, and foliage, Chinese, early 20th century, 10 in. high. **$300-$500**
COURTESY OF RICHARD A. BOWSER

Saucers, opaque white with fluted sides, each marked China, circa 1935, 5 in. diameter, set of 6. **$150-$225**

Vase, baluster form, green overlay carved through to a white ground with flowering branches, marked China, circa 1930, 6 in. high. **$150-$250**

Vase, globular form, milk glass with red overlay in a continuous pattern of prunus and rock-work, Chinese, 19th century, 8 1/2 in. high. **$1,500-$2,500**

Vase, globular form, milk glass with red overlay in a continuous pattern of prunus and rock-work, Chinese, 19th century, 8 1/2 in. high. **$1,500-$2,500**

Vase, yellow, baluster form with waisted neck, carved around the sides with meanders and stiff leaves above a band of lappets, Chinese, 19th century, 8 1/2 in. high. **$800-$1,200**

Vase, three-color overlay carved through to the milk white body with two blue dragons, a smaller green dragon on the neck, red foot rim, Chinese, 19th century, 6 in. high. **$600-$800**

Vases, baluster form, red overlay carved with a lotus, milky white ground, marked China, circa 1920, 8 in. high, pair. **$525-$725**

Vases, oviform, blue overlay carved with phoenix and peony blossoms to a milk white ground, marked China, circa 1935, 8 in. high, pair. **$300-$400**

Vases, ovoid, yellow, carved with bird and floral reserves, stiff-leaf border, rim nicks, Chinese, 19th century, 8 in. high, pair. **$1,500-$2,000**

Reverse Paintings on Glass

A beautiful lady seated beside a desk and holding a fan, an open book lying on the desk, gilt wood frame, Chinese, early 20th century, framed size 14 1/2 in. by 18 1/2 in. **$500-$700**

A beautiful mandarin lady lavishly dressed and seated on a bench, gilt wood frame, Chinese, early 19th century, framed size 7 3/4 in. by 7 1/4 in. **$700-$900**

A beautifully dressed mandarin lady holding a fan and seated beside a table, a vase full of flowers on the desk, gilt wood frame, Chinese, late 19th/early 20th century, framed size, 14 in. by 18 in. **$500-$700**

Chinese reverse painting on glass, late Ch'ing Dynasty, circa 1900, hardwood frame, framed size 17 in. by 21 in. **$300-$500**

A Chinese beauty seated beside a table, scattered fruit and lotus blossoms on the table, Chinese, early 20th century, 12 in. by 15 in. **$300-$500**

A Chinese beauty seated at a table, fixing her hair, through the open window beside her, a lake scene, black and gilt lacquer frame, Chinese, late 18th century, framed size 12 in. by 17 in. **$1,000-$1,500**

A court lady sitting beside a table, reading, her robe lavishly detailed, wood frame, Chinese, early 20th century, 18 in. by 24 in. **$550-$750**

A family gathered around the patriarch, who is seated on a high-back chair, wood frame, Chinese, early 20th century, 23 1/2 in. by 17 in. **$400-$600**

A European shepherdess and a young boy watching a lamb by a riverbank, gilt wood frame, Chinese, late 18th century, framed size 6 1/2 in. by 8 3/4 in. **$900-$1,200**

A lady holding a hand mirror and seated by a table piled high with books, hardwood frame, Chinese, early 20th century, framed size 12 3/4 in. by 18 in. **$350-$550**

A lady wearing a vibrant blue robe over pate red trousers, Chinese, early 20th century, 13 3/4 in. by 19 1/4 in. **$300-$500**

Five ladies on the terrace of a walled garden, watering flowers and picking blossoms, hardwood frame, Chinese, early 20th century, framed size 26 in. by 20 in. **$600-$800**

Three scholars chatting with attendants beneath a tree, all within a landscape, gilt wood frame, Chinese, early 20th century, framed size 18 1/2 in. by 14 in. **$500-$700**

Pair: Looking to the left, a Chinese beauty holding a fan, her long fingernails characteristic of Chinese ladies of the house, her robes apricot, looking to the right, she holds a book, Chinese, early 20th century, 24 in. by 37 in. **$1,300-$1,700**

Pair: Full-length portraits of a prince and princess, the prince seated on a throne and wearing elaborate gilt-decorated garments and jewelry, the princess leaning against a bolster holding a vina (stringed instrument), gilt wood frames, South Indian, late 19th century, framed size 10 in. by 14 1/4 in. **$400-$600**

Hard Stones

JADE

Note: The type of jade classified as nephrite was used by the Chinese until the late 18th century, when jadeite was imported from Burma. This type of jade was endowed with rich hues, and it soon surpassed nephrite in popularity, so much so that the emerald green variety became the property of the Emperor.

Archer's ring, light coffee-colored lustrous stone carved with eight horses in a mountain landscape, all in lifelike animated poses, 9/10 in. by 1 1/16 in., in embroidered silk pouch, Chinese, circa 19th century or possibly earlier. **$1,500-$1,750**

Archer's ring, green with ochre inclusions, plain, 19th century. **$100-$200**

Belt buckle, white, the two sections pierced with scrolling ruyi forming a pierced loop, Chinese, 19th century, 2 in. long. **$600-$900**

Belt hook, celadon with a dragon in relief, Chinese, early 19th century, 3 3/4 in. long. **$250-$400**

Left: Cylindrical soapstone brush pot, cut and pierced in deep relief on the side with a continuous broad band of pavilions nestling in pine and prunus, plus figures and travelers, all within narrow bands of formal key pattern, Chinese, mid-19th century, 6 in. high. Realized price (including the 10-percent buyer's premium), Christie's East, New York City. **$550.**

Covered box, carved in the form of a turtle with a lily pad on its back and a snake coiled on top of leaf, which acts as lid, 5 7/8 in. by 3 1/2 in. by 2 1/2 in. **$800**

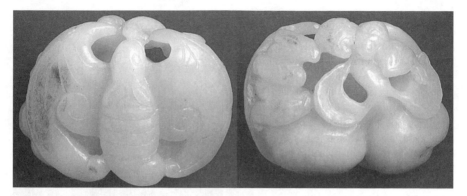

Carving, Chinese, circa 18th-19th century, openwork carving with one large bat and two smaller ones on two peaches, fine quality pale green mutton-fat nephrite jade, 2 1/3 in. by 1 5/8 in. by 1 1/4 in., a good luck charm. **$650-$750**

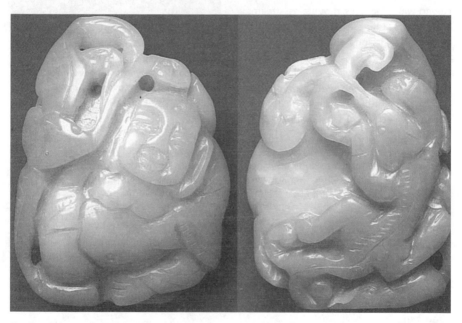

Carving, Chinese, circa 18th-19th century, openwork carving of a Lohan with bat and peach, fine quality pale green mutton-fat nephrite jade, 2 1/2 in. long, a good luck charm. **$650-$750**

Bi or pi (disk), hard jade, measuring approximately 2 in. in diameter and 5/8 in. in height, Chinese, dating to the Han Dynasty (206 BC-220 AD). The nephrite jade is an overall, rich chocolate brown in color. It has been carved in an openwork fashion to represent a dragon coiled around the traditional, ritual circular, or bi, shape. This shape had been used for ritual jades since neolithic times and was considered an emblem of wealth and power. The jade retains much of its original polish after burial and shows essentially no degradation. Fine original condition with no losses or repairs. **$150**

Boulder, celadon with brown mottling, carved with pine trees, mountains, streams, and horses, Chinese, late Ch'ing (Qing) Dynasty, 7 1/4 in. long. **$700-$900**

Bowl, green, lobed ovoid ring foot, boat-shaped body carved with three-lobed bands, each end with a duck's head finial, Indian, 19th century, 8 1/2 in. wide. **$1,200-$1,800**

Bowl, white, lotus-form, the body entwined with pierced lotus and vines, Chinese, 19th century, 3 3/4 in. long. **$500-$700**

Bowl, deep green, thin body, everted rim, mottled black flecks, Chinese, 18th century, 8 in. diameter. **$3,000-$4,000**

Bowl, celadon, straight sides, well-hollowed foot, Chinese, 19th century, 4 in. diameter. **$400-$600**

Box, apple green, oval with straight sides, Chinese, early 20th century, 3 in. wide. **$700-$900**

Brush washer, white, double-gourd form joined by scrolling tendrils, the sides with leafy, gnarled stems, Chinese, 19th century, 4 in. long. **$1,200-$1,500**

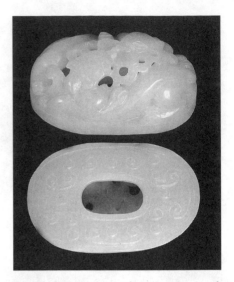

Carving, Chinese, circa 18th century, openwork carving of high-quality white mutton-fat jade with a lucky symbol on the flat bottom side, two entwined tigers whose tongues meet over a lotus pad on the curved top, 1 in. by 1 5/8 in. by 2 1/2 in., rare. **$850-$1,250**

Brush washer, green and white, the sides carved with gnarled branches and a leaf spray, Chinese, circa 1900, 3 in. wide. **$800-$1,200**

Censer, apple green and white, carved as a kylin standing four square with a bell around its neck, the head as the cover (its mouth open), fitted wood stand, Chinese, late 18th/early 19th century, 9 in. high. **$8,000-$10,000**

Censer, green and white, globular, three lion mask feet, lion mask and loose ring handles, Buddhistic lion cub finial, Chinese, 19th century, 6 1/2 in. high. **$2,500-$3,500**

Left: A green and lavender jade censer and cover, ornately carved, the body supported on four leaf-form carbriole legs with monster mask terminals and dragon head handles, the domed cover with a high pierced finial depicting a dragon pursuing a flaming pearl, the lavender stone with green inclusions carved to highlight details, late Ch'ing (Qing) dynasty, 5 3/4 in. high. Realized price (including the 10-percent buyer's premium), Christie's East, New York City. **$3,300.**

Right: A jade censer and cover with bands of rough, archaic foliage masks in crisp relief, open-work dragon handles and coiled dragon finial, the stone a mottled putty color with some russet and mustard clouding, carved in K'ang Hsi style, small chips to finial, 8 1/4 in. across the handles. Realized price (including the 10-percent buyer's premium), Christie's East, New York City. **$2,090**

Ewer and cover, celadon with brown mottling, loop handle, curved spout, panels of dragons on a floral ground, finial missing, Chinese, late 19th/early 20th century, 10 1/2 in. high. **$600 $800**

Figure of a recumbent boy carved from a pebble, celadon, Chinese, 18th century, 2 1/2 in. wide. **$750-$1,000**

Figure of a Buddhistic lion, recumbent with curly mane, celadon, Chinese, early Ch'ing (Qing) Dynasty, 4 in. long. **$2,500-$3,500**

Figure of a Buddhistic lion, recumbent, with brocade ball, Chinese, late 19th century, 3 in. long. **$450-$650**

Figure of Kuan Yin holding a flowering branch, the stone a pale green with light brown patches, Chinese, 19th century, 5 1/2 in. high. **$600-$800**

Chinese serpentine censer with tripod feet, the pierced cover surmounted by a recumbent kylin, 19th century, 5 in. high. **$250-$400**

Figure of a Lohan, white, wearing flowing robes and holding a sceptre, Chinese, late 19th century, 6 in. high. **$700-$1,000**

Figure of a water buffalo, gray, its legs tucked beneath its body, Chinese, early 20th century, 5 in. long. **$500-$600**

Figure, Ming Dynasty nephrite jade camel (1368-1644), measuring 7 in. by 6 in. by 2 1/2 in. The camel has been carved from a fine piece of green-brown nephrite jade by a master carver. Fine original condition. **$350**

Group, celadon with brown inclusions, a boy riding a carp, Chinese, 18th century, 3 in. wide. **$1,500-$2,500**

Group, mutton fat nephrite, a monkey climbing on a peach, the leaves forming the base, Chinese, 4 1/2 in. wide, circa 1900. **$800-$1,200**

Hand mirror, white-gray, carved with interlacing flowers below lotus buds, carved foliate borders, mirror replaced with modern glass, Indian, 19th century, 6 in. long. **$500-$675**

Inkwell, pale green, silver hinge and mount, fitted wood stand, the lid with Buddhistic lion finial, Chinese, late 19th century. **$600-$800**

Pebble, celadon and russet, carved as a peach with a leafy stem, Chinese, 18th century, 2 1/2 in. wide. **$900-$1,200**

Plaque, round, spinach green, carved with pavilions and pines, the reverse with an incised poem, fitted wood stand, Chinese, late 19th century, 5 3/4 in. diameter. **$900-$1,200**

Cosmetics jar, Ch'ing Dynasty, Kang Hsi period, 1660-1720, pale green jade with three carved animals on the side and knobbed lid, 3 1/4 in. by 3 7/8 in., excellent condition with areas of white patina. **$1,250-$1,350**

Plaque, white with pale green splashes, one side carved with a sage and waterfall, Ch'ien Lung (Qianlong) mark, but 19th century, 14 3/4 in. high. **$3,000-$4,000**

Plaque, celadon, carved with bats, ruyi heads, flowers, and leaves, Chinese, early 20th century, 2 1/2 in. wide. **$300-$450**

Plaques, pale green, oval, applied amethyst, quartz, and agate motif of birds perched on flowering branches, each in a fitted wood stand, Chinese, early 20th century, 16 in. high, pair. **$800-$1,200**

Scroll weight, dark green, rectangular, 7 1/2 in. long. **$300-$500**

Seal, celadon, square with a dragon handle, Chinese, circa 1900, 4 1/2 in. long. **$600-$900**

Figures of dancing women in traditional dress, mounted on marble bases, one holding a rose and a broad-brimmed hat, the other holding flowers on a tray and a handled swag, one figure has been reattached to its base with a resin, otherwise both are in excellent condition, circa 1900, 10 1/8 in. by 6 in. by 13 in., **pair. $6,500**

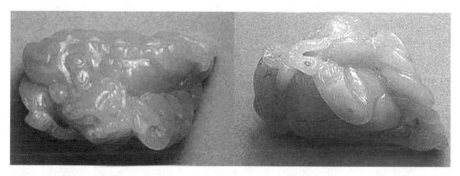

Figure, finely carved foo lion, circa 18th-19th century, in-the-round carving in pale green mutton-fat nephrite of a foo lion carrying a string of lucky coins in his mouth, believed to bring wealth to the owner, 1 1/4 in. by 1 5/8 in. by 2 3/8 in., excellent condition. **$375-$450**

Mask, white jade, Ming Dynasty, circa 1510-1600, finely carved protective horned mask with recessed back and suspension hole at top, 4 1/2 in. tall, rare. **$1,000-$1,250**

Ornament, Ming Dynasty, circa 1400-1600, carved both sides with mythic head, 2 7/8 in. tall. **$250-$350**

Teapot, stone pig, I Hsing, measuring approximately 5 1/2 in. by 3 1/2 in., dating to the 20th century. Fine original condition. **$65**

Ruyi sceptre, celadon, the handle carved with bosses and chrysanthemums, the underside with bosses, Chinese, 19th century, 10 in. long. **$1,500-$2,200**

Ruyi sceptre, pale green, carved with Taoist symbols in low relief, Chinese, 19th century, 8 1/2 in. long. **$600-$800**

Sceptre, green, the shaft and head carved with birds, Chinese, 19th century, 15 in. long. **$900-$1,400**

Vase, celadon, carved as a carp leaping from breaking waves, its mouth forming the rim, Chinese, 19th century, 7 in. high. **$800-$1,200**

Vase, celadon, the stone with brown patches, carved with birds at the base, Chinese, 19th century, 4 1/2 in. high. **$1,500-$2,000**

Vase and cover, celadon, flattened baluster form, pierced handles at the waisted neck, both sides carved with phoenix, Chinese, early 20th century, 9 1/4 in. high. **$600-$950**

Assorted Stones

Agate brush washer, the dish with lavender and brown hues, Chinese, early 20th century, 3 in. wide. **$1,200-$1,500**

Agate brush washer, brown-gray, carved as a lotus leaf with flower sprays, chipped, Chinese, late 19th century, 2 1/2 in. wide. **$175-$250**

Carved tiger eye agate figure of an alligator, on a carved wooden base, size with base, 3 1/2 in. by 1 3/8 in. by 1 3/4 in. **$125**

Large marble Buddha head, Ming or Ch'ing Dynasty, 8 1/2 in. tall, 13 lbs., carved in the round, detailed, generally excellent condition with light deposits. **$900-$1,250**

Monumental limestone head of Kwan Yin, Ching Dynasty, possibly older, over life-sized carved stone head of the goddess of compassion, 7 1/2 in. by 9 in. by 15 in., 55 lbs., light surface deposits. **$2,000-$2,500**

Soapstone and jade hinged box decorated with stylized flowers, possibly for cigarettes, in copper frame that has vine and floral pattern, excellent condition, 3 3/4 in. by 3 1/4 in. by 1 3/4 in. **$450**

Agate brush washer, honey-hued, oval and carved around the body with vines, Chinese, late 19th century, 2 in. wide. **$200-$300**

Agate wine ewer with ribbed body and domed lid, Chinese, early 20th century, 3 1/4 in. high. **$300-$450**

Amber brush washer carved with peony blossoms, reddish yellow, Chinese, 20th century, 4 in. wide. **$1,000-$1,500**

Amber figure of a ram, yellowish orange, naturalistically carved, Chinese, 20th century, 4 in. wide. **$1,000-$1,500**

Amber group, boulder form, fruit (including peaches and pomegranates), brownish red, Chinese, 19th century, 4 in. long. **$1,200-$1,500**

Amber group, yellowish orange, two dragons carved with C-scrolls, Chinese, circa 1900, 3 1/2 in. wide. **$600-$800**

Soapstone carving of a rabbit, excellent condition, 1 7/8 in. by 1 1/4 in. by 5/8 in. **$22**

Pair of carved soapstone seals in the form of an oxen and calf on a carved plinth decorated with animals and trees, bottoms engraved in seal characters, 7 3/4 in. by 3 in. by 3 in. **$350**

Chinese soapstone seal surmounted with a recumbent dragon and waves, gray with brown inclusions, 19th century, 4 in. high. $150-$225

Amethyst quartz, a recumbent Buddhistic lion, Chinese, circa 1900, 2 1/4 in. long. **$200-$300**

Carnelian agate vase carved as a large fruit with entwined vines, Chinese, 19th century, 6 in. high. **$900-$1,200**

Carnelian agate vase carved with fruiting plum branches, Chinese, 19th century, 4 in. high. **$1,500-$2,500**

Carnelian box and cover carved in the form of a cicada, Chinese, late 19th century, 3 in. long. **$250-$400**

Chalcedony agate vase and cover, flattened baluster form, gray-violet, lion mask handles and Buddhistic lion finial, Chinese, circa 1900, 9 3/4 in. high. **$1,000-$1,500**

Coral belt plaque with Shou character, Chinese, circa 1920, 3 3/4 in. long. **$225-$325**

Coral carved in the form of peony blossom arranged in a slender vase, Chinese, 20th century, 4 in. high. **$900-$1,200**

Coral group, two female deities, each below a phoenix, one standing on clouds and one leaning on a prunus branch, chipped, hardwood stand, Chinese, 20th century, 9 in. high. **$1,500-$2,000**

Lapis lazuli Buddhistic lions, bushy manes, one with a foot on a brocade ball, the other with a foot on its cub, Chinese, early 20th century, 6 1/2 in. high, pair. **$1,200-$1,800**

Lapis lazuli elephants, trunks raised, mottled stones with pyrite inclusions, Chinese, 20th century, 10 1/4 in. wide, pair. **$700-$1,100**

Lapis lazuli Lohan holding a fly whisk, the stone with gray and white inclusions, Chinese, early 20th century, 4 1/2 in. high. **$800-$1,200**

Malachite brush washer, gourd-shaped, fruit and leaves coiling around the surface, Chinese, early 20th century, 4 3/4 in. diameter. **$850-$1,200**

Malachite dragon, fierce expression, fitted wood stand, Chinese, 20th century, 5 in. long. **$400-$600**

Marble carpet weights, white, each on a square block, octagonal upper section with lotus-head finial, Indian, 19th century, 9 in. high, pair. **$850-$1,200**

Chinese soapstone artist's or collector's seal, top carved in the form of a garden scene with birds in bushes, 3 3/8 in. by 7/8 in. by 7/8 in. **$85**

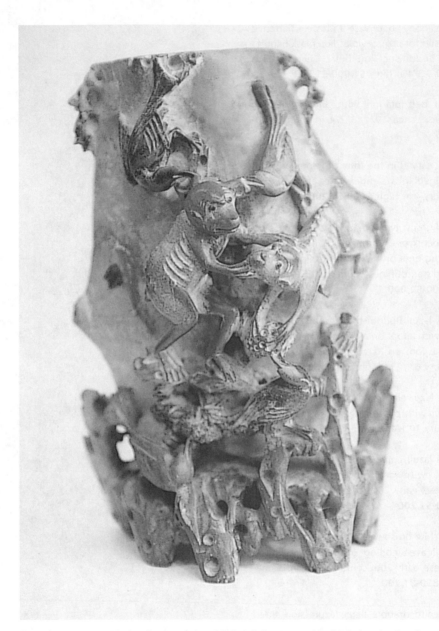

Carved soapstone vase showing monkeys with fruit being pursued by birds, hand colored, excellent condition, 5 1/2 in. by 8 1/4 in. by 3 1/2 in. **$225**

Marble dish, Pieta Dura work, rectangular, scrolling foliate design of carnelian, jade, lapis lazuli, and other inlaid flowering plants, lobed flower-head border, Indian, early 20th century, 10 in. by 8 in. **$500-$700**

Marble figure of a deer, white, standing on an oval base, Indian, 19th century, 17 in. high. **$750-$1,050**

Marble vase, baluster form, carved with dragons, bats, and cloud scrolls, Chinese, circa 1900, 9 1/2 in. high. **$500-$700**

Rock crystal, Kuan Yin seated on rockwork base and holding a ruyi sceptre, Chinese, 20th century, 4 1/2 in. high. **$1,200-$1,600**

Khmer stone head of the Buddha, circa 12th-14th century, 3 in. by 4 in., rare. $550-$650

Carved stone figure of two children riding a water buffalo who is standing over its calf, marked on the bottom "China," 6 1/4 in. by 5 3/8 in. by 3 1/4 in. $600

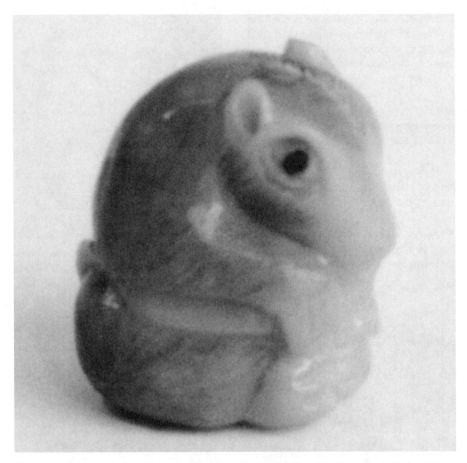

Stone carving of a rat holding its tail, painted eyes and fine detail on hair, 7/8 in. by 3/4 in. by 1 1/8 in. $225

Rock crystal, the Eight Immortals, each with attribute, Chinese, 20th century, 8 in. high, set. **$800-$1,200**

Rock crystal vase and cover, baluster form, loose ring handles below Buddhistic lion masks, lappet band at the base, chipped, Chinese, circa 1900, 11 in. high. **$700-$950**

Rose quartz censer, domed cover, globular body, loose ring and lion mask handles, Buddhistic lion finial, Chinese, late 19th century, 5 in. wide. **$500-$700**

Rose quartz figure of Kuan Yin holding a peony spray, mounted as a lamp, Chinese, early 20th century, 12 1/2 in. high. **$500-$700**

Rose quartz vase and cover, slender, carved with floral foliate branches, mounted as a lamp, Chinese, early 20th century, 14 in. high. **$700-$900**

Rose quartz vase and cover, pierced and carved with flowering branches on each side, floral finial, Chinese, circa 1910, 7 in. high. **$400-$600**

Rose quartz vase and cover, knob finial, Buddhistic lion handles at the shoulders, mounted as a lamp, Chinese, circa 1900, 6 1/2 in. high. **$300-$400**

Slate, panel carved in relief through a buff surface to a darker ground with cliffs and pavilions, Chinese, circa 1900, 13 1/2 in. by 11 in. **$900-$1,200**

Serpentine ruyi sceptre, the ends carved with Immortals, the stone a yellowish hue, chipped, Chinese, 19th century, 14 1/2 in. long. **$400-$600**

Soapstone figure of a guardian, bearded and wearing a layered tunic, Chinese, 19th century, 8 in. high. **$600-$800**

Soapstone figure of Kuan Yin, the stone with gray tones, chipped, Chinese, late 19th century, 8 1/2 in. high. **$300-$500**

Soapstone figures of the Eight Immortals, each with attribute, several chipped, Chinese, circa 1925, 7 3/4 in. high. **$400-$600**

Soapstone figure of Pu Tai holding staff and sack, Chinese, late 19th century, 22 in. high. **$500-$650**

Soapstone figure of a seated Lohan, Chinese, 19th century, 4 in. high. **$700-$950**

Soapstone seal, boulder-shaped, amber hue, carved with two Buddhistic lion cubs, Chinese, 7 in. high. **$800-$1,200**

Soapstone seal, rectangular, brown, surmounted by a Buddhistic lion cub, Chinese, circa 1910, 2 in. high. **$200-$300**

Soapstone seal carved as a rocky landscape, Chinese, late 19th century, 4 in. high. **$400-$700**

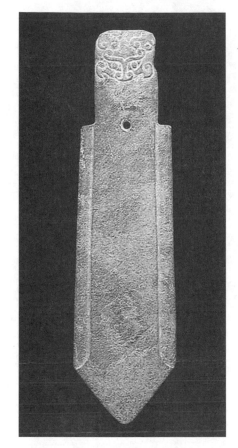

Taoist stone ceremonial blade, Ming Dynasty, 1368-1644, possibly earlier, blade carved with side ridges and Tao Tieh mask on both sides, a mounting hole drilled through the neck, 2 1/2 in. by 9 1/2 in., carved of purple gray stone, possibly serpentine, with wear and a couple of tiny age chips, rare. **$1,750-$2,250**

Soapstone seal, rectangular with rounded corners, greenish white, Chinese, 20th century, 4 1/2 in. high. **$200-$300**

Soapstone seal surmounted by a phoenix, Chinese, circa 1910, 2 3/4 in. high. **$200-$325**

Large Chinese black stone head of the Buddha, circa 17th-19th century, possibly earlier, carved of heavy black stone, 6 1/2 in. by 6 1/2 in. by 12 in., weight 28 lbs., some possible restoration, considerable light lime deposits. $1,000-$1250

Soapstone seal, plinth shape, cream color, the top carved with a Buddhistic lion, Chinese, early 19th century, 2 3/4 in. high. **$500-$700**

Soapstone tea caddy and cover carved in relief with pavilions, metal neck, Chinese, late 19th century, 6 in. high. **$900-$1,200**

Turquoise group of three children playing, Chinese, late 19th century, 4 in. high. **$800-$1,200**

Ink Stones

Boxed set of eight Chinese ink stones, in their fitted box, which measures 12 in. by 9 in., dating to the early to mid-20th century. Each stone is carved on the front with a scene of scholars that is highlighted with gold. The reverse sides have carved poems that are also highlighted. The box has had some water damage and shows stains on the interior but it is intact. The stones show some loss of the gold highlights, but the carved designs are crisp. None of the stones appear to have been used. **$150**

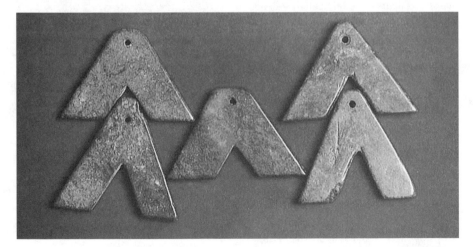

Five archaic style chimes, probably somewhat later copies but still with significant age, carved dark red stone in inverted "V" form, up to 1 3/4 in, set. $200-$250

Archaic style deep red blade form pectoral, probably somewhat later copy but still with some age, carved dark red stone, 2 3/6 in. long. **$200-$250**

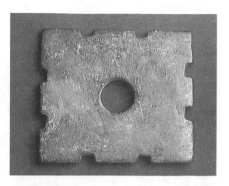

Archaic style red square Cong-form "pi" (flat disc with a hole in its center), probably somewhat later copy but still with some age, carved dark stone, 2 1/8 in. wide. **$200-$250**

Archaic style Tao Tieh faced pendant, probably somewhat later copy but still with some age, carved dark red stone, 2 in. long. **$300-$350**

Chinese tablet form pendant with kylin and scrollwork, probably somewhat later copy but still with some age, carved dark red stone, 2 1/4 in. long. **$300-$350**

Rounded rectangular duan ink stone (named for the Duanxi River, which runs at the foot of Mount Fuke, where the stone is found) carved with cosmic star patterns around the edges and at the sloping recess, a yi character in archaic script on the base in a recessed panel, Chinese, 17th century, 6 1/4 in. wide. **$1,500-$2,000**

Rounded rectangular duan ink stone carved on one side with a bird on a prunus branch above a hollowed crescent moon, Chinese, 17th century, 6 in. wide. **$800-$1,200**

Rounded rectangular duan ink stone mottled with green inclusions, an inscription on the base in a slightly recessed panel, Chinese, 18th century, 5 3/4 in. wide. **$875-$1,125**

Large Chinese stone carving, late 19th or early 20th century, finely carved variegated red stone scene with an adult water buffalo and three of its young, the adult ridden by three little Chinese boys one of whom plays a flute, 10 1/2 in. by 12 in. by 16 in., weight 45 lbs., signed, a masterpiece of Chinese stone carving, on custom wood stand. **$11,000-$12,500**

Square duan ink stone slightly recessed at one end with a cloud-pattern border, fitted wood box, dated 1936, Chinese, 6 1/4 in. wide. **$1,000-$1,500**

Trapezoidal duan ink stone with a raised border carved on the base (shui yen shen pin-underwater rock of the divine class), Chinese, 18th century, 3 3/4 in. wide. **$1,800-$2,400**

Trapezoidal duan ink stone carved to simulate a rock with a sloping recess to one side, Chinese, 18th century, 7 3/4 in. wide. **$2,000-$3,000**

Inro, Netsuke, Ojime,

AND RELATED ARTICLES

Because Japanese garments had no pockets, personal accessories had to be suspended from a cord worn around the carrier. In this assembly, known as sagemono, the netsuke was the toggle used to prevent the cord from slipping through the obi (sash or belt). The slide used for making the string tight or loose is called an ojime. In putting together the sagemono, the wearer would string the accessory through its runners (one on each side), adding the ojime as a slide, and fastening the netsuke at the end.

Types of Netsuke

Manju netsuke is named for its resemblance to the Japanese rice cakes of the same shape (round). This form of netsuke dates from the 18th century, unless it is made of ivory, in which case it originated around the mid-19th century. Manju netsuke may be made as one piece or two halves, and is slightly hollow inside (to take the cord). There may be a ring at the back used for the attachment of the cord, most manju netsuke have either one or two himotoshi (holes, or the aperture of a netsuke where the cord was fixed with which it was attached to the kimono's sash).

Ryusa is a more deeply carved variation of the manju. Kagamibuta is basically like a manju netsuke, but the lower half is well hollowed and the opening covered by a convex metal disc with a loop underneath. The cords are passed through a hole in the center and are then fastened to the loop on the lid.

Additional types of netsuke are as follows:

Katabori. Netsuke made to look like animals and figures, carved in wood or ivory.

Kurawa. Ashtray netsuke.

Ichiraku. Netsuke that has been woven or plaited in the form of baskets, gourds, and so on.

Trick or toy netsuke. Netsuke with moving parts.

Inro

The inro was the principle accessory worn by men. It originated as a box for holding a seal, and was later divided into two compartments to carry the ink as well. In the late 16th or early 17th century, the inro was further divided into as many as five-and sometimes even six-cases or compartments. Sometimes one or more of these main compartments was itself divided in half. At this point in the development of inro, they became medicine chests (yakuro) and were used to carry all sorts of medicines, drugs, and ointments.

Note that the bottom compartment of early inro is generally lined with silver or gold foil. In addition, inro (as well as ojime and netsuke) may be marked with a signature or seal. Like netsuke and ojime, inro can be found in a variety of materials and techniques, including ivory, wood, bone, antler, cloisonné, lacquer, wood, pottery, porcelain, and metal.

Other Accessories

Tonkotsu. Tobacco boxes that are larger than inro. Tonkotsu are usually wood, and are carved or decorated with lacquer and/or inlay.

Tobako ire. Pouches that were usually made of tanned leather or pieces of brocade.

Kinchaku. Money pouch.

Yatate. The case that contained the brush and ink, usually bronze.

Fudezutzu. A separate case for ink.

Hashi ire. Chopstick and knife.

Inro Values

Japanese gold lacquer over wood, four-case inro (small containers worn by men on cords attached to their sash, called obi in Japanese. They were used to store small things like seals, seal paste or medicine), decorated with both flat and raised gold, silver, brown, and red lacquer, dating to the late Edo or early Meiji periods. The front of the inro has a lobster, pine tree, and fruits. The reverse shows a flowering plant in a pot. The design shows this was intended for use during the New Year's celebration. The lobster is intended to bring long life, because its name in Chinese ideograph means "aged of the sea." The fruit is probably dried persimmon or bitter orange, both used at New Year's. The pine branch represents the "kado-matsu," a decoration traditionally placed outside the Japanese home only at the New Year as a hope for vigor and long life. The flowering plant is most likely apricot, which blooms in the season in spite of snow on the ground. The interior of the inro and the risers are completed in sprinkled, nashiki lacquer. The inro is closed with an orange lacquer-over-wood ojime and a lacquer-over-wood netsuke of a seated man preparing food. Both items are of the same period as the inro. There is some loss to the gold lacquer along the edges and to the gold leaves on the designs. They are unsigned. **$1,000**

Four-case inro in iroe takamakie (high relief) and hiramakie (low relief) and inlaid Aogai (abalone shell inlay) on a bark ground, clothing hung on a rope as if to air, inlay missing and chips, macabre staghorn ojime formed as a skull, signed Gyokumin. Realized price (including the 10-percent buyer's premium), Christie's, New York City. **$1,760**

Top, left to right: Inro, erotic, four-case decorated in orie togidashi (polished or rubbed lacquer, the design flush with the ground) on a nashiji ground with a couple united in sexual congress. Realized price (including the 10-percent buyer's premium), Christie's, New York City. **$2,200**

Unusual Japanese ivory two-case inro relief carved with the figure of what looks like a South Seas islander carrying a spear, dating to the Meiji Era (1868-1912). The inro measures 2 in. by 1 1/2 in. overall. The interior of the cases and the risers are covered in gold lacquer. This looks like elephant ivory but may be highly patinated marine ivory. It is accompanied by a glass bead ojime and a plain, well-worn ivory netsuke. **$500**

Japanese Meiji gunpowder container of wood, lacquer and bone, with a plain bone netsuke and ojime and an attached leather shot bag containing two lead shot and a cloth-covered barrel tamper, all dating to the Meiji, or late 19th/early 20th century. The container is in a disc shape measuring 4 1/2 in. in diameter and is covered in black lacquer that shows some wear and roughness from use. The fasteners and top are of bone, carved in detail with scalloped molding and a checkerboard pattern, alternating from black to white. The cap top is carved as a 16-petal chrysanthemum and was used to hold the powder measure for loading. The barrel tamper measures 7 in. in length and is made of wood wrapped in oil-stained cloth. All show evidence of use but no major damage and are redolent of gun oil and powder. **$250**

Unusual Japanese Meiji-period single-case wood inro with a bone inlay of a bat on the surface. The tonkotsu, or inro for tobacco, is made in a trefoil shape with the edges carved as waves. The case measures 3 1/2 in. in diameter and 1 1/4 in. in depth. The simple bone ojime is cone-shaped, the netsuke is a plain, flat, bone manju style. The inro is signed on the reverse in a bone reserve, or cartouche, with the name Kinto or Kanetaka. **$250**

The following inro are listed according to the number of cases:

Two-case, bamboo, carved with Chinese scholars, trees, and buildings, some wormage, 19th century. **$250-$350**

Two-case, hinoki wood (cypress) applied with tsuishu and black tsuikoku with two sides of an ink cake in low relief, chipped, cracked, wormage, attributed to Ritsuo. **$1,900-$2,500**

Two-case silver inro decorated with gold and silver peony and leaves, inlaid coral berries, coral-bead ojime and silver cloisonné manju netsuke, signed Fujimoto Kanekatsu (with kakihan [a written seal or signature]). **$4,000-$6,000**
COURTESY OF THE EDSON COLLECTION

Two-case, red lacquer with gold and silver reeds and marsh grasses, coral bead ojime, circa 1900. **$500-$600**

Three-case, gold hiramakie (low relief), takamakie heidatsu (high relief lacquer decoration with silver inlay) and togidashi (polished or rubbed lacquer, the design flush with the ground) on a black ground with a continuous motif of a bird perched on rockwork, chipped, late 18th century. **$1,200-$1,800**

Three-case, gold and silver hiramakie (low relief) with five insects on each side, black ground and interiors, relacquered, early Meiji period. **$900-$1,200**

Three-case, gold and silver hiramakie (low relief), hirame (large, irregular flakes of gold roughly sprinkled on a black lacquer ground, also fat gold flakes used in lacquer decoration [named for their resemblance to a flounder]), and nashiji (irregularly shaped flakes of gold suspended in clear or yellowish lacquer, also called "Pear ground," gold, silver or gold-silver alloys of reddish-yellow coloration used on lacquer, principally as a ground) with a continuous landscape showing an Emperor standing beside courtiers, top and bottom cases in need of restoration, 18th century. **$1,500-$2,000**

Three-case, hiramakie (low relief), mother-of-pearl, and silver on a gold ground, a continuous fence and floral motif, some inlay missing, late Meiji/Taisho period. **$500-$700**

Three-case, ivory with gold, silver, and red takamakie (high relief) with floral rounders, age cracks, plain, round, ivory ojime, ivory hako netsuke, the top with gold-lacquer fern, 19th century. **$1,500-$2,200**

Three-case, mura-nashiji decorated in gold and silver hiramakie (low relief) and hirame (large, irregular flakes of gold roughly sprinkled on a black lacquer ground, also fat gold flakes used in lacquer decoration [named for their resemblance to a flounder]) with a continuous motif of flowering chrysanthemums, gyobu interiors, signed Kajakawa saku, red tsubo-shaped seal, restored, early 19th century. **$1,885-$2,800**

Three-case roironuri (a waxy black or mirror black finish, a brilliant and highly reflective black lacquer), gold, silver, red, and brown hiramakie (low relief), takamakie (high relief), okibirame, and nashiii with the 12 zodiac animals, damaged, coral bead ojime, 19th century. **$600-$950**

Three-case, wood (natural) with lacquer, mother-of-pearl and enamel depicting lotus leaves in a continuous motif, shibuichi (gray-green patinated alloy of copper with varying quantities of silver) double gourd ojime, early 19th century, Ritsuo style. **$3,000-$4,000**

Three-case, wood carved in relief with a continuous motif of Shoki pursuing two Oni, ivory ojime carved with the Seven Gods of Good Luck, a wood netsuke of Shoki's hat, 19th century. **$1,500-$2,200**

Four-case, cherry bark decorated in iroe, hiramakie (low relief), and takamakie (high relief) on a red-brown ground with foliage and flowers, coral glass ojime, late Meiji period. **$1,200-$1,600**

Four-case, fundame (a matte finish of gold lacquer) decorated in gold and silver hiramakie (low relief), takamakie (high relief), and hirame (large, irregular flakes of gold roughly sprinkled on a black lacquer ground, also fat gold flakes used in lacquer decoration [named for their resemblance to a flounder]) with a hawk on a perch, nashiji (irregularly shaped flakes of gold suspended in clear or yellowish lacquer, also called "Pear ground," gold, silver or gold-silver alloys of reddish-yellow coloration used on lacquer, principally as a ground) interiors, rubbed, chipped, late 18th/early 19th century. **$1,875-$2,650**

Four-case, hirame (large, irregular flakes of gold roughly sprinkled on a black lacquer ground, also fat gold flakes used in lacquer decoration [named for their resemblance to a flounder]) and togidashi (polished or rubbed lacquer, the design flush with the ground) with a full moon behind pine branches, nashiji (irregularly shaped flakes of gold suspended in clear or yellowish lacquer, also called "Pear ground," gold, silver or gold-silver alloys of reddish-yellow coloration used on lacquer, principally as a ground) interiors, 19th century. **$1,500-$2,500**

Four-case, ivory, one side carved with Ebisu, the reverse with Daikoku, the panels within floral borders, floral runners, early Showa. **$400-$600**

Four-case, kinji (brilliant gold lacquer), decorated in gold, black, and red hiramakie (low relief), takamakie (high relief), hirame (large, irregular flakes of gold roughly sprinkled on a black lacquer ground, also fat gold flakes used in lacquer decoration [named for their resemblance to a flounder]), and nashiji (irregularly shaped flakes of gold suspended in clear or yellowish lacquer, also called "Pear ground," gold, silver or gold-silver alloys of reddish-yellow coloration used on lacquer, principally as a ground) with a cockerel standing on a drum, rubbed and chipped, early 19th century. **$1,800-$2,800**

Four-case, kinji (brilliant gold lacquer), decorated in gold, brown, and silver hiramakie (low relief), hirame (large, irregular flakes of gold roughly sprinkled on a black lacquer ground, also fat gold flakes used in lacquer decoration [named for their resemblance to a flounder]), nashiji (irregularly shaped flakes of gold suspended in clear or yellowish lacquer, also called "Pear ground," gold, silver or gold-silver alloys of reddish-yellow coloration used on lacquer, principally as a ground), and togidashi (polished or rubbed lacquer, the design flush with the ground) with a continuous motif of thatched houses among pine trees, slightly damaged and a minor repair to two cases, early 19th century. **$800-$1,200**

Four-case, kinji (brilliant gold lacquer) with gold, silver, red, and black takamakie (high relief), hiramakie (low relief), hirame (large, irregular flakes of gold roughly sprinkled on a black lacquer ground, also fat gold flakes used in lacquer decoration [named for their resemblance to a flounder]), and togidashi (polished or rubbed lacquer, the design flush with the ground), a dragon emerging from swirling waves, nashiji interiors, early 19th century. **$700-$900**

Four-case, kinji (brilliant gold lacquer) ground with a motif of berried branches, the berries of inlaid coral, gold takamakie (high relief) leaves, kinji (brilliant gold lacquer) interiors, signed Koma Ankyo, chipped, cracked, 19th century. **$1,200-$1,650**

Left: A sleeve inro, the sleeve decorated in gold hiramakie (low relief), kirigane, and nashiji, two scholars on a bridge with rock work beside and clouds above, seven-case inro decorated in iroe hiramakie
(low relief) to represent the grain of wood, minor chips and old damages, early 19th century. Realized
price (including the 10-percent buyer's premium), Christie's, New York City. **$1,230. Right:** Five-case inro
in gold hiramakie (low relief), nashiji, and kirigane on a fundame (a matte finish of gold lacquer)
ground, a pensive Dutchman leaning against a tree and watching a group of four puppies playing in a
field, late 19th century. Realized price (including the 10-percent buyer's premium), Christie's, New York
City. **$2,860**

Four-case, nashiji (irregularly shaped flakes of gold suspended in clear or yellowish lacquer, also called "Pear ground," gold, silver or gold-silver alloys of reddish-yellow coloration used on lacquer, principally as a ground) decorated in gold hiramakie (low relief), takamakie (high relief), and hirame (large, irregular flakes of gold roughly sprinkled on a black lacquer ground, also fat gold flakes used in lacquer decoration [named for their resemblance to a flounder]) with birds perched on branches, nashiji interiors, rubbed, chipped, crack on one cord runner, late 19th century. **$1,000-$1,500**

Four-case, roiro (black lacquer used for the ground) decorated with a floral spray on one side and a fan-shaped panel of flowers on the reverse in gold and colored takamakie (high relief), nashiji (irregularly shaped flakes of gold suspended in clear or yellowish lacquer, also called "Pear ground," gold, silver or gold-silver alloys of reddish-yellow coloration used on lacquer, principally as a ground) interior, chipped and worn, signed Kagikawa saku (with red pot seal), 19th century. **$2,000-$3,000**

Four-case, roironuri (a waxy black or mirror black finish, a brilliant and highly reflective black lacquer) decorated in gold and silver togadashi and hirame (large, irregular flakes of gold roughly sprinkled on a black lacquer ground, also fat gold flakes used in lacquer decoration [named for their resemblance to a flounder]) with a hut beneath leafy branches, interiors, very badly worn, early 19th century. **$700-$950**

Four-case, Somada school with a repetitive brocade motif of inlaid Aogai (abalone shell inlay) on a roironuri (a waxy black or mirror black finish, a brilliant and highly reflective black lacquer) ground, 19th century. **$2,000-$2,800**

Four-case, Somada style, roiro (black lacquer) ground with grazing horses in mother-of-pearl and gold foil, much of the inlay missing, 19th century. **$900-$1,200**

Four-case, Somada school, gold and silver gyobu nashiji (large nashiji flakes placed individually with a bamboo or steel needle), inlaid Aogai (abalone shell inlay) on a roirinuri ground with peacock, mums, and butterflies, the runners with aogai, round ojime and manju netsuke en suite, 19th century. **$5,500-$7,500**

Four-case, wood, both sides carved with a dragon and clouds, wood bead ojime, wood manju netsuke carved with a dragon, Taisho period. **$500-$800**

Five-case, one side with a cock perched on a drum, the reverse with a hen and three chicks, Shibayama inlay (mother-of-pearl and other materials), gold takamakie (high relief), togadashi (polished or rubbed lacquer, the design flush with the ground), and kirigane, some inlay missing, 19th century. **$2,000-$3,000**

Five-case, gold fundame (a matte finish of gold lacquer), gold, red, and black takamakie (high relief), hiramakie (low relief), and hirame (large, irregular flakes of gold roughly sprinkled on a black lacquer ground, also fat gold flakes used in lacquer decoration [named for their resemblance to a flounder]), Shibayama (mother-of-pearl and other materials) inlaid motif of cranes and peaches, nashiji interiors, signed Jokasai, metal ojime, ivory netsuke of a karako (child), old wear and damages, inlay missing. **$1,050-$1,100**

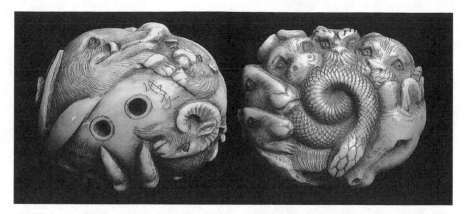

Japanese ivory netsuke, circa early 20th century, carved with all 12 animals of the oriental zodiac, 1 in. by 1 1/4 in. by 1 1/2 in., signed near the suspension hole. **$1,500-$1650**

Five-case, hiramakie (low relief), nashiji (irregularly shaped flakes of gold suspended in clear or yellowish lacquer, also called "Pear ground," gold, silver or gold-silver alloys of reddish-yellow coloration used on lacquer, principally as a ground), and togidashi (polished or rubbed lacquer, the design flush with the ground) with a continuous motif of a village beside a riverbank, quite worn, coral bead ojime, 19th century. **$2,000-$2,850**

Five-case, kinji (brilliant gold lacquer), decorated in gold, silver, red, and black hiramakie (low relief), takamakie (high relief), togidashi (polished or rubbed lacquer, the design flush with the ground), and heidatsu with a cockerel standing on a drum, the reverse with a floral spray, chipped, a hairline, orange glass ojime, early 19th century. **$1,500-$2,200**

Six-case, black with red-lacquer motif of a Koshin mask, another mask on the reverse, 19th century. **$600-$900**

Six-case, ivory carved in high relief with a continuous Chinese landscape, coral bead ojime, late 19th century. **$2,500-$3,800**

Left: Hirado netsuke of two carp molded in relief (yin and yang), late Edo period. $900-$1,200. Right: Hirado netsuke of a sparrow, molded in low relief, late Edo period. **$400-$650**

Netsuke Values

Japanese netsuke or okimono (a small object, usually a figure, that is placed somewhere for decoration) carved of antique marine ivory, measuring 3 1/4 in. by 2 in. by 1 1/2 in., dating to the Meiji Era (1868-1912). The piece shows a doomed rabbit in the grasp of a mountain lion, a rare subject in Japanese carvings. The inlaid horn eyes and unequal himotoshi are characteristic of the period. It is signed with seal characters in a cartouche. It has some small age cracks that do not affect the integrity of the carving. **$500**

Japanese netsuke or okimono (a small object, usually a figure, that is placed somewhere for decoration), made of elephant ivory, of Buwo, or Wen Wang, the founder of the Chinese Chou state, measuring approximately 3 in. high by 1 1/4 in. wide, dating to the mid-20th century. Buwo is a legendary figure in Chinese history as the victor over the last Shang king and founder of the Chou Dynasty around 1122 BC. This Bronze Age "Son of Heaven," as kings were referred to in those days, was protected by a dragon in battle. The netsuke-shi who carved this piece—it is signed on the base—depicts Buwo encircled by his protective dragon in detail. **$500**

Japanese Meiji-period netsuke carved from an ivory nut in the shape of a skull with a lizard crawling across the top. The himotoshi are formed by the base of the skull and one hole. It is unsigned and measures 1 1/2 in. by 1 in. A fine example of Meiji-period craftsmanship. **$200**

Unusual Japanese netsuke of a bug on a leaf, made of walrus ivory, measuring 2 1/2 in. by 1 1/4 in., and dating to the Meiji Era (1868-1912). Fine original condition. **$225**

Dark orange amber netsuke of Guanyin (a Buddhist deity called Avalokitesvara, known to the Chinese as Guanyin, the bodhisattva of compassion), standing 2 in. high, dating to the Meiji period (1868-1912). With hole-in-the-head himotoshi. **$200**

Japanese netsuke of frogs on a parasol and geta (raised wooden clogs), carved from elephant ivory, by the modern master, Hiroyuki. It measures 2 1/2 in. **$700**

Japanese netsuke of ivory, possibly marine in origin, of a monkey with a peach, dating to the mid-19th century. It measures 3 1/2 in. by 2 in. It has unequal himotoshi, which are characteristic of the period. The monkey's gentle appearance is similar to that seen in pieces by the great 18th and 19th century animal carvers. It is signed on the base by the artist, and appears to be Sanjusan. The netsuke has the yellowing and patina seen only in old ivory. Fine original condition with little wear. **$500**

Japanese netsuke carved from boxwood of two traveling medicine men with boxes on their backs, measuring approximately 2 1/2 in. in length, one with a repaired foot, unsigned, dating to the Meiji period. **$225**

Japanese netsuke or okimono (a small object, usually a figure, that is placed somewhere for decoration) carved from elephant ivory of the figure Bishamon, measuring approximately 3 1/2 in. in length, dating to the early-to-mid 20th century. It is signed on the base by the artist. Bishamon is one of the seven gods of good fortune. He is always represented in armor and often carries a spear and a small pagoda. He is also one of the Shitenno, or guardian deities of Buddhism and a commander of great armies. As one of these Four Heavenly Kings, Bishamon protects the North and is the guardian of great treasures. Fine original condition with no damage. **$500**

Left: Silver netsuke in the form of Daikoku's mallet with applied gold embellishments, Meiji period. $1,000-$1,500. Right: Carved coral netsuke of the Sneezer, signed Masakazu, late 19th century. **$2,000-$2,800**

Japanese netsuke, carved of marine ivory in an elongated, sashi style in the shape of a pheasant, measuring 3 1/2 in. long, dating to the Meiji Era (1868-1912). It has unequal himotoshi characteristic of the period and the patina that can be acquired only with age and careful use. It is unsigned. The pheasant is associated in Japan with a parent's devotion to children, because of the tendency for the pheasant to protect its eggs in the nest during a fire. The expression "Yakeno-no kigisu," or pheasants in the forest fire, is synonymous with parents sacrificing themselves for their children. **$325**

Japanese netsuke of a namazu, or earthquake, fish, measuring 1 3/4 in., carved of wood, and signed Kosei, dating to the 20th century. A very old Japanese legend states that namazu fish cause earthquakes by shaking their tails. This story may have come from the fact that these fish dwell in the mud at the bottom of ponds, much like our catfish. Kosei is a modern master carver who has used the grain and color of the wood piece to good advantage in representing his subject. The carving is detailed, the eyes are inlaid. Excellent original condition. **$750**

Japanese netsuke of stone, used as a seal with two characters in Chinese Zhuanshu, or seal script, measuring 1 in. by 1/2 in. by 1/4 in., dating to the Meiji period. **$50**

Japanese netsuke carved from antique elephant ivory in the shape of a walnut with relief carvings of a bird and flowers, measuring approximately 2 1/2 in. in length, signed Yasubasa, dating to the Meiji period (1868-1912). The netsuke is a solid piece of end-tusk ivory treated in a traditional way by the carver. Netsuke were originally meant to be worn as toggles on inro and pouches. Rough edges and sharp corners were discouraged because they would catch on the garments. This netsuke, with its rounded edges and smooth surfaces, was made to be worn, not just for decoration. **$350**

Japanese netsuke of elephant ivory, measuring approximately 2 1/4 in. by 1 1/2 in., dating to the early to mid-20th century. It shows a Chinese scholar at work at his desk, rubbing his eye. (Perhaps he is tired after practicing his calligraphy for his exams.) The netsuke is signed with what looks like Gyokuryu. Fine original condition. **$300**

Japanese netsuke, carved of antique elephant ivory, representing a rat on bale, from the modern master carver, Hiroaki, dating to the latter half of the 20th century. The artist has enhanced the piece with inlaid shell eyes. It measures 1 3/4 in. in length. **$550**

Japanese netsuke of ivory, possibly marine in origin, of a toad or frog seated on a lily pad, dating to the mid-19th century. The netsuke is large, measuring 3 in. by 1 1/2 in. It has inlaid shell eyes and unequal himotoshi, characteristic of the period. It is signed on the belly by the artist Shoitsu. It has the yellowing and patina seen only in old ivory. Fine original condition with little wear. **$350**

Japanese netsuke of ivory, possibly marine in origin, of two Chinese boys either embracing or having a disagreement over who will get the fan they are holding. The netsuke dates to the mid-19th century. It is carved to stand as an okimono (a small object, usually a figure, that is placed somewhere for decoration) and measures 2 1/2 in. by 2 1/2 in. by 1/4 in. It has unequal himotoshi, which are characteristic of the period. It is signed on the base by the artist Ranshu. An artist of this name was working in the mid-to-late 19th century. It has the yellowing and patina seen only in old ivory. Fine original condition with little wear. **$350**

Japanese marine ivory netsuke or okimono (a small object, usually a figure, that is placed somewhere for decoration) of a cicada, measuring approximately 3 1/4 in. by 1 1/4 in., dating to the Meiji Era (1868-1912). The inlaid eyes and unequal himotoshi are characteristic of the period. It is signed Shosai. The subject is unusual and shows the hand of an experienced carver. Fine original condition. **$350**

Daruma is also known as Bodhidharma, the founder of Chan Buddhism in China (known as Zen Buddhism in Japan). He is said to have lost the use of his arms and legs after meditating in front of a wall for nine years.

Japanese wood or ivory nut netsuke of a bull or ox, measuring approximately 1 1/2 in. by 1 1/2 in., dating to the Meiji Era (1868-1912). The netsuke-shi has expertly defined the bull with a minimum number of cuts. The unequal himotoshi and shell-inlaid eyes are characteristic of the period. It is unsigned. Fine original condition. **$150**

Japanese netsuke mask of an oni, or devil, measuring 2 in. by 1 in. and dating to the Taisho-Showa periods (Taisho [1912-1926], Showa [1926-1989]). The back is closed with a separate piece of ivory. Signed indistinctly. **$300**

Japanese fossil ivory manju netsuke of a coiled dragon, measuring approximately 1 1/2 in. in diameter, dating to the second half of the 20th century. It is signed by the modern master, Hiroaki, who has inlaid the eyes with horn or shell. Excellent original condition. **$300**

Japanese netsuke of carved amber in the shape of a sleeping ram, measuring 1 1/4 in., dating to the Meiji Era (1868-1912). **$150**

Japanese carved stone netsuke of a tiger's face, measuring 1 1/4 in. across, dating to the Meiji period (1868-1912). **$50**

Japanese netsuke of a pot-bellied man with a bemused expression carrying an exceptionally large rice bale, carved of fossilized ivory, measuring 2 1/4 in., dating to the Meiji period (1868-1912). The uneven himotoshi and patina are consistent with the age. **$300**

Japanese marine ivory netsuke or okimono of a boy climbing onto the back of an elephant using a ladder, measuring approximately 1 1/2 in. by 1 in., dating to the Meiji Era (1868-1912). There is minor wear on the surface, which is a good indication that the netsuke was been worn. It is unsigned. Fine original condition. **$250**

Japanese netsuke made of elephant ivory in a sashi style (long and thin) of an "oshidori," or mandarin duck, dating to the Meiji period (1868-1912). It is in excellent and original condition with one old sealed age crack. This netsuke has the rounded shape and unevenly sized himotoshi typical of Meiji pieces that were made to be worn, not just to display. Rich patina of age shows that this netsuke was indeed worn by one or more owners. The nestuke is signed by the artist, Hisamitsu. **$500**

Japanese wooden ivory nut netsuke of a boy with a rat and a bag, measuring approximately 1 1/2 in. in diameter, dating to the Meiji Era (1868-1912). The carving is crisp and shows essentially no wear. Fine original condition. **$200**

Japanese lacquered wood netsuke, dating to the Meiji period (1868-1912). The carving is oval in shape and measures 1 1/2 in. tall, indicating that this may have been carved from a fruit pit. Fine original condition. **$185**

Unusual and graphic Japanese wooden netsuke made in the shape of a penis, incised and carved with a raised dragon in gold accents, measuring 5 1/2 in. in length. This lifelike netsuke has through himotoshi in the base. Most likely a 20th century item. **$150**

Japanese bone netsuke in a manju or ryusa style, measuring approximately 1 3/4 in. by 1/14 in., dating to the Meiji Era (1868-1912). The netsuke has been expertly drilled and carved in a chrysanthemum form. It is not signed. Fine original condition. **$75**

Japanese netsuke carved of marine or fossil ivory, measuring approximately 2 1/2 in., dating to the Meiji Era (1868-1912). The netsuke-shi carved two beans on top of a chestnut, perhaps meant to be worn as a symbol of good harvest or during a festival. Fine original condition. **$350**

Japanese netsuke or ojime carved from natural amber, with inclusions and internal fractures, in the shape of Fukurokuju (the god of wisdom, wealth, and longevity), measuring 2 in. high, dating to the Meiji period (1868-1912). Unsigned, rich patina of age and translucency consistent with the material. **$75**

Japanese manju netsuke carved of stag horn or tusk, measuring 1 3/4 in. by 3/8 in., dating to the mid-19th century. The netsuke-shi has carved in relief a man or priest traveling on horseback. The center is unusual in that it uses wood to fill the core of the horn. It bears a brass pin. The carver's signature, Komin, is in a reserve. Several carvers by this name are known. Original condition with no damage and only minimal wear. **$275**

Japanese netsuke of elephant ivory in the shape of a man seated in front of a tea kettle and hibachi, stretching his arms over his head, measuring approximately 2 1/2 in., dating to the early 20th century. This may represent Daruma as he is awakening from his nine-year meditation. The netsuke is signed Miesan. This netsuke-shi is listed as a pupil of the modern carver Meigyokusai. The handle of the teapot may have been broken and reglued in the past. **$250**

Ivory netsuke of sumo wrestler squatting in front of his opponent, carved of mammoth ivory and measuring 2 1/4 in. by 2 in., dating to the latter 20th century. Signed by the carver. **$150**

Japanese manju (round and flat) netsuke carved of stag horn, measuring approximately 2 in. by 1/2 in., dating to the mid-19th century. The netsuke-shi has carved a long-haired warrior battling a dragon or sea serpent in the waves in relief on the front. The front shows the carver's signature, Nakashi, in a cartouche. The back has two inscribed maple leaves. No damage and only minimal wear. **$300**

Japanese ivory netsuke of a bending horse, measuring approximately 2 3/4 in. in height, dating to the first half of the 20th century. The himotoshi are positioned on the horse's flank so that the netsuke will hang appropriately. This is a good indication that the netsuke was made to be worn and was not just for the souvenir trade. The netsuke-shi has signed the piece on the reverse below the himotoshi. Fine original condition. **$400**

Japanese netsuke or okimono of antique marine ivory, measuring approximately 3 in. by 2 in. by 1 1/2 in., dating to the Meiji Era (1868-1912). The subject is most likely a sleeping Chinese sage or it might be Daikoku. Rich patina achieved only by human handling and age. The unequal himotoshi on the base are characteristic of the period. Fine original condition. **$450**

Japanese netsuke of antique marine ivory, measuring approximately 2 in. by 1 1/2 in., dating to the Meiji Era (1868-1912). The subject is a seated sennin or sage who is holding a fan. The top of the head was carved as a separate piece that was glued on by the carver. The material looks like a fossil or antique tooth. Himotoshi are on the back. Rich patina achieved only by human handling and age. There is a reddish stain on the top of the head, possibly from ink. **$350**

Japanese netsuke of bone, in cylindrical shape, with relief carving of Daruma awakening from his long sleep and stretching, measuring 1 1/2 in., dating to the mid-19th century. This is an old, plugged ojime. **$125**

Japanese rosewood netsuke of a man wrestling a tiger, measuring approximately 2 in. by 1 1/2 in., dating to the Meiji Era (1868-1912). The carver has placed the himotoshi to allow the front of the netsuke to show when it is worn. It is signed indistinctly. Fine original condition. **$350**

Japanese netsuke carved from ivory of a boy holding a peach, measuring approximately 3 1/2 in. in length, unsigned, dating to the Meiji Period. It is carved from end-tusk marine ivory that has been plugged on the base. There is one age crack in the boy's head that does not go through the ivory. The peach is revered by the people and is thought to have mysterious powers, usually to bring happiness. In one legend, the peach tree, or "momo," was given the name "Okantsumi-no-mikoto," or Great Sacred Fruit Deity, by Izanagi-no-mikoto, who threw peaches at the demons pursuing him. This netsuke most likely represents the children's story of Momotaro, a boy who was born from a peach found in a stream by an old woman. **$450**

Japanese netsuke/okimono (a small object, usually a figure, that is placed somewhere for decoration) carved of elephant ivory in what may be the figure of Jurojin, the Japanese god of longevity, dating to the early-to-mid 20th century. The piece measures 3 in. by 1 1/2 in. It is signed on the base indistinctly. Jurojin is one of the Seven Gods of Good Fortune in Japan. More specifically, he represents longevity. He is typically shown carrying a long staff with a book that supposedly carries the life-limit of everyone in the world. He is often accompanied by a 2,000-year-old black deer. Fine original condition. **$500**

Japanese wood or ivory nut netsuke of a man's head in a basket, measuring approximately 1 in. by 1 1/4 in., dating to the Meiji Era (1868-1912). The figure may represent an executioner's victim. Fine original condition. **$125**

The following netsuke are listed alphabetically by material and style:

Ivory, two sumo wrestlers engaged in combat, oval base, signed Shomin, 19th century. **$500-$700**

Ivory, three salmon struggling upstream, late Meiji period. **$175-$300**

Ivory, a bird emerging from a clamshell, inlaid eyes, 19th century. **$300-$500**

Ivory, Tokyo school, a Chinese boy dressed in Chinese attire and carrying a basket of fruit, 19th century. **$700-$1,000**

Ivory, Chokaro Sennin carrying a gourd on his shoulder, age cracks, 18th century. **$325-$500**

Ivory, a coiled snake, inset horn eyes, signed Toshitsugu, Meiji period. **$600-$800**

Ivory, a Dutchman, his coat engraved and stained with foliate designs, inlaid details, signed Hidegyoku, Meiji period. **$425-$600**

Ivory, Fukurokuju clasping his staff, late Meiji/early Taisho period. **$400-$600**

Ivory, Gentoku galloping his horse over the Dankei River, lightly stained, signed Mitsuo, 19th century. **$900-$1,250**

Ivory, a goose preening, boldly carved feathers, age crack, late 18th/early 19th century. **$1,000-$1,500**

Ivory, a grazing horse, head lowered to the left, engraved mane and tail, age cracks, early 19th century. **$1,200-$1,500**

Ivory, Hotei holding an uchiwa (rigid fan), a karako (child) on his back, signed Okakoto. **$300-$400**

Ivory, a man seated on a cushion, his arms and legs crossed, engraved and stained details, early 20th century. **$600-$800**

Ivory, a mask of Hannya, the female demon, the tips of her horns cut off, signifying repentance, 19th century. **$200-$300**

Ivory, a mask of Okina, late Meiji period. **$200-$300**

Ivory, an Oni in the disguise of Fukusuke, 18th century. **$400-$600**

Ivory, a peony blossom with finely rendered petals and stamen, the curled stalk forming the himotoshi, signed Ryuso. **$600-$900**

Ivory, a puppy lying on a roof tile, inlaid horn eyes, late Edo period, age cracks. **$425-$575**

Ivory, a rat seated beside two leaves upon a closed seashell, its tail trailing over the edge, inlaid horn eyes, signed Rantei, 19th century. **$800-$1,250**

Ivory, a recumbent cat, its eyes with inlaid ebony pupils, late Meiji period. **$900-$1,200**

Ivory, Tomotada style, a recumbent ox, the fur engraved and stained brown, its eyes with inlaid pupils, one missing, 19th century. **$600-$800**

Ivory, a skull with anatomical detail, Meiji period. **$600-$800**

Ivory, Masanao style, a sparrow with inlaid eyes, age cracks, 19th century. **$200-$400**

Ivory, a tortoise with six smaller ones clambering over its carapace, engraved details stained brown, late Edo period. **$500-$650**

Ivory, a seated Daruma, incised details, 19th century. **$900-$1,200**

Ivory, a seated, smiling Hotei, boldly carved with incised and stained details, late Edo period. **$450-$650**

Ivory, a seated Karako (child), details engraved and stained black, late 19th century. **$300-$400**

Ivory, Okatomo style, a seated monkey holding its offspring and clutching a stalk of kaki fruit, the legs forming the himotoshi, inlaid eyes, stained details, 19th century. **$750-$1,000**

Ivory, Kyoto school, a seated tiger with inlaid ebony eyes, engraved and stained details, early 19th century. **$600-$800**

Ivory, Kyoto school, a snarling tiger seated upon a section of bamboo, incised and stained details, 18th century. **$2,000-$3,000**

Ivory, a standing Dutchman wearing a wide-brimmed hat, his attire with incised details, 18th century. **$4,000-$6,000**

Ivory, a standing toy dog, knotted collar, tail looped to form himotoshi, late Meiji period. **$600-$800**

Ivory, Disappointed Rat Catcher kneeling and holding onto a box while the rat creeps over his shoulder, signed Tomomasa, 19th century. **$400-$600**

Ivory, Urashima (the fisherman) feeding the minogame (turtle-like beast) that is his future bride in disguise, contemporary. **$375-$500**

Ivory, a very plump sparrow, inlaid horn eyes, inscribed Masanao, late Edo period. **$500-$700**

Kagamibuta, in relief, the bronze plate with "Kinko on the carp" in various alloys, ivory bowl cracked, 19th century. **$200-$300**

Kagamibuta, shakudo (a dark metal alloy that mixes copper, gold and other materials), silver, and sentoku with a performer wearing a fox mask (scene from a No play), ivory bowl with age cracks, 19th century. **$1,000-$1,500**

Kagamibuta, in relief, a courtier wearing elaborate garb, the lid with various alloys, ivory bowl, 19th century. **$350-$550**

Kagamibuta, shakudo plate inlaid with a silver Mt. Fuji and gold clouds, ivory bowl, 19th century. **$400-$600**

Kagamibuta, the shakudo lid inlaid in gold and silver with a tiger and bamboo, ivory bowl, 19th century. **$900-$1,200**

Lacquer, in the style of the Nara school, a bearded Mongolian holding a vase, the sword strapped on his back forming the himotoshi, Taisho period. **$1,500-$2,000**

Lacquer, Somado style, box form with a motif of an uchiwa (single-stick fan), 19th century. **$900-$1,200**

Lacquer, a boy seated beside his dog, nashiji (irregularly shaped flakes of gold suspended in clear or yellowish lacquer, also called "Pear ground," gold, silver or gold-silver alloys of reddish-yellow coloration used on lacquer, principally as a ground), red, gold, and black takamakie (high relief), 19th century. **$1,000-$1,500**

Lacquer, a Daruma with arms stretched over his head, black and gold lacquer on a red ground, 19th century. **$500-$700**

Manju, ivory, a man smoking a tobacco pipe, Shibayama inlay (mother-of-pearl and other materials), stained ivory, some inlay missing, late Meiji period. **$375-$500**

Manju, ivory, carved in shishiaibori (low relief carving below the level of the surface), a performer dressed in a loose robe, the details inlaid in mother-of-pearl, signed Komin, 19th century. **$450-$650**

Manju, ivory, carved with Hotei holding an uchiwa (rigid fan) and leaning on a sack, the reverse with scroll designs, 19th century. **$425-$650**

Manju (kamakuri-bori), carved with three apes picking peaches, late Edo period. **$475-$650**

Manju, Raiden running amongst clouds, Hoshunsai Masayuki signature/seal, 19th century. **$1,500-$2,200**

Manju, Shibayama inlay (mother-of-pearl and other materials) with kiku (chrysanthemum) and foliage, age cracks, Meiji period. **$500-$700**

Manju carved with a Samurai's implements and armor, late Meiji period. **$425-$600**

Manju carved with shaped panels of the 12 zodiac animals, gilt-lacquer ground, 19th century. **$550-$775**

Manju formed with eight masks, signed Tomochika, 19th century. **$500-$750**

Manju, lacquer, fundame (a matte finish of gold lacquer) ground with lotus and leaf in silver and gold takamakie (high relief), hairlines, 19th century. **$600-$850**

Manju, porcelain, underglaze blue and white with a mountainscape, early 19th century. **$475-$675**

Manju, staghorn, pierced and carved with the legend of "Ono no tofu," the frog carrying an umbrella, the reverse with pine trees, 19th century. **$1,000-$1,500**

Manju, walrus, carved with egrets and a variety of flowers, 19th century. **$700-$1,000**

Manju, walrus, low relief carving of jurojin, 19th century. **$485-$625**

Porcelain, a celadon-glazed crane, Seto, late 19th century. **$225-$300**

Porcelain, a celadon-glazed Jurojin, Seto, Meiji period. **$250-$400**

Porcelain, a karako (child) seated upon an ox, white glaze, Meiji period. **$250-$375**

Pottery, a badger in a priest's garb, mid-19th century. **$275-$375**

Pottery, a bakemono (unreal things) kneeling down with two cha wan (bowls), his neck pierced with a pin (a nodding netsuke). **$665-$950**

Pottery, Kenzan style, a basket of bakemono (unreal things) from the story "The Tongue-Cut Sparrow." **$700-$900**

Pottery, a Daruma, his eyes in gilt, late Meiji period. **$200-$400**

Pottery, Okame with colored kiku mon (Chrysanthemum family crest) on her kimono, Meiji period. **$500-$700**

Silver, double gourd with engraved foliage, Meiji period. **$500-$700**

Silver, gourd shape with leaves and tendrils in relief, Meiji period. **$600-$800**

Stag antler, a brush pot, three bracket feet, one side carved with a tortoise, signed Hoshunsai with kakihan (a written seal or signature), 19th century. **$2,000-$2,800**

Stag antler, Tokyo school, a Buddhist temple gong (Mokugyo) hollowed out, the handles formed by two confronting dragons, 19th century. **$1,200-$1,600**

Stag antler, a group of mushrooms on a worn edge basket, 19th century. **$750-$1,050**

Stag antler, a man carrying a basket of flowers, 19th century. **$150-$225**

Stag antler, a recumbent boar, eyes with inlaid pupils, 19th century. **$100-$200**

Stag antler, a sashi netsuke carved as mask of Oni, 19th century. **$800-$1,200**

Stag antler, a Shishi leaning on a tama (jewel), inlaid ebony eyes, early 19th century. **$250-$375**

Wood, a chestnut naturalistically detailed (So school). **$1,000-$1,500**

Wood, a coiled dragon with inlaid ebony and ivory eyes, late Edo period. **$275-$375**

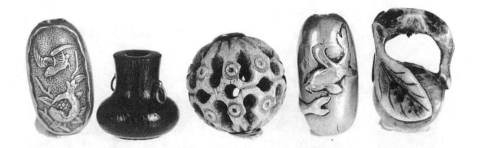

Left to right: Silver ojime with pomegranate, foliage, and birds in low relief, Meiji period. **$600-$900.** Wood ojime in the form of a vase with brass loose ring handles, Meiji period. **$300-$475.** Bone ojime with pierced and carved motifs, early 20th century. **$900-$1,200.** Silver ojime, carp in relief, 19th century. **$1,000-$1,500.** Stag antler ojime carved in the form of a peach and foliage, stained brown, late Meiji period. **$200-$375**

Wood, Gama Sennin, a toad perched on his back, he holds a staff and wears a mugwort (a plant also called by other names, including chrysanthemum weed) cloak, one crack, late Edo period. **$300-$400**

Wood, a Kappa astride a cucumber, 19th century. **$600-$800**

Wood, a karako (child) holding a puppy, 19th century. **$200-$300**

Wood, a kirin (mythical creature) with neck stretched upward, jaws open wide, finely detailed, 19th century. **$900-$1,300**

Wood, Tokyo school, a large and small chestnut with an inlaid ivory maggot, signed Gyokuso. **$500-$700**

Wood, a mask of Otobide, inlaid horn eyes, 19th century. **$400-$600**

Wood, Daikoku's mallet, ivory inlay, Meiji period. **$800-$1,200**

Wood, a rat clutching a chestnut, nicely patinated, inlaid horn eyes, late Edo period. **$300-$500**

Wood, a rat clutching a bean, his body curled, the curling tail forming the himotoshi, inlaid horn eyes, one ear damaged, 19th century. **$700-$900**

Wood, a seated monkey (Hear No Evil), his legs crossed to form the himotoshi, signed Masanao, late 19th century. **$1,000-$1,500**

Wood, a seated monkey with inlaid horn eyes, ittobori (single-cut) carving, 19th century. **$200-$300**

Wood, a Shishimai dancer dressed in full costume, late Meiji period. **$175-$225**

Wood, Nagoya school, a Shojo sleeping off the effect of sake, finely incised details, signed Ikkan, 19th century. **$3,000-$4,000**

Wood, a tea picker, ittobori (single-cut) carving, the female figure holds a bowl of recently picked tea, 19th century. **$200-$300**

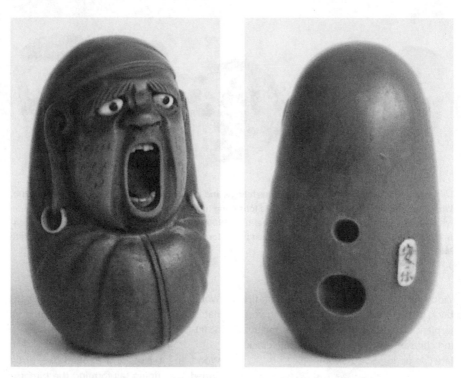

Carved and painted ojime of a man with wide open mouth and earrings, inset shell eyes, signed on the reverse, 2 in. by 1 1/8 in. by 1 1/8 in. $200

Wood, a Yamabushi emerging from a large conch shell blowing a horagi (conch), 18th century. **$750-$1,100**

Wood, an awabi (abalone) shell, 19th century. **$150-$250**

Wood, an inebriated man dancing on one foot, late Edo period. **$375-$575**

Wood, a mask of Oni, signed Ikko, 19th century. **$200-$300**

Wood, Disappointed Rat Catcher, signed Hisakazu, 19th century. **$500-$650**

Wood, the Sneezer, he makes himself sneeze by tickling his nose, late Edo period. **$500-$700**

Wood, Tokyo school, the Sneezer holding an ivory fan. **$800-$1,100**

Wood, two frogs on a lotus leaf, circa 1900. **$150-$250**

Wood, So school, two Kyogen players, one dancing with a fan, one tapping a drum, inlaid with ivory and ebony, signed Soya. **$2,000-$3,000**

Wood, two sages playing Go, carved details. **$350-$500**

Ojime

Japanese ojime of bone, in cylindrical shape, with a relief carving of a rat, measuring 1 1/4 in., dating to the mid-19th century. Fine original condition. **$75**

Japanese ojime of bone, in cylindrical shape, with relief carving of a man's face, measuring 1 5/8 in., dating to the mid-19th century. **$75**

Japanese ojime made of horn, measuring 1 1/2 in., in the shape of a horse, from the 20th century. **$35**

Japanese lacquer ball ojime measuring 5/8 in. in diameter, dating to the Edo-Meiji periods, or mid-19th century. It has minor chipping around the holes. **$50**

The following ojime are listed alphabetically by material and style:

Boxwood in the form of a persimmon, 19th century. **$100-$200**

Brass and copper with a carp in low relief, 19th century. **$400-$600**

Cloisonné, round, black ground with flowers in colors, silver wire, circa 1900. **$375-$525**

Gold (in the form of a tied purse), circa 1900. **$750-$1,050**

Gold, oviform with a floral and butterfly motif, dented, late 19th century. **$900-$1,200**

Iron (in the form of a finger citron), 19th century. **$300-$475**

Ivory carved with two Oni faces, Meiji period. **$150-$225**

Ivory with cranes carved in low relief, late 19th century. **$500-$700**

Ivory carved overall with five puppies, one spotted, 19th century. **$700-$900**

Ivory carved in relief with Rakan, 19th century. **$200-$400**

Ivory carved in the form of an octopus, 20th century. **$300-$400**

Ivory carved in the form of a peach, early 20th. **$200-$300**

Ivory carved in the form of a human skull, late 19th century. **$150-$250**

Ivory carved with the Three Wise Monkeys, early Showa period. **$475-$600**

Ivory, round, inlaid Shibayama (mother-of-pearl and other materials) motif of butterfly and flowers, Meiji period. **$750-$1,000**

Porcelain, underglaze blue and white leaves, the ojime a gourd shape, 19th century. **$300-$500**

Porcelain, Hirado, underglaze blue and white flower-and-leaf motif, the ojime oval in form, late Edo period. **$900-$1,200**

Porcelain, iron red and gold with two reserves, signed Eiraku, late Edo/early Meiji period. **$900-$1,250**

Shakudo in the form of Daikoku's mallet with silver and sentoku embellishment, 19th century. **$550-$700**

Shakudo in the form of a die with gold and silver inlaid stripes, 19th century. **$500-$700**

Shakudo with a shibuichi (gray-green patinated alloy of copper with varying quantities of silver) dragon, 19th century. **$700-$900**

Silver with a motif of bird and mums, the center of each mum inlaid in gold, 19th century. **$700-$1,000**

Silver chased overall with a design of chrysanthemums, late 19th century. **$500-$700**

Silver, oviform, with a design of dragon and clouds, late Meiji period. **$700-$900**

Silver, carved and pierced with kiku (chrysanthemum), late 19th century. **$600-$775**

Silver in the form of a peach, late Meiji period. **$500-$700**

Silver in the form of a seashell, late Meiji period. **$400-$600**

Silver, ovoid, open-work with applied gold kiku (a chrysanthemum), 19th century. **$800-$1,200**

Silver, round, pierced and carved with peony and foliage, late 19th century. **$450-$550**

Stag antler carved as a boat, 19th century. **$200-$300**

Stag antler carved in the form of a mushroom, 19th century. **$225-$325**

Stag antler carved in the form of a peach, late 19th century. **$200-$300**

Pipes

Tobacco, long-stem, decorated in gold hiramakie (low relief) with flowers, silver fittings, Japanese, 19th century, 19 1/2 in. long. **$500-$700**

Tobacco, long-stem, silver with butterflies and kiku (chrysanthemum), tortoiseshell decorated in hiramakie (low relief) en suite, Japanese, circa 1900. **$500-$700**

Tobacco, short-stem, Banko, two-tone brown with relief calligraphy, Japanese, circa 1900. **$375-$550**

Tobacco, short-stem, wood with carvings of birds and flowers, silver fittings, Japanese, circa 1910. **$150-$225**

Top: Japanese pipe in the form of an umbrella, early 20th century. $200-$300. Bottom: Chinese opium pipe, bamboo with silver hardware. $600-$800

Pipe Cases

Japanese inro, kizerazatsu (pipe case) and kizeru (pipe), the kizerazatsu carved of wood in an open style in the shape of an octopus, or "tako," the pipe of bamboo and brass, and the inro, or tonkotsu, carved from wood in a cylindrical, single-case, box form with wave designs from the natural wood grain, dating to the Meiji Era (1868-1912). The tonkotsu measures 3 in. by 3 in. by 2 in. The kizerazatsu measures 7 1/2 in. in length, the pipe measures 9 1/2 in. The set is signed on the base of the tonkotsu Shuraku. The wood has a rich patina. There is one, small rim chip repair near one of the cord holes on the tonkotsu. The octopus is featured in many Japanese tales, including the story of the carpenter Hassan, of Edo, who swore off eating octopus to get rid of his warts. This octopus is carved in typical style as a somewhat comical figure with a pouting mouth. He is often shown with a cloth around his head, holding a fan and dancing. From this figure has come the term Tako-Nyudo, or octopus monster, which is used to refer to bald-headed people. **$700**

Bamboo carved in low relief with four No masks, brass pipe, carnelian glass ojime, late 19th century. **$175-$250**

Bone carved in high relief with Tobosaku holding a peach, 19th century. **$400-$600**

Ivory, one side carved with a man leaning on the pole he is holding, the reverse with pine branches, age crack, 19th century. **$300-$500**

Stag antler carved in relief with scholars playing Go, the upper section with two cranes, signed Gyokko, 19th century. **$300-$400**

Stag antler carved with Ashinga and Tenaga, signed Shoryu, 19th century. **$350-$550**

Stag antler carved with three seals, age cracks, 19th century. **$250-$350**

Wood decorated in kebori (fine hairline engraving) and shishiaibori (low relief carving below the level of the surface) with a girl and a cat, circa 1900. **$250-$350**

Wood lacquered to simulate bamboo, 19th century. **$150-$200**

Tobacco Pouches

Leather with silver kanamono (various small metal plates that decorate and hold armor together, the various rivets, and the ornaments), ivory bead ojime, and stag antler obihasami, netsuke carved and pierced with gourds, 19th century. **$800-$1,200**

Carved wood tonkotsu with silver and copper ojime, late Edo period. **$250-$350**

Tonkotsu, wood formed from a section of branch and decorated with stained ivory water lilies, early 19th century. **$375-$575**

Tonkotsu, wood inlaid with ivory, horn, and shell in a motif of seashells and fish, signed Tokoku (school of), late 19th century. $700-$950

Tonkotsu, wood with brown and black hiramakie (low relief) in a motif of flowering branch and a wasp, chestnut-form ivory ojime, wood netsuke in the form of a lotus pod, 19th century. **$450-$650**

Ivory, Horn, Shell, and Tortoiseshell

Is It Genuine Ivory?

BY BERNARD ROSETT

The title of this article is perhaps the question most frequently asked in antiques and art galleries. Since prehistoric days, ivory has been known and loved as an artistic medium. Artificial and substitute materials have been known almost as long.

Ivory comes from the tusks, the upper incisors, of the pachyderm (elephant). Like all teeth, these are mainly composed of calcium phosphate. The structure of a tusk consists of large numbers of minute tubules, each about 1/15,000 inch in diameter, and filled with an oily substance that serves to give nourishment to the tusk.

The fine structure of the tusk explains the great elasticity of the material. The severe depletion of the vast herds of Asian and African elephants is a direct result of the suitability of ivory for fundamental, ornamental, and occasional objects.

A cross-section of tusk invariably exhibits a reticulated crisscross pattern that is unique-ivory. Also visible is the wood-grain pattern of a longitudinal portion of an ivory sample. The oily tubules mentioned are responsible for the typical gleam and patina of ivory. Another characteristic of ivory is its density: 1.70-1.95 times that of water, which often serves to quickly distinguish it from plastics and other light materials. The microstructure of ivory helps to explain its good heat conductivity, whereby it usually feels cold to the touch. Experienced shoppers are often seen touching a suspect piece of ivory-the cheek.

The Bible contains frequent mention of ivory, as in passages describing the glories of King Solomon's temple. The museum at Oxford University in Great Britain boasts ivory works of art from Egypt that predate 3000 BC. Although the centuries have made them somewhat dry and brittle, they still retain some of the gleam and polish of their youth.

There are other natural materials that have some resemblance-elephant ivory, but none have the crosshatched appearance already described.

Hippopotamus teeth (canines and incisors) are the hardest of all the ivorylike materials. The grain lines are wavy and all run in one direction. The surface has a gleaming whiteness. Netsuke are sometimes carved of this material.

Walrus tusks, the upper canines, are also encountered in netsuke and other sculptured work, but are also often seen in Middle Eastern and Scandinavian dagger handles. Walrus "ivory" is often identified by sections of characteristic mottling. Moderately deep carving brings out this handsome effect. The mottled interior has been found-be harder than the outer layer.

Whale teeth are most often encountered in scrimshaw. Whale teeth have a striated grain pattern.

Narwhal tusk comes from the elongated left tusk of a species of Arctic whale. This often grows to a length of six to eight feet. It is thought that the mythological unicorn originated in stories of the rarely met narwhal. These tusks are seldom cut into sections, usually being preserved intact as walking sticks. Occasionally, small sections are made into netsuke, which have historically been made of almost any material that might be named. The center of most of the narwhal tusk is hollow, and the transverse and longitudinal sections resemble the pattern of a tree trunk.

Boar's tusks, the upper canines of the wild boar (or of the wart hog), make a particularly fine, white "ivory" beloved by one school of netsuke carvers. The cross-sections of these tusks are approximately triangular. Since these tusks are relatively small (under six inches in length), many carvings contain complete tusks.

Vegetable ivory, which comes from the nut of a tropical South American palm (phytelephas), was often used in the fabrication of buttons. The grain pattern, mostly circular, is dull and indistinct. This material is softer than bone or ivory.

Bone-shin bones or tibia from any reasonably sized animal-is the most commonly used imitation ivory substance. All mammal bones are hollow, the center filled with spongy material. A bone carving will usually show, in transverse section, a pattern of black dots resembling a stubbly beard. A longitudinal section shows the bone channels (foramina) as a series of brown or black streaks. The surface of bone is generally duller than that of polished ivory. A good magnifying glass (3X-6X) makes it easy to identify many of these materials. Bone is usually less dense than ivory.

Stag antlers, the antlers of reindeer, elk, and the like (sometimes erroneously called staghorn), have long been of common use for knife or dagger handles, as well as for small carvings. Antlers have a spongy center, but the outer zones are denser than bone. The color of an antler varies from yellow to rich brown. The longitudinal section shows many irregular openings, unlike the regular, dark streaks seen in bone.

Plastic ivory substitutes. Many types of plastic have been employed since the invention of celluloid at the turn of the century, in the vain attempt to simulate the properties of ivory. There is even a material called ivorine that has alternating streaks of dark- and light-colored plastic to simulate the grain of ivory. This, however, does not approach the density of real ivory, and the grain pattern in no way resembles the crosshatched pattern of ivory. Even the straight-line pattern is far too regular to deceive a careful observer. It is also much softer than bone or ivory.

The following properties offer more specific guidelines for distinguishing among the materials already discussed here.

Hardness or scratchability. With the point of a sharp penknife, scribe a short line on an unobtrusive part of the piece in question. A well-defined incision will be seen in the case of plastic. Bone, ivory, or other animal materials will barely show a scratch.

Heat and conductivity. Plastics are poor conductors of heat. The minute canals of bone or ivory, however, conduct heat quite well. Therefore they feel cool to the touch. A needle or safety pin, heated red hot and quickly applied to an inconspicuous place on the piece in question, is a good method of testing. Animal materials will not be affected, but a small puff of smoke or a brand-like scar are proof of plastic.

Kyoto Pottery

FRONT ROW, LEFT TO RIGHT: Ash pot, gosu (blue) ground with flowers and scrolls, 18th century, 3 1/2 in. high, **$1,800-$2,200**; blue-ground bowl with flowers and foliage, 18th century, **$2,500-$3,500**; box in the form of a drum with tomoe mon, 18th century, **$2,000-$3,000**; tea caddy with wood lid, impressed Ninsei mark, **$2,800-$3,800**; miniature cup with impressed Ninsei mark, **$1,200-$1,600**

BACK ROW, LEFT TO RIGHT: Sake pot with wire bail handle, the motif including mushrooms and foliage, the top with Tokugawa mon, 18th century, 6 in. high, **$2,500-$3,500**; three-piece censeræetray, bowl, and open-work cageæthe bowl featuring a wheel motif, the cage with foliage and branches, marked Ninsei, 8 in. high, **$3,000-$5,000**; ewer in the form of a tree trunk with foliage and large peaches, 18th century, **$2,700-$4,000**; gourd-shaped bottle with open work and good luck and long life characters, 18th century, **$3,500-$4,500**; tea caddy with T-pattern motif, Ninsei mark, **$4,000-$5,000**

19th Century Chinese Porcelain

LEFT TO RIGHT: Yellow-ground bowl decorated with lotus and meandering scrolls and foliage, Tao Kuang mark (and of the period), 8 in. diameter, **$2,500-$3,500**; white-ground square-form bowl with high foot, the motif featuring beautiful Chinese women, Kuang Hsu mark (and of the period), 11 in. diameter, **$800-$1,200**; turquoise-ground bowl featuring a mother and many children in various poses, Chia Ch'ing mark (and of the period), 4 1/2 in. diameter, **$1,000-$1,500**

Japanese Imari

LEFT TO RIGHT: Meiping bottle/vase, the reverse with an inscription that indicates that this piece was a gift at a Shinto wedding, circa 1880, 16 in. high, **$800-$1,200**; plate, a Sumo wrestler in low relief, circa 1870, 9 in. high, **$500-$700**; covered jar, hen-and-cock finial, early 18th century, **$2,500-$3,500**; charger (this piece has a box, not shown, which indicates the date of manufacture as March 1871), 24 in. diameter, **$4,500-$6,500**

Vase, tree-bark cloisonné, ceramic body in urn form, showing a four-toed dragon, signed on the bottom, excellent condition, 4 1/2 in. by 2 1/4 in. **$150**

Cloisonné jar and cover, small, with stylized floral motifs, numbered on the bottom "1722," excellent condition, 4 3/8 in. by 3 1/2 in. **$600**

Imari plate, hand-painted with rich blue, rust-red, green, and gold, with center decoration of flowers in a vase, rim chips, 8 1/2 in. diameter. **$75**

Porcelain snuff bottle, blue and white, showing two figures (master and student?) in a landscape, with red painted ceramic stopper, signed on the bottom, 2 1/8 in. by 2 5/8 in. by 1 in. **$220**

Carved wood figure of a Chinese nobleman in elaborate robes, with lacquered and gilt decoration, late 19th century, 9 1/2 in. by 4 in. by 3 1/2 in. **$175**

Handbag, silk (possibly made from sleeve bands) with stitched designs of coins, flowers, and squared scrolls, clasp also decorated with applied coins, with woven strap, Chinese, overall 24 in. by 6 3/4 in. **$1,200**

Lacquer table decoration, centerpiece, elaborately carved and lacquered with gilt details, showing court scenes, with six legs in the form of foo lions, one finial missing, possibly made for export, circa late 19th century, 14 in. by 6 in. by 9 3/4 in. **$800**

Japanese Cloisonné

LEFT TO RIGHT: Shallow rectangular tray with two finches on bamboo before the rising moon, the reverse with a design of cherry blossoms, silver mounts, signed Namikawa Sosuke, 12 in. by 10 in., sold at Christie's, New York City. Realized price (including the 10-percent buyer's premium): **$8,800**; baluster vase with a bird perched on a leafy branch above flowering chrysanthemums, silver rims, signed Kyoto Namikawa, sold at Christie's, New York City. Realized price (including the 10-percent buyer's premium): **$1,980**; globular-form covered jar with domed lid and brass bud finial, copper wire with birds flying among lilies, morning glories, daisies, and hydrangeas, signed Kyoto Namikawa, 4 in. high, sold at Christie's, New York City. Realized price (including the 10-percent buyer's premium): **$1,045**; incense burner and cover, baluster form, five cabriole feet, pierced dome cover, 5 3/4 in. high, signed Kyoto Namikawa, sold at Christie's, New York City. Realized price (including the 10-percent buyer's premium): **$12,100**

Satsuma

FRONT ROW, LEFT TO RIGHT: Censer with perforated silver wire cover, 17th century, **$1,000-$1,500**; tortoise-form sake kazu (wine pot) in bekko gusuri (tortoiseshell glaze), 18th century, **$1,800-$2,500**; bowl featuring panels of seasonal flowers, the interior with a diaper band and center motif of a phoenix in flight, late Edo period, 7 in. diameter, **$900-$1,200**; teapot with Shishi motif, blue mon on base, late Edo period, **$1,000-$1,500**

BACK ROW, LEFT TO RIGHT: Chaire, same gusuri (sharkskin glaze), 18th century, **$2,500-$3,500**; plate, the Masanobu mark on the back accompanied by a blue mon, circa 1810, 10 in. diameter, **$3,500-$5,500**; bottle, late 18th century, 7 in. high, **$2,000-$3,000**; censer in the form of Hotei (with sack) and child, designed so that the essence emits from his mouth and perforations on the sack, late 18th/ early 19th century, restored, **$1,200-$1,600**

Snuff Bottles

FRONT ROW, LEFT TO RIGHT: Snowflake glass with red overlay motifs of 100 Antiques, 18th century, **$1,200-$1,600**; famille rose porcelain bottle with motifs in relief, late 18th/early 19th century, **$900-$1,200**; I Hsing cylindrical bottle, blue ground with flowers and birds, late 18th/early 19th century, **$800-$1,200**; porcelain bottle, a dragon on one side and a phoenix on the reverse, molded in high relief, Tao Kuang period, **$1,800-$2,500**

SECOND ROW, LEFT TO RIGHT: Silver bottle with flower and bird motifs in low relief, Ch'ien Lung mark (and of the period), **$2,000-$3,000**; inside-painted crystal bottle signed Yeh Chen San, continuous motif of fish and aquatic plants, the exterior carved with sea animals, carved ears, **$2,500-$3,500**

BACK ROW, LEFT TO RIGHT: Amethyst bottle carved in high relief, early 20th century, **$1,200-$1,800**; lapis lazuli bottle in the form of a carp, 20th century, **$700-$900**; pear-shaped clear glass bottle with red overlay motifs of carp, waves, and bats, 18th century, **$2,000-$2,800**

Cloisonné platters, round, showing birds and flowers on a turquoise background, excellent condition, 12 in. by 1 1/2 in., pair. **$1,300**

Chinese export porcelain shallow bowl, possibly Lowestaff, decorated with scenes of acrobats and musicians performing before a royal (?) household, with a floral-decorated rim, 8 3/4 in. by 1 5/8 in., minor paint chipping. **$225**

Cloisonné vase, wisteria design, drilled for a lamp base, late 19th century, 17 1/2 in. by 7 in. **$2,950**

Lacquered stool and storage box made of bamboo with painted panels of leaves and birds, front opens to reveal storage area, original tacked leather upholstery, Japanese, late 1800s, 21 in. by 19 1/2 in. by 14 1/2 in. **$750**

Jade figure of dancing woman in traditional dress, mounted on marble base, holding a rose and a broad-brimmed hat, excellent condition, circa 1900, 10 1/8 in. by 6 in. by 13 in., one of a pair, single figure. **$3,500**

Soapstone and jade hinged box decorated with stylized flowers, possibly for cigarettes, in copper frame that has vine and floral pattern, excellent condition, 3 3/4 in. by 3 1/4 in. by 1 3/4 in. **$450**

Plate from a set of Japanese Kakiemon foliate dinnerware, made circa 1700, decorated with stylized flowers and roosters, plate measures 8 3/4 in. diameter, part of an 81-piece set that includes cups, saucers, covered bowls, and assorted serving pieces. **$25,000/set**

Japanese Studio Ceramics

FRONT ROW, LEFT TO RIGHT: Red-ground bowl with flambe glaze, signed Makuzu Kozan, circa 1900, 6 in. diameter, **$1,500-$2,200**; bowl with black ground, crackled interior, motif of Tokugawa mon, signed Tanzan, circa 1910, **$1,800-$2,800**

BACK ROW, LEFT TO RIGHT: Blue-ground vase with flowers (in low relief), birds, and trellis, signed Hansuke, late 19th century, 10 in. high, **$900-$1,200**; green-ground vase with wave motif at the base, applied gun metal-hued lizard around the rim, base signed Makuzu Kozan, circa 1900, **$3,000-$4,500**; blue and white vase, motif of puppies frolicking in the snow, signed Kawamoto Masakichi, circa 1882, 13 in. high, **$1,600-$2,500**; covered jar with chrysanthemums and waves, the base signed Ito Tozan, Meiji period, 7 in. high, **$3,000-$4,000**

Blue and White Porcelain

LEFT TO RIGHT: Japanese Hirado covered jar, 18th century, masked feet and ears, the reverse with dragon and clouds motif, **$2,000-$3,000**; Chinese blanc de chine, Shou Lao (with staff, gourd, castanets, and peach of long life), 18th century, 11 in. high, **$5,000-$7,000**; beaker-form vase, K'ang Hsi period, 14 in. high, **$1,800-$2,500**; Hirado carp-form vase, Meiji period, 12 in. high, restored, **$500-$650**

Chinese Cloisonné

Candle holders, each formed as a standing crane, and well-grained, carved-wood, fitted stands, Ch'ien Lung period, 19 in. high, sold at Christie's, London. Realized price (including the buyer's premium), pair: **$5,294**; vessels and covers in the form of standing Buddhistic lions, one looking to the left and the other looking to the right, 18 1/2 in. high, sold at Christie's, London. Realized price (including the buyer's premium), pair: **$2,647**

Pair of figures of pigeons with glossy black finish, cast bronze, taller figure is 6 1/2 in. by 7 1/4 in. **$800**

Rosewood carved figure of a woman with a bird, Chinese, late 19th or early 20th century, probably a tourist item, on a rosewood base, 14 1/2 in. by 6 in. by 4 in. **$185**

Brass figure of Buddha on stand, Tibetan, 21 1/2 in. by 27 in. by 13 in. **$1,200**

Japanese celluloid showing a geisha riding in a covered cart being pulled by an ox that is led by a man in a broad hat, 6 1/4 in. by 3 3/8 in. by 2 1/8 in. **$100**

Moriage (raised decoration used on some Japanese pottery) umbrella stand showing members of the nobility and attendants, some restoration, 25 1/2 in. by 10 1/2 in. **$900**

Bronze vase decorated with five-towed dragons, inscribed with symbols and flowers in a landscape, early 20th century, 16 1/4 in. by 8 1/4 in. **$400**

Jewelry box with musical mechanism, decorated with a peacock in a moonlit landscape, interior has mirror and is lined in blue velvet, with two hinged compartments and one drawer, with ring holder, marked Japan on the bottom, excellent condition, 12 in. by 5 7/8 in. by 8 1/4 in. **$200**

Chinese Monochromes
LEFT TO RIGHT: Cherry red bottle/vase (lang yao), 4 1/2 in. high, Ch'ien Lung period, 18th century, **$3,000-$5,000**; blue water coupe, K'ang Hsi period, 3 in. diameter, **$2,500-$3,500**; lime green bowl with incised dragons and flaming pearl, Kuang Hsu mark (and of the period), 6 1/2 in. diameter, **$1,200-$1,600**; liver red bowl, Yung Cheng mark (and of the period), **$3,000-$5,000**

Famille Rose Export Porcelain

FRONT ROW, LEFT TO RIGHT: Rose Mandarin two-handled bouillon, circa 1825, large size, **$375-$600**; Rose Mandarin punch bowl, circa 1830, 15 in. diameter, **$3,000-$4,500**; Rose Medallion barrel-form covered box, first half of the 19th century, **$600-$900**

BACK ROW, LEFT TO RIGHT: Rose Mandarin platter, circa 1820, 16 in. diameter, **$1,200-$1,600**; Rose Medallion spittoon, Tao Kuang period, **$1,500-$2,200**

Japanese Lacquer

FRONT ROW, LEFT TO RIGHT: Tea caddy with a motif of maple leaves going upstream, late Edo period, **$1,500-$2,500**; kogo (a covered box, usually for incense), circa 1915, 3 1/4 in. diameter, **$1,000-$1,500**; cloud-shaped tray, one of a set, late Meiji period, set of five, **$1,200-$1,500**

BACK ROW, LEFT TO RIGHT: Writing box (suzuribako) with silver rims and silver water dropper, Meiji period, **$2,000-$3,000**; inro case (containing pullout drawers in which inro are housed), silver hardware, Shibayama-inlay motif, Meiji period, **$3,500-$5,500**; tiered box with nashiji interiors, late 17th/early 18th century, **$4,000-$6,000**

Kutani
FRONT ROW, LEFT TO RIGHT: Kutani bowl in yellow and aubergine with dragon and flaming pearl motif, Yoshidaya revival (named for an 18th century Japanese merchant), circa 1810, 5 in. diameter, **$2,000-$2,800**; fan-form okimono with rats, late 19th century, **$1,200-$1,500**; vases, late 19th century, 5 in. high, **$400-$600**
BACK ROW: Plate with Japanese lacquer repair, late 19th century, **$450-$700**

Solubility test. A drop of acetone (lacquer thinner) placed on an inconspicuous area of the suspect piece will leave a definite mark if the piece is plastic because it starts to dissolve or soften under the drop of acetone. Animal materials are not affected. For vegetable ivory, a specific test involves the application of a drop of sulfuric acid, which leaves a brown stain on this substance.

Grain. Careful observation through a magnifying glass reveals a great deal of detail, and study of the many grain patterns will aid in identifying the material. It is also important to have good illumination to bring out the fine grain.

Color and luster. True ivory can vary from white to cream to yellow to brown, according to its preparation and history. The color and luster of plastics can be controlled.

Density or specific gravity. As mentioned earlier, bone and ivory are measurably denser than plastics. However, the clever faker can put heavier fillers or ivory dust in his mix to make this a dangerous criterion for the buyer-trust.

Smell. The sense of smell is sometimes helpful in identifying materials. Probably everyone is familiar with the characteristic odor of celluloid that has been subjected to friction. Likewise, some of the acrylics and epoxies have a distinctive sweet odor when rubbed on a wool sleeve. Real bone and ivory are usually odorless unless burned at high temperatures.

Horn (Rhinoceros)

Libation cup carved with a variety of flowers, including peony, chrysanthemum, and sunflower, among rock-work; the handle formed by complex branches of peony by a rock, the plant extending over the rim into the interior beside a large cricket among rocks; the horn a honey tone; Chinese, 18th century, 6 in. wide. **$7,000-$9,000**

Libation cup carved with monkeys, deer, birds, and ducks among the Three Friends motif (pine, plum, and bamboo), with pine trunks forming the handle and petals forming the interior, Chinese, 18th century, 6 1/2 in. wide. **$3,000-$4,000**

Libation cup carved with a sampan (flat-bottomed Chinese skiff usually propelled by two short oars) moored by a lakeside and two figures on a promontory near retreats in a mountainous landscape, deeply carved pine trees forming the handle and extending over the rim, the horn a deep color, Chinese, 18th century, 6 1/2 in. wide. **$6,000-$7,000**

Libation cup carved with a continuous garden scene, main buildings, pavilions, and trees within a household compound, the trunk of a sturdy pine tree forming the handle and extending over the rim into the interior, the horn a dark tone, Chinese, 18th century, 7 in. wide. **$3,500-$4,500**

Libation cup carved with overhanging, projecting cliffs rising from breaking waves, a twisting pine forming the handle and extending over the rim, the inside rim carved with formalized clouds, the horn a dark color, Chinese, 17th century, 1 3/4 in. wide. **$5,000-$6,000**

Libation cup carved with a river landscape, a boat with four figures approaching two scholars on a bank, rock-work forming the handle and extending over the rim, the horn a reddish brown color, Chinese, 18th century, 5 3/4 in. wide. **$3,000-$4,000**

Libation cup carved with pine and other foliage among rocks and a waterfall, the trunk of the pine forming the handle and extending over the rim into the interior, carved rock-work details, the horn a honey tone, minor repair, Chinese, 17th century, 6 in. wide. **$3,000-$4,000**

Libation cup carved with mythical animals, including dragons, a tortoise, and a Buddhistic lion, among breaking waves, craggy banks around the rim area, a rocky grotto with a pine tree above forming the handle and extending over the rim; repair-foot and rim chips, Chinese, 17th century, 6 in. wide. **$5,000-$6,500**

Ivory

Box and cover carved as an elephant supporting Jurojin and a small boy, Shibayama details, signed Gyokuzan, Japanese, circa 1900, 4 3/4 in. high. **$700-$900**

Box and cover carved and pierced in high relief and low relief with birds, their eyes inlaid in horn, details stained black, age cracks, Japanese, circa 1900, 5 in. wide. **$1,000-$1,500**

Box and cover carved with the Seven Gods of Good Luck, stained details, Japanese, circa 1920, 3 1/4 in. high. **$600-$800**

Box and cover, double gourd form with relief carvings of flowers, leaves, and gourds over trelliswork, Chinese, 19th century, 4 in. wide. **$250-$400**

Box and cover with Shibayama motifs of three cranes standing beneath a prunus, some inlay missing, Japanese, circa 1900, 3 3/4 in. long. **$900-$1,200**

Brush holder carved and pierced with children, trees, and buildings, Chinese, Kuang Hsu (Guangxu) period, 5 1/4 in. high. **$550-$750**

Brush pot carved overall with numerous figures and pavilions, Chinese, circa 1885, 4 in. high. **$800-$1,200**

Brush pot, cylindrical with incised motifs of birds, insects, bats, and bamboo, Chinese, early 20th century, 4 1/4 in. high. **$300-$475**

Card case densely carved with figures and pavilions, Chinese, first half of the 19th century, 4 1/8 in. long. **$450-$600**

Carving, Japanese, circa 19th century, sphere finely carved with a young prince among five masters or immortals and a dragon and foo lion, no doubt illustrating a scene from Japanese legend, rich golden patina, signed. **$3,500-$3,750**

Figure, Japanese elephant ivory okimono (a small object, usually a figure that is placed somewhere for decoration) of a farmer, dating to the early 20th century. The farmer holds a sack and a staff as he leans to the side. The carved and fitted figure is attached to a wooden base by way of a separate ivory piece. Overall, the okimono measures 5 1/2 in. tall. The base is 4 in. wide. The ivory is in fine original condition with minor age cracks and patina. The staff was cut intentionally at a diagonal. **$300**

Letter rack, the arched top carved and pierced with two confronting dragons and flaming pearl, Chinese, circa 1885, 6 in. high. **$400-$600**

Group, two men playing Go, signed Toshikazu, Japanese, late Meiji period, 4 in. diameter. **$1,500-$2,500**

Group, three dragons, all intertwined, inlaid horn eyes, Japanese, late 19th century, 9 1/2 in. high. **$850-$1,250**

Group, four seated Buddhas, dhyana mudra, each on waisted lotus thrones, Burmese, 19th century, 4 in. high. **$650-$900**

Japanese ivory, 19th century, representing a Japanese folk tale with the hero besieged by nine monkeys, 7 in. long, several small losses, protruding details, rich patina, signed on the base; provenance: Ex. Robert Lang collection. **$1,500-$1,750**

Box, circular form, carved with figures and pavilion, all in high relief, Chinese, late 19th century, 2 3/4 in. diameter. **$200-$300**

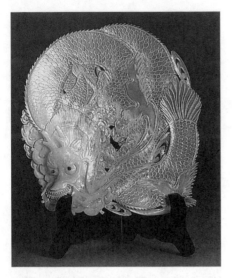

Shell, abalone, carved in the form of a dragon, inlaid eyes, Japanese, Meiji period, 7 in. high. **$800-$1,200**

Shell, abalone, carved with a monkey catching a butterfly, inlaid horn eyes and stained details, Japanese, late 19th century. **$800-$1,000**

Shells carved in low relief with officials, children, and pavilions, the eyes inlaid, Chinese, late 19th century, pair. **$1,000-$1,500**

Staghorn

Candlesticks, tree-trunk form with fruiting peach branches, Japanese, late Meiji period, 9 in. high, pair. **$900-$1,200**

Model of two monkeys seated beneath a lantern, Japanese, late Meiji period, 5 in. high. **$300-$450**

Parasol handle carved as a kappa holding a sake bottle, inlaid eyes, Japanese, late 19th century. **$300-$400**

Tortoiseshell

Box and cover, circular, densely carved with figures, pagodas, and trees, sides and base similarly carved, Chinese, early 19th century, 5 in. diameter. **$1,200-$1,800**

Shell entirely carved in the style of the Western Chou (Zhou) Dynasty, but late 19th/early 20th century, Chinese. **$450-$700**

Carving, Chinese, circa late 19th or early 20th century, with female musicians/dancers, 7 in. tall, signed, age cracks, otherwise intact, on custom wood base. **$850-$1,250**

Carving (okimono) of a hawk attacking a monkey, stained details, Japanese, late 19th century, 5 in. high. **$800-$1,200**

Carving, (four views) Japanese, circa 19th century, sphere finely carved with a young prince among five masters or immortals and a dragon and foo lion, no doubt illustrating a scene from Japanese legend, rich golden patina, signed. **$3,500-$3,750**

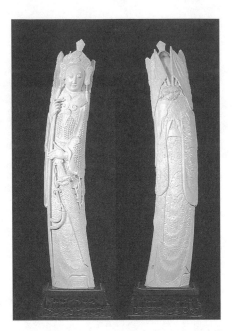

Figure, Chinese, circa mid-20th century, carved from the larger half of a tusk with a finely modeled ancient Chinese warrior in meticulous detail, 28 in. long, weight 16 lbs., a few tiny chips, signed on the bottom, on custom two-tiered carved hardwood stand, rare. **$2,500-$2,750**

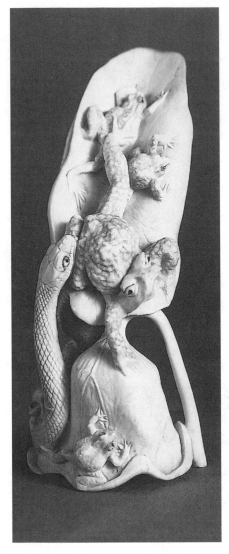

Carving of five frogs, varying in size, and a serpent, all upon an aquatic plant, Japanese, late 19th century. **$800-$1,200**

Group, a father holding his son, the father wearing a kimono jacket and trousers, the boy held at his shoulder, a basket at his feet, cracked, signed Gyokushin, Japanese, circa 1910, 8 1/4 in. high. **$1,000-$1,500**

Model of a bamboo shoot, the interior hollowed and carved and pierced with the old man from the "Tongue-Cut Sparrow" story, signed Minghoku, Japanese, Meiji period, 7 1/2 in. high. **$450-$750**

Model of a basket seller wearing a kimono jacket and holding a bamboo pole with wares hanging from it, details lightly painted in colors, signed Masahide, Japanese, circa 1900, 6 in. high. **$700-$1,000**

Figure, warrior, Chinese, circa mid-20th century, meticulous detail, 7 3/4 in. tall, excellent condition, on silver-inlaid custom rosewood stand. **$1,500–$1,750**

Figure, Buddha, Chinese, circa mid-20th century, seated with one leg raised on custom stand, 2 in. tall, excellent condition. **$300–$350**

Model of Benten wearing elaborate headdress and flowing robe and holding a biwa (a stringed instrument similar to a lute or guitar), signed Shugetsu, Japanese, late Meiji period, 12 in. high. **$1,500–$2,000**

Model of a Bijin (Japanese beauty), her kimono and obi with chased kiku (chrysanthemum), she holds a flowering branch, signed Nobuyuki, Meiji period, 11 1/4 in. high. **$1,200–$1,800**

Model of a Bijin standing and wearing a patterned kimono and obi, her hands repaired, signed Shingyoku, Japanese, Meiji period, 10 3/4 in. high. **$600–$900**

Model of a bird catcher holding a bird in one hand, a basket tied about his waist, the pole missing, age cracks, Japanese, circa 1920, 12 1/2 in. high. **$700–$900**

Model of a Chinese sage holding a writing brush and leaf fan, damaged, Japanese, Taisho period, 8 1/2 in. high. **$700–$900**

Model of Daikoku holding a mallet and standing on rice bags, signed Tamiyuki, Meiji period, 6 3/8 in. high. **$350–$600**

Figure of the Disappointed Rat Catcher holding a truncheon, looking over his shoulder as the rat escapes, Japanese, Meiji period, 2 1/2 in. high. **$900–$1,200**

Figure, Japanese, circa late 19th, early 20th century, polychrome figure of a yukata-clad (a lightweight cotton garment) man holding a fan and a birdcage with door that opens to reveal a songbird inside, 12 3/4 in. tall, signature carved on the bottom of one sandal, on curled rosewood base. **$3,500-$3750**

Model of a drum seller carrying his wares on a bamboo pole held over his shoulders, Japanese, Taisho period, 5 3/4 in. high. **$1,000-$1,500**

Model of Ebisu carrying a fishing pole (with fish dangling at the end) over his back, signed Tomokazu, Japanese, late 19th century, 5 in. high. **$675-$900**

Model of an elder smoking a pipe and holding a lantern, his tonkotsu hanging from his waist, signed Koko, Japanese, Taisho period, 8 in. high. **$825-$1,075**

Model of a farmer carrying a small boy on his back and holding a basket of grain, engraved details stained brown, chipped and cracked, Japanese, circa 1900, 7 1/2 in. high. **$300-$500**

Model of a fisherman seated before a tree repairing his nets, signed Kyoshu, Japanese, Meiji period, 10 3/4 in. high. **$750-$1,125**

Model of Fukurokuju holding a staff and uchiwa (single-stick fan), walrus ivory, signed Tomochika, cracked, Japanese, late 19th century, 4 3/4 in. high. **$325-$500**

Model of a geisha holding a lantern, her kimono engraved with cranes and stained brown, Japanese, Taisho period, 10 in. high. **$1,800-$2,200**

Model of Hotei seated against treasure sack and holding an uchiwa, signed Gyokumin, Japanese, Meiji period, 8 1/4 in. high. **$400-$575**

Model of an Immortal holding a fly whisk, the ivory a mellow honey shade, Chinese, Ming Dynasty, 8 in. high. **$2,000-$3,000**

Model of Kuan Yin standing on a lotus-and-wave base and holding a vase, age cracks, Chinese, late 19th century, 13 1/2 in. high. **$900-$1,200**

Model of Liu-hai (an Immortal) with a toad on his shoulder, flowing robe, scroll under left arm, cracked, replaced foot, Chinese, 17th century, 7 1/4 in. high. **$1,200-$1,500**

Model of a phoenix on rock-work, the details picked out in colors and black, cracked, Chinese, circa 1920, 8 1/2 in. high. **$500-$700**

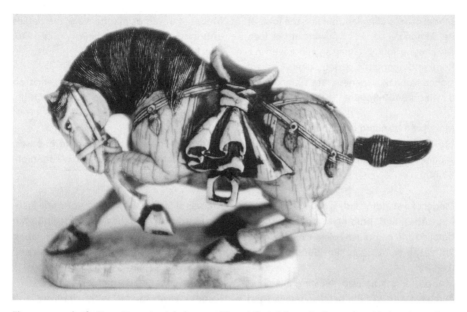

Figure, carved, of a Tang Dynasty-style horse with saddle, bridle and stirrups, hand painted, excellent condition, 5 1/8 in. by 3 1/2 in. by 2 in. **$900**

Model of a smiling Immortal wearing flowing robes with wide sleeves, right arm and left leg raised, cracked, extremities damaged, Chinese, 17th century, 7 in. high. **$700-$1,000**

Model of an Immortal carrying a ruyi sceptre, age cracks, the patina a soft yellow, Chinese, Ming Dynasty, 7 in. high. **$1,200-$1,600**

Model of an Immortal with a long beard, chipped foot, Chinese, 18th century, 5 1/2 in. high. **$750-$1,000**

Model of a monkey trainer (called a "Sarumawashi") seated on a bench holding a small bowl of rice, a monkey at his side, the details stained brown, signed Muneharu, Japanese, late 19th century, 5 in. high. **$400-$600**

Model of a rat seated on Daikoku's sack, Japanese, late Meiji period, 5 in. long. **$525-$675**

Model of a Samurai holding a fan and leaning on his katana, a wakezashi tucked beneath his obi, engraved and stained details, Japanese, late Meiji/early Taisho period, 7 1/4 in. high. **$1,000-$1,500**

Model of Shou Lao holding a gnarled staff from which a gourd is suspended, age cracks, Chinese, 17th century, 7 in. high. **$1,400-$1,800**

Model of a skeleton pulling at a woman's kimono, marine ivory, Japanese, Meiji period, 6 in. high. **$700-$1,200**

Model of a standing lady holding the folds of her kimono, a basket of flowers at her feet, the kimono lightly stained and engraved in a floral and geometric pattern, digits broken, signed Nobuaki, Japanese, late 19th century, 8 in. high. **$400-$600**

Model of a standing lady, Shibayama details on her kimono in a motif of flowers, Japanese, circa 1885, 9 in. high. **$2,000-$3,000**

Model of a standing lady wearing long flowing robes and holding a teapot, finely detailed and painted in colors, Chinese, early 20th century, 10 1/2 in. high. **$900-$1,200**

Model of a standing lady wearing a kimono engraved with wisteria, her hair detailed and stained black, she holds a peony blossom, signed Isshin, Japanese, late 19th century, 8 1/4 in. high. **$775-$985**

Model of a street vendor holding a pole over his shoulder, drums and baskets suspended from the pole, engraved details stained brown, small pieces missing from the baskets, signed Eishin, Japanese, late 19th century, 7 1/2 in. high. **$500-$700**

Model of a sumo wrestler with his arms by his side; he wears an elaborate kesho-mawashi (the ceremonial apron worn by sumo wrestlers during their "dohyo-iri" or ring-entering ceremony), signed Ryusui, Japanese, Taisho period, 8 1/2 in. high. **$975-$1,400**

Model of a woman holding a floral spray, finely painted in colors, Chinese, early 20th century, 10 3/4 in. high. **$900-$1,200**

Model of a young girl holding her hagoita (battledore), her kimono carved with peony blossoms, Japanese, late Meiji period, 6 1/2 in. high. **$1,000-$1,500**

Model of a warrior, marine ivory, the details engraved and stained, Japanese, circa 1910, 6 in. high. **$300-$500**

Models: an Emperor and Empress, each on horseback, Chinese, 20th century, 13 in. high. **$1,500-$2,200**

Models of phoenix on rock-work bases, Chinese, early 20th century, 5 1/2 in. high, pair. **$750-$1,000**

Models of Shou Lao, mirror images, one leaning left, the other to the right, each with a fan and gnarled staff and long flowing robes, age cracks on each, Chinese, 19th century, 12 in. high, pair. **$1,000-$1,500**

Needle case carved with dragons and clouds, Chinese, early 19th century, 6 1/2 in. long. **$125-$200**

Plaques carved as a cross-section of a gourd, with 18 Lohan carved in relief (nine on each plaque), details in polychrome, Chinese, 19th century, 7 in. wide, pair. **$900-$1,200**

Plaques carved and pierced with crabs, frogs, fish, and seashells, Chinese, circa 1900, 8 1/2 in. long, pair. **$1,200-$1,800**

Plaques deeply carved with figures, mountains, and pavilions, polychrome highlights, Chinese, late 19th century, 12 in. wide, pair. **$800-$1,200**

Plaque painted with Kuan Yin holding a flower, details executed in famille rose, plaque set into a panel for display, Chinese, 18th century, size of wood panel 10 in. by 6 in. **$600-$800**

Puzzle ball and stand, 20 concentric balls carved with various designs, floral exterior, floral base, Chinese, early 20th century, exterior ball 5 in. diameter. **$1,000-$1,500**

Seal surmounted by a Buddhistic lion, Chinese, circa 1900, 3 1/2 in. high. **$200-$300**

Table screen carved in relief with a kingfisher perched on a flowering branch, the reverse with figures in a mountainscape, Chinese, 20th century, 7 in. high. **$350-$500**

Table screen with Shibayama and lacquered panels featuring birds on flowering branches, some inlay missing, Japanese, circa 1900, 12 1/2 in. high. **$1,500-$2,500**

Takarabune (treasure ship) with the Seven Gods of Good Luck on deck, the wood stand carved as breaking waves, some attributes missing, cracks, Japanese, early 20th century, 19 in. by 18 1/2 in. **$2,500-$3,500**

Takarabune with the Seven Gods of Good Luck on deck, stained and engraved details, Japanese, circa 1925, 15 in. long. **$1,500-$2,000**

Tea caddy, rectangular, densely carved with scenes of scholars, boats, pavilions, and trees, the edges carved as bamboo, sliding top, cracked, Chinese, mid-19th century, 3 3/4 in. wide. **$1,000-$1,500**

Tusk carved in high relief with two dragons and clouds, the eyes inlaid with horn, Japanese, Meiji period, 32 1/4 in. long. **$3,600-$4,200**

Tusk heavily carved with figures and pavilions, Chinese, 19th century, 35 in. long. $2,500-$3,500

Tusk vases inlaid in Shibayama with birds, insects, trees, and flowers; silver rims, fitted wood bases, some losses to inlay, Japanese, late 19th century, 11 in. high, pair. **$2,000-$3,000**

Tusk vases, Shibayama with lacquer, takamakie, tortoiseshell, and mother-of-pearl, designs of branches, birds, and flowers, cracked, losses to inlay, Japanese, circa 1900, 14 in. high, pair. **$5,000-$7,000**

Vases, tusk on wood stand, carved in low relief with insects and foliage, Japanese, early Meiji period, 15 1/2 in. high, pair. **$2,200-$3,200**

Vase carved with four vertical ribs, age cracks, Chinese, 18th century, 4 in. high. **$400-$600**

Vases, ovoid, carved with 18 Lohan, each delicately painted in colors, loose ring handles, Chinese, early 19th century, 3 3/4 in. high, pair. **$900-$1,200**

Vase and cover carved and pierced with four panels of landscapes, Buddhistic lion and loose ring handles, Buddhistic lion finial, Chinese, early 20th century, 12 1/2 in. high. **$1,200-$1,500**

Vases, trumpet-shaped necks, applied foliage handles, the bodies carved with panels of Lohan, both damaged, Chinese, circa 1900, 7 3/4 in. high, pair. **$450-$600**

Wrist rests carved in low relief as sections of bamboo, the underside with high-relief landscapes, Chinese, 19th century, 10 in. long. **$500-$750**

Shell

Shell, abalone, mounted on three silver ball feet, the shell inlaid with three silver characters reading health, happiness, and long life, Chinese, circa 1910, 7 in. by 8 in. **$500-$700**

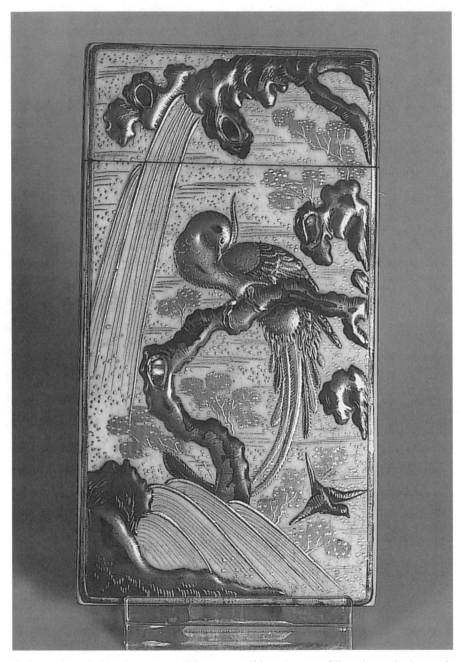

Card case decorated in a lacquer and Shibayama motif featuring waterfalls and a perched peacock, Japanese, late 19th century, 4 3/4 in. high. **$1,500-$2,000**

Japanese Pottery and Porcelain Marks

Kiyen factory

Akahada/Kishiro maker

Akahada

Sampei Gashu maker

Kashiu Mimpei maker

Kashiu Sampei maker

Cho maker

Eizan maker

Kichi maker

Kashiu Mimpei maker

Yoskiage

Good Fortune/Long Life

Good Fortune

Good Fortune

Hibarabayashi maker

Japanese Pottery & Porcelain

JAPANESE CERAMICS

Arita

A Japanese feudal lord brought a troupe of Korean potters to Japan in the late 16th century. In 1616, the potters discovered superior white porcelain stone at Izumiyama (Izumi Mountain) near Arita. The height of Arita production was reached about 1690, though pieces known as Arita ware (or Imari-Arita) continue to be made today.

Blue and white transfer charger of blue-white porcelain, measuring 12 1/4 in. across and 1 3/4 in. high, dating to the mid-19th century. The charger is decorated with a transfer pattern of a central roundel of a basket of flowers in early 19th century Chinese style, complemented by three fan-shaped floral reserves of peonies alternating with three separate peonies in an overall pattern of plum or cherry blossoms, all done in underglaze blue. The reverse shows spur marks and a four-character mark in a double square in underglaze blue. There are floral sprays around the undersurface rim. The charger has one old, sealed age crack measuring approximately 1/2 in. and one restored 1/8 in. rim chip. **$285**

Ash pot, square form, blue, Indian red, green, gilt, and colors, supported on four legs, two panels, Shishi and cash symbols, Japanese, circa 1800. **$700-$900**
COURTESY OF RICHARD A. BOWSER

Censer in the form of a treasure ship (tarak-abune) with a deck that can be lifted off, the back of the sail with perforated openings in the form of cash, polychrome and gilt, Japanese, late 18th century, 8 in. long. **$1,200-$1,600**
PRIVATE COLLECTION

Model of a monkey, white biscuit, Japanese, early 19th century, 4 in. high. **$700-$950**

Dish, Kakiemon style and palette, central roundel of phoenix on rock-work with flowers, the rim with rocks, pine, plum, and bamboo, late 17th century, 8 in. diameter. **$1,500-$2,000**

Dish, underglaze blue with scrolling floral motif, 19th century, 5 in. diameter. **$50-$75**

Dish, fish-shaped, Arita or Imari blue and white, measuring 9 in. by 1 1/2 in. The dish has a Chinese zuanshu (seal script) mark on the base but it is Japanese and dates to the 20th century. Fine original condition. **$135**

Dishes, blue and white, each painted with three fish, floral scroll on the reverse, 18th century, 8 1/2 in. diameter, pair. **$1,500-$2,000**

Ewer, underglaze blue and white, three square panels, two with foliage and figure, the other with herons on plum branches, the neck with a band of stylized flower heads, loop handle, minor chips, late 17th century, 9 in. high. **$1,200-$1,600**

Jar and cover, underglaze blue and white, ovoid form with a motif of phoenix and flowering trees with formal borders, the cover restored, late 17th century, 20 in. high. **$1,500-$2,500**

Jar and cover, octagonal ovoid form, underglaze blue and white, the motif consisting of flowers and rock-work beneath formal bands, restoration to cover and rim, late 17th century, 25 1/4 in. high. **$3,500-$5,000**

Kendi, ribbed globular body with underglaze foliate branches, the neck and everted rim similarly decorated, early 18th century, 8 in. high. **$700-$1,000**

Joss-stick holder in colors and gilt, Japanese, late 18th/early 19th century, 3 in. long. $500-$700

Model of a leaping carp, iron red, underglaze blue and gilt, fin restored, 18th century, 4 3/4 in. high. **$600-$800**

Model of a seated tiger, white biscuit, naturalistic detail, late Edo period, 5 in. high. **$900-$1,200**

Model of a sleeping cat, red, black, and gilt, the tail curled to one side, late 19th century, 7 in. long. **$300-$500**

Vase and cover, ovoid, underglaze blue and white, panels of kiku (chrysanthemums) bordered by cloud bands, the cover similarly decorated and surmounted by a tear-shaped finial, early 18th century, 19 in. high. **$1,500-$2,200**

Vase, blue and white Arita, measuring approximately 9 in. in height, decorated in raised panels of figures, dating to the early-to-mid 20th century. Two opposite side panels have raised figures of a geisha and a samurai. The other panels are decorated in underglaze blue floral and vine patterns. The flared, square mouth tapers to a high waist, flowing into a tapered square body. **$175**

Model of a puppy, white biscuit, black pupils, Japanese, late Edo period, 3 in. high. $1,000-$1,500

Vases, beaker form, gosai with motif of dragons and flowers, raised ribs and animal-head ears, archaic style, one with minor repair, late 18th century, 10 in. high, pair. **$600-$800**

Wine pot and cover, underglaze blue and white, a continuous band of chrysanthemum flower heads, loop handle, rim and spout with karakusa (scroll), knob finial, late 18th century, 7 1/2 in. high. **$700-$900**

Banko Wares

For many years, the name Banko has been abused and misunderstood, which in turn has led to great confusion. Collectors and dealers alike have incorrectly used the term Banko in conjunction with references to Korean wares, Poo ware, and combinations thereof, in an effort to describe the Sumida Gawa wares attributed to Inoue Ryosai (see Sumida Gawa Wares, which follows). Because of the misuse of terminology, Banko wares were almost entirely neglected by the collecting community. Today, however, Banko wares are highly collectible.

Rozan (Numanami Gozaemon), also known as Numanami Shigenaga, was the first Banko. Born in Ise Province (now called Mie Prefecture), about 1718, he was a wealthy merchant and amateur potter. He used two seals on his wares, Banko (meaning 10,000 or enduring) and Fueki (eternal or unchanging).

Numanami Gozaemon produced wares in the styles of Ninsei and Kenzan. He also produced wares styled after Korean prototypes, Kochi wares, along with his original formulas. Around 1787, word of this potter's accomplishments reached the capital. Shogun Inyenari was so impressed with these reports that he summoned Numanami Gozaemon to the capital and made him an "official" potter.

During his stay at the capital, Banko was able to study new methods and soon became skilled at using the techniques developed by the Chinese. Among his reproductions or copies were those styled after Ming Dynasty red and green (Wan Li style), famille verte, famille rose, and Delft wares.

The original Banko died at the end of the 18th century, and if not for a mere accident, collectors might not even be aware of his work today. Mori Yesetsu (Banko II), born in 1808, was originally a wood carver and bric-a-brac dealer with some degree of skill in the art of the potter. In 1830, he accidentally found the original Banko formulas, which contained descriptions of methods for the manufacture and application of enamels. As it was not uncommon for Japanese marks and seals to be copied, bartered, and/or forged, Mori Yesetsu was able to purchase the recipes and seals (both Banko and Fueki) from the grandson of Banko I.

The wares produced by Mori Yesetsu and his brother, Yohei (who adopted the Fueki seal), were somewhat different from those of the original

Banko. Mori Yesetsu was inventive and quite creative. Rather than using molds in the manner of his peers, he reversed the process by pressing the clay against the exterior of the mold. With this new method, the wares retained the design on the interior as well as the exterior of the piece. Another result is that the potter's finger marks appear on many forms of the later Banko wares.

For the most part, the paste of these creations was thin and translucent, yet quite strong. From two to as many as 12 molds, all having movable and interchangeable parts (basically made of wood), were used to produce many cleverly molded pieces.

In general, each type of Banko ware has distinguishing characteristics. Among the most easily recognizable varieties are marbleized wares, gray wares, tapestry wares, white wares, and brown wares. The marbleized wares are brown and white, with the density of the hues depending upon the ratio of white to brown clay. They are usually quite thin and bear evidence of the potter's finger marks, especially on lids and rims. Gray wares vary in consistency of paste. The early pieces seem quite thick, whereas later pieces are generally thin. Often one finds gray wares with enameled and/or sprigged-on ornamentation, or with stenciled motifs and Chinese-style glazing. Tapestry wares were made of various pale-colored clays, including green, white, cream, gray, brown, and blue. The clay was rolled out to a very thin consistency, pressed together, and then rolled out again and again. Several of these variously colored rolls were slipped together (in and out) and the composite package of clay was then sliced. In turn, the slices were slipped in and out to form the desired patterns and delineations of color. Tapestry wares are thin and translucent and glazed on the interior. They feel gritty to the touch, much like the texture of a blackboard.

Movable handles are peculiar to Banko wares, as are knobs that pivot in their sockets; these were used on teapots, sake pots, and pieces with finials. Motifs found on Banko wares can be incised, impressed, enameled, molded in relief, or applied in relief, and they can be used singularly or in combinations.

Banko II's wares were quite popular in the Japanese domestic market. Before long, numerous potters such as Shibata and Shitomei Sohei were copying his style, including some pieces hand-turned on the potter's wheel.

For the most part, these potters produced wares in the district of Yokkahchi. Generally, all the potters who produced wares styled after those of Mori Yesetsu used either a Banko or Fueki mark, either alone or in combination with their own marks and seals.

In the West, the first important recognition of Banko wares came during the 1878 Paris Exhibition, where more than 15 producers of Banko wares participated.

Bowl with monkeys around the rim, the interior with a crackle glaze, the monkeys' garb in colors, Japanese, circa 1910, 7 3/4 in. diameter. **$700-$950**

Censer in the form of Hotei's sack with Hotei and child in low relief, primary colors, Japanese, circa 1900, 3 in. diameter. **$300-$400**

Left: Candlestick in the form of an iris with applied iris and leaves, shades of green and lavender, Japanese, circa 1890. $200-$300. Right: Vase, one of a pair, gray ware with basketweave motif and applied branches, colors and gilt, Japanese, circa 1880, 3 1/2 in. high. **$400-$600**
COURTESY OF RICHARD A. BOWSER

Bowl, marbleized, round, decorated with flowers, butterflies, and insects, late 19th century, 6 1/2 in. diameter. **$700-$900**

Censer in the form of a house, the roof perforated, circa 1910, 4 3/4 in. high. **$275-$350**

Group of monkeys: Hear, See, and Speak No Evil, circa 1920, 3 in. high. **$150-$185**

Group of monkeys: Hear, See, and Speak No Evil, circa 1920, 5 1/2 in. high. **$300-$400**

Group of monkeys: Hear, See, and Speak No Evil, 6 1/2 in. high. **$400-$500**

Group of monkeys, one holding a broom, circa 1915, 7 in. wide. **$350-$475**

Group of monkeys grasping for a fish, circa 1915, 6 1/2 in. wide. **$400-$500**

Humidor, marble and white glaze with no masks in low relief, 6 1/2 in. high, circa 1920. **$450-$600**

Humidor, a contorted face, gray ware, 6 in. high, circa 1920. **$450-$600**

Nodder, a child carrying a fan, circa 1920, 4 1/2 in. high. **$400-$600**

Nodder, a monkey reading a book, circa 1910, 5 in. high. **$300-$500**

Plate, gray ware, the clay in basketweave form, late 19th century, 7 in. diameter. **$375-$500**

Teapot, four military generals in relief, Taisho period. **$300-$400**

Teapot, gray with enameled motifs of 100 Treasures in relief, reed handle and tea strainer, circa 1900. **$375-$500**

Two monkeys, each holding a vase, Japanese, circa 1910, 3 in. high, each. **$200-$300**

Teapot (with strainer) in the form of Ebisu holding a fish, gray ware with colored enamels, Taisho period, 6 in. by 7 in. **$275-$375**

Teapot in the form of a cat, the head as the lid, the raised paw as the spout, gray ware with dainty enameled flowers, circa 1915. **$400-$500**

Teapot in the form of a duck, woven reed handle, circa 1915. **$300-$400**

Teapot, glazed white in imitation of Chinese blanc de chine, applied lotus, late 19th century. **$400-$500**

Teapot, gray ware in the form of a house, the roof as the lid, applied flowers, branches, and birds, reed handle, circa 1910. **$350-$450**

Teapot, white ware with applied flowers in low relief, the flowers in pastel hues, Japanese, late 19th century, 7 in. high. **$300-$400**

Teapot in the form of a goat, gray ware with enameled flowers, circa 1920. **$375-$475**

Vase, gray ware, motif of enameled crustaceans, impressed Banko seal, circa 1875, 8 in. high. **$650-$800**

Marbleized teapot in shades of brown, Japanese, 3 1/2 in. high, circa 1900. **$300-$400**

Teapot in the form of a quail, gray ware with colors and gilt highlights, insect finial, Japanese, circa 1900. **$375-$450**

Teapot, gray ware with the Three Wise Monkeys in low relief, the teapot in the form of a pumpkin, deep green the primary color, Japanese, circa 1919. **$350-$475**

Vase, gray ware, in the form of a Japanese lantern, painted green at the top and bottom, red body, naturalistically enameled motif of running rabbits, 8 1/2 in. high, circa 1900. **$350-$500**

Vase, gray ware, painted green in a basket-weave pattern with a cat and mouse motif, late Meiji period, 6 1/2 in. high. **$275-$375**

Vase, brown ware, with an enameled motif of flowers, late 19th century, 6 in. high. **$450-$650**

Wall pocket, gray ware enameled in colors and gilt, in the form of Daikoku with sack and mallet, Taisho period, 7 in. by 5 in. by 2 in. **$200-$275**

Wall pocket in the form of Hotei (the god of contentment and happiness), gray ware painted green, yellow, and red, Taisho period, 7 1/2 in. by 4 1/2 in. by 2 in. **$200-$275**

Wall pocket, gray ware in the form of a hawk perched on a branch, Taisho period, 4 1/4 in. by 8 1/4 in. **$300-$375**

Wall pocket in the form of a woman with a green basket on her back, early Showa period, 9 1/2 in. high. **$125-$175**

Vase in brown tapestry with applied flowers in low relief, polychrome and gilt, impressed Banko mark in base, circa 1900, 6 in. high. **$350-$500**

Vase with a scenic motif in relief, ring handles, beige and brown, Japanese, circa 1930, 7 in. high. **$100-$150**

Vase, gray ware, one panel with monkey (in low relief) retrieving fruit, the reverse with cranes in relief among grasses, polychrome and gilt highlights, Japanese, circa 1880, 8 in. high. **$650-$950**

Fukagawa

Although the Fukagawa family has been engaged in the production of porcelain since about 1650, the wares produced from the Meiji period into the early 20th century–when Japanese porcelains were first being exported to the West–are of special interest to collectors.

In 1876, the head of the family, Fukagawa Ezaiemon, established a ceramic society called Koransha (the company of the fragrant orchid). The markings used on the wares of this company included an orchid spray and leaves. Several members of the society left in 1880 to form new companies, leaving Koransha with the Fukagawa family. In 1894, Chuji Fukagawa, the head of the company at the time, adopted a new trademark, or backstamp: Mt. Fuji. When Fukagawa Porcelain was appointed purveyor to the Imperial Household in 1910, the company became the representative of Japan's chinaware society.

The Fukagawa company has always produced wares of the highest quality, but collectors tend to concentrate on those with the Imari palette and on those judged representative of the arts and crafts movement (studio ceramics).

Jardinière, globular, ribbed with motif of peony and sparrow in shaped reserves, blue, red, and gilt, base marked Fukagawa sei, late 19th century, 14 in. diameter. **$800-$1,200**

Jardinière, globular, painted in blue, red, yellow, and gilt with continuous tree peony, the base marked Fukagawa sei, late 19th century, 15 1/2 in. diameter. **$600-$900**

Plate, Imari palette, ribbed, fluted, and scalloped, paneled motif of flowers, trees, and maple leaves, center with a kiku (chrysanthemum) spray, Koransha orchid spray mark, early Meiji period, 10 in. diameter. **$900-$1,200**

Spittoon, cherry blossom mouth and plum blossom interior, the upper band with dragon and pearl, the vertical bands with plum and diapers, Mt. Fuji mark, circa 1905, 10 1/2 in. high. **$2,000-$2,750**

Vases, pair, matte brown background decorated in a bird and floral motif with overglaze enamels, measuring 6 1/2 in. high by 5 in. at their widest, dating to between 1875 and 1883. The vases have expertly rendered designs of Ho-o birds (a mythological bird of Chinese origin, which resembles a phoenix), flowers, a tree, and auspicious fungus in multicolor enamels. Each vase has the red orchid mark of the Koransha, the Company of the Scented Orchid. Fine original condition with some rubbing of the gold on the rims. **$300**

Vase, bulbous with short neck, birds on branches, Mt. Fuji mark, circa 1915, 6 in. high. **$200-$300**

Vase, colors and gilt with courtiers holding fans, the shoulder and foot with stylized phoenix, Fukagawa in red characters, 16 in. high. **$1,200-$1,500**

Kogo (incense box) in the form of a Shishi decorated with mon in blue, red, and gilt, the base and interior with an orchid-spray mark, Japanese, early Meiji period, 2 1/2 in. high. **$500-$700**

Punch bowl with the dragon and cloud motif, the base with an orchid-spray mark, gilt highlights, Japanese, late 19th century, circa 1885, 16 1/2 in. diameter. **$1,000-$1,500**

Vase with café au lait (coffee hue) ground and mon, various chrysanthemum forms in colors and gilt, orchid-spray mark on base, Japanese, early Meiji period, 4 in. high. **$750-$975**

Vase, iron red, blue, and gilt with a band of cranes and waves below a lappet border; the neck with ruyi bands, late 19th century, 23 in. high. **$1,500-$2,000**

Vase, motif of fish and blossoming plum trees, Mt. Fuji mark, circa 1910, 6 7/8 in. high. **$300-$500**

Vases, pair, each with misty forest scenes in underglaze blue and gilt above and below floral bands, Meiji period, 10 in. high. **$900-$1,200**

Vases, ribbed, ovoid with flared necks, panels of cranes, pheonix, and prunus, circa 1890, 12 in. high, pair. **$1,500-$2,200**

Vase with motif of irises in red, blue, and gilt, the base with an orchid-spray mark, Japanese, early Meiji period, 8 in. high. **$500-$750**

Vases, ovoid with inward-curving rims painted with panels of cranes amongst pine and bamboo reserved on a ground of kiku mon (chrysanthemum crest) and scrolling foliage, red, blue, and gilt, Koransha mark, 19th century, 25 in. high, pair. **$7,000-$10,000**

Hirado

Hirado Island is located off the northwest coast of Kyushu, Japan. It was on this island, in the mid-18th century, that the renowned Hirado porcelains were introduced. Although the daimyo (feudal lord) of Hirado, Matsura Shizunobu, had brought over Korean potters at the end of the 16th century, production of fine quality porcelains was not initiated there until about 1750. At that time, a fine clay (used in combination with other materials) had just been discovered. The resulting porcelain was excellent for its glaze and modeling.

Like other Japanese daimyo, the Lord of Hirado financially supported the production of ceramic wares. Prior to the Meiji restoration (1868), Hirado porcelain wares were produced for the sole use and discretion of the daimyo.

Regulations were enacted forbidding the sale of Hirado porcelains. The wares were used as presentation pieces, given to the Court of the Tokugawa and to other daimyo and noblemen. Among these pieces, the ones produced during the late 18th and early 19th centuries are considered the best Hirado porcelains. Still, the collecting community has shown great interest in later Hirado wares, many of which were uniquely and exquisitely modeled.

The paste of Hirado wares is white (milky) and free of grit, which is sometimes found in the paste of other varieties of Imari. The glaze is lustrous and almost void of the kind of granulation present in the glaze of other Imari porcelains.

Hirado wares produced in white were so cleverly modeled that any addition of color would have distracted from the overall artistry of the object. Other pieces were done with a single shade known as Hirado blue. Hirado blue is a soft, delicate color that was used to enhance and enrich motifs such as landscapes, floral sketches, and karako (children) at play. The blue was applied to the surface of an article once it had reached the biscuit stage of firing. Hirado blue is not as smudged or runny in appearance as that found in other Imari.

Prices for Hirado porcelain vary from dealer to dealer, as is the case with just about all forms of Orientalia, and are dependent upon profit margins and so on. However, like many other areas of Orientalia, Hirado continues to progress steadily in terms of both prices and appeal to collectors.

Bottle with underglaze blue motif of birds perched on branches, Japanese, late Meiji period, circa 1900, 13 1/2 in. high. **$900-$1,200**

Bottle/vase, globular body with phoenix and a leafy branch, the long neck with inverted stiff-leaf border, late Meiji/early Taisho period, 12 in. high. **$1,500-$2,000**

Box and cover in the form of a seashell, the shell finial with a pearl inside, blue, brown iron oxide, and white, motifs of crustaceans and shells, late Edo period, 5 in. diameter. **$1,000-$1,500**

Box and cover, underglaze blue and white in the form of a rat on a melon, chipped, late Edo period, 4 1/2 in. high. **$600-$800**

Candlesticks, underglaze blue and white, each modeled as a karako (child) holding a branch, petal rim, damages to both, late Meiji period, 5 in. high, pair. **$400-$600**

Censer, globular, underglaze blue and white, pierced lid, the body with plants and karako, early Meiji period, 3 in. high. **$600-$800**

Cup, the center with a basket-weave band, the top band with a continuous landscape, late Meiji period, 4 1/2 in. high. **$700-$900**

Ewer, underglaze blue and white, a seated karako with a dog in his arms, the dog's head forming the spout, the cover modeled as a hat, circa 1910, 7 3/4 in. high. **$350-$500**

Ewer, brown and cobalt blue in the form of a Hotei (the god of contentment and happiness) and treasure sack, a late 19th century copy of an 18th century specimen, 8 in. long. **$500-$700**

Bottle, globular with an elongated neck, underglaze blue and white with karako (children), the neck with ruyi sceptre below stiff leaves, late Edo period, 8 in. high. **$1,000-$1,500**

Bowl and cover modeled as a seashell and decorated with small shells in low relief, iron oxide and underglaze blue, late 18th century, 5 in. wide. **$1,000-$1,500**

Group, Shishi (fanciful dog or lion, five in all) clambering over one another, underglaze blue and white, chips to tails and ears, late 19th century, 7 3/8 in. **$600-$900**

Jar and cover, conch shell with applied barnacles and seashells, brown and underglaze blue, 6 in. diameter, 19th century. **$900-$1,200**

Joss-stick holder in the form of a rabbit, cash-shaped opening at the top, repair to one toe, early 19th century, 6 in. high. **$1,000-$1,500**

Model of a cockerel, the tail feathers arched upwards, white ware, 19th century, 6 1/2 in. high. **$600-$800**

Model of a puppy, white glaze, bow tied around his neck, late 19th century, 4 1/2 in. long. **$700-$900**

Model of a Shishi (fanciful dog or lion) in underglaze blue and white, late 19th century, 5 in. high. **$350-$550**

Model of a recumbent tiger, white glaze, 19th century, 7 1/2 in. long. **$650-$800**

Teapot, brown and underglaze blue with stippled ground, white flower heads and foliage, late 19th century, 5 1/2 in. high. **$300-$500**

Vase, ovoid, high shoulder, flared mouth, incised plum-branch motif, all white, Meiji period, 12 1/2 in. high. **$800-$1,200**

Vase, applied tripod dragon feet, the globular body decorated with a blue cloud pattern, damaged, circa 1910. **$300-$500**

Vase, globular, underglaze blue dragon motif and a dragon in relief around the neck, the dragon's spikes broken, circa 1900, 7 1/2 in. high. **$300-$400**

Bucket with underglaze blue motifs of birds above breaking waves, 7 in. high, Japanese, early Meiji period. **$500-$700**

Left: Dragon upon waves, all white, Japanese, late Edo period. **$750-$950**. Right: Hirado carp, all white glaze, Japanese, early Meiji period. **$500-$700**

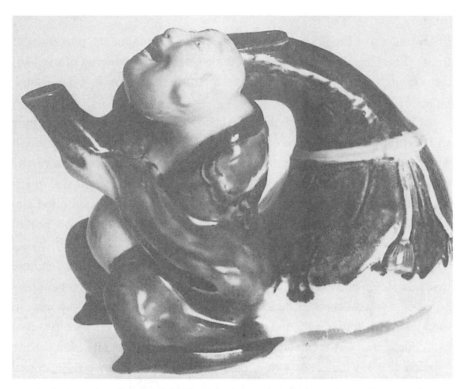

Ewer in the form of Hotei and sack in gos (blue), brown iron oxide and white, 18th century. **$2,500-$3,500**

Model of Hotei and sack, underglaze blue and white, Japanese, late Edo period, 2 in. by 1 1/2 in. **$900-$1,200**

Imari

Imari refers to a broad group of ceramic wares named for the port town of Imari. These ceramics have been produced since the early part of the 17th century in Hizen province (Saga prefecture), northern Kyushu Island, Japan.

The first Imari wares (shoki Imari) show the Korean influence in style and decoration. The basic decorations were executed in underglaze blue and white. Overglaze polychrome decorations were not developed until the middle of the 17th century. At that time, Dutch traders brought vast quantities of ko Imari (early Imari) to Europe, where it was greatly admired and sought after. It was so successful that it cut into the Chinese export porcelain market, thus forcing the Chinese to produce Imari.

There are distinguishable variances between Japanese and Chinese Imari. Japanese porcelain is heavier. Its glaze is thicker and may contain pinholes. It may also show evidence of spur marks (caused by the supports in the kiln). The blue hues found on Japanese Imari are darker than those of its Chinese counterpart, and are often characterized as "runny." Unlike the Chinese Imari, which used a thin, coral red, Japanese Imari was decorated with thick, opaque Indian red. Certain varieties of Japanese Imari can even have lacquered motifs.

Color categories of Japanese Imari include sometsuke, decorated in underglaze blue and white; nishikide, decorated with patterned polychrome designs; gosai, generally not more than five colors; and sansai, decorated in three colors. The descriptions following give further details on popular types of Imari.

Barber's bowl, iron red, underglaze blue, and gilt with flowering shrubs, the everted rim with kiri (a type of tree, also called paulownia) and phoenix, late 17th century, 10 3/4 in. diameter. **$750-$1,050**

Bottle, Three Friends motif, Kakiemon style, 18th century, 12 7/8 in. high. **$1,650-$2,175**

Bottle/vase, long neck with butterfly mon and floral patterns in iron red, underglaze blue, and gilt, circa 1870, 10 in. high. **$300-$400**

Bowl, Indian red, blue, and gilt, scalloped rim, four reserves on the interior and exterior, divided by panels of diapers, the center with a vase filled with flowers, Japanese, early 19th century, 9 in. diameter. **$700-$950.**

COURTESY OF LEON AND TONI ANDORS

Bowl with leafy motif, outer rim decorated with rust-colored textured design, early 20th century, 12 in. by 2 1/2 in. **$175**

Bowls, design-matched pair, measuring 6 1/4 in. by 2 1/2 in. and 4 1/4 in. by 1 in. in size, dating to the early 20th century. The bowls have waterfront landscape designs in underglaze blue, accented by red and gold enamels. The artist has signed the pieces with a seal in red and gold on the front. Each bowl bears a Fuku, or happiness and good luck mark, in underglaze blue on the base, which is typical of this period of Imari (from the region of Arita, named after the port, where it was shipped for export). The larger bowl has a 1/8 in. smooth chip from the foot rim that dates to their manufacture. Otherwise, the bowls are in fine original condition. *$120*

Bowl, sansai, scholar's table, chest, and mon with floral, scroll, and bat motifs, circa 1830, 6 in. diameter. **$700-$900**

Bowl, sansai, the motif with a center medallion of phoenix and paulownia, 16 petals forming the contour, the interior with radiating bands of mon diapers, crane, and florals, which are repeated on the exterior, the foot decorated with X's and O's, circa 1775, 7 3/4 in. diameter. **$3,500-$4,500**

Bowl in an elongated, foliate rim design, measuring 6 1/2 in. by 5 in. by 1 1/2 in., dating to the mid-to-late 19th century. The bowl is decorated in overglaze enamels with thick, red leaves and a tree and bird, using the palette consistent with early 19th century painters. The cream crackle glaze is consistent with the period. The origami crane, fan, and flowers on the sides are Buddhist symbols. The base bears a Fuku, or happiness-good luck mark. Excellent, original condition with no damage and only minimal wear. **$125**

Bowl, gosai, scalloped with a central medallion of pomegranates and foliage in underglaze blue and gilt, a band of blossoms and leaves form the contour, wide band of six panels with reserves, pseudo Ming mark, circa 1800, 8 in. diameter. **$750-$900**

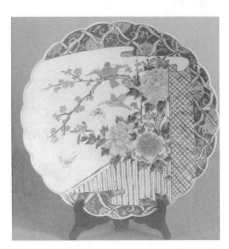

Charger, Indian red ground with cranes in gosu (blue), white, black, and gilt, Japanese, late Edo period, 18 in. diameter. **$1,200-$1,600**

Charger with scalloped rim; red, blue, yellow, green, aubergine, and gilt, Japanese, late 19th century, 18 in. diameter. **$550-$800**

Bowl, sansai, fluted, ribbed, and scalloped, a motif of florals and phoenix, circa 1800, 6 in. diameter. **$700-$900**

Bowl, gosai, a center medallion with a torri (gate) in a waterscape, the border divided into three reserves, each featuring waves and carp, circa 1860, 6 in. diameter. **$375-$500**

Footed bowl measuring 4 1/2 in. by 2 3/4 in., dating to the late Edo or early Meiji Eras. The bowl is decorated in kinrande style (gold decoration on red background) with alternating floral medallions. The high foot shows an X and O pattern in underglaze blue. The base is unmarked, consistent with earlier Imari pieces. The gold on the rim is worn and a small (1/4 in.) rim chip has been filled with a gold lacquer technique. The bowl could have been used either as a tea bowl or a food dish during the tea ceremony. **$100**

Censer, square with canted corners, four panels with shrubs and flowers on a diaper ground, a pierced wood cover added later, pseudo Cheng Hua mark, late Edo period, 7 in. square. **$1,200-$1,600**

Charger measuring 16 in. in diameter, dating to the late 19th or early 20th century. The center is decorated with a wave design in underglaze blue. It is surrounded by alternating panels of flowers in the typical Imari palette. The reverse has three underglaze blue designs. There are no marks. Minor surface wear from use. **$430**

Charger, gosai, mum and leaf motif with six alternating bands of tree and veranda with beehive and bird, raised enamels, the reverse with leaf and scroll in an underglaze blue, circa 1870, 12 in. diameter. **$1,700-$2,200**

Charger, sansai, shell-shaped, fluted, ribbed, and scalloped, the motif featuring kame and garden, the reverse with blue scrolls, circa 1885, 13 in. diameter. **$900-$1,200**

Charger, gosai, phoenix and six varied floral cartouches, impressed Katkana mark, circa 1925-34, 12 1/2 in. diameter. **$200-$300**

Left: Imari figure with musical instrument in blue, red, green, and gilt, circa 1920, 6 in. high. **$100-$150.** Right: Imari figure with fan, her kimono in gilt, blue, and red, Japanese, circa 1890, 3 1/2 in. high. **$350-$550**

Pitcher, vertical diapers in colors and gilt, Japanese, late 19th century, 8 in. high. **$400-$500**

Charger, gosai, fluted, ribbed, and scalloped, three sprays of peony and foliage in the center, three phoenix cartouches divided by three bands of kiku (chrysanthemum) and mon (family crest), the reverse with red and underglaze blue rhinocerous horn and coin patterns, circa 1870, 12 1/4 in. diameter. **$1,800-$2,500**

Charger, sansai, fluted, scalloped, and moderately ribbed, flower/phoenix and two alternating mon overall, circa 1850, 14 in. diameter. **$1,000-$1,500**

Charger, sansai and gilt, the central roundel containing peonies and bamboo branches, the rim with shaped panels filled with phoenix on a cherry branch, Shishi (fanciful dog or lion), and Buddhistic emblems, chipped, crack in base, Genroku period, 22 in. diameter. **$2,500-$3,500**

Charger, blue and white, a village scene, Meiji period, 22 in. diameter. **$2,000-$2,500**

Dishes, set of five, decorated in Kakiemon style with floral designs in underglaze blue and overglaze green, red, and black enamels, measuring approximately 4 1/2 in. in diameter, dating to the Edo period, or late 18th or early 19th centuries. The dishes have scalloped edges and are all in excellent condition with no damage or repairs. **$750**

Dish, sansai, persimmon center medallion, motif of fruit, foliage, and scrolls, circa 1850, 7 1/2 in. diameter. **$175-$225**

Dish, sansai, the pattern featuring pine and a four-petaled leaf with six alternating mon and floral bands, underglaze blue scrolls on the reverse, circa 1880, 6 1/4 in. diameter. **$150-$225**

Plate, hand-painted with rich blue, rust-red, green, and gold, with center decoration of flowers in a vase, rim chips, 8 1/2 in. diameter. **$75**

Dish, sansai, fish form with mon and floral motif, Meiji period, 4 1/4 in. diameter. **$300-$500**

Dish, sansai, fish form with floral motif and gilt highlights, Meiji period, 15 in. diameter. **$700-$1,100**

Dish, sansai, in the form of a boat, the stern with a notch, the exterior ornamented with waves, the interior with floral motifs and diapers, Meiji period, 12 in. by 7 1/4 in. **$800-$1,200**

Model of chonin (meaning "civilian" or "villager") holding a fan, his undergarments iron red and gilt, his kimono black, 7 in. high. **$900-$1,200**

Model of a bijin ("beautiful woman," sometimes a prostitute) holding a scroll, her kimono decorated with florals in red, blue, and gilt, circa 1890, 16 in. high. **$900-$1,200**

Model of a bijin ("beautiful woman," sometimes a prostitute) playing a biwa, gosai, her kimono decorated in floral patterns, circa 1910, 6 in. high. **$300-$500**

Model of a bijin ("beautiful woman," sometimes a prostitute) seated and playing with a cat, mounted as a lamp, circa 1920, 5 in. high. **$125-$185**

Plate, sansai, slightly scalloped, the center with a flower vase and low table, floral border with landscape cartouche, five spur marks on the base, late 18th century, 11 in. diameter. **$3,000-$4,000**

Plate, sansai, scenic landscape center medallion with six panels of mon and garden views, the reverse with underglaze blue scrolls, circa 1880, 8 1/4 in. diameter. **$300-$400**

Plate, gosai, scalloped rim, the center with a dragon medallion, three large leaf cartouches and overall motifs of cherry trees, the reverse with underglaze blue and red cash and ginger, circa 1800, 8 1/2 in. diameter. **$700-$900**

Plate, sansai, fluted and scalloped, three-leaf pattern with reserve of Kotobuki (congratulations) and diaper mon, the reverse with underglaze blue treasure bags, circa 1800, 8 1/2 in. diameter. **$900-$1,200**

Plate, sansai, fluted, ribbed, and scalloped with floral medallion in the center and 12 radiating bands of varied floral motifs, circa 1830, 8 1/2 in. diameter. **$900-$1,200**

Plate, gosai, fluted, ribbed, and scalloped; the center medallion surrounded by radiating bands of florals and paulownia, the reverse with underglaze blue pearl and ginger, circa 1860, 9 1/2 in. diameter. **$300-$425**

Plate, gosai, motif of fungus and scrolls on the reverse, the center with a flower vase, the border with sages in landscapes, circa 1850, 8 1/2 in. diameter. **$300-$400**

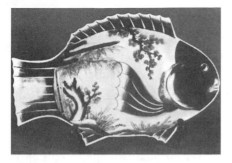

Plate, fish-shaped, celadon, blue, and white, Japanese, circa 1875, 11 in. diameter. $500-$750

Plate, gosai, hexagonal, the center with a floral cartouche, the border with alternating bands of flowers and birds, scrolls and cash on the reverse in underglaze blue, circa 1880, 11 in. diameter. **$850-$1,200**

Plate, octagonal, the motif featuring clouds, insects, and flower baskets, circa 1800, 7 1/2 in. by 9 1/4 in. **$1,000-$1,500**

Plates in the form of abalone shells, blue and celadon with gilt highlights, the motif of pine and plum with diapers, the plates molded in low relief, circa 1875, 8 1/2 in. by 9 1/2 in., pair. **$500-$600**

Plates, sansai, shell-shaped, fluted, ribbed, and scalloped, phoenix and tree pattern in Chinese style, circa 1875, 9 in. diameter, pair. **$350-$475**

Platter, oval, fluted, ribbed, and scalloped, the motif including waves, cranes, pine, and kame (turtle) diapers with kiku (chrysanthemum), the reverse with cash and scroll motifs and moon year characters in underglaze blue, circa 1850, 9 1/2 in. by 12 1/2 in. **$700-$900**

Platter, oval, a band of shells and medallions of scholar's utensils on the rim, the center with wisteria and toys that have wheels in the form of the wheel of life, late Edo period, 13 in. wide. **$600-$900**

Saucers, sansai, petal-shaped, slightly ribbed, dragon medallion surrounded by six formal cartouches, circa 1850, 5 in. diameter, set of six. **$1,000-$1,500**

Tokkuri (sake bottle), sansai, rectangular with canted shoulders, short neck, dragon and vines, body crack, late 17th century, 7 in. high. **$700-$900**

Tokkuri (sake bottle), rectangular, angled shoulders, short neck, panels of cranes, red, blue, and gilt, late 18th century, 7 1/4 in. high. **$1,200-$1,600**

Umbrella/cane stand, sansai, the upper and lower bands with underglaze blue flowers, the center with flowering branches and fence-work, stenciled patterns, circa 1910, 24 in. high. **$800-$1,200**

Umbrella/cane stand, underglaze blue and white with overall floral motifs, stenciled patterns, circa 1910, 24 in. high. **$400-$600**

Vases, sansai, fluted, ribbed, and scalloped with overall floral reserves, circa 1860, 8 in. high, pair. **$1,200-$1,500**

Bottle vase, measuring 15 in. in height and 6 in. in diameter at the base, dating to the 18th or 19th century. Decorated in underglaze deep blue enamels and overglaze reds in a floral pattern. The vase has a slight tilt if viewed from one side. The base is unmarked, as is characteristic of earlier pieces. Fine original condition. **$350**

Cabinet vase measuring 3 1/2 in. high and 2 in. at its widest, dating to the early 1800s. **$45**

Kakiemon

Kakiemon is a name synonymous with the line of potters who worked at the Nangawa kiln near Arita (a district in Hizen, which was the center for porcelain manufacture). It is also the name given the superb porcelain, motifs, and palette produced by this line of potters during the 18th, 19th, and 20th centuries.

Sakaida Kizaemon (Kakiemon I), circa 1596-1666, was among the first potters to produce porcelain in Japan. He is also acknowledged as the producer of the first overglaze enamels used on Japanese porcelain. During the Kwanei era (1624-1644), he was a student of Takahara Goroshichi, a Korean potter known for his underglaze blue decorations. Goroshichi and Kizaemon worked together at Shoten-ji temple, a Buddhist monastery where the latter had taken refuge because of the political turmoil of the times. There they produced porcelain wares with blue and white motifs.

At the same time, Kizaemon began experimenting with methods that could enable him to produce colored enamel glazes. In the process he used techniques learned from the formulas given to him by a friend named Tokuemon. Tokuemon, an Arita merchant, had been in Hagasaki (approximately 60 miles from Arita) while a Chinese ship was in the harbor, and had bought formulas unknown in Japan from a Chinese potter traveling on the ship. After much experimentation, Kizaemon was successful in producing a red ornamentation (like the color of persimmon), which he presented to the head of the Nabeshima clan in the form of a decoration for an okimono for tokonoma (an object for display purposes in an alcove). The lord of Nabeshima was so struck by the new glaze that he changed Kizaemon's name to Kakiemon (derived from the Japanese kaki, which means persimmon).

The earliest Kakiemon polychrome porcelain wares were made from clay obtained from Izumi yama, in Hizen province. This clay was of the highest quality, and the porcelain was thin. The glaze was white, and the clarity of the polychrome enamels added further richness to the wares. Motifs were simple and naturalistic, quite the opposite of the busy patterns one associates with Imari. They never included diapers or geometric motifs, and generally either two-thirds or one-fourth of a given article was left undecorated.

From the end of the 17th century, Kakiemon wares had a more lustrous glaze and richer motifs, which did include geometrics in addition to traditional styles.

The Kakiemon palette includes blue (blue-black, blue-gray, and blue-green); iron red (light); yellow; black; and aubergine (eggplant purple). Occasionally gilt has been added. Also note that some early wares have a brown or brownish-red edge.

Bottle, the motif of a phoenix in colors, the reverse with sparse cloud forms in colors, Japanese, early 18th century, 13 1/2 in. high. **$4,000-$6,000**

Bottle/vase with a motif of cherry and peony blossoms, 18th century, 9 in. high. **$1,800-$2,500**

Bowl, exterior divided into 10 panels alternating with ladies and blossoms, brown rim, star crack in base, circa 1700, 8 1/2 in. diameter. **$2,500-$3,500**

Bowl, lobed form, Three Friends (pine, plum, and bamboo) motif on the interior, exterior with peony sprays in colors, brown-edged rim, chipped, 18th century, 7 in. diameter. **$3,000-$4,000**

Bowl, oval, typical palette with a band of dragons bordered by waves, exterior with flower heads, late 18th century, 8 3/4 in. long. **$1,200-$1,800**

Bottle, hexagonal with a tail neck, underglaze blue, iron red, green, and yellow with pine, prunus, and bamboo amidst rocks, chip and hairline, late 17th century, 10 3/4 in. high. **$7,000-$9,000**

Bowl, pierced-ring rim, Kakiemon palette, motif of morning glory against a trellis, hairline and rim chip, late 17th century, 6 1/2 in. diameter. **$2,000-$3,000**

Bowl, Kakiemon style, painted colors and gilt with phoenix and clouds, the exterior with butterflies and flowering branches, late 19th century, 9 1/2 in. diameter. **$400-$600**

Bowl, everted, brown-edged rim, the interior with two birds above pine and prunus and banded hedges within a floral band in colors and gilt, late 17th century, 5 1/2 in. diameter. **$1,500-$2,200**

Bowls, kiku (chrysanthemum) form, typical palette, courtesans amongst flowering plum, the well of each with a stylized floral motif, 19th century, 6 1/2 in. diameter, pair. **$800-$1,200**

Censer, hexagonal, three ball feet, iron red, green, yellow, aubergine, and blue, two birds above prunus and rocks, no cover, late 17th/early 18th century, 5 1/4 in. high. **$7,000-$9,000**

Dish, lobed, foliate with two floral sprays, a bird perched on a branch, a Shishi (fanciful dog or lion), and a moth, rim chips, late 17th century, 9 3/4 in. diameter. **$2,000-$3,000**

Kendi, globular with short spout, tall neck, everted rim, blue, red, and green motif of flowers and foliage, spout damaged, no stopper, late 17th century, 8 in. high. **$3,500-$5,000**

Censer with copper lid, the motif in colors, Japanese, circa 1720, 4 in. high. **$6,000-$8,000**

Dish, porcelain, Kakiemon style, the base marked Occupied Japan, 7 in. diameter. **$100-$150**

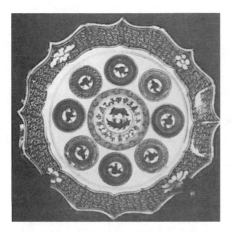

Plate, zodiac, underglaze blue and white, Year of the Horse, brown edge, Japanese, circa 1726, 8 in. diameter. **$2,000-$3,000**

Mizusashi (water jar), underglaze blue and white with flowering peony and rock-work on the body and lid, 18th century, 8 in. high. **$2,000-$3,000**

Saucer dish, foliate rim, underglaze blue, iron red and colors with gilt, two birds amongst rocks, the reverse with a band of plum blossom, brown-edged rim, circa 1700, 11 in. diameter. **$2,500 $3,500**

Saucer dish, green, blue, red, black, and gilt with Three Friends motif, rim chips and hairlines, late 18th century, 4 1/2 in. diameter. **$700-$900**

Teapot and cover, typical palette, continuous band of plum blossoms and grasses, karakusa (scroll design) on spout and handle, kiku (chrysanthemum) knob finial, finial restored, end of the 17th century, 5 3/4 in. long. **$700-$900**

Vase, ovoid, painted with prunus trees and chrysanthemum among rock-work, circa 1800, 10 in. high. **$2,500-$3,500**

Plate from a set of Japanese Kakiemon foliate dinnerware, made circa 1700, decorated with stylized flowers and roosters, plate measures 8 3/4 in. diameter, part of an 81-piece set that includes cups, saucers, covered bowls, and assorted serving pieces. $25,000/set

Kutani

Baluster jar, covered, porcelain, from the late Edo period name of the area where it was originally produced, measuring 14 in. high and 8 in. in diameter, dating to the 20th century. The jar has a circular band of lohans and dragons painted in multiple overglaze enamel colors with gilt accents. The cover, shoulder, and base have scroll and flower designs done in the typical Kutani red. The base bears a green and black Kutani mark similar to those found on "ko," or old Kutani. However, this looks like an early-to-mid 20th century piece. Fine original condition. **$400**

Bottle/vase painted with shaped, scattered reserve filled with figures and landscapes, circa 1910, 11 in. high. **$350-$500**

Bowl, the interior painted with a bird beside a flowering plant, clouds on exterior, Yoshidaya, early 19th century, 4 1/2 in. high. **$1,000-$1,500**

Bowl, called a "chawan", measuring approximately 4 1/2 in. by 3 in., dating to the early-to-mid 20th century. The bowl is decorated on the outside in overglaze enamels in typical Kutani colors with three reserves, one featuring two gentlemen, the others showing landscapes. The upper and inner rims have brick red diapers with gold accents. The bowl bears a Kutani place mark in red on the base. Excellent condition. **$100**

Bowl, underglaze blue in a floral motif, 17th century, 8 1/2 in. diameter. **$300-$500**

Bowl and cover, the domed cover with a section of bamboo forming the finial, painted red-orange and gold with shaped panels of courtiers seated on horseback with attendants, the bowl with panels of birds and branches, white interior, marked Dai Nihon Kutani, circa 1890, 10 1/2 in. diameter. **$300-$450**

Censer, measuring 3 in. by 3 in., dating to the early 20th century. The earthenware body of the censer stands on three feet. The typical red/brown surface glaze is decorated with landscape design done in muted, old-style colors. The base bears both the kanji for Kutani and the artist's signature. The latter indicates that this was a more valued piece, being worthy of the artist's name. Minor wear to the top with some gilt rubbing. **$125**

Censer, the domed, pierced cover with a Shishi (fanciful dog or lion) finial, the body with a dragon chasing the pearl above waves, colors and gilt, marked Fuku on base, late 19th century, 6 in. high. **$250-$350**

Censer, three short legs, the body with orange and gilt foliage, the lid missing, marked Fuku, 1 in. high, circa 1900. **$300-$400**

Censer modeled as a Shishi (fanciful dog or lion), the head forming a pierced cover, orange and gilt, marked Kutani, circa 1900, 4 1/2 in. high. **$175-$250**

Charger, the central motif of six cranes flying over a beach above minogame (tortoises) on rocks, the red sun rising in the horizon within a floral border, Taisho period, 18 in. diameter. **$900-$1,200**

Chopstick rest, double gourd with an orange cord, Meiji period, 3 in. long. **$100-$150**

Dish decorated in red and gilt with shaped panels of flowers, cockerel, and hen, the base marked Kutani; late 19th century, 14 in. diameter. **$600-$900**

Dish, the well with the Seven Gods of Good Luck in a woodland setting, the border with flowers and scrolls, red and gilt, circa 1880, 14 in. diameter. **$900-$1,200**

Figure of a bijin ("beautiful woman," sometimes a prostitute), polychrome and gilt, circa 1920, 12 in. high. **$200-$300**

Tray, two open-leaf-form handles, scalloped rim, motif of hawk perched on branch above breaking waves, red-orange and gilt, Japanese, late 19th century, 16 in. diameter. **$750-$950**

Vase with applied foliage and toad, the body decorated with insects, white, red-orange, and gilt, Japanese, late 19th century, circa 1885, 4 in. high. **$300-$400**

Figure of Hotei (the god of contentment and happiness, he has a laughing face and a big belly), measuring 7 1/2 in. tall and 5 in. at his widest, dating to circa 1920. The buff body is accented by the artist in both flat and raised enamels. The closed base is marked with the kanji for Kutani. Excellent original condition. **$200**

Figure of a standing Hotei (the god of contentment and happiness) with treasure sack and fan, brown-toned skin, colored attire, impressed Kutani mark on the base, the base with a cheesecloth finish, circa 1935, 8 in. high. **$100-$125**

Figures, Seven Gods of Good Luck, orange, green, brown, and gilt attire, each with an attribute, circa 1925, 3 in. high, set. **$200-$300**

Figure of a hawk perched on a tree stump, naturalistic decoration, late 19th century, 12 in. high. **$300-$400**

Figure of a sleeping cat, gold splashes on the body, a red ribbon collar with gilt bell, Showa period (1926-1989), 10 in. long. **$150-$200**

Plate, iron red and sepia with gilt floral sprays within gilt foliage border, the exterior with a leaf-blade band in iron red, circa 1910, 9 in. diameter. **$200-$300**

Plate, red and gilt with sepia flowers, the exterior with a red diapered band, late Meiji period, 8 in. diameter. **$100-$150**

Plate, red-orange and gilt with fan-shaped panels of women doing various domestic chores, rim restored, marked Kutani, late 19th century, 10 1/2 in. diameter. **$500-$700**

Vase with a panel featuring Kinko on a carp, red-orange and gilt, Japanese, late 19th century, circa 1885, 6 in. high. $500-$700
COURTESY OF RICHARD BOWSER

Sake (or saki) bottle (tokkuri), AO (blue-green palette), rectangular, tall neck, everted rim, green, blue, aubergine, and black with panels of riverscapes and landscapes, Yoshidaya revival, marked Fuku on base, early 19th century, 10 1/2 in. high. **$2,000-$3,000**

Sake bottle (tokkuri), double gourd, AO (blue-green palette) with motif of vines, marked Kutani on the base, circa 1875, 8 1/2 in. high. **$300-$400**

Sake bottle (tokkuri), double gourd with designs of dragon and kirin with clouds, waves, and geometric patterns, Yoshidaya revival, marked Fuku on base, early 19th century, 8 in. high. **$1,200-$1,800**

Sake bottle, pear-shaped, 1000 Faces in red, black, and gilt, circa 1915, 6 in. high. **$200-$300**

Sake cups, set of three, Japanese, measuring 2 in. across and 1 1/4 in. high, dating to the mid-20th century. Each cup is decorated on one side in typical Kutani red, brown, black, and gold overglaze enamels with the figure of Daruma. The obverse bears a poem or inscription written in Kanji in black. The base bears the Nine Mountains Kanji characters for Kutani. Two of the cups have had small rim chips repaired with gold. **$85**

Salt shaker in typical colors, measuring 3 in. by 2 1/2 in., dating to the early 20th century. The shaker is missing its cork and shows some wear on the gilt. The base is signed with the characters for Kutani. **$45**

Teapot, orange and gold with flowering branches, circa 1915, 5 in. diameter. **$125-$175**

Tea set: teapot, covered sugar and creamer, six cups and saucers, and six cake plates, scenic motif featuring Mt. Fuji, marked Kutani, circa 1910. **$275-$350**

Tea set: teapot, open sugar and creamer, six cups and saucers, eggshell porcelain, red-orange and gilt with landscape motif, circa 1910. **$250-$300**

Tea set: teapot, covered sugar and creamer, eight cups and saucers, two serving plates, and eight cake plates, orange and gold with samurai and attendants and a riverscape, marked Dai Nihon Kutani, circa 1910. **$300-$500**

Pair of vases, crane neck, measuring 9 in. high and 4 in. at their greatest width, dating to the Meiji era(1868-1912). The vases are decorated with bird and floral designs using the typical orange-red, brown, and gold Kutani palette. The designs are painted in four double-gourd, scroll, and cherry blossom reserves. These are accented by gold lozenges and circles with scrolling on the necks. The bases are signed by the artist. A 1/4 in. chip of the rim of one vase has been repaired with a gold lacquer technique. **$250**

Vase, "AO" or blue-green palette, ribbed, oviform, tall, slender neck, panels of various diapers, early 19th century, 7 in. high. **$800-$1,200**

Vase, "AO" or blue-green palette, birds flying above peony, marked Fuku on the base, circa 1900, 8 in. high. **$200-$300**

Vase, gourd-shaped, red-orange and gilt motifs of birds perched on flowering branches, circa 1885, 8 1/2 in. high. **$225-$300**

Vase, 1000 Faces pattern, orange, black, and gilt, circa 1900, 6 in. high. **$150-$200**

Vase, oviform, red-orange foliage and blossoms overall with gilt highlights, marked Kutani on the base, circa 1890, 14 in. high. **$600-$800**

Kyoto Ceramics

The early 17th century opened a golden age of ceramic production in what was then Japan's capital city as potters filled the orders of Kyoto's prosperous merchants and courtiers, who demanded high-quality ceramic wares for use in the tea ceremony (called Cha no yu or temae) and for food service. Even in the most ordinary ceramics, Kyoto potters set the standard for style and craftsmanship.

Although the works of certain potters achieved magnificent acclaim, similar characteristics reappear regularly in all ceramics from Kyoto. The works are distinguished by eclecticism, a selective use and sophisticated interpretation of many styles and techniques inspired by objects from other periods and cultures.

And Kyoto's artists were among the first in Japan to master the overglaze enamel decoration closely associated with Kyoto ceramics.

Among the artists whose works are highly sought by collectors of Kyoto ceramics are Ninsei, Kenzan, Hozan, Eiraku, Ogata Kenzan, and Dohachi. In addition, objects made in the style of these artists are desirable, whether they were produced during the time in which the artist lived, or in later periods.

Box and cover in the form of a brocade ball, green, blue, red, and gilt, Ninsei style, early 19th century, 1 1/2 in. high. **$800-$1,200**

Box and cover in the form of a mandarin duck painted in colors and gilt, Ninsei style, early 19th century, 3 7/8 in. long. **$1,000-$1,500**

Box and cover, circular with chrysanthemums overall in gilt, gosu blue, and red on a cream ground, Ninsei seal, 18th century, 2 7/8 in. diameter. **$2,200-$3,200**

Box and cover, circular with red, green, blue, and gilt Buddhistic symbols on a cream ground, inscribed Ninsei on the base, 18th century, 3 1/2 in. diameter. **$3,500-$5,000**

Censer modeled as a Shishi (fanciful dog or lion), its head forming the cover; ochre, blue, and iron oxide details with gilt lacquer repairs, late 18th/early 19th century, 7 1/4 in. high. **$1,200-$1,500**

Censer, pierced and molded with lotus and foliage in pastel hues, the base with a diapered band, Meiji period, chips on rim, 10 1/2 in. high. **$700-$900**

Ash pot, gosu (blue), green, and cream with carved motif of flowers and scrolling foliage, Japanese, late 18th century, 4 1/2 in. high. **$1,500-$2,200**

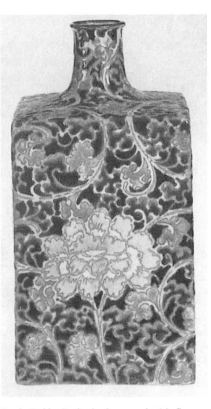

Bottle (tokkuri), the body carved with flowers and foliage in gosu (blue), green and cream, Japanese, 18th century, 10 in. high. **$3,500-$5,500**

Bottle, underglaze motif of Three Friends (pine, plum, and bamboo), Japanese, late 17th early 18th century, 8 in. high. **$2,000-$3,000**

Censer and cover painted with leaf-shaped panels of flowers, signed Kenzan, but actually only done in his style, late 19th century, 2 in. high. **$800-$1,200**

Chaire (tea caddy), globular form, everted rim, mottled brown glaze, ivory lid, the base marked Ninsei, but actually only done in his style, early 19th century. **$600-$900**

Chawan decorated with brown slip, Indian red, and gilt, flowering plum branches; the base marked Kenzan, but actually only done in his style, early 19th century, 3 in. diameter. **$600-$900**

Bowl, the motif of flowers and foliage carried out to the rim, which is cut as buds and blossoming flowers in pale hues and gosu (blue) with gilt highlights, Japanese, 18th century, 10 in. diameter. **$2,500-$3,500**

Chawan, raised ring foot, the gray glaze with plum blossoms in iron red and iron oxide, Kenzan style, early 19th century. **$500-$700**

Figure of Hotei (the god of contentment and happiness) carrying treasure sack and holding a fan, colors and gilt, realistically modeled, late Edo/early Meiji period, 12 in. high. **$1,200-$1,800**

Jar and cover, green, blue, and gold motif of willow trees, Ninsei style, early 19th century, 8 1/4 in. high. **$1,200-$1,800**

Mizusashi (water jar), cylindrical, a variety of open and closed fans in colors and gilt, inverted lid with loop handle signed Gyozan and sealed Cho, late Edo period, 6 in. high. **$1,200-$1,600**

Censer surmounted by a Shishi and tama, the body with flying phoenixes, the entire piece in red-orange and gilt, the base with impressed Eiraku (Hozen) mark, early 19th century, 6 in. high. **$2,000-$2,500**

Censer, open-work lid, the motif including mon and foliage in colors and gilt, the base with a Ninsei impressed mark, Japanese, 5 in. high. **$2,500 $3,500**

Mizusashi (water jar), cylindrical, inverted lid with loop handle, a motif of standing cranes in blue, black, and iron red with gilt highlights, signed Gyozan, late Edo period, 8 in. high. **$1,000-$1,500**

Sake bottle, bulbous, short neck, flowering chrysanthemum and lotus in red, white, green, and gilt on a creamy glaze, early 19th century, 8 1/2 in. high. **$1,000-$1,500**

Sake bottle, cylindrical, short spout, crackled glaze, blue, white, and green motif of camellia sprays, late 18th century, 8 3/8 in. high. **$2,000-$3,000**

Sake bottle, cylindrical with short neck, two lobed-handle bosses, blue, green, and gilt motif of pine trees below a band of scrolling foliage in iron red, late 17th/early 18th century, 6 1/2 in. high. **$2,500-$3,500**

Sake bottle, double gourd, green and blue motif of plum and bamboo, early 19th century, 12 in. high. **$900-$1,200**

Sake bottle, rectangular, short neck, blue overall, each side with a panel filled with a blue mountainscape on a cream ground, chipped on corners, hairline on foot, last half of the 18th century, 6 in. high. **$800-$1,200**

Left: Chaire (tea caddy) with underglaze blue and brown iron oxide motif of the Imperial kiku mon, the base marked Taizan, Japanese, early 19th century. **$800-$1,200.** Right: Matching furo (brazier), the base also impressed with a Taizan mark, 8 in. high. **$1,500-$2,500**

Chaire (tea caddy) with wood lid, the black body decorated with diapers in gilt, red, and blue, base with impressed Ninsei mark, 3 in. high. **$4,000-$5,000**

Vase, modified, elongated pear shape, decorated with flowers and foliage, a diaper band above the colors and gilt, the base marked Taizan, Japanese, circa 1870, 8 in. high. **$500-$700**

Vase, four handles, bright shades of red-orange, blue, colors, and gilt, base marked Kiyomidzu, Japanese, late 19th century, 12 in. high. **$650-$950**

Vase, Japanese Kyo-mizu, or old Kyoto, bottle-shaped, white porcelain, covered with a tan, ray-skin glaze, and decorated in moriage (a special type of raised decoration used on some Japanese pottery) style flowers of pink, white, green, and blue enamels, dating to the Meiji era (1868-1912). The vase measures 9 in. by 3 in. by 5 in. Excellent original condition with no cracks, chips, or repairs. **$300**

Vase, globular, a motif of 100 Treasures in red, blue, and gilt; green and aubergine, 18th century, 11 in. high. **$3,500-$5,000**

Chaire (tea caddy), the base with impressed Ninsei mark, an ivory lid, Japanese, 4 in. high. **$3,000-$5,000**

Chawan, the black ground decorated with butterflies in colors and gilt, Ninsei style, Japanese, late 19th century. **$300-$400**

Chawan decorated with a mandarin duck, Japanese, late Edo/early Meiji period. **$300-$500**

Sake bottle, ribbed, ovoid form, sparsely decorated with pine, plum, and bamboo, late 18th century, 7 3/4 in. high. **$1,500-$2,200**

Sake bottle, squat form, elongated neck, blue mountainscapes on a large, crackled glaze, early 19th century, 8 1/2 in. high. **$600-$800**

Teapot, Japanese earthenware, measuring 3 in. in height by 3 in. across the body, decorated on the lower half with a pebbled, or ray skin, tan glaze accented by a green and white floral moriage (a special type of raised decoration used on some Japanese pottery) enamel design, dating to the early-to-mid 20th century. The spout, handle, and lid are decorated in underglaze blue and white. Typical of Kiyomizu pottery pieces produced in Kyoto. **$80**

Ewer decorated in colors and gilt, the base with a Taizan mark, Japanese, early 19th century. **$750-$1,000**

Mizusashi (water jar) for the tea ceremony, bands of motifs upon a crackled ground decorated in overglaze colors, by Eiraku Hozen, Japanese, early 19th century, 7 in. high. **$3,000-$5,000**

One of a set of mukozuke (set of five), with motifs of maple leaves in colors on a beige-cream ground, each piece signed Kenzan. **$3,000-$5,000**

Vase, four handles, bright shades of red-orange, blue, colors, and gilt, base marked Kiyomidzu, Japanese, late 19th century, 12 in. high. **$650-$950**

Vase, modified, elongated pear shape, decorated with flowers and foliage, a diaper band above in colors and gilt, the base marked Taizan, Japanese, circa 1870, 8 in. high. **$500-$700**

Dohachi

Box and cover modeled as a bird and decorated in blue glazes, seal on the base, early 19th century. **$800-$1,200**

Bowl, a motif of maple leaves in colors, Dohachi seal, early 19th century, 6 in. diameter. **$700-$1,000**

Figure of Okame (a goddess of luck in Japan), kimono in colors and gilt, marked on the base, early 19th century, 6 in. high. **$1,200-$1,650**

Eiraku

Chawan (tea bowl), green-brown glaze, pottery, impressed mark, circa 1870. **$900-$1,200**

Bowl, Chochin (Japanese lantern) style, flowers and Shishi (fanciful dog or lion) with key fret border, late Edo period, impressed mark, 8 in. diameter. **$1,500-$2,200**

Vase, globular, decorated in red-orange with phoenix and butterflies above clouds, porcelain, Eiraku seal, early Meiji period, 7 in. high. **$1,200-$1,800**

Circular box and cover, the overall motif in green and gosu (blue) kiku mon (16 petals), brown iron oxide bands, the interior decorated with wheels of life in colors and gilt, the base with an impressed Ninsei mark, 6 in. diameter. **$3,000-$4,000**

Kenzan

Basket, cherry and hawthorn motif, Kenzan style, late 19th century, 6 in. high. **$250-$350**

Bowl, irregular, shallow form, painted with a bamboo pattern in white slip and under-glaze iron brown, the base signed and dated 1705, 10 in. diameter. **$3,000-$5,000**

Studio bowl made of a pottery base with cream, crackle glaze, and overglaze multicol-or designs of monks in abstract forms, bear-ing the Kenzan signature in overglaze brown, measuring 5 in. by 2 1/4 in., and dat-ing to the 20th century. **$125**

Bowl, motif of bamboo in iron brown and white, signed Kenzan, but actually only done in his style, late 18th century, 11 in. diameter. **$1,000-$1,500**

Bowl, irregular form with a pierced rim, bam-boo and snow motif in white slip and under-glaze iron brown, the base with a white reserve signed Kenzan, early 18th century, 9 in. diameter. **$1,500-$2,000**

Kyoto-ware bowl with floral motifs and cranes above, the rim cut out to simulate flying cranes, brown iron oxide and gosu (blue), the base signed Kenzan, Japanese, 18th century. **$3,000-$5,000**

Sake jar with a tea-dust glaze, decorated in overglaze enamels in moriage (a special type of raised decoration used on some Japanese pottery) style with a samurai and calligraphy, measuring 5 1/4 in. in height and 2 1/2 in. at its widest, signed and consistent with work by Kenzan. A crack in the rim has been repaired with gold lacquer technique. **$150**

Tea bowl (chawan) with white glaze, gosu (blue), and brown iron oxide floral motifs on exterior and interior, signed Kenzan, Japanese, 18th cen-tury. **$3,000-$5,000**

Box in the form of a cloud with a floral motif, the interior decorated with blue and gilt, the base marked Kenzan, Japanese, 18th century, 5 in. wide. **$2,500-$3,500**

"Made in Japan"

Bank in the form of a cat, one paw raised, porcelain, decorated with polychrome flowers, 14 1/2 in. high. **$150-$200**

Dinner set, Seiji ware (celadon) in a pale green with Mt. Fuji in white slip (low relief):

Bread and butter plate, 6 in. diameter. **$10-$20**

Breakfast plate, 8 1/4 in. diameter. **$15-$25**

Butter tub, perforated bottom. **$50-$75**

Creamer and sugar. **$75-$100**

Cream pitcher. **$50-$75**

Cup and saucer (tea). **$15-$25**

Cup and saucer (demitasse). **$25-$35**

Dinner plate, 9 3/4 in. diameter. **$35-$45**

Egg cup. **$20-$30**

Mayonnaise server and spoon, 6 1/2 in. diameter. $**35-$50**

Oval platter, scalloped, 9 1/2 in. wide. $**50-$75**

Oval platter, scalloped, 10 1/2 in. wide. **$60-$80**

Oval platter, scalloped, 15 in. wide. **$75-$100**

Salad bowl, 8 1/2 in. diameter. **$50-$75**

Soup bowl, 7 1/4 in. diameter. **$35-$45**

Tea plate, 7 1/4 in. diameter. **$15-$25**

Teapot (four-cup capacity). **$45-$65**

Teapot with removable strainer (six-cup capacity). **$50-$75**

Tile, 6 1/2 in. diameter. **$25-$50**

Tile, 6 in. square. **$25-$45**

Tray in bamboo basket with open handles, 8 1/2 in. by 14 1/2 in. **$100-$150**

Vegetable dish/cover, round, 10 in. diameter **$25-$45**

Vegetable dish/cover, oval, 10 1/2 in. **$27.50-$40**

Vegetable dish with three feet, round. **$50-$75**

Vegetable dish, oval with three feet, 7 1/4 in. wide. **$35-$45**

Figures, the Seven Gods of Good Luck, porcelain with luster colors and gilt, mounted on a long stand, circa 1930, each figure 7 in. high. **$300-$500**

Flower bowl, nine white swans surrounding the blue, blue luster, 8 in. diameter. **$175-$200**

Phoenix Pattern-Blue and White:

Cereal bowl, 6 in. diameter. **$18-$22**

Cup and saucer (tea). **$10-$15**

Creamer and sugar (loop handle). **$40-$50**

Egg cup. **$15-$20**

Platter, 12 in. wide. **$40-$55**

Platter, pierced handles, 11 in. **$35-$45**

Salad bowl, 7 1/2 in. diameter. **$20-$22.50**

Scalloped bowl, 5 1/2 in. diameter. **$15-$18**

Serving bowl, oval, 10 in. wide. **$45-$55**

Teapot (cozy). **$65-$95**

Teapot, 7 1/2 in. wide. **$40-$55**

Teapot, 9 in. wide. **$50-$60**

Sweetmeat set: seven fan-shaped dishes around a central round dish (each piece with a floral motif), and black lacquer box with matching motif on the cover, 12 in. diameter. **$125-$175**

Tea set: teapot, sugar and creamer, and six cups and saucers, moriage, a floral pattern on a deep green ground, marked Made in Japan (with a plum-blossom trademark), circa 1930. **$150-$175**

Tea set: teapot, covered sugar and creamer, and six cups and saucers, moriage, a landscape motif in autumnal shades, circa 1925. **$100-$200**

Tea set: teapot, sugar and creamer, six cups and saucers, and six cake plates, tan and blue luster. **$100-$125**

A pair of salt and pepper shakers, yellow ground with moriage dragons in gray, blue, and pink, black band at top and base, Japanese, circa 1920. **$10-$15**

Scalloped dish, muted black-gray ground with moriage dragon in gray, blue, and pink, the wicker handle missing, Japanese, circa 1930, 8 in. diameter. **$50-$75**

Porcelain vase with coralene dragon in gold and yellow, Japanese, circa 1925, 6 in. high. $125-$175

Miscellaneous

Bowl, Japanese covered porcelain, measuring 5 in. by 3 1/2 in. with the lid, dating to the late 18th to early 19th centuries. The bowl is decorated on the exterior with rich overglaze enamels and gilding of flowers, birds, and auspicious fungus. Geometric pattern diapers of blue, red, and gold encircle both the bowl rim and lid. The lid has a central floral medallion. The interiors are glazed with white, which has black speckles from the kiln. The glazed base is unmarked. The rim shows minor fritting. There is a very small hairline on the interior glaze of the lid. The bowl has a wooden stand of later manufacture. Fine original condition. **$400**

Pair of food bowls, earthenware, measuring 6 in. by 3 in., covered with a shiny, white glaze and decorated in overglaze iron designs of pine trees, dating to the mid-to-late 20th century. **$75**

Demitasse set with rose red flowers and green foliage, gilt trim, marked Shofu Nagoya, Japanese, circa 1935, service for six. **$125-$150**

COURTESY OF MRS. FLORENCE SIMON

Seto-ware stepped bowl, the body with reticulated floral motifs, the interior of the bowl decorated with carp, all in greens and blues, Japanese, 18th century, 6 in. high. **$4,000-$5,000**

Seto-ware triple gourd bottle with applied tie, brown glazes, lacquer repair at the lip, Japanese, 8 in. high, 18th century. **$900-$1,200**

Pair of soba (noodle) cups, blue and white, dating to the late 19th century. The cups measure 3 1/4 in. by 2 3/4 in. The landscape design on the surface is transfer printed. One has a hairline age crack. **$100**

Kendi of porcelaneous body with a blue-white glaze and underglaze red design of vines, measuring 7 1/2 in. long and 7 in. tall, dating to the Meiji era(1868-1912). The kendi was used as a device for smoking and should not be confused with a ewer for liquids. The kendi is typically a Chinese ceramic piece that was made for the Middle Eastern market. **$250**

Earthenware kendi covered with a sea-green celadon glaze, dating to the early 20th century. The kendi is decorated in underglaze, darker green, free-hand plant and geometric designs, giving it a Korean appearance. It stands approximately 9 in. in height. Fine original condition. **$250**

Sake jug that stands 9 1/2 in. high and measures 7 in. in its greatest diameter. It is circa 1900 Arita, with a typical blue-green tinged white porcelain body decorated under the glaze with a deep cobalt blue in a simple pine tree design. No marks on the base. Mint condition. **$125**

Bizen ewer with applied gourds and foliage in relief, twisted handle, modified double-gourd form, Japanese, early 19th century, 16 in. high. **$750-$950**

Bizen sake bottle, pinched form, with Daikoku in low relief, Japanese, late Edo period, 6 in. high. **$300-$500**

Teapot, porcelain, with rich blue glaze and gilt trim, decorated with mutli-colored medallions and stylized motifs, wire-wrapped metal handle, 1930s, size with handle down, 6 in. by 5 1/4 in. by 5 in. **$75**

Bottle neck pottery vase with a rich celadon wide-crackle glaze, accented by overglaze decorations of a bird and flowers done in brown lacquer with gold and black highlights, measuring 11 in. in height by 3 in. at the base, dating to the late 19th or early 20th century. Minor wear of the lacquer surface but no evidence of cracks, chips, or repairs. **$125**

Tokoname planter with dragon and cloud motif in low relief, Japanese, late Meiji/early Taisho period, 7 in. by 9 in. **$300-$400**

Seto-ware vase with scaleless dragon in high relief, the vase with a flambé glaze, Japanese, circa 1900, 7 in. high. **$300-$500**

COURTESY OF RICHARD A. BOWSER

Double gourd vases, circa early 20th century, matching pair decorated with scenes of birds and flowering cherries in natural settings, the necks with gilded molding, 21 1/2 in. tall, excellent condition, **pair.** **$2,500-$2,750**

Turquoise crane-neck vases measuring 12 in. (height) by 5 in. (waist) by 3 1/2 in. (base), dating to the early 20th century. These vases are done in imitation of the Kang Hsi glazes (named for the emperor who ruled China from 1661 to 1722). The thick glaze has run onto the foot of each vase. The foot rims are rough, showing that they have been cut from the kiln floor. There are some expected glaze bursts. One vase has a linear mark across the back. **$300**

Pottery vase with a fine, cream-white earthenware body, measuring 5 3/4 in. by 3 in., dating to the Meiji or Taisho periods. The vase is covered with a fine crackle, cream glaze and is accentuated by slips of red, blue, and tan that run down from the rim. The artist has used these glazes as clouds to hide an elegant coiled dragon done in raised gold lacquer. The base has underglaze cracks produced during one of the several firings needed to make the piece. They are not through cracks and do not affect the structural integrity. **$150**

Nabeshima

Officially, the first kiln for Nabeshima was set up at Iwayakawachi about 1628. Toward the end of the 17th century, the kiln was moved to Okochiyama. Prior to the Meiji restoration (1868), Nabeshima wares were produced under the patronage of the daimyo of Saga prefecture, Lord Nabeshima. Similar to other wares produced during the Edo period, Nabeshima porcelains were only intended for the use of the daimyo. Nothing less than perfection was acceptable, and only the finest of specimens were used by the daimyo as special presentations and/or gifts. Then, from 1868 on, Nabeshima wares were produced for domestic use and Western export. However, quality and perfection did not decline as quantity increased. Thus, whether late or early, these wares have high market values.

Nabeshima porcelain was produced from the same materials used at other Arita kilns. However, it is much finer than other Arita wares, which sometimes have a coarse and roughly textured paste. Another distinction of Nabeshima wares is that their decorators drew outlines in underglaze blue, then filled in the motif using either broad or fine strokes. Other Arita porcelains have somewhat careless drawings, by comparison, for their enamels were applied prior to the outlining process.

Nabeshima wares, moreover, were enameled with subdued or paler hues, as compared to the more vibrant or brilliant hues found on other Arita porcelains. Among the colors used on polychrome articles are iron red, underglaze blue, yellow, green, and seiji (celadon, which has a green tint). Unlike the slightly raised application of enamels found on other varieties of Arita wares, Nabeshima enamels are flat, becoming one with the glaze.

The motifs found on Nabeshima wares are usually simple, naturalistic, and structurally bold. Designs can cover as little as one-third of the surface of an entire object. Geometric motifs in polychrome enamels were generally used in combination with a monochrome ground to cover the entire surface of an object.

Nabeshima wares are well known for their high foot rim. Generally, bowls and plates have a high foot rim enhanced with an underglaze blue comb pattern. The reverse rims of articles may also be enhanced with repetitive flowers and leaves, or with the cash pattern in underglaze blue.

Dish, underglaze blue and white, two mandarin ducks among water weeds and grasses, comb pattern on the foot, tasseled cash on the reverse, late 19th century, 8 in. diameter. **$500-$700**

Dish, underglaze blue and white, camellias on a pale blue ground, comb pattern on the foot, tasseled cash on the reverse, late Edo period, 7 1/2 in. diameter. **$500-$600**

Dish, underglaze blue and white, chrysanthemums and foliage, comb pattern on the foot, 18th century, 8 1/4 in. diameter. **$800-$1,200**

Dish, underglaze blue and white, everted rim, motif of flowering camellia branch, the reverse with tasseled cash, tapered comb pattern on the foot, 18th century, 8 1/4 in. diameter. **$4,000-$6,000**

Dish, polychrome motif of peonies, comb pattern on the foot, the reverse with tasseled cash, two hairlines, 18th century, 7 3/4 in. diameter. **$1,000-$2,000**

Saucer dish, polychrome motif of wisteria and foliage curling upward, comb pattern on the foot, gold lacquer repairs on the rim, 18th century, 4 1/4 in. diameter. **$2,500-$3,500**

Saucer dish, a motif of plum blossoms, foliage, and peaches in iron red, blue, and green, comb pattern on the foot, three groups of cash on the reverse, late Meiji period, 8 in. diameter. **$600-$750**

Dish decorated with a takarabune (treasure ship) in colors and gilt, comb pattern on foot, early Meiji period, 8 in. diameter. **$600-$800**

Plate decorated in underglaze blue, Japanese, 18th century, 8 in. diameter. **$900-$1,200**

Plate with an underglaze blue motif of a flower basket, Japanese, 18th century, 8 in. diameter. **$1,800-$2,200**
PRIVATE COLLECTION

Plate with high foot decorated with a comb pattern, the motif a copy of an Utamaro print, Japanese, late Meiji/early Taisho period, 8 in. diameter. **$400-$700**

Nippon Era Ceramics

Pottery bowl with purple flambé glaze on the interior and exterior, the base marked Nippon, Japanese, circa 1900, 6 in. diameter. **$175-$200**
COURTESY OF THE VIRGINIA KERESEY COLLECTION

Bowl, open handles, lakeside scene with swans in autumnal hues. **$100-$150**

Bowl, two open handles, windmill scene, 6 1/2 in. diameter. **$100-$125**

Bowl, two open handles, orange and gold border, interior and exterior with ladies standing in a garden. **$125-$175**

Bowl, two reticulated handles, autumnal hues with a lakeside scene and a moose. **$100-$125**

Bowl, cobalt with gilt trim, interior with fan-shaped reserves of seated Rakan (Buddhist disciples), 7 in. diameter. **$100-$150**

Bowl, cobalt and gold with red and pink roses, 8 in. wide. **$175-$225**

Bowl in a woven silver basket with twisted silver handles, pale blue exterior, white interior with small blue flowers, 4 1/2 in. diameter. **$150-$185**

Bowl, red ground, dark blue border, Bird of Paradise motif, 9 1/4 in. diameter. **$150-$185**

Chocolate set: pot (10 1/2 in. high) and six cups and saucers, slip-trailed dragon (moriage), the ground shaded black-gray and pink with blue and pink flames, gray dragon. **$350-$450**

Chocolate set, orange and gilt handles and trim, bijin ("beautiful woman," sometimes a prostitute) amongst cherry trees in a village scene. **$375-$500**

Black pottery box and cover decorated with calligraphy, the base marked Nippon, Japanese, circa 1900, 4 in. diameter. **$100-$150**
COURTESY OF KYLE HUSFLOEN

Dish, the central motif of flower vases in pastel hues, the border with alternating yellow and blue reserves, 9 1/2 in. diameter. **$150-$200**

Baking dish and cover, pottery, bamboo design in brown and green, 6 in. diameter. **$75-$100**

Fruit basket, wicker handle, bamboo motif in green on white porcelain, 7 in. diameter. **$100-$125**

Fruit dish, black ground with flowers and bird perched on a branch in yellow, blue, and pink, a blue border, Chinese-style motif, 7 1/8 in. diameter. **$100-$125**

Fruit dish, black ground with flowers and birds in yellow, blue, and pink with a blue and yellow border, Chinese-style motif, 8 1/2 in. diameter. **$125-$175**

Fruit dish, black ground with flowers and a bird perched on a branch, shades of blue, yellow, and pink, 10 in. diameter. **$175-$220**

Humidor, Rakan (Buddhist disciple), molded in relief, 7 1/2 in. high. **$1,000-$1,500**

Humidor, windmill scene in shades of brown and yellow. **$300-$400**

Jar and cover, moriage dragon motif in shades of gray, 7 in. high. **$250-$350**

Juice set: elephant-form pot and six tumblers, moriage dragon in shades of gray with pink and blue flames. **$300-$400**

Juice set: covered pitcher (9 1/2 in. high) with six tumblers, Satsuma style, diapers in gold and red, the panels with figures of children. **$300-$450**

Nut set: one large bowl (6 in. diameter), small bowls (each 3 in. diameter), scalloped with iris motif. **$100-$150**

Pitcher, cobalt and gold with brilliant red roses, 8 in. high. **$350-$475**

Pitcher, Satsuma style, scalloped foot and rim, diapers in gold and red, two scenic panels with children at play, 7 in. high. **$200-$275**

Plaque, three herons huddled amongst marsh grasses, 8 1/2 in. diameter. **$200-$300**

Plaque, Egyptian scene, two camels and two riders, 10 in. diameter. **$200-$300**

Plaque, oval, two dried salmon in relief, 18 in. wide. **$1,000-$1,500**

Plate, cobalt and gold with red spider mums, 9 in. diameter. **$225-$300**

Plate, moriage, slip-trailed dragon motif in shades of gray, 8 in. diameter. **$100-$150**

Smoking set: humidor, cylindrical cigarette container, match holder, and tray, Egyptian scene with camel and rider. **$500-$600**

Snack set, pale blue with huddled white herons, tray 8 1/2 in. long, service for four. **$200-$300**

Tea set, lotus finial, a motif of pink cherry blossoms and branches, six pieces. **$275-$325**

Tea set: teapot, sugar and creamer, and six cups and saucers, moriage dragon motif in shades of gray. **$200-$300**

Tea set: teapot, sugar and creamer, and six cups and saucers, orange ground with silver dragons, Chinese style. **$250-$325**

Tea set, Satsuma style, motif of Rakan (Buddhist disciples), and Kannon (goddess of mercy), gilt trim, knob finials, service for six. **$225-$350**

Vase, beaker form, black with irises and a band with a continuous lake scene, 10 1/2 in. high. **$200-$275**

Vase, cylindrical, motif in Longwy style, 10 1/2 in. high. **$200-$250**

Vase, green pottery in a woven silver basket, marked Awaji Nippon, 12 in. high. **$125-$175**

Vase, yellow pottery in a woven wicker basket, marked Awaji Nippon (with an impressed trademark of a bird), 14 1/2 in. high. **$200-$250**

Vase, moriage, square form, a motif of plum blossoms and branches with perched birds, dragon and ring handles, biscuit ground, 9 in. high. **$225-$300**

Vase, moriage, dragon motif in shades of gray. **$200-$250**

Vase, moriage, motif of cranes and lotus, 10 in. high. **$200-$300**

Vase, moriage, motif of flowering prunus branches, 10 in. high. **$200-$300**

Vase, moriage, bird perched on a flowering branch, two open handles, 12 in. high. **$200-$300**

Wall pocket, pottery, black with bird (in relief) painted in colors and gold, 12 in. long. **$200-$300**

Noritake (Art Deco)

Ashtray, circular, orange luster, 3 1/2 in. diameter. **$15-$25**

Ashtray, orange luster border, hexagonal, the well with a standing lady, 4 1/4 in. wide. **$75-$100**

Ashtray, flower form, orange luster with a seated nude on the rim, 7 in. wide. **$275-$375**

Box (powder), blue and orange luster with blue bird finial, 4 1/2 in. wide. **$150-$185**

Cake plate, round with two open handles, cobalt and gilt border, the center with a lake scene at dusk, 10 1/2 in. diameter. **$125-$150**

Candlesticks, a lake scene in autumnal hues, 5 1/2 in. high, pair. **$150-$225**

Celery dish, oval with open handles, lake scene in autumnal hues, 12 1/2 in. long. **$50-$100**

Chamber sticks, orange luster, black-rimmed loop handles, 2 1/2 in. high. **$100-$150**

Condiment set: salt and pepper, mustard pot and spoon, toothpick holder, and tray, orange and blue luster with small floral motifs, 5 in. diameter. **$150-$175**

Decanter, primary hues with a Mexican motif, 8 1/2 in. high. **$300-$400**

Dresser doll, bobbed hairdo, cylindrical form, gold luster with red-orange plum blossoms, 5 1/2 in. high. **$275-$325**

Humidor, continuous desert scene in shades of red, 5 1/2 in. high. **$320-$375**

Dish with lemon and flowers in relief, bright orange luster ground, the motif in bright yellows and greens and black, Noritake, Japanese, circa 1925. $100-$150
COURTESY OF MARK FOGEL

Humidor, lake scene in autumnal hues, 4 in. high. **$175-$225**

Inkwell, clown form, primary colors, 4 in. high. **$285-$350**

Luncheon set: four kidney-shaped plates and four cups, gold luster border with a floral motif in primary colors on the plate, a floral motif on the interior of the cups, 7 in. long, each. **$50-$75**

Plaque, autumnal lake scene with waterfowl, 10 in. wide. **$175-$225**

Smoking set: two-handled oval tray, match holder, and cylindrical cigarette container, blue luster with floral sprays, 7 in. long. **$220-$260**

Sweetmeat set: blue and gold luster with six fan-shaped dishes surrounding a circular dish, each with a motif of fruit in primary colors. **$150-$225**

Dish with center handle hand-painted in shades of green and blue, green and gilt rim and handle, base marked Noritake, Japanese, circa 1930, 9 in. diameter. **$100-$125**
COURTESY OF MARK FOGEL

Tea set, orange luster and white with a motif of roses and foliage, service for six. **$275-$350**

Tea set: teapot, sugar and creamer, four cups and saucers, and four cake plates, two shades of orange-luster borders with gold-luster bodies and black bands, knob finials. **$200-$275**

Tea set: teapot, sugar and creamer, six cups and saucers, and six cake plates, deep orange with a pattern of two perched cockatoos. **$300-$400**

Tea set: teapot, sugar and creamer, and six cups and saucers, a desert scene in shades of red. **$225-$325**

Vase, orange luster with geometric bands and stiff-leaf (archaic) motif, 8 1/4 in. high. **$175-$225**

Vase, jack in the pulpit, autumnal lake scene, 7 3/4 in. high. **$225-$325**

Vase, tree-trunk form with a peacock in red, blue, yellow, and green; 5 in. high. **$250-$275**

Wall pocket, blue luster with a motif of a lake scene in autumnal hues, 8 in. high. **$100-$135**

Wall pocket, orange luster below and above a lake scene with swans at sunset, 8 in. high. **$100-$150**

Occupied Japan

Ashtray, interlocking square form, decorated with a bird perched on a flowering branch, orange and gold, base marked Kutani Occupied Japan, 4 in. long. **$55-$85**

Candy dish and cover, circular, Imari palette with motif in red, blue, and gold, 6 1/2 in. diameter. **$100-$125**

Candy dish, magenta lacquer with gold flowers on the lid, 7 in. diameter. **$100-$175**

Figures, Dutch boy and girl, each carrying buckets suspended from strings, blue and white, 4 in. high. **$15-$20**

Figures, mandolin players, attire with lace trim, marked Moriyama, 6 1/2 in. high. **$200-$250**

Figures, Dutch boy and girl, polychrome, 3 1/2 in. high. **$20-$25**

Figures, Thai dancers, polychrome, 5 1/4 in. high. **$45-$65**

Figures, Imari style, male and female dressed in Japanese costumes, polychrome, 6 1/2 in. high. **$200-$300**

Group, a Japanese gentleman with a lady by his side (she appears to be cleaning his ear), Imari palette, 9 in. long. **$250-$300**

Group, a seated bijin ("beautiful woman," sometimes a prostitute) playing with cat, Imari palette, 4 in. high. **$200-$300**

Sake set: a whistling bottle and six cups, white with red dragons. **$75-$100**

Sake set: a whistling bottle and five cups; moriage with gray dragons. **$75-$100**

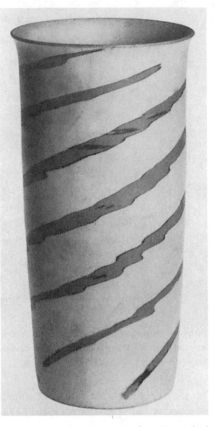

Pottery vase, cylindrical, one of a pair, marked Occupied Japan, 14 in. high. **$100-$175**

Tea set: teapot and five cups, traditional, Imari palette. **$100-$125**

Tea set: teapot, sugar and creamer, six cups and saucers, and six cake plates, hand-painted with bright orange flowers and green foliage, gilt trim. **$100-$175**

Vase, red-over-black rubbed lacquer-over-pottery, decorated with finely executed autumn grasses in raised, flat, and sprinkled gold and silver lacquer techniques, measuring 12 1/2 in. tall, 4 in. across the base, and 8 1/2 in. across the top. Not marked but probably Occupied Japan period (1945-52). In excellent condition with no chips, cracks, damage, or losses. **$300**

Oribe

Oribe ware is named for the famous tea master, Furuta Oribe (1545-1615), who invented the style.

Covered bowls, set of seven, dating to the late 19th or early 20th century. Each bowl measures 4 1/4 in. across and 2 in. high (2 1/2 in. with the covers on). Each piece has a pottery body, a cream glaze, underglaze brown geometric designs, and a splash of lustrous green/blue glaze—all characteristics of Oribe wear. Five are in excellent, original condition. Two of the bowls have had small rim chips repaired using a gold lacquer technique. This technique is used only for pieces to be considered valuable enough to warrant the expense. Fine, rare and original condition. **$300**

Bowl, short foot ring, turned rim, brown slip and green glaze with autumnal flowers and trellis pattern, gold lacquer repair, late 17th/early 18th century, 9 in. diameter. **$2,000-$3,000**

Censer, cream body with a green glaze and brown flower and trellis pattern, late 19th century, 8 3/4 in. high. **$300-$500**

Chawan, fences and plum-blossom design, late Edo period. **$250-$325**

Food dishes, three, made of earthenware and covered with a cream glaze and designs of flowers in overglaze enamels, measuring 6 1/2 in. by 1 1/2 in., dating to the early-to-mid 20th century. Each plate is shaped like a leaf and bears a different floral design in brown, white, and green, similar to the palette seen in Oribe ware. The design is consistent with the Kyoto Kenzan school. The dishes are signed on the reverse in a white cartouche, Kozan, from the Makuzu Kozan studio. Minor rim chips professionally restored. **$300**

Dish, round and scalloped, green glaze with incised cranes and foliage, rim chips, 17th century, 7 in. diameter. **$1,200-$1,800**

Dish for the tea ceremony, made with a piecrust edge and decorated in brown with a mountain and pine trees, dating to the late 19th or early 20th century. The Oribe blue-green glaze runs over one corner. The dish measures 5 1/2 in. by 4 in. by 2 1/2 in. **$100**

Four-lobed dish for the tea ceremony, decorated with a brown thatched roof and tree with a splash of typical Oribe green running to red glaze in a leaf-like design, dating to the early 20th century. The dish measures 6 in. by 5 1/2 in. and has a rough, unsigned base. **$100**

Mukozuke, boat-shaped dishes, loop feet, green and white glaze on a brown ground with interlocking diamond shapes, the exterior with wave patterns, two restored, early Edo period, 7 1/2 in. long, set of five. **$700-$900**

Boat-shaped dish, green and yellow, hand modeled by an expert potter, measuring 10 in. by 5 in. by 2 in., dating to the Meiji era(1868-1912). The yellow and green glaze accents the modeling and wave patterns scribed into the sides. An unusual ceramic piece that has characteristics of Oribe ware in the glaze. This may have been used in the tea ceremony or in ikebana (Japanese flower arrangement). **$300**

Sake jars, pair, measuring 5 1/4 in. in height and 2 1/2 in. at their greatest width, hand potted and shaped from clay coils, then decorated with enamels in typical Oribe style with brown and white fruits and a rich blue/green glaze, signed in a cartouche, Tai Ten Ki Nen. **$400**

Patterned Dinnerware

Tree in the Meadow

This pattern, otherwise known as the Sunset Pattern, is highly collectible (like the Azalea pattern below). Its scenic motif features a house set with a tree in the background. The motif is generally found in autumnal hues, but has been identified in shades of blue and green as well. Values for Tree in the Meadow dinnerware are comparable, for the most part, to the values listed for Azalea.

Azalea

The Azalea pattern contains pink and white azalea blossoms. The blossoms have yellow stamens and red shafts. The foliage is yellow-green with dark green accents between the blossoms. Prices are as follows:

Bouillon (two handles). **$15-$20**

Bouillon. **$20-$25**

Basket. **$100-$185**

Bonbon dish. **$25-$40**

Bowl (two handles). **$15-$20**

Bowl (soup). **$15-$25**

Bread and butter plate. $10-$15

Butter tub with liner. **$35-$45**

Cake plate. **$45-$55**

Celery dish**$100-$125** (Tree in the Meadow, **$30-$45**)

Cheese dish. **$100-$125**

Chocolate cup and saucer. **$20-$25**

Coffee pot. **$400-$500**

Creamer. **$20-$35**

Cup and saucer (demitasse). **$30-$45**

Cup and saucer (tea). **$20-$30**

Dinner plate, 9 3/4 in. diameter. **$20-$30**

Egg cup. **$20-$30**

Four-o'clock-tea cup and saucer. **$25-$35**

Gravy dish. **$40-$55**

Ice cream set (seven pieces). **$220-$250**

Jam jar (with under-plate). **$75-$100**

Lemon plate. **$20-$30**

Luncheon plate. **$20-$30**

Two sets of creamers and sugars in the Azalea pattern. See listing for current values.

Mayonnaise set (three pieces). **$30-$45**

Mustard set (three pieces). **$40-$50**

Nut dish. **$17-$22**

Oatmeal bowl. **$12-$15**

Pickle dish. **$20-$25**

Platter, 12 in. **$40-$50**

Platter, 14 in. **$40-$60**

Platter, 16 in. **$300-$350**

Relish dish (two-handled). **$125-$175**

Salad plate. **$15-$25**

Salt and pepper. **$20-$30** (and up)

Sauce dish or berry bowl. **$10-$15**

Spoon holder. **$45-$55**

Sugar (covered). **$20-$30**

Sugar (open). **$17-$22.50**

Sugar shaker. **$75-$100**

Tea and toast set (one cup and tray). **$20-$25**

Teacup and saucer (breakfast). **$20-$30**

Tobacco jar. **$250-$325**

Vase. **$200-$250**

Vegetable dish (oval or round), covered. **$100-$125**

Vegetable dish, open and divided. **$100-$125**

Raku

A type of hand-formed pottery that originated in Japan in the 16th century, with a soft, lead glaze, the pieces low-fired, characterized by a rough, hand made appearance with exposed patches.

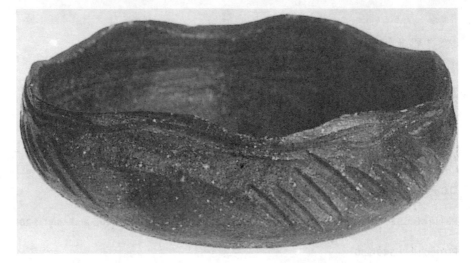

Ash pot with knife-cut motifs, Japanese, 18th century, 7 in. diameter. **$900-$1,200**

Chawan, black glaze stopping short of the foot, chips on the rim and foot, impressed Raku seal, 18th century. **$300-$400**

Chawan, black and brown glaze stopping short of the foot, 18th century, 4 1/2 in. diameter. **$1,800-$2,500**

Chawan, flaring mouth, short ring foot, black glaze, Raku seal, 19th century, 5 7/8 in. diameter. **$600-$900**

Chawan, short ring foot, temmoku glaze, impressed Raku seal, 19th century, 2 1/8 in. high. **$800-$1,200**

Chawan, short ring foot, mottled red glaze, impressed seal (Cho Raku), 19th century, 3 in. high. **$700-$1,000**

Chawan with black glaze and splash of white and green, Japanese, Edo period. **$1,500-$2,000**

Satsuma

The collector/dealer who hears the word Satsuma thinks of a long-admired form of Japanese ceramics in which faience (pottery) is covered with a glaze that produces a beautiful network of crackles and is itself ornamented with polychrome enamels.

Near the end of the Momoyama period (1574-1603), Shimazu Yoshihiro, the daimyo of Satsuma and Osumi provinces, launched an attack against Korea as a prelude to the conquest of the Chinese Empire. Although the Japanese armies had gained some strong victories, after six years of fighting, they were recalled to their homeland by Hideyoshi Toyotomi. Upon returning to Japan in 1598, Shimazu Yoshihiro brought with him approximately 20 families of Korean potters, who settled in Kagoshima and Kushinko. Shortly before the start of the Edo period (1615-1868), these Korean potters were divided into two groups. One group was relocated in Chosa, Osumi province. The second group was resettled in the area around Naeshiragawa, Satsuma province. Reasonably good clay was found in and around these locations, and the potters soon began to practice their craft.

Early productions included articles for use in Cha no yu (the Japanese tea ceremony). Monochromes, flambé glazes, same gusuri (sharkskin glaze), bekko gusuri (tortoiseshell glaze), and shiro gusuri (white glaze) were all popular. Objects were generally small in size and modeled after Korean prototypes. Grandiose objects such as palace vases and urns were, for the most part, products of the Meiji period (1868-1912), and were made for Western export.

It was not until the Kwansei era (1787-1800) that Satsuma wares were decorated in the manner recognized today. The employment of polychrome enamels, including silver and gold, was initiated, with artists using gold under the direction and instruction of Shimazu Narinobu, the daimyo at that time.

Early motifs were simple, elegant, graceful interpretations of nature. They included florals, birds, insects, and animals (both real and mythological), used singularly or in combinations. Shortly before the end of the Edo period (1850-68), figures in the forms of processionals, Rakan (Buddhist disciples), warriors, and so on were incorporated into motifs.

At the London International Exposition in 1862, Satsuma was displayed for the first time in a Western country. This was followed by displays in Paris (1867) and in Vienna (1873), and at the Philadelphia Centennial in 1876. From its first appearance in the West, Satsuma was extremely well received and in overwhelming demand. As a result, the so-called imitation Satsuma wares were created (near the beginning of the Meiji period) to meet the new demand.

Actually, the "imitations" should be classified as Satsuma: For the most part, there is little variation in the quality of the paste, or in the technique and methods of decorating, used to produce these wares. For the layman, in fact, they are hardly distinguishable from the productions of Kagoshima prefecture.

Satsuma was created by individuals whose great technical skills were combined with gracefulness of form and a careful mixture of compounded hues. The endless variety of wares produced attest to their excellence.

Basket, flattened circular form with a motif on each side featuring seated children in colors and gilt, signed Hattori, late Meiji period, 3 in. high. **$175-$225**

Bowl, black matte ground on the interior and exterior with gilt flowers and birds, early Showa period, 8 1/2 in. diameter. **$200-$300**

Bowl decorated with clouds and two dragons on the interior below a lappet border, the exterior with mums, iron red, blue, and gilt, signed Masanobu, circa 1810, 8 in. diameter. **$3,500-$5,000**

Bowl, deep, rounded form with shaped panels filled with women engaged in a variety of domestic pursuits, the panels divided by bands of diapers, colors and gilt, late 19th century, 6 in. diameter. **$400-$600**

Bowl, hexagonal, the motif with mums and butterflies on the interior, the exterior with a band of flower heads at the rim, circa 1930, 6 in. diameter. **$100-$175**

Bowl, the interior with shaped panels filled with bamboo, dragons, plum blossoms, and phoenix on a formal ground, the exterior with phoenix, key pattern, and lappets on the rim, signed Masanobu (with blue Shimazu mon), first quarter of the 19th century, 12 in. diameter. **$4,000-$5,000**

Bowl, the interior with a seated Kannon (goddess of mercy), colors and gilt, the exterior with gilt diapers, late Meiji period, 8 in. diameter. **$400-$500**

Blank decorated in the United States with a motif of pink cockatoos and flowers in shades of pink and fuchsia, circa 1926, 8 in. high. **$300-$500**

Bottle decorated in colors and gilt with floral motif, Japanese, circa 1900, 8 in. high. **$300-$500**

Bowl, lobed rim, roundels of kiku (chrysanthemum) and kiri (a type of tree, also called paulownia) mon (family crest) in blue and gilt on the interior and exterior, signed Shokuzan, early Meiji period, 8 1/2 in. diameter. **$1,000-$1,500**

Bowl, the interior with a peacock on rockwork among blue and salmon-hued peony and flowering prunus, the exterior with rounders, a diaper border, signed Chikusai, Meiji period, 12 1/4 in. diameter. **$700-$950**

Bowl, black matte ground on the interior and exterior with a motif of gilt butterflies overall and a diaper border, chipped, early Showa period, circa 1930, 4 in. diameter. **$100-$150**

Bowl, flower form, decorated with figures in a village scene with a lake, colors and gilt, Taisho period, 5 1/4 in. diameter. **$150-$185**

Bowl in the shape of Mt. Fuji, the interior with samurai on horseback, the exterior with floral rounders and diapers, signed Kinkozan, late Meiji period, 6 1/8 in. wide. **$500-$850**

Left: Covered box decorated in gosu (blue), red, and gilt, Japanese, late Edo period, 4 in. diameter. **$1,500-$2,000**. Right: Covered box with 1000 Butterflies motif in gosu, red, and gilt, late Edo period, 4 in. diameter. **$1,500-$2,000**
COURTESY OF THE EDSON COLLECTION

Left: Box with floral motif in colors and gilt, late Edo/early Meiji period. **$700-$900**. Right: Box and cover with floral motif in gosu (blue), red, and gilt, the interior painted with flowers, late Edo period, 3 3/4 in. diameter. **$1,800-$2,400**

Bowl, square form with canted corners, the interior and exterior in the 1000 Flowers pattern in colors and gilt, signed Yozan, Meiji period, 4 1/4 in. diameter. **$300-$500**

Bowl, the interior with objects for the scholar's table, the rim with lappets, the exterior with chrysanthemum and foliage, iron red, blue, white, and gilt, late Edo period, 5 in. diameter. **$2,000-$3,000**

Censer (sans lid) decorated with floral motifs in colors and gilt, signed Kinkozan, circa 1910, 4 in. diameter. $900-$1,250

COURTESY OF HOWARD AND FLORENCE KASTRINER

Box and cover, fan-shaped, the lid decorated with figures picnicking beneath flowering cherry trees, the sides with diapers, circa 1910, 4 1/2 in. wide. **$500-$600**

Box and cover, hexagonal, the lid with ladies in a garden, colors and gilt, signed Kinkozan, circa 1920, 3 in. wide. **$300-$400**

Box and cover, the lid with sprays of flowers and rock-work in gilt, blue, and colors, the sides with brocade patterns, late Edo period, 6 in. diameter. **$1,200-$1,600**

Box and cover, the lid with a writhing gold dragon, signed Kozan, Meiji period, 3 1/4 in. diameter. **$300-$475**

Box and cover, flower form, the exterior with gold phoenix, the interior with bamboo and prunus, early Meiji period, 3 in. diameter. **$650-$800**

Charger with Kanzan and karako in colors and gilt, late Edo period, Japanese, 15 1/2 in. diameter. $1,000-$1,500

Coffee set made for export, circa 1950s, including pot, creamer, sugar, six cups and six saucers (sets made for internal use have five- or 10-cup sets), decorated with red maple leaves and gilt handles, spouts and rims. **$185/set**

Box and cover in the form of a drum, overall motif of fruit and flowers, colors and gilt, 3 in. diameter, circa 1900. **$350-$550**

Bucket, the body with a continuous landscape and birds in flight, gilt handle and bar, circa 1885, 7 in. high. **$200-$300**

Bucket, the body with blue and lavender morning glories and green foliage, gilt trim, circa 1890, 6 1/2 in. high. **$225-$325**

Buttons, set of four, 1930s vintage, done in a floral design, each measuring 1 in. across. **$85/set**

Censer and cover decorated with panels of warriors and court ladies, the cobalt blue ground with gilt foliate scrolls, signed Kinkozan, late Meiji period, 5 in. high. **$2,000-$2,700**

Censer and cover decorated with figures in a garden, trailing purple and white wisteria and gilt highlights, Meiji period, 6 in. high. **$400-$600**

Censer and cover, the sides with panels of figures including bijin ("beautiful woman," sometimes a prostitute), courtiers, and entertainers (as well as birds) in a landscape, the pierced cover with overall gilt diapers, hairlines, Meiji period, signed Seikozan, 6 in. high. **$2,000-$3,000**

Censer and cover decorated with children playing various games, the pierced cover and ground with 1000 Flowers pattern, restored chips and finial, hairline, signed Yabu Meizan, circa 1910, 3 1/2 in. high. **$2,000-$2,500**

Ewer, motif of Rakan, Kannon, and dragon, gilt and colors, Japanese, 1915-25, 6 1/2 in. high. **$500-$700**

Ewer with cover, decorated in colors and gilt, the base signed Toyosai, late Edo period. **$1,800-$2,700**

Censer and cover, samurai and attendants within diapered patterns in colors and gilt, late 19th century, 8 in. high. **$200-$300**

Censer and cover, the body with panels of foliage and mums, the ground with scattered mon and scrolls, angular handles, mask and tongue legs, Shishi (fanciful dog or lion) finial, gilt, iron red, and blue, rim cracks, signed Masanobu, early 19th century, 9 in. high. **$2,800-$3,700**

Censer and cover, the silver lid pierced with peony, the cylindrical body decorated with foliate rounders on a diaper ground, iron red, gilt, white, black, and turquoise, early 19th century, 4 in. high. **$1,500-$2,000**

Censer and cover, reticulated overall, gilt borders, circa 1910, 4 in. high. **$1,000-$1,500**

Censer and cover, hexagonal, each side with floral lappets in colors and gilt, pierced shakudo, shibuichi, and silver lid, blue mon on the base, late Edo period, 6 in. high. **$3,500-$4,500**

Censer and cover, lozenge form with fan-shaped panels of kiku (chrysanthemum) surrounded by dragons and clouds, a mixed alloy lid, the base with a blue mon, late Edo period, 7 in. high. **$2,000-$3,000**

Censer and cover, the body with 1000 Flowers pattern, replacement lid (pierced wood), signed Yabu Meizan, circa 1900, 3 in. high. **$1,000-$1,500**

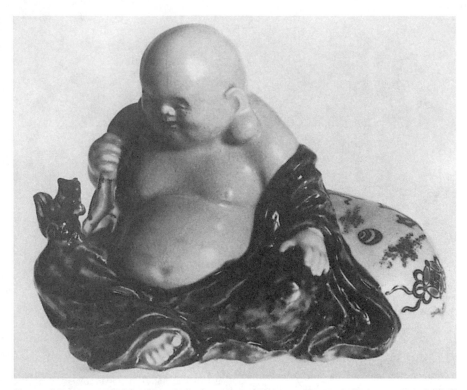

Figure of Hotei, seated with sack, a squirrel perched at his knee, colors and gilt, Japanese, early Meiji period, 6 in. high. **$500-$750**

Chaire (tea caddy) with a continuous scene of children in colors and gilt, 2 1/2 in. high, Meiji period. **$600-$800**

Charger, foliate, colors and gilt, Rakan (Buddhist disciples) and Kannon (goddess of mercy), and their attributes, diapered rim, the halos in raised gilt, circa 1915, 12 in. diameter. **$700-$1,000**

Chawan decorated with fan-shaped panels filled with flowers and foliage, Meiji period. **$300-$500**

Chawan decorated with phoenix and flowers, late Edo/early Meiji period. **$500-$600**

Chawan decorated with fan-shaped panels filled with flowers and foliage in colors and gilt, Meiji period. **$300-$450**

Chawan decorated with phoenix and flowers, late Edo/earty Meiji period. **$500-$600**

Chawan decorated with the Seven Gods of Good Luck and their attributes; iron red, blue, and gilt, with a diapered rim and a lappet band; the base with a blue mon; circa 1860, 4 in. diameter. **$1,000- $1,500**

Cricket cage, the pierced body held by a cloth formation (which is also the handle), painted with fans and flowers, finial missing, late Meiji period, 8 in. high. **$500-$700**

Figure of a dog, Bekko (tortoiseshell) glaze, Japanese, late Edo period, 8 in. high. $3,000-$5,000

COURTESY OF HOWARD AND FLORENCE KASTRINER

Dish, colors and gilt with a large gathering of Rakan (Buddhist disciples), and attendants in a landscape, diaper band around the rim, signed Hododa, Taisho period, 12 in. diameter. **$450-$650**

Dish, kiku (chrysanthemum) form, the diapered petals radiating from a central panel of figures, colors and gilt, circa 1910, 6 1/8 in. diameter. **$800-$1,200**

Dish supported by a monkey at one end and a dog at the other, landscape motif, the dog's neck cracked and restored, signed Kinkozan, late Meiji period, 6 1/2 in. long. **$400-$600**

Dish, the interior with karako playing within a formal band which is bordered by chrysanthemum sprays, signed Meizan, 5 1/4 in. diameter. **$800-$1,200**

Dish, leaf shape with motif of a suzuribako (writing box) in colors and gilt, Meiji period, 9 1/4 in. diameter. **$425-$575**

Dish, colors and gilt with three birds amongst flowers and grasses, floral border, signed Kinkozan, late Meiji period, 8 in. diameter. **$600-$800**

Figure of Hotei (the god of contentment and happiness), dating to the late 19th-early 20th century. The piece measures approximately 7 in. across and 5 in. high. It has a paper tag on the base with eight Japanese names in English from the Surveillance Office, Yoshino Storage Area, and the date: 5 Sept 1953. The figure is very well done with a buff glaze body and moriage (a special type of raised decoration used on some Japanese pottery), multicolor and gilt designs. Fine original condition. **$500**

Figure of a bijin (meaning "beautiful woman," sometimes a prostitute) holding a hand scroll, her robes decorated in clouds motif, colors and gilt, one hand restored, hairlines coming up from the base, late 19th century, 14 1/2 in. high. **$500-$750**

Figure of a seated Daruma, his robe and cowl in iron red, blue, and gilt, and decorated overall in repetitive kiku mon (chrysanthemum crest); mid-19th century, 7 1/2 in. high. **$1,500-$2,500**

Figure of Daikoku holding mallet and standing on a rice bail, his attire in red, blue, white, gilt, black, and turquoise, mid-19th century, 8 in. high. **$2,000-$2,700**

Figure of an elder seated on a tatami mat, colors and gilt, early 20th century, 5 in. wide. **$400-$600**

Figure of a standing elephant, the saddle decorated in blue, iron red, gilt, and colors, circa 1800, 7 in. high. **$3,500-$4,500**

Figure of a standing elephant, brown body with orange, green, and gold saddle, early Showa period, 6 in. high. **$200-$275**

Figure of Hotei (the god of contentment and happiness), his robes in black, green, and gold with phoenix medallions, late Meiji period, 10 1/2 in. high. **$700-$1,000**

Figure of Hotei (the god of contentment and happiness) seated on sack and holding a fan, hands and feet repaired, late Meiji period, 10 1/4 in. high. **$200-$375**

Figure of an Immortal, his patterned robe in colors and gilt, his beard and mustache black; he holds a fan which has been restored; hairlines and chips; Meiji period, 27 1/2 in. high. **$1,200-$1,800**

Figure of Kannon (goddess of mercy), her robes and cowl heavily gilded with repetitive geometric designs, circa 1900, 12 in. high. **$375-$500**

Figure of Kannon (goddess of mercy), her robe and cowl decorated in brown, red, orange, blue, and green with gilt accents, overall floral diapers, circa 1925, 12 in. high. **$200-$300**

Figure of Kannon (goddess of mercy), her loose robes and cowl in colors and gilt, repaired hands, early Showa period, 16 in. high. **$200-$300**

Figure of Kanzan (a wise mountain hermit, also the name of a cherry tree), attire decorated in floral patterns, colors, and gilt, signed Gahokoku, Meiji period, 10 in. high. **$1,000-$1,500**

Jar and cover decorated in green, gosu (blue), red, white, and gilt, bird finial, the lid with a Shishi motif, Japanese, late 18th century, restored, 8 in. high. **$1,200-$1,500**

Figure of Okame (goddess of luck) holding a fan, her robes in colors and gilt with floral motifs, late 19th century, 12 in. high. **$400-$600**

Figure of Rakan (Buddhist disciple) seated on rock-work, his loose-fitting robe decorated in colors and gilt, damaged, early Meiji period, 10 1/4 in. high. **$750-$1,000**

Figure of a Shishi (fanciful dog or lion) with gilt, circular designs, early 19th century, 7 in. high. **$1,200-$1,500**

Figure of a Shishi (fanciful dog or lion) and tama (sacred Buddhist jewel), brown with colors and gilt, Showa period, 7 1/2 in. high. **$100-$125**

Figure of a standing woman, her kimono in colors and gilt with a motif of maple leaves and streams; she holds a fan; early Meiji period, 12 1/2 in. high. **$1,000-$1,500**

Vase antique lamp, vase circa 19th century, the lamp circa early-to-mid 20th century, with 19 Lohans and saints and a dragon rendered in gold and pigments, the four central figures and the dragon being raised molded figures; the vase 12 in. by 6 1/2 in., the total height of the lamp 24 1/2 in.; lamp of solid bronze, the shade retainer can be adjusted upward up to an additional 3 1/4 in. to accommodate a larger shade if desired; unobtrusive crack in one small ring around the metal base, the vase with required non-visible drill hole in base but in excellent condition, shade not included. **$2,500-$2,750**

Figure of a woman; her robes in brown with red, orange, green, and gilt mon; Showa period, 14 in. high. **$150-$185**

Figures of a pair of pottery Foo dogs, measuring 12 in. by 12 in., dating to the 20th century. The dogs are done in earthenware decorated in multiple colors and moriage (a special type of raised decoration used on some Japanese pottery) motifs similar to both Satsuma and Kutani ware. The base is covered with green felt. Excellent original condition with no evidence of damage or repair. **$400**

Jar and cover, ovoid body with three panels of peony between formal borders, matching lid with knob finial, circa 1850, 9 in. high. **$1,800-$2,500**

Jar and cover, two panels with village and lakeside scenes, the ground with 1000 Flowers pattern, cover painted to match, signed Yabu Meizan, late Meiji period, 10 in. high. **$2,500-$3,500**

Jar and cover, the body with oval reticulated panels between panels showing figures in a garden with maple and wisteria, the shoulder and foot with flowers, reticulated cover, signed Kinkozan, late Meiji period, 8 in. high. **$2,500-$3,500**

Jar, the ovoid body decorated with peony and Shishi (fanciful dog or lion), colors and gilt, cover missing, marked Satsuma yaki (in gold on a black reserve), circa 1915, 9 in. high. **$200-$275**

Jardinière decorated with the Seven Gods of Good Luck, colors and gilt, signed Dai Nihon Satsuma yaki, Meiji period, 11 1/4 in. diameter. **$700-$900**

Jardinière, panels of samurai and attendants; brown ground decorated with trailed yellow, red, and blue enamels, circa 1915, 9 in. diameter. **$225-$375**

Napkin holder, cylindrical, Three Friends motif in iron red, blue, gilt, and colors, late Edo period, 4 in. high. **$800-$1,000**

Mizutsugi with motif of fans, moriage motifs within the fans, color and gilt, late 18th/early 19th century. **$2,000-$3,000**

Mizusashi (water jar) with delicate motifs of peacocks and foliage highlighted in gilt, late Edo period, 6 in. high. **$1,500-$1,800**

Napkin holder, cylindrical, decorated with Tomoe mon in colors and gilt, late Meiji period, 3 3/4 in. high. **$400-$600**

Plate, cobalt and gilt ground surrounding a central motif of three women in a garden, late Taisho period, signed Kinkozan, 8 in. diameter. **$1,000-$1,500**

Plate, colors and gilt with a seascape, several boats, the narrow border worked in a gilt diaper, signed Kinkozan, late Meiji period, 9 1/2 in. diameter. **$400-$500**

Plate, fan shape supported on three stub legs, motif of maple leaves in autumnal colors and gilt, circa 1930, 10 in. wide. **$175-$275**

Platter, oval, a wizard and his monkey, colors and gilt, Japanese, early Meiji period, 16 in. wide. **$500-$750**

Plate, iron red, blue, and gold, a mountain-scape, the border with a lappet band that is carried over to the reverse, marked Satsuma yaki with a blue mon on the base, late Edo period, 10 in. diameter. **$3,000-$4,000**

Plate, rectangular, dragon and Rakan (Buddhist disciples), in gilt and colors, late Taisho period, 8 1/2 in. by 12 in. **$300-$500**

Plate, the central motif (warrior's headgear and flowers) in colors and gilt, a gilt diaper border, circa 1900, 8 1/2 in. diameter. **$600-$775**

Plate, two girls in low relief in a garden scene, gilt diaper border, the motif in colors with heavy gilt, Taisho period, 7 in. diameter. **$200-$300**

Plate, enamel and gilt, showing the Buddhist pantheon, circa 1900, 7 in. diameter. **$85**

Satsuma-style tea set decorated in colors and gilt with Rakan, Kannon, and dragon, Japanese, circa 1925, service for six. **$200-$250**

Teapot decorated with a mass of flowers on the lid, spout, handle, and two-thirds of the body, signed Kinkozan, late Meiji period, 7 in. high. **$300-$500**

Teapot, discus form with alternating bands of flowers and foliage, supported on three legs, bail bamboo handle, early Showa period, 5 in. diameter. **$200-$275**

Teapot modeled as a cockerel and decorated in colors, blue, and gilt, realistic in appearance, legs restored, handle damaged, early 19th century, 7 1/2 in. long, **$1,200-$1,600**

Teapot decorated with figures of seated Rakan (Buddhist disciples), and dragons, with Kannon (goddess of mercy), in colors and gilt, marked Hododa, early 20th century. **$250-$375**

Tea set: teapot, sugar and creamer, six cups and saucers, and six cake plates, a motif of bamboo in green with gilt highlights, circa 1935. **$200-$300**

Tea set, brown ground with Rakan (Buddhist disciples), Kannon (goddess of mercy), and dragon, dragon spouts, circa 1935, service for six. **$250-$350**

Tea set: teapot, covered sugar and creamer, six cups and saucers, and six cake plates, each piece decorated with wisteria pattern, circa 1935. **$300-$475**

Tea set, each piece decorated with a woman seated next to a child in a garden setting, circa 1920, service for four. **$300-$500**

Tea set: teapot, covered sugar, open creamer, and six cups and saucers, overall motif of 1000 Flowers, signed Yabu Meizan, circa 1905. **$2,000-$3,000**

Pair of tokkuri, or sake bottles, measuring approximately 5 1/2 in. high, dating to the third quarter of the 20th century. The bottles are painted in floral designs in overglaze enamels. The bases have the artist's signature. **$100**

Punch or fruit bowl decorated in the United States, colors and gilt, signed Mabel Dibble, 1909, 18 in. diameter. **$900-$1,200**

Tokkuri (sake bottle), double-gourd form with two diapered panels and two panels of scattered kiku (chrysanthemum) and foliage, blue, iron red, and gilt, first half of the 19th century, 6 1/2 in. high. **$1,500-$2,500**

Tokkuri (sake bottle), double-gourd form with birds and flowers in colors and gilt, the neck with gilt diaper, Meiji period, 8 1/2 in. high. **$350-$550**

Tokkuri (sake bottle), the body with brown and blue glazes and flowers and foliage in gilt, Edo period, 7 1/2 in. high. **$2,000-$3,000**

Umbrella stand, brown ground with panels of warriors and attendants, overall designs in trailed colored enamels, circa 1915. **$300-$550**

Vase, two reserves of figures on a floral ground, circa 1930, 6 in. high. **$200-$300**

Vase in beaker form, applied motifs of young girl, her dog, basket of fruit, trees, foliage, and grasses, Mt. Fuji in low relief, colors and gilt, Japanese, circa 1900, 16 in. high. **$3,500-$5,500**
COURTESY OF HOWARD AND FLORENCE KASTRINER

Vase, baluster form, measuring 18 in. high and 8 in. in diameter, dating to the Meiji era, circa 1880; the earthenware body rests on a flared, recessed foot. The body swells gently to the shoulders where it cuts back in to form a cylindrical neck and flared mouth. There are two applied leaf handles. The typical, crackled, off-white Satsuma glaze can be seen on the interior and the base. The outside of the vase is covered in a deep green glaze. The central area has overall flowers in an orange sky design in multicolor overglaze enamels. The neck is decorated with painted yellow-green leaves. The vase is marked with a size or number mark (No. 13) that was used for European customers to designate a pattern and size. The artist has signed the vase on the base in gold, but too much of the signature has worn off to read it accurately. There are some old, gold fill-ins where some colors have worn around the base and shoulders. Otherwise the vase is in fine original condition. **$350**

Vase, baluster form with a continuous rural scene (including huts and a procession), the neck and foot with cobalt and gilt scrolls, signed Kinkozan, Taisho period, 6 in. high. **$1,000-$1,500**

Vase, barrel form with birds perched on flowering prunus branches above and below gold diaper bands, Taisho period, 9 in. high. **$200-$300**

Vase, beaker form, decorated with figures in a garden, signed Ryozan, late Meiji period, 6 in. high. **$450-$600**

Vase with handles in the form of Daikoku's mallet, the motif in gosu (blue), gilt, and red, base with blue mon, late Edo period, 5 in. high. **$1,500-$1,800**

Cylindrical vase on tripod feet, colors and gilt with a floral motif, base marked Kinkozan, Japanese, circa 1915, 5 in. high. **$500-$700**

Vase, colors and gilt with Rakan (Buddhist disciple), molded in relief on a scenic ground, the neck with a band of dragons, chipped rim and foot, late Meiji period, 14 in. high. **$300-$500**

Vase, two panels of figures in garden landscapes divided by a cobalt ground filled with gilt flowers, signed Shuzan, late 19th century, 5 1/4 in. high. **$300-$475**

Vase, a processional, the shoulders with a floral band, colors and gilt, cracked, signed Kinkozan, circa 1900, 4 in. high. **$150-$200**

Vase with motif in colors and gilt, Japanese, circa 1955, 8 in. high. **$75-$100**

Vase, modified pear shape, gosu (blue), gilt, and red, late Edo period, 8 in. high. **$3,000-$4,500**

Vase decorated with 100 Antiques between ruyi bands and chrysanthemum lappets, iron red, blue, and gilt with colors, blue mon on the base; 9 in. high. **$2,500-$3,500**

Vase, double gourd, cobalt blue with gilt dragons, signed Kinkozan, late Meiji period, 4 in. high. **$400-$600**

Vase, double gourd with panels of courtiers kneeling before a daimyo, the ground with brocade patterns, colors and gilt, late 19th century, 5 in. high. **$375-$485**

Vase, globular with a short neck, the body with two Shishi (fanciful dog or lion) and tama (sacred Buddhist jewel) on each side, lappet band on the foot and neck, late Edo period, 7 1/2 in. high. **$1,200-$1,800**

Vase, globular, colors and gilt with chrysanthemums and butterflies above and below lappets, marked Satsuma yaki (and with blue mon), Edo period, 11 in. high. **$3,000-$4,000**

Vase, hexagonal with Rakan (Buddhist disciples), molded in relief, a writhing dragon in relief, colors and gilt, late Taisho/early Meiji period, 11 in. high. **$500-$700**

Vase, motif of flowers and grasses beside a stream, the shoulder with butterflies and a fan, colors and gilt, 6 in. high, circa 1915. **$300-$400**

Vase, a peacock in colors and gilt perched on a flowering branch, colorful plumage, late 19th century, 8 1/2 in. high. **$450-$600**

Vase, a continuous scene of figures in a village beside a lake, the shoulder with birds and flowers, colors and gilt, circa 1915, 4 in. high. **$200-$300**

Vase, baluster form, molded in low relief with warriors and women in gardens, cobalt blue ground with gilt scrolls, signed Kinkozan, circa 1910, 8 in. high. **$500-$750**

Vase, continuous pattern of Immortals and attendants beneath trees, colors and gilt, late 19th century, 4 in. high. **$300-$400**

Vase, the motif includes three egrets, bamboo, and flowering grasses in colors and gilt, signed Kinkozan, 6 1/2 in. high. **$450-$675**

Vase, ovoid body decorated with orchids and a stream, the shoulder with phoenix and kiri (a type of tree, also called paulownia) leaves, iron red, blue, green, and gilt, the base marked Satsuma yaki, late Edo period, 17 in. high. **$4,000-$6,000**

Vase, the body decorated with frogs in various poses in colors and gilt highlights, early Meiji period, 7 in. high. **$500-$700**

Vase, double gourd, decorated with figures overlooking a lake, a village scene in the background, brocade borders, colors and gilt, rim and foot damaged, signed Yabu Meizan, circa 1910, 4 3/4 in. high. **$700-$950**

Vases, ovoid form, colors and gilt with chrysanthemum and bamboo fences above and below a blue border with gilt floral rounders, marked Satsuma yaki, Meiji period, 11 in. high, pair. **$1,200-$1,800**

Vases, slender baluster form with motifs of vases and koro in iron red, blue, gilt, and colors, marked Satsuma yaki, late Edo period, 7 1/2 in. high, pair. **$1,500-$2,000**

Vases, brown ground with Rakan (Buddhist disciples), in colors and gilt highlights, early Showa period, 12 1/2 in. high, pair. **$200-$300**

Vase, moriage (a special type of raised decoration used on some Japanese pottery), measuring 18 1/2 in. high, dating to the late 19th or early 20th century. The vase has an overall moriage, or cake icing, design in brilliant colors of geisha, samurai, and flowers. The tip of one handle has been restored and there is an age hairline crack in upper rim that does not affect the vase's integrity. **$300**

Vases decorated with pheasants and bamboo in colors and gilt highlights, the neck, foot, and side panels in cobalt blue with gilt foliage, circa 1920, 8 in. high, pair. **$300-$500**

Vase, 1000 Flowers motif in colors and gilt, signed Kinkozan, Taisho period, 7 in. high. **$1,000-$1,500**

Vase, modified mallet shape, the four squared sides with two panels of gardens and diaper neck, the panels within the diaper contain village scenes with townspeople, rim and foot in colors and gilt, Tokyo school, late 19th century, 9 in. high. **$900-$1,200**

Vase, modified pear shape with slender neck, alternating bands of flowers, diaper, and figures in a processional, signed Meizan, circa 1900, 4 1/2 in. high. **$1,500-$2,500**

Satsuma water coupe, undecorated, early 20th century, 4 in. high. **$200-$300**

Vase, oviform, iron red, blue, gilt, and colors with birds flying below wisteria and above capped waves, blue mon on the base, late Edo period, 8 in. high. **$2,000-$3,000**

Satsuma blank decorated in the United States with a motif of pink cockatoos and flowers in shades of pink and fuchsia, circa 1926, 8 in. high. **$300-$500**

Vase, ovoid, scholars beneath trees in colors with gilt highlights, applied chrysanthe-mum-form handles, Taisho period, 5 3/4 in. high. **$200-$300**

Vase supported on the back of a Shishi (fan-ciful dog or lion), the vase with panels of fig-ures, chipped, hairlines, circa 1920, 9 in. high. **$600-$800**

Vases decorated in orange and gold maple leaves and branches, signed Kinkozan, circa 1920, 4 1/2 in. high, pair. **$300-$450**

Vases, mirror image, the shoulders with a procession of figures attending a festival, the neck and foot with gilt diapers, circa 1910, 18 in. high, pair. **$1,500-$2,100**

Studio Ceramics

Pieces associated with a specific maker or group of potters.

Boat with removable roof, all white, the base with an impressed Kozan mark, circa 1905, Japanese, 18 in. diameter. **$1,000-$1,600**

Stemmed bowl, the interior in aubergine and mustard with symbol of long life, the exterior a blue-green with blue motifs of insects, the base marked Makuzu Kozan, late 19th century, 5 in. high. $2,000-$3,000

Bottle, squat and square, temmoku glazes, fitted wood box signed Kawai Kanjiro, 7 in. high. **$2,000-$3,000**

Studio bowl, six-sided, with a crane design, measuring 8 in. across by 3 in. high, dating to the early-to-mid 20th century. The piece is made of an earthenware body, covered on the exterior with a dark brown/black glaze and on the interior with a crackle blue glaze and figure of a stork among the reeds in white and green overglaze enamels. It bears the artist's seal impressed on the base. One small chip of the blue interior glaze professionally restored. **$150**

Unusual Japanese studio bowl painted on the interior with three geisha in a garden on a famille noire, or black, background, dating to the late 19th or early 20th century. The garden scene contains rich colors of trees, flowers, and auspicious fungus as well as the detailed kimono of the ladies. There is a floral outer rim diaper and a brown palm leaf base diaper. The bowl measures 10 in. across and 3 1/2 in. high. The base has a kakihan ("written seal, signature") mark of the artist. It is in original condition except for the restoration of a 1/8 in. rim chip. Possibly Fukagawa. **$200**

Studio bowl of pottery covered with a milk chocolate brown exterior glaze on the body with a dark brown rim glaze, a crackled gray interior glaze, and an underglaze blue and black design of crabs and sea grass, dating to the late 19th or early 20th century. There is a 1/4 in. chip loss of the interior glaze characteristic of this type of ware. The bowl measures 8 in. by 3 in. **$125**

Bowl, measuring approximately 8 in. by 3 in., dating to the early to mid-20th century. This bowl has a buff body with a finely crackled cream glaze overall. It is sparsely decorated with a bamboo node and leaves in two shades of dark green. The artist has executed this drawing in a sumi-e style ("ink painting"). The rim is glazed black. The bowl is most likely Satsuma in origin, given the body and glaze as well as the signature on the base, which reads "Zan." Fine original condition. **$150**

Bowl, leaf form, porcelain, the blue ground with stem and ribs in low relief, impressed mark (Makuzu Kozan), late Meiji period, 12 1/4 in. long. **$1,500-$2,200**

Bowl, porcelain, flower heads on a white ground, the base with a seal (Seifu), late 19th century, missing lid. **$500-$700**

Kozan censer in celadon with a white slip motif of clouds and cranes, the base with a Kozan mark, the lid copper with perforations in the form of Tokugawa mon, Japanese, circa 1900, 5 in. high. **$1,500-$1,800**

Censer with silver lid, the floral motif featured on two panels of the body is cut out in the lid, the base is signed Tomimoto Kenkichi, Japanese, 5 in. high. **$2,500-$3,500**

Ewer in the form of an animal with archaistic motifs and mon with rabbits, gun metal, blue-green, and white, Japanese, Tanzan, circa 1910. **$1,800-$2,500**

Box and cover, the cover of flower form, 3 1/8 in. diameter, Kanjiro. **$600-$900**

Box and cover, circular, pottery decorated with cranes nesting in a pine tree beneath a full moon, colors and gilt, signed Taizan, circa 1900, 5 1/8 in. diameter. **$800-$1,200**

Brush pot, hexagonal, cream glaze over splashed iron abstract patterns, wood box, Shoji Hamada, 7 3/4 in. high. **$900-$1,200**

Censer, tripod, globular body, celadon glaze, signed Seifu, porcelain, late 19th century, 3 in. high. **$1,000-$1,500**

Charger decorated with a design of Mt. Fuji in hand-painted iron oxide glaze with overtones of yellow ochre, a thick, Seiji celadon background, and a frosted white mountain peak. The charger is signed on the base in sometsuke (cobalt blue underglaze). Measures 11 in. by 1 3/4 in. No chips, cracks, or repairs but some kiln glaze faults on surface. **$300**

Chawan, blue and yellow peony sprays, the base marked Seifu, early 20th century. **$300-$500**

Dish, circular, colored glazes depicting leaves in a river bed, signed Ro (Rosanjin), 7 1/2 in. diameter. **$1,500-$2,500**

Dish, square, gray with orange-brown streaks, a motif of glass in white, Shino style (pure white glaze), Rosanjin (Kitaoji Rosanjin [1883-1959] was one of Japan's most important 20th century ceramists), 10 1/2 in. square. **$2,500-$3,500**

Dish, squared with upturned corners, Iga style, Rosanjin (Kitaoji Rosanjin [1883-1959] was one of Japan's most important 20th century ceramists), 7 1/2 in. diameter. **$900-$1,200**

Inkwell with silver mounts, glass inserts, motif of crustaceans and waves in green, silver pen with writhing dragon in low relief, Japanese, circa 1910, the inkwell, **$500-$750**, the pen **$300-$500**.
COURTESY OF RICHARD A. BOWSER

Model of two egrets in pottery, the details painted gray, beaks broken, marked Kozan (Miyagawa Kozan), circa 1885, 4 1/4 in. high. **$600-$900**

Mizusashi, cylindrical, the ground shaded pink to white with clouds and Mt. Fuji, the cover glazed black to simulate lacquer, Seifu, circa 1900, 7 1/4 in. high. **$2,000-$3,000**

Plate, underglaze blue and white with a moon through bamboo, the motif carried over to the reverse, late 19th century, signed Seifu, 8 1/4 in. diameter. **$1,000-$1,500**

Plate enameled in gilt and colors with ferns and daisies, signed Taizan, circa 1910, 8 1/2 in. diameter. **$600-$800**

Oil dish in deep mustard-brown and brown-black, scenic motif, Seto style, the base with impressed Makuzu Kozan mark, late 19th century, Japanese, 6 in. diameter. **$1,800-$2,400**

Pitcher in blue-green, white, beige, and black with motifs within motifs, together with caricatures, Japanese, Tanzan, circa 1900, 8 in. high. **$1,500-$2,200**

Two sake ewers in blue-green, white, and beige with motifs within motifs and diapers, each marked Tanzan, circa 1900, the largest 6 in. high. Left: Restored. **$500-$800**. Right: **$1,500-$1,800**

Vase, flattened rectangular form, red and blue iris spray on a cream ground within blue bands, Kawai Kanliro, 9 in. high. **$700-$1,000**

Vase, café au lait ground with blue and white roundels filled with birds and foliage, porcelain, signed Kawamoto Masakichi, circa 1880, 18 in. high. **$5,000-$7,000**

Vase, globular body, round ring foot, everted rim, motif of kiri (a type of tree, also called paulownia) and phoenix set against a scrolling vine, underglaze blue and white and café au lait with celadon ground, porcelain, signed Kawamoto Masakichi, 10 1/4 in. high. **$3,000-$4,000**

Vase, copper red ground with a motif of morning glories in lavenders, signed Kozan, circa 1900, 6 1/2 in. high. **$1,400-$1,800**

Vase, baluster form, a dragon and waves in colors and underglaze blue, the base marked Makuzu Kozan sei, circa 1905, 10 in. high. **$1,400-$1,800**

Vase, baluster form, decorated in shaded-green-to-mauve ground with a motif of wisteria coming down from the neck, the base marked Makuzu Kozan, 12 1/2 in. high, circa 1900. **$2,500-$4,000**

Vase, underglaze blue and red with band of foliate scrolls, Ju characters and stylized longevity symbols, cracked, signed Katie zo, 11 1/2 in. high, Meiji period. **$400-$600**

Vase, baluster form, underglaze blue and white with bamboo and leaf motif, signed Makuzu Kozan, circa 1900, 24 1/2 in. high. **$3,500-$4,500**

Vase, ovoid form, porcelain, pale green graduated glaze with motif of huddled herons, signed Seifu, Meiji period, 4 in. high. **$700-$900**

Vase, porcelain, copper red glaze, impressed mark (Seifu), 5 in. high. **$900-$1,200**

Vase, beaker form, pale pink with white herons and plum blossoms, signed Makuzu Kozan, circa 1900, 7 in. high. **$1,500-$2,200**

Vase, bulbous with a short neck, yellow ground with underglaze blue and white dragons and clouds, marked Kozan sei (Miyagawa Kozan), late 19th century, 7 in. high. **$1,200-$1,600**

Vase decorated with three fish, pottery, colors and gilt, base marked Makuzu Kozan, late 19th century, 4 in. high. **$2,000-$3,000**

Vase, double gourd, decorated with flowers, stems, and foliage on a brown ground, restored, base marked Tanzan, late 19th century, 4 3/4 in. high. **$800-$1,200**

Vase decorated with cranes in flight above breaking waves, colors and gilt, marked Tanzan, circa 1900, 4 in. high. **$750-$950**

Vase, hexagonal with birds flying among flowering peony branches, marked Taizan, 9 in. high. **$600-$850**

Vase, conical form, turquoise, beige, brown, and blue-green glazes with white accents, a play of motif within motifs, the base marked Tanzan, Japanese, circa 1900, 7 in. high. **$1,500-$1,800**
COURTESY OF HOWARD AND FLORENCE KASTRINER

Left: Double gourd vase, deep blue ground with silver overlay motifs of maple leaves and scrolls. Right: Vase, deep-chocolate-colored ground with silver overlay irises and foliage. Both marked Tanzan, 5 in. high, each. **$900-$1,200**
COURTESY OF HOWARD AND FLORENCE KASTRINER

Porcelain vases with pink and green motifs, mei ping form, the bases signed Makuzu Kozan, Japanese, circa 1910, 3 1/2 in. high, each. **$900-$1,200**

Vase, globular form, trumpet neck, pottery, motif of maple leaves in gilt and autumnal hues against a cream-colored glaze, base signed Makuzu Kozan (seal), late 19th century, 9 1/8 in. high. **$3,500-$5,000**

Vase, globular, the motif of peaches and foliage in underglaze blue and copper red, base marked Kozan, circa 1900, 6 in. high. **$2,000-$2,500**

Vase, double gourd, underglaze blue and white with groups of birds in flight above flowering branches, signed Kawamoto Masakichi, circa 1885, 15 in. high. **$1,500-$2,200**

Vase, baluster form, pastel-hued magnolia and foliage, chip on base, underglaze blue seal, signed Ryosai, circa 1900, 7 1/2 in. high. **$800-$1,200**

Vase, baluster form, blue and violet morning glories in low relief, base signed Ryosai, circa 1890, 10 in. high. **$1,200-$1,800**

Vase, beaker form, underglaze blue and white with a motif of bamboo stalks, signed Ryosai, late 19th century, 8 1/8 in. high. **$1,000-$1,500**

Vase, globular form with a tall neck, graduated celadon ground with a pink and white floral motif, marked Ryosai, circa 1885, 8 in. high. **$1,000-$1,500**

Vase, baluster form, light green graduating to pink and yellow with blossoming peony branches, marked Shofu, circa 1885, 7 1/2 in. high. **$700-$900**

Vase, oviform, shaded green to white, two herons in a pond with marsh plants, marked Shofu, circa 1885, 9 in. high. **$600-$900**

Vase, ovoid, carved with kiku (chrysanthemum) on a pale blue glaze, signed Seifu, circa 1900, 5 1/4 in. high. **$3,200-$4,000**

Vase, ovoid with a graduated green ground and a motif of cranes in flight, impressed Seifu mark, late 19th century, 3 1/2 in. high. **$900-$1,200**

Vase, cylindrical with three bands containing pomegranates and foliage, scrolls, and chrysanthemums, signed Taizan, circa 1890, 6 in. high. **$800-$1,200**

Vase, double gourd with birds perched on flowering prunus in colors and gilt, pottery, the base signed Taizan, circa 1900, 7 1/2 in. high. **$1,200-$1,500**

Vase, flared neck, bulbous body, decorated with panels of flowering branches, base marked Taizan, circa 1905, 7 1/2 in. high. **$1,000-$1,500**

Vase, creamy pink crackled glaze with a motif of a goose and marsh grasses under a full moon, lacquer repair on rim, signed Tanzan, 8 in. high, circa 1900. **$1,200-$1,500**

Vase, double gourd, muted shades of green, brown, and blue in a leaf motif, marked Tanzan, late 19th century, 7 1/2 in. high. **$600-$800**

Porcelain vase with carved motif of flowers and grasses, the full moon above, five curled legs, shades of pale blue and white, eggshell porcelain, Japanese, circa 1905, 6 in. high. **$900-$1,200**

Vase decorated with three Tai fish in shades of brown and ochre on creamy glaze, rolled lip, pottery, marked Tanzan, circa 1900, 7 in. high. **$1,200-$1,800**

Vase, bulbous body with long, tapered neck, a motif of flowers in colors and gilt on the neck and down one-third of the body, pottery, the base marked Ito Tozan, circa 1900, 9 in. high. **$600-$900**

Sumida Gawa Wares

The Asakusa district of Tokyo actually saw the birth of Sumida Gawa wares. Tokyo is located on East Central Honshu, on the Kanto plain. This region is intersected by the Sumida Gawa (gawa means river), for which the ceramics produced nearby were named.

Until the arrival of Inoue Ryosai, a Seto potter, there had been little in the way of porcelain manufacture in Tokyo. Then, in 1875, Inoue Ryosai formed a partnership with Shimada Sobei, a pottery dealer, and established a porcelain kiln in the Asakusa district. Materials for the production of his wares were likely secured from Aichi prefecture, where Seto is located, so there was little difference in the quality of his paste as compared to that of Seto (Owari) producers.

His style of decoration, for the most part, was more in line with that of the Tokyo school. The Asakusa kiln produced pottery wares, including articles for use in Cha no yu, as well as porcelain wares contemporary to the late 19th and early 20th centuries, which were fashioned there until the end of the Taisho period.

It appears that during the late 1890s, porcelain-bodied wares with heavy transmutation (flambé) curtain glazes and applied figures in relief were developed; the earliest Sumida Gawa wares date from this time. (In 1899, a Sumida Gawa vase standing 48 inches high and having a porcelain body, red ground, and applied motifs of the 500 Buddhist Disciples won first prize in a Tokyo exhibition.) Hayata Takemoto, with whom Inoue Ryosai had worked earlier in establishing a kiln for the daimyo of Settsu Province (Osaka prefecture), was a specialist in the use of transmutation glazes, especially in the Chinese style. It seems reasonable to assume that his working relationship with Hayata Takemoto allowed Inoue Ryosai to develop the glazes so closely associated with the later Sumida Gawa wares.

The earliest wares usually had a red, green, or black ground, distinguished sometimes by a leathery look. The smaller, ornamental pieces, especially figures, were often entirely covered with glaze.

In 1924, the kiln was moved from the Asakusa district to Yokohama. Despite the change in location, the name of the wares remained the same. Several new hues, however, were added to the palette: orange, brown, blue, and lavender.

Among the other characteristics of later pieces is an unglazed ground, which may be flicked off with a fingernail or removed with a strong hand and a dampened cloth. Some of these pieces were made with the use of a mold (including the figures done in relief), which can be detected by examining the interior of an object and/or its motif. In general, motifs-which feature monkeys, dragons, scenics, florals, Rakan (Buddhist disciples), elders, and karako-are applied in high relief.

Ashtray, black ground with the Seven Gods of Good Luck peering over the rim, late Meiji period, 5 1/2 in. diameter. **$400-$500**

Ashtray in the form of a badger, cartouche, circa 1910. **$250-$350**

Ashtray, red body with a boy seated on the rim, cartouche, circa 1925, 2 1/2 in. diameter. **$200-$300**

Ashtray, circular with a house near the rim, impressed mark, 4 In. diameter. **$175-$225**

Bottle/vase, a skeleton carrying a sake bottle, plus a badger on rock-work, 7 1/8 in. high. **$900-$1,200**

Censer (and cover) on three legs, elephant handles, the finial in the form of an elder, lid perforated, 5 in. high. **$400-$500**

Coffeepot, Toby form, blue glaze, 9 in. high. **$400-$600**

Cookie jar, temple form with a figure seated on the lid, the roof forms the lid, 9 in. high. **$500-$700**

Flower bowl, three children peering over the rim, red ground, 3 1/2 in. by 7 in., Taisho period. **$250-$325**

Flower dish for cut flowers, ten men peering over the rim, green body, Taisho period, 9 in. diameter. **$300-$400**

Figure of Hotei (the god of contentment and happiness) and sack (which is glazed blue), incised mark, 8 in. high. **$700-$1,000**

Figure of Daruma (the founder of Chan Buddhism in China, known as Zen Buddhism in Japan), large, loose-ring earrings, black and white cowl and flowing robe, impressed mark on base, 9 in. high. **$700-$1,000**

Figure of Rakan (Buddhist disciple), seated on a temple bell, his robe and cowl glazed, the bell with a red ground, 9 in. high. **$900-$1,200**

Group, Three Wise Monkeys, 3 in. by 4 in., circa 1925. **$300-$400**

Hanging basket, canoe form, five monkeys climbing into the canoe, cartouche, 12 in. by 4 in. by 3 in. **$1,000-$1,500**

Bowl with three figures peering over the rim, red ground, Japanese, early 20th century, 6 1/2 in. diameter. **$225-$300**

Pitcher in the form of a man, his queue forming the handle, purple glazes, Japanese, early 20th century, 4 1/4 in. high. $250-$325

Humidor in the form of a man, his face contorted, his arms wrapped around his knees, the lid with a finial in the form of a boy, incised mark, 5 1/2 in. high. **$600-$900**

Jardinière, pale curtain glazes, worn red ground, large, bold morning glories and foliage in relief, cartouche, 5 in. by 6 in. **$450-$650**

Jardinière and stand, red ground, writhing dragons in gray, the bowl 12 in. diameter, total height 26 in. **$2,500-$3,500**

Mug, a goat in relief, black ground, cartouche. **$200-$275**

Pitcher, red ground, black glaze, figures in various poses (drinking sake and burning incense, for example), cartouche, 12 in. high. **$700-$950**

Shoe, red ground and curtain glazes, applied design of a child near the toe, incised mark, 6 in. long. **$500-$600**

Teacup and saucer, red ground, glazed around the rim, handle, and border of the saucer, both pieces with a child engaged in play near a vase; incised mark; 3 3/4 in. high. **$200-$300**

Teapot in the form of a sampan with a boy, a woven reed handle and waves at the base, incised mark, 7 in. long. **$700-$900**

Teapot, red ground, curtain glaze on the handle, spout, lid, and upper body, the decoration includes a child at play, incised mark, 7 in. high. **$400-$600**

Teapot, reed bail handle, black ground, blue curtain glaze, applied figures shooting a cannon, incised mark. **$700-$900**

Toothpick in the form of a man's head, incised mark, 2 in. high. **$250-$350**

Vase, green ground, two children on one side, a seated elder on the reverse, incised mark, 7 in. high. **$275-$325**

Vase, irises in low relief on a red ground, cartouche, 24 in. high. **$2,500-$3,500**

Vase, oviform with red ground, covered with monkeys wearing haori, damage to some of the monkeys, circa 1915, 14 in. high. **$1,000-$1,500**

Vase, pinched form, black ground with a tiger on rock-work, incised mark, 8 1/2 in. high. **$800-$1,200**

Vase, red ground with Benten seated on rock-work and playing a biwa, low relief, 11 in. high. **$400-$500**

Vase, red ground with morning glories and foliage in high relief, pinched form, white flambé curtain glaze, Japanese, circa 1900, 10 in. high. **$550-$750**

Vase, the Seven Gods of Good Luck in low relief, marked Made in Japan, 8 in. high. **$200-$300**

Vase with figures of two elders on rock-work, cartouche, 7 in. high. **$500-$700**

Vase, one side of the base modeled as a grotto with a family of monkeys in various poses (being seated at a table and drinking tea, for example), cartouche, 18 in. high. **$2,000-$2,700**

Vase, red ground with an octopus in relief, cartouche, 2 1/4 in. high. **$500-$600**

Vase, red ground with three children in low relief, incised mark, 8 in. high. **$200-$300**

Vase with floral motif in high relief, early 20th century. $500-$750
COURTESY OF GARDNER POND

Japanese Pottery and Porcelain Marks

Kiyen factory

Akahada/Kishiro maker

Akahada

Sampei Gashu maker

Kashiu Mimpei maker

Kashlu Sampei maker

Cho maker

Eizan maker

Kichi maker

Maker's mark

Yoskiage

Good Fortune/Long Life

Good Fortune

Good Fortune

Hibarabayashi maker

Japanese Pottery and Porcelain Marks

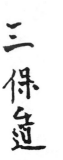

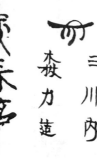

Zoshuntei maker

Mori Chikara, Mikawachi
(maker and place)

Fukagawa maker

Yamaka maker

Fukagawa maker

Hichozan Shimpo maker

Shimodo maker

Hirado

Found on Hirado wares

Mikawaji

Zoshuntei maker

Happiness

Banko
(impressed mark)

Japanese Pottery and Porcelain Marks

Banko (impressed mark)

Yusetsu maker (Banko)

Fuyeki maker (Banko)

Banko (impressed marks)

Banko-Tekizan maker

Ganto-Sanzin maker

Fuyeki maker

The Yofu factory

Banko ware

Kutani (place name)

Kutani (place name)

Kutani (place name)

Kutani (place name)

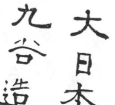

Kiokuzan maker

Yuzan maker

Kutani/Kayo (place name)

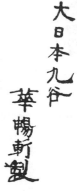

Kochoken maker

Japanese Pottery and Porcelain Marks

Tozan maker

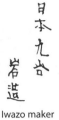
Iwazo maker

Kawamoto Masukichi
maker / Seto, Japan

Kawamoto
Hansuke maker

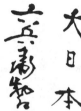
Rokubeye maker

Iwata, Aichi, Japan

Toyosuke maker

Eizan maker

Owari (place
mark)

Nagoya (place mark)

Kawamoto Masukichi
maker

Hokuhan maker

Fuwa Sodo maker

Ide maker

Kai maker

Nakajima
maker

Gyokuzan maker

Satsuma (place mark)

Satsuma (place mark)

Hoju maker

Hohei maker

Hoyei maker

Japanese Pottery and Porcelain Marks

Koko maker

Siekozan maker

Kinko factory maker

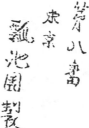

Hiocheyen Tokyo maker

Gosaburo maker

Gozan maker

Tsuji/Tokyo, Japan
(maker and place mark)

Kozan (Makuzu) maker

Denka maker

Myakawa Kozan maker

Makuzu Kozan maker

Meizan maker

Kenya maker

Ryozan maker

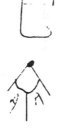

Inoue Ryosai

Inoue Ryosai

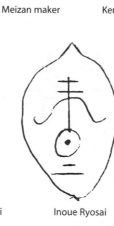

Inoue Ryosai

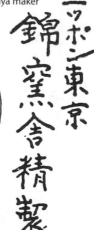

Kinsho Company, Tokyo
(maker and place mark)

Japanese Pottery and Porcelain Marks

Kitei maker

Zoroku maker

Hichibeye maker

Sahei maker

Seifu maker

Raku

Eiraku maker

Eiraku maker

Kanzan Denshichi maker

Makuzu Kozan maker

Shuzan maker

Kinunken maker

Taizan maker

Taizan maker

Tanzan maker

Dai Nippon (Great Ja

Bizan maker

Seikozan maker

Shuhei maker

Kanzan maker

Kinkozan

Hozan maker

Awata (place mark)

Ryozan

Kinkozan

Dohachi

Kenzan

Ninse

Japanese Tea Ceremony Articles

Japanese tea ceremony articles can include chasyaku (teascoop), chawan (tea bowl), chaire (tea container), chasen (tea whisk), chakin (linen cloth), fukusa (silk cloth), furo (brazier), futa (lid), futaoki (lid rest), hisyaku (ladle), kensui (waste-water receptacle), kama (kettle), kashiki (container for sweetener), kashikiri (small knife for sweetener), mizusashi (fresh-water container), natsume (tea container for thin tea), and tatami (mat made of rushes).

Chawan, or tea bowl, in temmoku (a mountain between China's Zhejiang and Anhui provinces) shape, measuring 4 1/2 in. by 2 in., dating to the early-to-mid 20th century. This bowl is made of fine white clay that is covered with a celadon glaze. The artist has painted designs of wheat sheaves and circles in iron oxide that have fired to a rich brown and deep black. This bowl was made in England, possibly by a disciple of Bernard Leach. Fine original condition. **$150**

Pair of Japanese Oribe green chawan, or tea bowls, measuring 2 1/2 in. high by 5 in. across, dating to the 20th century. The bowls have a lustrous Oribe green glaze on an earthenware body. Fine original condition. **$80**

Japanese sake cup, measuring 3 in. by 1 in., dating to the mid-1900s. The cup is made of metal and is plated in 24K gold. It has an embossed central chrysanthemum figure. Fine original condition, with box. **$125**

In Chinese, the name, "qingci" means "greenish porcelain." So why is this known as "celadon"? Celadon was the hero of the French writer Honore d'Urfe's romance "L'Astrée" (1610), the lover of the heroine Astrée. He was presented as a young man in green, and his dress became fashionable in Europe. It was about this time that the Chinese qingci made its debut in Paris. People compared its color to Celadon's suit and started to call the porcelain "celadon."

Japanese sake cup, measuring 3 in. by 1 in., dating to the mid-1900s. The cup is made of metal and is plated in 24K gold. It has an embossed central crane figure. Fine original condition. **$75**

Japanese sake cup, measuring 3 1/2 in. by 1 1/2 in., dating to the mid-1900s. The cup is made of metal and appears to be either silver or silver plate. It has an embossed central bean design. The cup has an upward bend in one portion of the rim that appears to be intentional. **$50**

Japanese hand-potted green teacup or tea bowl, measuring 2 1/2 in. by 3 3/4 in., dating to the early-to-mid 20th century. Fine original condition. **$35**

Japanese yellow Shigaraki or Seto chawan, or tea bowl, with a folded shape, dating to the Meiji period (1868-1912). The bowl is handmade from coiled clay. There is a subtle blue and brown floral design on the inside of one edge of the rim. The bowl measures 6 1/2 in. by 5 in. by 2 1/4 in. It is unsigned. There is an old rim chip measuring 3/8 in. that has been repaired with gold lacquer technique. **$200**

Japanese tea caddy made of tin, measuring 5 in. overall in height, dating to the late 19th or early 20th century. The caddy is coated with a layer of brown-red lacquer. It is accented by both flat and raised gold and tree-bark lacquer in a bird in tree design. The top has a stylized lion finial. There is an interior cap to the compartment. There is loss of some of the lacquer on the reverse and some overall scratches. **$150**

Japanese Oribe chawan or tea bowl, measuring 5 in. by 2 1/2 in., dating to the early-to-mid 20th century. The bowl has the typical Oribe green glaze and brown geometric figures. Fine original condition. **$100**

Japanese Kutani chawan, or tea bowl, measuring 5 in. by 3 in., from the mid-to- late 20th century. The chawan has a sunflower design in typical Kutani orange and green colors. The bowl bears the impressed mark "RIJU" on the base. Fine original condition. **$100**

Boxed set of pottery and porcelain Japanese chaire or tea caddies, consisting of two chaire and two tea scoops, from the mid-to-late 20th century. The first chaire measures 2 in. by 1 1/4 in. and is covered with a yellow-brown Seto glaze on fine, creamy clay with a black glazed top. The second chaire measures 2 1/2 in. across and 1 in. high and has a crackled, cream glaze interior, a black exterior and three cuts in the foot. The lid is signed on the interior in black. The top has a unique bamboo knot handle. The wooden box measures 3 1/4 in. by 3 1/4 in. by 6 1/2 in. and is signed and sealed on the front. **$285**

Complete set of three Japanese sake cups and pourer, made of earthenware with a rich green celadon crackle glaze, dating to the early 20th century. The cups and server have overglaze red enamel horse and abstract designs on the front and back. They are from the Soma Obori kiln in the northeastern Japanese region of Hokkaido, known as Tohoku. They measure 3 in. across and 2 in. tall. The set is in original excellent condition. **$125**

Japanese temmoku (an iron-rich pottery glaze) chawan, or summer tea bowl, measuring 7 in. by 2 in., from the mid-to-late 20th century. The bowl has a soft white matte glaze that creates a hare's fur effect on the interior and spills over the outside. The rim carries a blue-green glaze reminiscent of Oribe pottery. It is signed on the base by the artist. This work of a tea ceremony master potter. **$250**

Japanese chawan, or tea bowl, made of a fine cream earthenware body covered with an overall fine crackle Satsuma-like glaze, dating to the mid-to-early 20th century. The bowl is decorated on the exterior in over-glaze enamels of red, brown, white, and green with gold highlights in a garden lantern and plant design. The bowl measures 4 3/4 in. by 3 in. and is in original condition. **$150**

Japanese chawan, or tea bowl, made in the style of Sung and Tang Dyansty bowls with a temmoku (a mountain between China's Zhejiang and Anhui provinces) shape and a dark brown glaze. The surface glaze is pebbled in texture. It is signed "Fushin" on the foot rim. One way to translate this literally is "not the ape." From the mid-to-late 20th century. Fine original condition. **$85**

Japanese Negoro lacquer incense box, or "i. ko-bako" carved in Kamakura bori style of light wood, with a landscape surface scene, measuring 4 7/8 in. by 3 3/4 in. by 1 in., dating to the Meiji Period (1868-1912). The sides of the box are carved with a Greek key design. The interior and base are covered in black lacquer. The term Kamakura bori originated during the Muromachi Period (1392-1568) and refers to designs copied from the Chinese, wherein a wooden piece was carved into a design, then covered with layers of lacquer. This box has been finished in the typical Japanese Negoro style, in which red lacquer is followed by black lacquer. When the black is partially rubbed off, the red shows through. Excellent condition with no evidence of damage and only minimal wear. **$300**

Japanese boxed traveling tea ceremony set, consisting of three chawan, or tea bowls, one "mizusashi," or water container, a bamboo water ladle, a bamboo tea brush, a bamboo tea scoop and napkins—eight pieces in all—dating to the mid-20th century. One bowl measures 5 in. by 3 in., has an unglazed white foot and is decorated in blue and white dragonflies. The second bowl measures 4 1/2 in. by 3 in., has an unglazed terra-cotta foot, and and brown-speckled, white glaze. The third bowl is temmoku (a mountain between China's Zhejiang and Anhui provinces) in shape, measures 5 1/2 in. by 2 in., has an unglazed pottery foot, and is decorated with bamboo designs in brown and underglaze blue on white. The bowls are impressed with the name that may be "TOKO." The water container measures 6 in. in height and is decorated with a rich, dark, chocolate brown glaze with bamboo designs on one half. The other half has a brown/ivory glaze with some unglazed areas. This piece is unsigned. All eight pieces fit into compartments in the box. No losses or damage to any of the pieces. **$500**

Jewelry

Bar pin, Komai, scenic design, signed, Japanese, circa 1900. **$400-$600**

Bar pin, silver inset with six settings of topaz between filigree leaves, Chinese, circa 1900. **$200-$250**

Silver beads, China trade, late 19th century, 3 in. diameter, each. **$50-$75**

Belt, silver with eight rectangular sections, each section with a repoussé motif of flowers and leaves joined by plain loops, Chinese, late 19th century, extended to 27 in. **$450-$600**

Belt buckle, silver, oblong, cherry blossoms in relief, Japanese. **$135-$175**

Belt buckle, silver set with coral and turquoise in three hinged sections, the stones set amongst filigree scrolls, Nepalese, 19th century, 7 1/2 in. diameter. $500-$700

Belt hook, celadon jade, tongue-shaped fitting with dragon head pierced across its mouth, the underside with a flower head, button, Chinese, 18th century, 5 1/2 in. long. **$2,000-$2,500**

Bracelet, bangle, carved ivory with dragon motif, Chinese, circa 1925. **$100-$150**

Matching bracelet and pin, silver and black enamel, marked Siam, pin, $50-$75, bracelet. $50-$75
COURTESY OF RONI SIMON

Bracelet, Komai, seven round medallions with plain links, each of the medallions with a floral motif, Japanese, circa 1925. **$500-$700**

Bracelet, Komai, the plaques in silver mounts, plain silver links, each plaque with a varied motif (including a landscape, a lake scene, and a view of Mt. Fuji), Japanese, circa 1925. **$450-$650**

Bracelet, gilt, repoussé work, riders on horseback in a landscape, key borders, Chinese, mid-19th century. **$2,550-$3,500**

Bracelet, gold, eight tiger-eye discs, each set in 14-karat gold with a Fuku character at its center, plain links, Chinese, 20th century. **$200-$275**

Bracelet, pewter, bangle engraved with birds and flowers, Chinese, circa 1930. **$25-$50**

Bracelet, silver, five green jade plaques carved with Shou characters and two rows of plain silver links, Chinese, circa 1935. **$200-$300**

Bracelet, silver, hinged form, closed by a pin attached to a chain, three rows of pierced rosettes and two large clusters of plain silver beads attached to the terminals, Indian. **$300-$400**

Brooch, Komai with design of birds and flowers, marked S. Komai, Japanese, circa 1910. **$550-$750**

Brooch, Satsuma, dragon and clouds in gilt and colors, mounted in silver, Japanese, circa 1930, 2 1/2 in. diameter. **$400-$600**

Bracelet, Komai, with inlaid gold and silver floral and scenic plaques, Japanese, circa 1925. $500-$700

Brooch, silver with carved coral rose inset, Chinese, circa 1935. **$100-$125**

Brooch, silver with malachite insert carved with three flowers, Chinese, circa 1930. **$150-$200**

Cabochon, jade, brilliant, translucent green, 7 mm by 53 mm by 2 mm, realized price at an auction conducted by Christie's in Hong Kong (January 1986). **$9,000**

Cigarette case, Sentoku with gold, silver, and shakudo motifs of bamboo and flowers, Japanese, circa 1925. **$100-$150**

Clip, silver with gold wash, round and flat, set with a carved red lacquer plaque in a floral motif, Chinese, circa 1930. **$20-$30**

Cuff links, cloisonné, green ground, white peony blossoms, silver rims, dark green backs, Japanese, circa 1910. **$225-$350**

Cuff links, Komai, round with paulownia leaves in gold and silver, signed Komai, circa 1910. **$275-$400**

Cuff links, Satsuma, a motif of bamboo in colors and gold, silver mounts, Japanese, circa 1935. **$150-$200**

Cuff links, silver set with a round green jade plaque carved in low relief with a flower and foliage, Chinese, circa 1925. **$50-$75**

Earrings, carnelian drops, silver mountings, Chinese, circa 1920. **$100-$185**

Earrings, pale green cabochons set in 14 karat gold, pierced backs, Chinese, early 20th century. **$300-$500**

Earrings, plain carnelian loops, screw backs, Chinese, circa 1935. **$35-$65**

Bracelet, mother-of-pearl and silver button, Chinese, late Ch'ing (Qing) Dynasty. **$225-$300**

Earrings, carved celadon jade with a phoenix motif below seed pearls, screw backs, Chinese, circa 1925. **$175-$275**

Earrings, silver with gold wash and carved red lacquer drop bead, screw backs, China, circa 1930. **$20-$30**

Fingernails, silver inset with turquoise and coral beads, Chinese, early 20th century, pair. **$250-$325**

Comb, ivory with Shibayama inlay in a motif of flowers and butterflies, Japanese, late 19th century, 3 1/2 in. wide. **$900-$1,200**

Comb, tortoiseshell with seed pearls, Chinese, circa 1900. **$200-$300**

Comb, tortoiseshell with seed pearls along the top, two pearls missing, Chinese, circa 1910. **$150-$250**

Comb, tortoiseshell decorated with gold hiramakie (low relief) and hirame (large, irregular flakes of gold roughly sprinkled on a black lacquer ground, also fat gold flakes used in lacquer decoration [named for their resemblance to a flounder]) and inlaid in aogai (abalone shell) on a gold ground, Japanese, late 19th century, 3 3/4 in. wide. **$500-$700**

Hair ornament, lacquered tortoiseshell set inlaid with mother-of-pearl and coral, Shibayama, gold lacquer, Japanese, circa 1920. **$600-$900**

Hair ornament, kingfisher on a metal sheet forming a phoenix, embellished with semi-precious stones, Chinese, late 19th century, 7 in. long. **$200-$300**

Bracelet, silver with gold wash, the motif including a scenic design with warriors on horseback, mother-of-pearl and bamboo leaves, hallmarked CW (and Chinese characters), the mark of Cum Woo, Queen's Road, Hong Kong, circa 1850. **$2,000-$3,000**

Bracelet, silver with green enameled oval reserves containing silver characters for long life and good fortune, marked Siam, circa 1920. **$150-$225**

Earrings, celadon jade and 14 karat gold (for pierced ears), Chinese, circa 1900. **$500-$600**

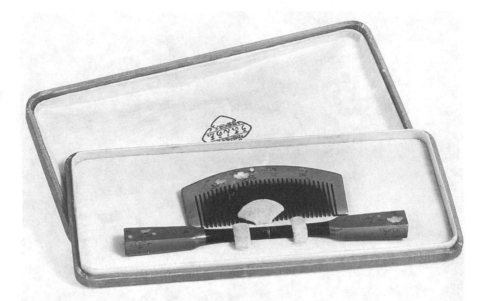

Hair ornament set, gilt lacquer on tortoiseshell with Shibayama inlay, circa 1910. **$700-$900**

Pendant, silver metal, in the form of an up-ended horse, with remnants of original green and red enamel on saddle, 3 7/8 in. by 3 in., with silver metal multi-strand chain with clasps in the form of bats, that measures 20 1/2 in. long, Chinese. **$250**

Pin, ivory, in the double happiness character, Chinese, circa 1925. **$100-$150**

Hair ornament, gold, circular, the border pierced with flower heads, a peacock medallion at the center, the whole set with rubies, Indian, 3 1/4 in. diameter. **$1,200-$1,500**

Hairpin, jade and pink tourmaline, Chinese, circa 1920. **$300-$500**

Hairpin and comb, roiro (black lacquer) ground with large flower heads, Zeshin style, Japanese, Taisho period. **$600-$900**

Hairpin, kingfisher resembling a phoenix, Chinese, early 20th century. **$100-$150**

Hat pin, Komai with motif of a willow tree and crane, Japanese, circa 1900. **$250-$350**

Headdress, kingfisher feathers with jade, rose quartz, and glass beads, some stones missing, Chinese, 19th century. **$300-$500**

Pin, Komai inlaid with gold, the back reads S. Komai, 3 3/4 in. diameter, circa 1910. **$400-$650**

Necklace, turquoise and silver bead with pendant, measuring 16 in. in length, with beads ranging from 10 mm to 20 mm. The pendant is made of hollow silver in the form of a fleur-de-lis, which measures 2 1/2 in. by 2 in. Chinese. **$100**

Necklace, 33 reticulated celadon and brown jade beads, each carved with the character for long life (Shou), restrung, Chinese, 19th century. **$1,500-$2,200**

Necklace, 73 graduated jade beads, each measuring anywhere from 8 mm to 3 mm in diameter, the beads are brilliant, translucent emerald green, diamond and gold clip attachment. **$60,000-$70,000**

Necklace, 24 uniform beads of carved red lacquer, hand-knotted, choker, Chinese, circa 1930, 16 in. long. **$50-$85**

Necklace, carnelian and 14 karat gold beads, 32 in. long. **$500-$700**

Necklace, carved ivory beads (uniform in size), hand-knotted, Chinese, circa 1925, 18 in. long. **$250-$350**

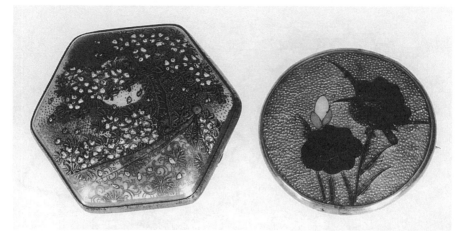

Left: Satsuma pin set in silver, gilt and raised enamels of a flowering tree with full moon above, Japanese, circa 1910, 3 3/4 in. diameter. **$200-$300**. Right: Cloisonné pin set in silver, ginbari (foil) with floral motif set against a silver-blue ground, silver wire, Japanese, circa 1920. **$275-$375**

Necklace, jade beads of various colors, hand-knotted, Shou character on clasp (14 karat gold), 18 in. long. **$400-$550**

Necklace, lapis lazuli, 21 round beads alternating with woven silk and metal discs, Indian, 21 1/4 in. long. **$250-$350**

Necklace, pink coral beads, graduated, Chinese, circa 1920, 18 in. long. **$150-$225**

Nose rings, six crescentic rows of small pearls, one row inside with a crystal inset lozenge at the top, the whole strung on gold wires and fringed with seed pearls and blue glass beads, Indian, 1 3/4 in. diameter. **$450-$600**

Pendant, aquamarine carved with a bat in flight, the stone with natural faults, Chinese, early 20th century, 2 in. long. **$300-$400**

Pendant, aquamarine carved as a peach, Chinese, late Ch'ing (Qing) Dynasty. **$300-$500**

Pendant, carnelian carved as a length of bamboo with a carved centipede, pierced for hanging, Chinese, late 19th century, 2 3/4 in. long. **$200-$300**

Pendant, carnelian, a spider carved from the lighter skin, Chinese, circa 1920. **$200-$400**

Pendant, celadon jade carved as the celestial twins, Chinese, late 19th/early 20th century, 2 1/2 in. wide. **$300-$500**

Pendant, celadon jade carved as two peaches with foliage, Chinese, late 19th century, 2 1/2 in. wide. **$200-$300**

Pendant, gold with a central turquoise surrounded by 11 coral insets, the whole surrounded by 14 turquoise inset petal forms with open-work sections in between, Indian, 3 in. diameter. **$300-$425**

Pendant, 14 karat gold Shou character, 1 in. diameter. **$200-$275**

Left: Silver pin, the character reading good fortune, marked D'argent and Saigon, made in Saigon for export to France, circa 1930. **$100-$150.** Right: Silver pin with fan below a bamboo-form bar (the character translates good fortune), Japanese, circa 1920. **$175-$200**

Pendant, ivory, oval, carved in high relief with flowers and filigree, black silk cord, ivory bead slide, silver clasp, Chinese, circa 1920, 36 in. long. **$175-$225**

Ring, pale green jade cabochon, 14 karat gold mounting. **$700-$900**

Ring, silver with a design of a seated Buddha, Chinese, circa 1900. **$150-$200**

Ring, silver with gold wash, set with oblong plaque of carved red lacquer, Chinese, circa 1935. **$50-$75**

Ring, silver with square turquoise inset and carved with Fuku character, Chinese, circa 1930. **$75-$100**

Ring, white gold set with a green jade cabochon measuring 252 mm by 16.2 mm by 6 mm, realized price at an auction conducted by Christie's in Hong Kong (January 1986). **$60,000**

Stick pin, Komai, round medallion with floral pattern, Japanese, circa 1900. **$250-$350**

Stick pin, Komai, diamond-shaped, scenic motif, Japanese, circa 1900. **$250-$350**

Tiara, kingfisher feathers, semiprecious stones and glass beads, Chinese, circa 1900. **$200-$300**

Korean Ceramics

Koreans have produced pottery since the prehistoric era. Lo-lang area pottery exhibited Chinese influences. Kimhae pottery from modern-day Pusan was the first truly indigenous ceramic ware. The pottery looked like a wide-mouth pot with a flaring rim and a horn-shaped handle. A cord pattern was produced by beating the gray clay with a stringed paddle. This was the predecessor to Old Silla high-fired stoneware from the fourth century AD.

The information known about ancient pottery is from the ceramics buried with the dead. They included pots, covered cups with a knobbed lid on a pedestal, and a long-necked jar requiring a stand. Clay figurines of animals and humans are also known. It is assumed that many of these figures are meant for decorative attachment to pots.

With the introduction of Buddhism, cremation became prevalent, so ceramic burial objects decreased in number. However, ceramic urns began to appear.

Ceramic tiles and roof tiles with inscribed images are common and are thought to have ceremonial and religious significance.

The pottery of the later Three Kingdoms period (57 BC- 668 AD) are identified by the kingdom in which it was produced. Koguryo and Paekche ceramics are noted for their brown and green glazes. Silla ceramics are recognized by their random glaze patterns.

Bottle, blue and white with large peony blossom, Yi Dynasty, 12 in. high. **$350-$550**

Bottle/vase, blue and white, faceted pear shape painted with a sparrow perched on a blossoming branch, the long neck ending in a rounded lip, Yi Dynasty, 11 in. high. **$700-$950**

Bowl, celadon, inlaid with cranes and clouds, Yi Dynasty, 5 in. diameter. **$125-$175**

Bowl, white glaze stopping high above a spreading foot, Yi Dynasty, 5 in. high. **$50-$100**

Stem bowl, celadon, measuring 6 in. diameter by 3 1/2 in. tall, dating to the 18th century. The bowl is foliate in design and is covered in rich, olive-green celadon glaze. A central floral design in overglaze, raised white and black enamel is surrounded by five similar designs in the cavetto (a concave molding having a curve that approximates a quarter circle). The foot shows the fine, whitish clay of the body and adherent grains of sand from the kiln. Fine original condition, with fitted box. **$300**

Box and cover, mishima inlay (stoneware made of gray clay to which white slip is applied using a variety of decorative techniques), flying cranes, rim chips, 13th century, 7 in. diameter. **$750-$1,000**

Underglaze blue bottle set on recessed ring foot with cylindrical neck and decorated in underglaze blue over an incised rambling-flower-spray pattern, covered in a clear glaze, Korean, Yi Dynasty, 19th century, 8 1/2 in. high. Realized price (including the 10-percent buyer's premium), Christie's, New York City. **$2,200**

Box and cover, mishima inlay, cranes inlaid in black and white slip on a stylized-cloud ground with flower-head medallion, lacquer repair, Koryo Dynasty, 6 1/2 in. diameter. **$500-$750**

Left to right: Blue and white jar with underglaze blue phoenix flying amid clouds, Korean, Yi Dynasty, 19th century, 8 1/4 in. high. Realized price (including the 10-percent buyer's premium), Christie's, New York City. **$4,400.** Blue and white dish, recessed ring foot, decorated in underglaze blue with a crane flying amid clouds, covered in a creamy white overall glaze, Korean, Yi Dynasty, 19th century, 6 in. diameter. Realized price (including the 10-percent buyer's premium), Christie's, New York City. **$3,080.** Blue and white bottle, pear-shaped, recessed ring foot, everted rim, underglaze blue hanging grapevine design, white glaze, Korean, Yi Dynasty, 7 1/2 in. high. Realized price (including the 10-percent buyer's premium), Christie's, New York City. **$2,640**

Brush pot, blue and white with a scenic motif including a fenced terrace, Yi Dynasty, 4 3/4 in. high. **$600-$850**

Brush pot, white glazed, open-work motif including confronting phoenixes and clouds, Yi Dynasty, 5 1/2 in. high. **$475-$700**

Charger, blue and white, measuring 16 in. in diameter, dating to the mid-20th century. The charger is decorated with a Chinese-style landscape and a poem in calligraphy. Small areas of brownish discoloration to the glaze. **$100**

Dish, short ring foot, flaring sides, pale green glaze, Yi Dynasty, 5 in. diameter. **$100-$200**

Serving dish, blue and white, measuring 12 1/2 in. by 2 1/2 in., dating to the mid- 20th century. The dish is decorated with cranes in a landscape design with flow-blue characteristics. Excellent condition. **$50**

Jar, short, everted neck painted in underglaze blue with peony, rim chips, Yi Dynasty, 7 in. high. **$175-$250**

Jar, globular, blue and white with a motif of flowering peony branches below a collar of florets and fret pattern, minor rim chips, Yi Dynasty, 4 1/2 in. high. **$1,500-$2,500**

Jar, opaque gray glazed stoneware, lacquer repair on rim, Yi Dynasty, 8 1/2 in. diameter. **$500-$700**

Jar, blue and white, painted with stylized foliage, Yi Dynasty, 8 1/2 in. high. **$150-$200**

Spittoon, celadon, flaring neck, globular body, olive green glaze, biscuit foot fired brown, Koryo Dynasty, 13th/14th century, 7 1/2 in. diameter. **$1,500-$2,200**

Offering vessel, Old Silla Dynasty, circa 3rd-6th century AD, decorated gray glazed cover with knob handle sits on high pedestal base with openwork rectangles, 5 7/8 in. by 5 in., rare. **$650-$750**

Offering vessel, Old Silla Dynasty, circa 3rd-6th century AD, decorated gray glazed cover with knob handle sits on high pedestal base with openwork squares, 5 1/2 in. by 5 1/2 in., rare. $650-$750

Vase, ovoid, flattened lip covered with a translucent green glaze, Yi Dynasty, 7 in. high. **$200-$300**

Vase, pear-shaped, decorated in white mishima on a celadon ground with floral medallions below a lappet band on the shoulder, lacquer repair on lip, Koryo Dynasty, 7 in. high. **$275-$375**

Vase, oviform body with short, ribbed neck and deep, cup-shaped lip, celadon glaze, 15th/16th century, 10 1/2 in. high. **$300-$500**

Water dropper, blue and white, square form with bamboo motif, Yi Dynasty, 3 1/4 in. high. **$100-$200**

Lacquer

CHINESE LACQUER

Lacquer was commonly applied to wooden objects, sealing off their surfaces with a protective coating. Originally, however, the Chinese had an altogether different use for this preservative. Because it turns black when exposed to air, lacquer was first used-with a stylus-for writing on bamboo slips wrapped together or tied to form books. During the Han Dynasty, lacquer was colored by the addition of metallic salts: Vermilion, or cinnabar, was produced with sulfide of mercury. With the discovery of ways to generate other hues, including black, brown, yellow, silver, gold, turquoise, olive green, and purple, lacquer became as popular for its ornamental value as it had been for its practicality.

Producing lacquer ware was a lengthy process. A base such as wood had to be planed very thin, then polished, after which a piece of paper, silk, or linen was applied to its surface. Next, layer after layer (20 to 30 coats) of lacquer was smoothed on, with each coat drying thoroughly. When enough coats had been applied, the lacquer could be painted. If the lacquer was to be carved, 200-300 coats were applied to create the necessary thickness.

JAPANESE LACQUER

The Japanese, besides using standard forms of lacquer production, created many aesthetically appealing innovations: raised work in colors; marbled lacquer; inlaid shell, gold, and silver leaf; pear-skin finishes; relief work using shell, foil, and so on prior to the application of the final coat; and using metal filings instead of gold or silver foil on the surface. Their lacquer wares may have metal, wood, paper, or ceramic bodies (bases).

Among the functional and decorative objects produced in Japanese lacquer are netsuke, inro, ojime, and hair ornaments.

DATING CHINESE LACQUER

During the Tang Dynasty, the dry hollow method of producing lacquer ware was developed. Layers of cloth saturated in lacquer were pressed onto a clay or wooden mold. When the lacquer had dried, the mold was removed, and the resulting cloth-based piece could be painted.

Sung (Song) Dynasty objects included red lacquer with carved landscapes, as well as small boxes with gold or silver bodies. In addition, mother-of-pearl inlay (laque burgauté-technique of decorating lacquer ware with inlaid designs employing shaped pieces of iridescent blue-green shell) was used for Imperial wares. (As laque burgauté evolved, it also included gold and silver foil inlays.)

The Yüan Dynasty brought new techniques such as red lacquer carved in deep relief, painted lacquer with gold relief, and pierced lacquer.

During the Ming Dynasty, some pewter bodies were used for Chinese lacquer ware, and reign marks were added. Ming designs were bold; with the onset of the Ch'ing Dynasty, designs became intricate and delicate by comparison.

Red lacquer was especially prominent in the Ch'ien Lung period of the Ch'ing Dynasty.

KOREAN LACQUER

Korean lacquer is highly polished with a mirror finish. It is usually found on metal bases. Most prominent are black or red objects sparsely decorated with mother-of-pearl motifs. Patterns include flowers, dragons, and flying cranes.

Album for postcards, motif of flowers and birds with Shibayama inlay (mother-of-pearl, coral, and horn) on a black ground, Japanese, circa 1910, 14 in. by 11 in. **$200-300**

Bowls, covered, set of five, Japanese lacquer over wood bowls with five accompanying shallow bowls, dating to the mid-20th century. The bowls are covered with a rich brown lacquer on the exterior and with black lacquer on the interior. The covers are decorated with cranes in flat and raised gold lacquer with red highlights. The covered bowls measure 4 3/4 in. by 3 3/4 in.; the shallow bowls measure 4 3/4 in. by 1 in. Excellent original condition with no damage and no significant wear. They are clearly the work of a master craftsman and were intended for use as a wedding gift. **$250**

Food bowls and stand for a doll's set, Japanese lacquer, rare, dating to the Meiji Era (1868-1912) but perhaps earlier. The set consists of a stand and six food bowls, four of which are covered. The items are made of a wood base with red lacquer interiors and black lacquer exteriors, decorated with a running vine and flower design in flat, gold lacquer, typical of Edo pieces. The gold edge of the stand is worn evenly, and the black lacquer has taken on the rich, dark brown patina characteristic of age and exposure to light. Two of the bowls have rough inner edges but no chips or cracks. Fine original condition. The stand measures 5 in. square and stands 4 1/4 in. tall. The bowls measure 2 in. by 2 in., 2 in. by 1/2 in., and 1 3/4 in. by 1 3/4 in., respectively. **$200**

Hinged box, Japanese black lacquer over wood with raised gold and silver lacquer designs of a palm tree, morning glories and a bird, measuring 10 in. by 8 in. by 2 1/2 in., dating to the early 20th century. The interior and back are finished in sprinkled nishiki-e (prints in several colors) using multicolored gold and silver powders. The box has a lock but no key. The black surface shows some wear consistent with aging. The raised lacquer is in excellent condition with only minimal wear. The box is signed on the front surface in gold lacquer sosho characters (cursive style Japanese calligraphy). **$350**

Book cover decorated in silver and gold takamakie (high relief) and applied in aogai (abalone shell inlay) and ivory, Hotei sitting on bag of treasures before a frog dressed as a fisherman and two seated mice dressed in priest's garb, minor damages, chips and scratches, Japanese, circa 1883, 15 1/2 in. by 12 1/2 in. Realized price, Christie's East, New York City. $825

Japanese suzuribako, or writer's box, made of black lacquer over wood, decorated with cloud and mon, or crest, designs in brown and gold flat lacquer, measuring 8 in. by 5 1/2 in. by 1 1/4 in., dating to the Taisho-Showa periods. The box is signed with a red kakihan (written seal, signature) on the reverse. The box has an interior compartment but none of the tools of the writer are present. Minor scuffing of the lacquer. **$300**

Box and cover, black ground, the cover is a group of gourds in takamakie (high relief), aogai (abalone shell inlay), and gold hiramakie (low relief), signed Zeshin, Japanese, late 19th century, 3 in. diameter. **$3,000-$4,500**

Box and cover, black, the lid carved with elephants and soldiers, a green floral border, Thai, 19th century, 11 in. long, 8 in. wide, 4 1/2 in. deep. **$200-$300**

Bowl with gilt motif of waves in Korin style, silver rim, Japanese, late Meiji period, 14 in. diameter. **$1,000-$1,750**

Box and cover, black with gold and silver togidashi (polished-out or rubbed lacquer, the design flush with the ground) in a motif of huts and Mt. Fuji, Japanese, circa 1910, 2 in. square. **$150-$200**

Box and cover, circular, gold hiramakie (low relief) on a red ground with kiku (chrysanthemum) and trellis pattern, nashiji interiors (irregularly shaped flakes of gold suspended in clear or yellowish lacquer, also called "pear ground," gold, silver or gold-silver alloys of reddish-yellow coloration used on lacquer, principally as a ground), Japanese, late 19th century, 3 in. diameter. **$1,500-$2,200**

Box and cover, circular, the domed lid inlaid with a mother-of-pearl floral spray in brown lacquer, overall mother-of-pearl coin pattern, old minor damages, Korean, Yi Dynasty, 18th century, 4 in. diameter. **$800-$1,200**

Covered bowl, cinnabar, Qing Dynasty (1644-1911), dated 1792, Imperial seal carved on cover, 13 1/2 in. by 5 in. **$2,000**

Storage box, lacquer over metal, measuring 6 in. by 4 in. by 1 1/2 in., Japanese, made by the Maruni Co. in Occupied Japan (1945-'52). The box is decorated on the outside with gold lacquer accented by a design of palm fronds or leaves in red, green, silver, and gray. The interior is gold lacquer. The base is footed. An example of Occupied Japan work that turned scrap metal into fine art. **$80**

Wooden box with an interior divider, decorated on the surface with irises in gold, green, white, and pink lacquer colors and three, accenting diagonal lines, measuring 10 in. by 8 in. by 1 1/2 in., Japanese, dating to the early to mid-20th century. The interior is finished in black lacquer. The tray, or divider, is finished in red lacquer and has a rest for pens or brushes. The interior of the lid is signed. Minor scratches on the under surface. **$125**

Box and cover, fan-shaped, nashiji interiors (irregularly shaped flakes of gold suspended in clear or yellowish lacquer, also called "pear ground," gold, silver or gold-silver alloys of reddish-yellow coloration used on lacquer, principally as a ground), kinji (brilliant gold lacquer) ground, the lid covered with mums, Shibayama inlay, Japanese, late 19th century, 6 in. wide. **$1,500-$2,000**

Box and cover (kogo), red lacquer ground with black motifs of insects, flowers, and foliage in a continuous motif (continued on the reverse), Japanese, 4 in. diameter, Taisho period. $1,000-$1,500

Box and cover, fish form, red and black, Japanese, circa 1935, 12 in. long. **$100-$150**

Box and cover, guri (carved lacquer), carved with scroll design, age cracks, Japanese, 18th century, 4 1/4 in. diameter. **$600-$900**

Kimono box, lacquer on wood, measuring 14 in. by 10 in. by 4 1/2 in., Japanese, dating to the mid-20th century. The box is covered in a glowing, deep chocolate brown lacquer, both inside and out. It contains a fitted interior tray. The exterior is decorated with inlaid shell in a design of two cranes on the surface and auspicious Buddhist symbols on the edges. The tray has a 16-petal chrysanthemum on one side and a kiri mon associated with the empress on the other, both in iridescent inlaid shell. There are minor scratches on the base but no other damage. The workmanship is typical of that known as Ryukyu lacquer from the island of Okinawa. Korean lacquerers do similar work, but the designs of this box are Japanese. **$600**

Box and cover, laque burgauté (technique of decorating lacquer ware with inlaid designs employing shaped pieces of iridescent blue-green shell), circular, inlaid with gilt foil in hexagonal cells around a mother-of-pearl flower head, Chinese, 18th century, 2 in. diameter. **$350-$500**

Box and cover, lacquer and leather, hand-painted with landscape scenes on a brown ground, brass fittings, Chinese, circa 1920, 15 in. long, 9 in. wide, 8 in. deep. **$125-$185**

Box and cover, lacquer and leather, hand-painted with landscape scenes on a red ground, brass fittings, Chinese, circa 1920, 15 in. long, 9 in. wide, 8 in. deep. **$200-$275**

Box and cover, rectangular, cinnabar (red) lacquer carved overall with peony sprays, black interiors, the lid with a carved white serpentine oval plaque set in the red lacquer, Chinese, circa 1925, 9 in. by 12 in. **$400-$600**

Box and cover, rectangular, brown ground decorated with tsuba (sword guard) and kozuka (small knife accompanying a short sword) in gold and colored takamakie (high relief) simulating various alloys, restored, Japanese, circa 1900, 4 1/2 in. by 7 3/4 in. by 5 in. **$1,800-$2,500**

Box and cover, round, cinnabar lacquer, black interiors, the lid carved with Shou Lao, overall scrolling vines, Chinese, late 19th century, 4 in. diameter. **$350-$500**

Box and cover, round, cinnabar lacquer, the cover with a relief garden landscape and figures of three Immortals, overall squared spiral ground, Chinese, mid-to-late 19th century, 5 1/2 in. diameter. **$500-$750**

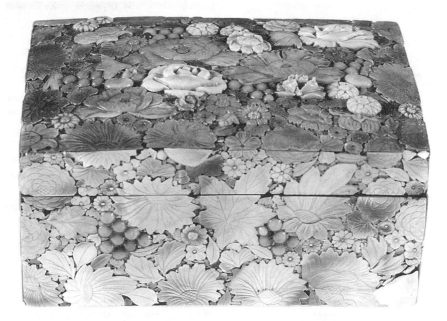

Box, Shibayama-on-lacquer, the overall motif of flowers, foliage, and berries in mother-of-pearl, ivory, coral, and jade, Japanese, late 19th century, 4 1/2 in. by 3 1/4 in. **$3,500-$5,500**

Box and cover, tsuishu, round, carved in relief, one side with a Rakan, the other with cell patterns, Japanese, 19th century, 3 in. diameter. **$700-$1,000**

Box and hinged cover, rectangular, the cover with relief motif of birds and flowers, pewter interiors, Chinese, early 20th century, 9 in. diameter. **$200-$300**

Box, tiered, cinnabar carved lacquer, old damages, Chinese, Ch'ien Lung (Qianlong), 18th century, 11 1/2 in. high. **$1,500-$2,500**

Brush pot or holder, bamboo, measuring 5 in. tall by 1 1/2 in. in circumference, covered with Negoro lacquer (a type of Japanese lacquer named after the Negoro Temple in Kü prefecture, where it was first made), Japanese, dating to the mid-20th century. It is decorated with a carved design of bamboo leaves. It is signed indistinctly on the bottom. **$125**

Candy dish and cover, orange and gold with silver mums on the lid, orange interiors, Japanese, circa 1935, 10 in. diameter. **$50-$75**

Box, cylindrical, tiered, carved red lacquer (cinnabar, the top with a scenic motif, black lacquer interiors, Chinese, 18th century, 6 in. high, minor damage. $1,200-$1,800

Censer, gold hiramakie (low relief), roiro (black lacquer) ground, sparse motif of bamboo sprays, nashiji interior (irregularly shaped flakes of gold suspended in clear or yellowish lacquer, also called "pear ground," gold, silver or gold-silver alloys of reddish-yellow coloration used on lacquer, principally as a ground), Japanese, circa 1915, 3 in. diameter. $100-$185

Chest and cover decorated in gold hiramakie (low relief) with mon, nashiji ground (irregularly shaped flakes of gold suspended in clear or yellowish lacquer, also called "pear ground," gold, silver or gold-silver alloys of reddish-yellow coloration used on lacquer, principally as a ground), copper mounts, cracked and faded, Japanese, Edo period, 25 in. by 60 in. $6,000-$8,000

Coasters (six) with matching container box, black with gold peony blossoms, Japanese, circa 1935, set. $20-$30

Crumb tray made of wood covered with black and red lacquer that has been rubbed to create a variegated design. The handle of the tray is carved in a floral design. The back is coated in black lacquer. The tray measures 9 in. by 8 in. Both front corners show loss of lacquer and there are surface scratches. Japanese. Probably late 19th or early 20th century. $25

Dishes, set of five, lacquer over wood, measuring approximately 5 in. in diameter, Japanese, dating to the mid-1900s. The dishes are coated with a rich, purple-red lacquer that is decorated with grapes in gold-orange and silver. Minor rim chips on two. $95

Dishes, set of five, lacquer, made of wood covered with offset deep reddish-brown lacquer over black, with five different designs of flowers and plants done in flat and raised gold lacquer, measuring 5 in. in diameter. They are signed and sealed by the artist. Japanese, early-to-mid 20th century. $250

Document box (bunko) and cover, gold hiramakie (low relief), nashiji (irregularly shaped flakes of gold suspended in clear or yellowish lacquer, also called "pear ground," gold, silver or gold-silver alloys of reddish-yellow coloration used on lacquer, principally as a ground), takamakie (high relief), and hirame (large, irregular flakes of gold roughly sprinkled on a black lacquer ground, also fat gold flakes used in lacquer decoration [named for their resemblance to a flounder]) on roironuri (a waxy black or mirror-black finish, a brilliant and highly reflective black lacquer) ground with pine, grasses, and flowers in a continuous pattern, silver rims, chipped and cracked, cover warped, Japanese, late 18th/early 19th century, 10 in. wide, 13 1/2 in. long, 3 3/4 in. deep. $2,000-$3,000

LEFT: Gofun brush with top in brown lacquer with gilt motifs, Japanese, circa 1900, 3 in. high. **$250-$375.** RIGHT: Box and cover (kogo), nashiji (irregularly shaped flakes of gold suspended in clear or yellowish lacquer, also called "pear ground," gold, silver, or gold-silver alloys of reddish-yellow coloration used on lacquer, principally as a ground) with gold motifs of bamboo and long-tailed tortoise (kame), Japanese, late 19th century, 3 in. high. **$900-$1,250**

Stacking food boxes, set of four, lacquer on wood, Japanese, decorated with a base of black lacquer on the outside and red lacquer on the inside, then covered with intricate scrollwork and mon in gold flat and raised lacquer in a style consistent with the late Edo period, or early-to-mid 18th century. The boxes rest on a pierced, lacquered wood tray and stand 8 in. overall in height. The tray measures 5 in. by 5 in. by 2 1/2 in. The boxes measure 4 in. by 4 in. by 1 1/2 in. The mon in raised gold lacquer is of a six-lobed passion flower, which has a central motif similar to the chrysanthemum. This crest was chosen by several Samurai families because of its simple beauty and similarity to the Imperial crest. The interior base of one of the boxes is cracked, some of the corners have minor chips, there is some rubbing of the gold, and mild loss of luster of the original black lacquer. **$450**

Inro storage box ("inrobako") with five drawers, detachable front lid, gold and silver togidashi (polished-out or rubbed lacquer, the design flush with the ground) with water plants and grasses on a mura nashiji ground (irregularly shaped flakes of gold suspended in clear or yellowish lacquer, also called "pear ground," gold, silver or gold-silver alloys of reddish-yellow coloration used on lacquer, principally as a ground), silver pulls and mounts, chipped and cracked, warped, three drawer pulls missing, Japanese, late Meiji period, 10 1/2 in. by 11 1/4 in. by 8 3/4 in. **$1,200-$1,800**

Jewelry box with musical mechanism, decorated with a peacock in a moonlit landscape, interior has mirror and is lined in blue velvet, with two hinged compartments and one drawer, with ring holder, marked Japan on the bottom, excellent condition, 12 in. by 5 7/8 in. by 8 1/4 in. **$200**

Jewelry box, black lacquer with painted scenic motif, musical, Japanese, circa 1955, 12 in. by 10 in. by 12 in. $50-$75

Kodansu, one hinged door enclosing three drawers, the kinji (brilliant gold lacquer) ground decorated in shades of gold and orange takamakie (high relief), hiramakie (low relief), kirigane (a lacquer technique used for details, with gold and silver particles), muranashiji (lacquer with small gold flakes in irregular clusters), and togidashi (polished-out or rubbed lacquer, the design flush with the ground), buildings and landscapes, the drawers with grasses, silver mounts, mura nashiji interiors (irregularly shaped flakes of gold suspended in clear or yellowish lacquer, also called "pear ground," gold, silver, or gold-silver alloys of reddish-yellow coloration used on lacquer, principally as a ground), Japanese, 19th century, 4 1/4 in. by 4 in. by 3 1/2 in. **$5,700-$7,000**

Kushidai, or traveling cosmetics case, wood and lacquer, Japanese, dating to the Edo period. The case is constructed of wood covered with black lacquer and gold flat and slightly raised lacquer scrolling vine patterns with variations of the Kutsuwa, or bit, mon design adapted from the pieces on the side of the horse's bit. Originally a military design, this crest was used by Christian families in the later Edo years because of the hidden cross design. The kushidai has four drawers with interior sprinkled nashiji lacquer (lacquer technique used for the ground, coarse gold powder), each with a circular, crest copper alloy pull. There is some wear to the side handles and to the lacquer, especially on the top, but the piece is in otherwise great condition. **$650**

Lazy Susan, orange and gold with gold and silver mums in low relief, Japanese, circa 1935, 12 in. diameter. **$50-$75**

Mirror case, gold hiramakie (low relief) and togidashi (polished-out or rubbed lacquer, the design flush with the ground) with dragonflies, nashiji interior (irregularly shaped flakes of gold suspended in clear or yellowish lacquer, also called "pear ground," gold, silver, or gold-silver alloys of reddish-yellow coloration used on lacquer, principally as a ground), badly chipped, Japanese, early 20th century. **$200-$400**

Model of Buddha seated with legs crossed, dry lacquer, jeweled necklaces showing through open robes, red and gold, old damages, Chinese, 17th century, 16 1/2 in. high. **$900-$1,200**

Model of Buddha seated on hexagonal lotus base with hands clasped around the right knee, traces of red, black, and gilt, some old damages, Chinese, 17th century, 14 1/2 in. high. **$800-$1,200**

Model of Daikoku's mallet, gold with wood-grain body, restored, Meiji period, 5 1/2 in. long. **$900-$1,200**

Model of a dignitary seated on a throne, red, gold, and black lacquer, beard made of human hair, some flaking, Chinese, circa 1900, 10 1/2 in. high. **$200-$300**

Model of Kuan Yin, carved cinnabar lacquer, the robes with repetitive square patterns and flower heads, both hands raised, Chinese, late 19th century, 12 1/2 in. high. **$900-$1,200**

Model of Shou Lao holding a staff and peach, cinnabar, his robe with Shou characters and cell patterns, some chipping at the bottom of the robe, Chinese, late 19th century, 14 in. high. **$900-$1,200**

Panel (taken from a cabinet door and framed), black and gold takamakie (high relief) with two birds perched on a branch beneath the full moon, Japanese, Taisho period, framed size 15 in. by 20 in. **$200-$325**

Pair of plates, luncheon or occasional, lacquer over wood, measuring 7 in. in diameter, Japanese, dating to the late Meiji-early Taisho periods (1868-1912). Each plate has a gold tendril or scrolling vine design accenting a central design of a seaside mountain scene done in raised gold and red lacquer. There are some small frets to the edge noticeable only by touch and some minor wear of the gold, otherwise fine original condition. They have no marks on the base, meaning either that they predated the tariff acts of 1891 or that they were part of a set that was marked on the box. Both the design and workmanship are typical of early 20th century—pre-World War II—work for the tourist trade. **$85**

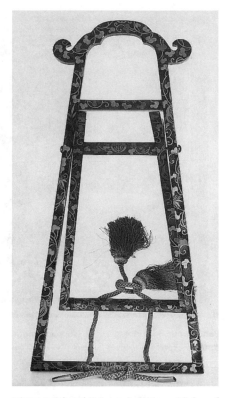

Mirror stand, nashiji (irregularly shaped flakes of gold suspended in clear or yellowish lacquer, also called "pear ground," gold, silver, or gold-silver alloys of reddish-yellow coloration used on lacquer, principally as a ground) with gold motifs and scrolls, Japanese, late Edo period. **$1,800-$2,500**

Sake barrel, red and black, the sides carved in relief to simulate twisted ropes, Japanese, late Meiji period, 23 in. wide. **$400-$600**

Sake cup, red lacquer over wood, measuring approximately 4 in. by 1 1/4 in., Japanese, dating to the mid-20th century. The cup has a gold five-petal blossom in the center, representing a family crest, or mon. Both the mouth and foot rims are gold edged. The base has five Kanji characters that represent the maker. Fine original condition. **$45**

Panel, wood, with gold lacquer, ivory and mother-of-pearl inlay, Japanese, circa 1900, 20 in. by 14 in. **$800-$1,200**

Sake kazu (wine pot), globular with gold kiku (chrysanthemum) and scrolls on a silver ground, black lacquer handle, Japanese, late Meiji period, 5 1/2 in. diameter. **$400-$650**

Screen, three-panel, each panel with a continuous scene of children playing, the upper portion of each panel having floral clusters and old damages, Chinese, early 20th century, each panel 18 in. by 72 in. **$1,000-$1,500**

Sewing box, oblong, black and gilt, hinged cover, interior with ivory accessories, Chinese, early 19th century, 14 in. wide. **$1,200-$1,600**

Shrine (portable "zushi"), black case containing Amida Nyorai standing on a lotus pedestal, gilt wood figure of Bodhisattva on each door, copper hinges, mandala missing (Hindu or Buddhist graphic symbol of the universe, specifically, a circle enclosing a square with a deity on each side; also a graphic and often symbolic pattern usually in the form of a circle divided into four separate sections or bearing a multiple projection of an image), Japanese, early Meiji period, 28 1/2 in. high. **$3,000-$4,000**

Tea caddy (natsume) with silk brocade pouch, motif of maple leaves flowing upstream, late Edo period. **$1,500-$2,500**

Tabako-bon (smoking implements) in gold and silver hiramakie (low relief), hirame (large, irregular flakes of gold roughly sprinkled on a black lacquer ground, also fat gold flakes used in lacquer decoration [named for their resemblance to a flounder]), and heidatsu (gold foil covered in lacquer, which is afterwards polished so that the gold is visible) with flowering cherry trees, one wide drawer below two smaller drawers, the top with silver liners and silver covers, silver carrying handle, cracked and chipped, Japanese, late 19th century. **$2,500-$3,500**

Tabako-bon, rectangular, rounded corners, gold hiramakie (low relief) and heidatsu (gold foil covered in lacquer, which is afterwards polished so that the gold is visible) with mother-of-pearl inlaid motif of maple and cherry branches floating in a river, silver rims, nashiji interiors (irregularly shaped flakes of gold suspended in clear or yellowish lacquer, also called "pear ground," gold, silver, or gold-silver alloys of reddish-yellow coloration used on lacquer, principally as a ground), scratched and minor chipping, Japanese, late Meiji period, 11 1/2 in. by 9 in. by 6 in. **$4,500-$6,500**

Tabako-bon, roironuri (a waxy black or mirror-black finish, a brilliant and highly reflective black lacquer) decorated in gold, silver, and red takamakie (high relief), hiramakie (low relief), hirame (large, irregular flakes of gold roughly sprinkled on a black lacquer ground, also fat gold flakes used in lacquer decoration [named for their resemblance to a flounder]), nashiji (irregularly shaped flakes of gold suspended in clear or yellowish lacquer, also called "pear ground," gold, silver, or gold-silver alloys of reddish-yellow coloration used on lacquer, principally as a ground), and heidatsu (gold foil covered in lacquer, which is afterwards polished so that the gold is visible) with red-capped Manchurian cranes in the sunset above peony blossoms and branches; the base fitted with a drawer below two smaller drawers, the top with two copper liners and silver covers, sentoku (yellow metal alloy consisting of copper, zinc, and tin) carrying handle, damaged, Japanese, late 19th century, 9 in. wide. **$1,200-$1,500**

Tea caddy (natsume) in gold hiramakie (low relief) and heidatsu (gold foil covered in lacquer, which is afterwards polished so that the gold is visible) on a red-brown ground with a motif of seashells, nashiji interior (irregularly shaped flakes of gold suspended in clear or yellowish lacquer, also called "pear ground," gold, silver, or gold-silver alloys of reddish-yellow coloration used on lacquer, principally as a ground), chipped and cracked, Japanese, early 19th century, 3 1/2 in. high. **$650-$850**

Tea caddy, carved wood covered with gold lacquer, measuring 5 1/2 in. by 4 1/2 in., dating to the early-to-mid 20th century. The interior is coated in black lacquer. Fine original condition. **$50**

Tea or luncheon set, complete, black and gold lacquer over wood, 36 pieces, Japanese, dating to around 1950. The set is decorated in varying floral motifs in gold lacquer over black. It includes a tea or coffeepot with lid, sugar with lid, creamer, six cups, six saucers, six luncheon plates, six spoons, two service plates, and a tray. **$200**

Table screen, cinnabar, rectangular, carved with figures before a pavilion, the reverse with ladies in a landscape, the base and sides carved with lotus heads and foliage on a spiral pattern ground, restored, Chinese, circa 1900, 16 in. high. **$800-$1,200**

Tray, black with sparse gold plum branches, Japanese, circa 1930, 15 1/4 in. by 20 in. **$150-$250**

Tray, laque burgauté (technique of decorating lacquer ware with inlaid designs employing shaped pieces of iridescent blue-green shell), inlaid with iridescent shell in a scenic motif with pairs of figures, Chinese, 18th century, 4 1/2 in. square. **$375-$485**

Tray, cinnabar, canted rectangular form, the central pattern with children in a garden, the border with peony scrolls that continue on the underside, Chinese, early 19th century, 9 in. by 11 in. **$900-$1,200**

Tray for kimono, gold hiramakie (low relief) with a mon, nashiji underside (irregularly shaped flakes of gold suspended in clear or yellowish lacquer, also called "pear ground," gold, silver, or gold-silver alloys of reddish-yellow coloration used on lacquer, principally as a ground), Japanese, circa 1920, 25 in. long. **$1,000-$1,500**

Tray, oval, gold takamakie (high relief) on a nashiji ground (irregularly shaped flakes of gold suspended in clear or yellowish lacquer, also called "Pear ground," gold, silver or gold-silver alloys of reddish-yellow coloration used on lacquer, principally as a ground) with a scene featuring Samurai with banners, Japanese, late Meiji/early Taisho period, 14 1/4 in. long. **$300-$400**

Tray, oval, motif of a warrior on horseback, gilt on black, Burmese, circa 1900, 18 1/4 in. diameter. **$150-$300**

Tray, lacquer/papier-mâché, red ground with gold designs of birds in flight, marked Made in Japan, circa 1930, 7 1/2 in. by 13 in. **$200-$275**

Tray, lacquer/papier-mâché, black ground with gold motif of blossoming branches, marked Made in Japan, circa 1930, 10 1/2 in. by 13 1/2 in. **$150-$225**

Tray, rectangular, gold takamakie (high relief) on a nashiji ground (irregularly shaped flakes of gold suspended in clear or yellowish lacquer, also called "Pear ground," gold, silver or gold-silver alloys of reddish-yellow coloration used on lacquer, principally as a ground) with a motif of clam shells, Japanese, late Taisho/early Showa period, 15 1/2 in. long. **$300-$500**

Tray, red with an incised pattern of a peacock and tree peony, overall cell pattern, cracked, Chinese, early 19th century, 18 in. wide. **$600-$800**

Tray, round, lacquer/papier-mâché, black ground with sparse decoration of flowers in colors and gilt, marked Japan, circa 1935, 12 1/2 in. diameter. **$200-$250**

Tray and box, silver with gold and black hiramakie (low relief) dragonflies, Japanese, Taisho period, 9 in. wide. **$500-$700**

Pair of vases, Chinese, made for the mantle of molded lacquer resin over brass bodies, covered with orange/red cinnabar designed with two panels of birds and flowers amidst overall Greek key and scrollwork designs. These vases were initially molded, then finished by hand, in a manner of production in use since the Han Dynasty, so it is impossible to date them precisely, probably early to mid-20th century. Excellent condition with no evidence of damage. **$650**

Vase, archaic beaker form, black surface on pewter inlaid with mother-of-pearl and gold foil, a continuous mountainscape, some losses, Chinese, early 18th century, 10 1/2 in. high. **$600-$800**

Writing box (suzuribako), black lacquer with gold and silver flowers and foliage, the interior with ink stone and water dropper, Japanese, late Meiji/early Taisho period. **$1,000-$1,500** Private Collection

Vase for ikebana (Japanese flower arranging), lacquered wood, made from a tree limb or trunk, measuring 11 1/2 in. high and 6 in. at its widest, Japanese, dating to the Meiji-Taisho periods. The vase has lacquered leaves and a bird in raised red, gold, and silver lacquer. There is a metal insert for the flowers. Minor wear. **$200**

Vase with detachable stand, cinnabar carved with Shou rounders and floral bands, old damages, Chinese, early 19th century, 14 in. high. **$575-$750**

Vase, ovoid form, trumpet neck, kinji (brilliant gold lacquer) ground with writhing dragon and nashiji interior (irregularly shaped flakes of gold suspended in clear or yellowish lacquer, also called "pear ground," gold, silver, or gold-silver alloys of reddish-yellow coloration used on lacquer, principally as a ground), Japanese, late Meiji period, 8 in. high. **$1,000-$1,500**

Vase and cover, cinnabar, carved with sages and attendants set in rocky landscapes, Chinese, 20th century, 10 in. high. **$225-$325**

Vases, carved cinnabar lacquer, globular form, two panels, each inlaid with jade, mother-of-pearl, and coral in a motif of cranes and pine with trellis, carved ground, key pattern at the shoulders and necks, Chinese, circa 1900, 19 1/2 in. high, pair. **$1,500-$1,900**

Water bucket, deep red lacquer over metal, in traditional shape, measuring 9 in. high and 3 in. across the base, decorated with a cricket in silver and gold flat lacquer, Japanese, signed by the Maruni Co. and dated to the Occupied Japan period (1945-1953). Minor surface scratches. **$200**

Writing box (suzuribako), brown ground with mura nashiji (irregularly shaped flakes of gold suspended in clear or yellowish lacquer, also called "pear ground," gold, silver, or gold-silver alloys of reddish-yellow coloration used on lacquer, principally as a ground) decorated with a cherry tree, pine, and prunus in gold, silver, and colored togidashi (polished-out or rubbed lacquer, the design flush with the ground); the interior with a fitted tray, ink stone, and water dropper (suiteki), cover chipped and cracked, Japanese, 19th century, 8 1/4 in. by 9 1/2 in. **$2,500-$3,500**

Writing box, hiramakie (low relief) and togidashi (polished-out or rubbed lacquer, the design flush with the ground) on a roiro (black lacquer) ground with motif of a large pine, gold hiramakie interior on a nashiji ground (irregularly shaped flakes of gold suspended in clear or yellowish lacquer, also called "pear ground," gold, silver, or gold-silver alloys of reddish-yellow coloration used on lacquer, principally as a ground) with wide-leaf bamboo, silver water dropper, the cases of the writing implements in gold nachiji (lacquer technique used for the ground, with coarse gold powder) with silver fittings, corner chipped and repaired, Japanese, Meiji period, 9 1/4 in. wide, 10 1/8 in. long, 2 3/8 in. deep. **$4,000-$5,000**

Writing box, gold, silver, and red hiramakie (low relief) inlaid in aogai (abalone shell) on a gold-speckled black ground, motif of a gateway, trees, and foliage; the interior with nashiji ground (irregularly shaped flakes of gold suspended in clear or yellowish lacquer, also called "pear ground," gold, silver, or gold-silver alloys of reddish-yellow coloration used on lacquer, principally as a ground) and a willow motif, fitted with ink stone and silver water dropper, chips and crack, Japanese, late 18th/early 19th century. **$3,500-$5,000**

Metalwares

CHINESE BRONZE

Emperor Huang Ti, the Yellow Emperor (approximately 2697-2597 BC), is recorded as having conceived of the idea for casting metal, thereby opening the door to the development of decorative and functional metalworks. The first bronze vessels, however, were not cast until approximately 2205 BC, during the reign of Emperor Yu, the fifth emperor to follow Huang Ti. His reign saw the production of the tripod, in the form of three-legged bronze cauldrons. Eventually, the tripod became a symbol of Imperial power.

Collectors consider Shang/Yin era (1766-1122 BC) vessels as the focal point among early bronze pieces. Produced for religious and court ceremonies as well as domestic purposes, these vessels helped determine the rank or standing of a household; the more bronze a person or family owned, the more highly they were esteemed.

Early bronze pieces were finished with tools. Some of them were inlaid with black pigment or with gold and/or silver. They could also be partially gilded and inlaid with semiprecious stones (mainly turquoise). Shang bronzes might even be ornamented with geometric motifs, animal designs, or bands of designs. A frequently used motif was (and still is) the t'ao t'ieh (mythical Chinese creature called the beat of gluttony), or monster mask, a grotesque face having two eyes, eyebrows, nostrils, and only an upper lip.

Shang bronzes should be covered with a patina (corrosion produced by oxidation of the metal), which is a bluish green, yellowish, or reddish efflorescence. This patina is highly prized.

The defeat of the Shang brought about a new reign, the Chou Dynasty. Chou bronzes fall into periods: early, 1027-900 BC; middle, 900-600 BC; and late, 600-256 BC, followed by the Warring States period, 255-222 BC. At first, Chou bronzes were copies of Shang pieces, distinguished only by their more elaborate designs. Then came the heavier objects of the middle period, with handles and legs decorated with lower relief (not as sharp or high as Shang specimens).

Late Chou bronzes were given more delicate and intricate motifs. There was more use of silver, gold, and/or copper inlays. Pieces included dagger hilts, swords with turquoise stones inlaid, realistic human figures, animals, and personal accessories such as belt hooks, combs, hairpins, mirrors, and so on. Longer inscriptions were another characteristic of later Chou bronzes.

The short-lived Ch'in Dynasty, 221-206 BC, was an oppressed time during which bronzes with historical inscriptions were melted down. Following it was the Han Dynasty, 206 BC-220 AD, when bronze was fashioned in a variety of functional forms (and sizes) such as dishes, bells, ewers, and basins. During this time, casting was done with the lost wax method. An exact model of the desired vessel was produced in wax, around which a clay mold was formed. A few holes were left in the clay mold so that the wax could be melted, drained, and replaced with molten metal. When the bronze hardened, the mold was usually broken off. If a mold composed of several pieces was used, the pieces could be separated to allow removal of the cast bronze, in which case the mold could be reused.

Han vessels, for the most part, contained 83 percent copper and 17 percent tin. Inlays included gold, silver, turquoise, and the addition of malachite; many pieces were silvered or gilded overall. Bowls, for instance, were usually void of motifs and covered with silver.

In general, bronzes of the Han Dynasty were simpler and more realistic than those from previous eras. Real animals were depicted instead of mythological ones, and the animals were elongated to produce the effect of motion: Horses, for example, are shown with outstretched feet.

During the Ming Dynasty, new processes for variegating the surface of the metal were developed. Reign marks came into use, and vessels based on ceramic shapes, in addition to those with fish-form, rope, phoenix, and elephant handles, were developed.

Included among bronze surfaces were chestnut brown, yellow gold, and crab apple, some of which featured gold raindrop forms or forms similar to gold snowflakes (splashed gold).

In the succeeding dynasty and into the 20th century, fine Chinese bronzes continued to be produced. Collectors, therefore, have a tremendous range of objects to study. Accordingly, they must consider many factors, among them, stylistics, patina, and markings, in order to make proper age and value identifications. Early specimens often need testing in order for their ages to be accurately determined.

JAPANESE ALLOYS

About 200 BC, during the Han Dynasty, the influence of Chinese and Korean art and industry in producing metalwares reached Japan. The Japanese, quick to learn new methods from travelers, were not satisfied with copying bronze and iron objects, and began to produce their own: mirrors, swords, and bells, for instance. With the introduction of Buddhism in the 6th century AD and the resulting demand for images and other religious articles, Japanese metalwork progressed still further. By the 8th century, coinage had been introduced. Finally, the civil wars of the 12th century brought weapons and armor into great demand, and with that, families of quality metalworkers and swordsmiths rose in prominence.

Later developments continued to strengthen the need for metalwork. With the advent of the tea ceremony, the manufacture of kettles and other utensils became significant. The opening of trade with the West in the 16th century led to the introduction of firearms.

During the Tokugawa period, 1615-1868, peace reigned and the art of the metalworker flourished. The bronze makers' art included architectural accoutrements, shrines cast entirely in bronze, and gates for temples. Large bronze lanterns were produced to line the courtyards of shrines.

As both the science of preparing metals and the art of designing them advanced, the Japanese developed a number of interesting alloys. Plentiful copper, known to some collectors for its successful application in hammered and enameled objects, was used chiefly in alloys such as bronze, shakudo (dark pickled alloy, a mixture of copper, gold, and other materials), shibuichi, and sawari.

Shakudo is three to six percent gold. Suitable treatment by pickling and polishing produces a beautiful glossy patina of dark brown or bluish black on objects formed from this alloy. Shakudo makes a perfect ground for inlaid designs of gold, silver, and/or copper.

Similarly, shibuichi has physical properties that make it excellent for inlays. It may consist of one part silver to three parts copper, one part silver to two parts copper, or a 50/50 mix of the two. The value of this alloy is dependent, in part, on its patina. When shibuichi is first cast, its color is that of pale gunmetal. Its beauty comes with the gray tones that the mix produces.

Sawari, a mix of copper, tin, and lead, was used quite often for creating Buddhistic ceremonial articles.

Box and cover in the form of a helmet, gold-inlaid mon and clouds, Japanese, early Meiji period, 2 1/2 in. high. **$800-$1,200**

GOLD

Few gold objects were produced because the use of this metal was restricted in Japan. However, it was very popular in the gilding of copper, bronze, and so on, as well as for inlays and as part of the alloy shakudo. Gold was also suitable for lacquering, or was used alone in small articles such as ojime, menuki (sword pegs), and pouch clasps.

KOMAI

In 1855, the Komai family originated a form of damascene (or Japanese zogan) used to ornament swords, guns, and various types of sword furniture. With the major changes brought about by the Meiji restoration, beginning in 1868, the Samurai were no longer allowed to wear swords, so the Komai family, like many others, had to find another form of livelihood. They applied their damascene craft to creating objects in Western and traditional Japanese styles. Their wares were very well received in the West and are highly prized today.

There were two makers of Komai wares working in Kyoto: S. Komai and O. Komai. Each used a different mark, but the quality of their work is the same. Komai-style works, on the other hand, look like genuine Komai, but were produced with a different metal body.

The following outline describes the process used to create damascene ware.

1. On a ground of steel, double hatch lines were cut with a chisel.
2. The outline of the design was drawn on paper and transferred onto the ground by means of the tracing method, in which a design could be copied through paper onto the ground with a small needle point.
3. Some combination of gold, silver, and/or copper was then pounded into the ground, following the pattern of the copied dots.
4. At this point, approximately 20 coats of lacquer were applied, each being baked onto the object before the next application.
5. The object was then rubbed and polished to a bright finish.

CHINESE SILVER

Silver has always been abundant in China. Among the many articles produced from this abundance, perhaps the finest are those of the Tang Dynasty. During this period, silver was alloyed with tin and lead, cast into the desired shape, and finished with hammering. Handles and ring feet were soldered on, and sometimes a lining was added, especially when the motif came through to the other side. Many of the objects produced feature a ground closely packed with circles that were punched with a die on which the lines and surfaces of the design had been traced.

Yuan Dynasty silver, for the most part, had plain, beaten surfaces, with a floral medallion or flower-and-phoenix motif. During the Ming Dynasty, the limited amount of silver produced was either cast, engraved, traced, or finished with repoussé.

Chinese silver of the Ch'ing Dynasty enjoyed immense export popularity. This silver matched the shapes of Chinese export porcelains and was, for the most part, designed to meet the requirements of Western tastes, with patterns based on English and American patterns.

The following remarks from Charles L. Tiffany tell a great deal about why Chinese silver was in such demand. They were made following a visit to a silversmith on Old China Street, 1844.

"He can manufacture any article-from a salt spoon to a service plate-in the most elegant manner. He will line a pitcher with its coating of gold or produce a favorite pattern of forks in a very short time. The silver is remarkably fine and the cost of working it a mere song. Its intrinsic value is, of course, the same as in Europe, but the poor creatures who perspire over it are paid only enough to keep the breath in their bodies. Filigree baskets or card cases seem to be favorites with these silversmiths. It is much cheaper to have a splendid service of plate in China than in any other country, and many Europeans send out orders through supercargoes."

The earliest Chinese maker of export silver was Pao Yun (circa 1810-1840). He was joined by a number of other makers who worked during the early to mid-19th century (or shortly thereafter), many of whom copied English hallmarks. Some used initials and/or Chinese marks: "W" was used by Wo Shing or Wohing; an "H" by Lee Ching of Hong Kong and Hoachings;

"WH" by Wang Hing from Queens Road, Hong Kong; "CW" by Cum Wo; "SS" is associated with Synshing; and "YS" is associated with Yutshing.

JAPANESE SILVER

Although pure silver ore is rare in Japan, lead ore containing considerable proportions of silver is common, and from ancient times has been the major source of silver for the Japanese. Extraction of the silver begins with the smelting of the lead ore, followed by cupellation, a process that involves melting the metal in a porous cavity in the ground so that the lead sinks into the pores, and leaves only the silver. The extraction process is very wasteful of lead, and as a result, silver has found only a small place in Japanese metalwares. However, during the last three centuries, a method has been used to extract silver from copper ore.

Japanese silver has been used in conjunction with cloisonné and the art of enameling, as well as for inlays and in the alloy shibuichi, which is valued for its patina. Since the eighteenth century, kettles, vases, ornaments, and such-some of which are masterpieces of chasing-have been produced. Other works of Japanese silver include personal accessories and occasional objects. Unlike the Chinese counterparts, these objects were made with an emphasis on Japanese style rather than on Western styles.

Japanese silver objects generally have a higher silver content than Chinese silver objects.

OTHER CHINESE ALLOYS

Often, Chinese silversmiths worked in other metals including gold. One such metal was paktong, an alloy made of copper, nickel, and zinc, and used exclusively for export objects such as candlesticks.

Pewter was another metal popularly used for exports, with the largest amount of pewter exported from China during the 19th century, around the time of the U.S. Centennial. Chiefly used for tea caddies, incense-stick holders, pricket sticks, jars, teapots, and so on, pewter was sometimes inlaid with brass, copper, or semiprecious stones (especially in the late Ch'ing Dynasty and early 20th century).

Archaic Chinese Bronzes

BY MICHAEL B. KRASSNER

Archaic bronzes are considered by many collectors to be the finest examples of Chinese art, and it was only during the 20th century that Shang Yin, Chou, and Han bronzes have come onto the Western market.

The following are types of bronze vessels from the Shang Yin to the Han Dynasties (1525 BC-220 AD). They served as models for countless copies through the centuries.

LI. A tripod vessel with hollow legs (one of the most ancient pottery forms) and having two upright loop handles through which a stick could be passed for lifting. Used for cooking meat.

TING. Similar to a Li, but with solid legs; also used for cooking meat. This is referred to in early Chinese dictionaries as a sacred vessel for blending the Five Tastes (acrid, sour, salt, bitter, and sweet), a vessel for cooking food, or a vessel for boiling well-cooked food.

HSIEN. This is really two vessels: a steamer, formed like a li, with an upper part consisting of a colander with handles. Used for cooking vegetables and cereals. One of these vessels bears the inscription For use while campaigning, while traveling, to make soup from rice and millet.

KUEL (OR CHIU). A bowl, with or without a cover, sometimes with handles, resting on three or four feet, or on a hollow base. Used as a container for grain.

TOU. A shallow dish-with handles and a cover-on a round base; used for offering fruit. The circular projection on the cover served as a foot when the cover was inverted.

FU. A rectangular covered dish with straight, sloping sides, sometimes with four feet. (The cover is almost a duplicate of the vessel.) Used for cooked cereals.

HSU. A shallow oval dish with handles and cover. As with the tou, the projection on the cover served as a foot when inverted. This is not a ritual vessel. Many are inscribed Traveling Hsu and were used during expeditions.

I (ALSO WRITTEN YI AND IH). A ewer from which water was poured, often shaped like a sauce boat. The name "i" is also used as a general term for sacrificial vessels.

KUANG. A squat vessel, elongated from front to back, with a handle at the back and a cover extending over an open spout. Also shaped like a sauceboat, but larger than an "i" (as described above).

HU. A large wine vessel with a bulbous body, narrow neck, and usually ring handles. Used for storing food.

LEI. A large vase, or jar, for wine. It is like a hu, but with the widest part of the body just below the neck.

TSUN. A ceremonial wine vessel that is rectangular and has a flaring lip.

CHIA. A round tripod, or square and four-legged, vessel with a handle on one side and two uprights on the lip. The legs are hollow so that when the vessel is filled with wine or water and pushed down onto a glowing bed of coals, the maximum surface will be exposed to the heat.

KU. A tall, slender wine beaker with a

wide foot and trumpet mouth.

Chiieh (formerly written Chio). A tripod cup with a handle and a pointed lip.

YU. A large, deep, covered vessel with a flaring lip, with or without handles, for storing wine or water.

P'AN. A shallow basin (usually round) for washing. Used in ceremonial rites and in domestic life.

CHIEN (OR HSI). A large, deep basin with two handles, also used for washing.

NOTE: In addition to the vessels listed here, there were many that were made in the form of animals-notably tigers, elephants, goats, deer, and birds.

Bronze Shapes

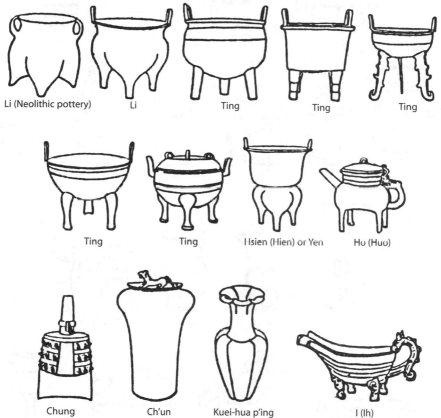

Li (Neolithic pottery)　　Li　　Ting　　Ting　　Ting

Ting　　Ting　　Hsien (Hien) or Yen　　Ho (Huo)

Chung　　Ch'un　　Kuei-hua p'ing　　I (Ih)

Bronze Shapes

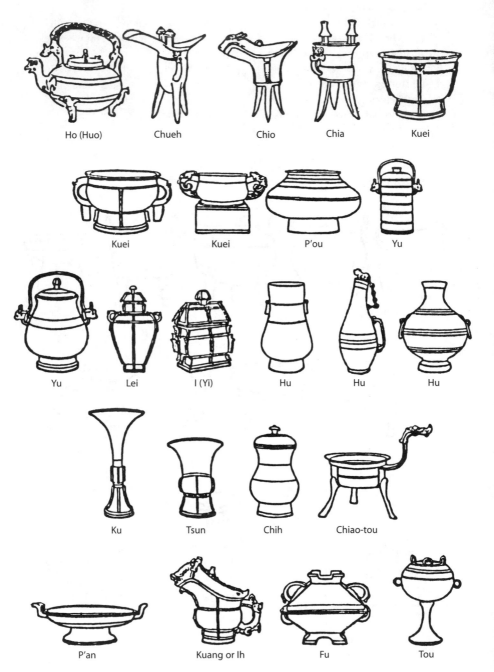

Ho (Huo)　　Chueh　　Chio　　Chia　　Kuei

Kuei　　Kuei　　P'ou　　Yu

Yu　　Lei　　I (Yi)　　Hu　　Hu　　Hu

Ku　　Tsun　　Chih　　Chiao-tou

P'an　　Kuang or Ih　　Fu　　Tou

Brass

Ashtrays, oblong with fluted edge, marked China, circa 1935, nest of four. **$25-$45**

Bonbon dish, fluted edge and base, engraved with a floral motif, marked China, circa 1925, 3 in. by 5 1/2 in. **$45-$65**

Finger bowl, two handles, embossed floral motif, marked China, circa 1930. **$30-$50**

Bowl engraved with two confronting dragons, hardwood stand, both pieces marked China, circa 1915, 14 in. diameter. **$125-$175**

Candelabra, two-light, marked China, circa 1930, 4 3/4 in. by 9 3/8 in. **$35-$65**

Candelabra, three-light, the center holder upon an S shape, marked China, circa 1937, 8 3/4 in. high. **$75-$100**

Candlesticks, dragons entwined on stems, marked China, circa 1935, 4 in. high. **$45-$65**

Censer, four stub feet, two bamboo-form handles, the body with radiating bamboo leaves, Japanese, circa 1925, 5 1/2 in. high. **$150-$220**

Censer, tripod, the body with a carp and wave design, the lid with lotus blossoms and leaves, Japanese, circa 1925, 4 in. by 5 in. **$125-$175**

Cigar box, wood roller top painted with a landscape, Japanese, circa 1930, 8 1/2 in. high. **$50-$75**

Dinner bell and hardwood stand, the bell embossed with a dragon, the stand similarly carved, marked China, circa 1925, overall height 15 in. **$150-$250**

Dinner gong, set of three bells, graduated in size, strung on silk cords, decorated with red flowers, striker missing, Japanese, circa 1925. **$50-$75**

Censer with three interlocking sections and top with fine grid pattern, assembled measures 3 3/4 in. by 3 1/4 in. by 3 1/4 in., Chinese. **$125**

Figure of Buddha on stand, Tibetan, 21 1/2 in. by 27 in. by 13 in. **$1,200**

Flatware service with carving knife, fork and salad servers, each piece decorated with Ganesh, marked Siam, circa 1928, service for eight. **$200-$350**

Figure of a bull standing on a rectangular base with flat, lobed rim, arched tail, beaded trappings and bells around his neck, Indian, 19th century, 5 1/2 in. high. **$300-$450**

Kettle (for hot water) with stand and alcohol lamp, hammered, Fuku character surrounded by etched floral patterns, silver lining, Japanese, circa 1915. **$200-$325**

Pair of medallions in the shape of butterflies and water lilies, pierced-brass, Chinese, measuring 2 1/2 in. by 2 1/2 in., dating to the mid-20th century. **$50**

Smoker's set: tray, cigarette holder, cigar holder, ashtray, and match-box holder, etched floral motif, Japanese, circa 1930, tray size 12 in. by 9 in. **$125-$175**

Smoker's set: round cigarette jar, ashtray, and match holder on a brass smoking stand with removable round tray, Chinese, circa 1925, 21 3/4 in. high. **$300-$500**

Spittoon (Bidri) with overall design of leaves within bulbous medallions, shoulder and neck in a herringbone pattern, Indian, 19th century, 8 1/2 in. high. **$325-$500**

Mini-teapot with glass bead finial and glass flowers, foliage in low relief, Chinese, circa 1925, 2 1/2 in. high. **$50-$75**

Match case, circa late 19th or early 20th century, in the form of dragon holding a ball, the case hinged to open at the dragon's mouth, Japanese, 1 1/2 in. by 3 in. **$700-$750**

Tray incised with panels of calligraphy within a trellis border, Indian, early 20th century, 22 1/2 In. diameter. **$200-$300**

Vase (Bidri), straight flaring sides decorated with silver-inlaid flowers and scrolling stems, Indian, 19th century, 8 3/8 in. high. **$375-$550**

Vases (Bidri), squared foot with turned stem and ribbed ovoid body, tall neck with floral mouth, overall silver-inlaid flowering plants, Indian, 19th century, 14 in. high, pair. **$900-$1,200**

Vase with gold and silver fish, foliage and waves on a gunmetal ground, the work incised overall, Japanese, circa 1955, 12 in. high. **$100-$125**

Bronze

Brazier decorated with cranes, scroll feet and ring handles, Chinese, 19 1/3 in. by 11 3/4 in. by 5 1/8 in. $2,500

Bottle/vase, long, tapered neck, enameled butterflies scattered over the body, Japanese, circa 1900, 8 in. high. **$1,200-$1,600**

Bowl, lotus-petal band around the base, lion mask loose-ring handles and scrolling lotus band below the rim, Hsüan Te (Xuande) mark, but early Ch'ing (Qing) Dynasty, 5 1/2 in. diameter. **$700-$1,000**

Box and cover, circular, decorated with birds and grasses, the patina overcleaned and scratched, Japanese, circa 1915, 4 3/4 in. diameter. **$75-$100**

Cauldron, tripod, annular handles, vertical rope pattern on the sides between cicada lappets, C-, L-, and S-shaped scrolls, encrustation and damage, Chinese, Han Dynasty, 9 in. wide. **$800-$1,100**

Censer in the form of a standing duck, the feathers incised, traces of gilt, Chinese, 17th century, 6 in. wide. **$950-$1,350**

Censer, late 19th or early 20th century, topped by a foo lion finial, tripod base, lobed sides with foliate scrolls, Chinese, 6 1/2 in. by 4 in. $125

Censer in the form of Kinko seated on a carp (the figure of Kinko is removable), Japanese, late Edo period, 12 in. long. **$1,600-$2,200**

Censer in the form of a Takarabune (treasure ship), Japanese, circa 1900, 5 3/4 in. high, 4 1/2 in. wide. **$175-$225**

Censer, globular, two bamboo node-shaped handles, three legs, Hsüan Te (Xuande) mark but early 20th century, Chinese, 7 1/2 in. wide. **$325-$450**

Censer, rectangular form, four feet with rope handles, the sides with Buddhistic symbols, Ch'eng Hua (Chenghua) mark, but 19th century, Chinese, 4 1/2 in. wide. **$250-$375**

Censer cast on three short feet, late Ming Dynasty, Chinese, 11 3/4 in. diameter. **$1,000-$1,500**

Censer, three conical feet with wide, arched loop handles at the rim, Chinese, 18th century, 6 1/2 in. diameter. **$900-$1,200**

Censer, tripod, gilt-splashed, wide, flaring sides, pierced upright handles, flat base, elephant-head feet, Hsüan Te (Xuande) mark, but early Ch'ing (Qing) Dynasty, 5 1/2 in. wide. **$1,000-$1,500**

Censer, tripod, mask feet, continuous motif of dragon and flaming pearl, S-shaped handles, Tao Kuang (Daoguang) six-character mark (and of the period), cover missing, Chinese, 20 in. high. **$1,000-$1,500**

Censer, tripod with bamboo-form handles, the body with phoenix in flight, repatinated, Japanese, circa 1875, 13 in. wide. **$500-$700**

Censer, tripod, with two open-loop handles: Chinese, the base with Wan Li mark, but early 20th century, 5 in. diameter. **$100-$125**

Warring States "ding," 475-221 BC, rare bronze tripod vessel with a band of molded ornamentation beneath the rim, 8 in. by 9 1/2 in., excellent condition with light encrustation. **$6,000-$6,500**

Pair of guardian figures, cast bronze, Japanese, late 19th century, 17 1/2 in. by 8 1/2 in. by 6 3/4 in., one figure holding broken sword in right hand. **$2,400/pair**

Dish, tripod, bucket form, flared lip, bracket feet, encrustation, Korean, Koryo dynasty, 4 in. diameter. **$500-$700**

Drum, ribbed, waisted circular form, the top cast with a star medallion and concentric bands, four open-work frogs on the rim, the sides with double pierced strap-work handles, Shan States, Chinese, 24 1/4 in. diameter, 18 1/4 in. high. **$2,000-$3,000**

Figure of Avalokitesvara, gilt, on stepped rectangular plinth, the feet on a lotus base, jeweled tiara, arms draped with flowing robes, Sino-Tibetan, 19th century, 7 1/2 in. high. **$600-$900**

Figure of a beetle, naturalistic, articulated joints, Japanese, circa 1930, 1 1/2 in. long. **$300-$500**

Left to right: Gilt bronze figure of a multi-armed deity seated in dhyanasana (meditation pose with hands in lap), the primary left hand in dhyana mudra (a pose or gesture of meditation and concentration in the attainment of spiritual perfection) (a pose or gesture of meditation and concentration in the attainment of spiritual perfection) and the right slightly raised, the secondary hands raised, the right holding a vajra, wearing a flowing dhoti with coral-studded pectoral jewelry and diadem, a double lotus base, gilt-rubbed, Tibetan, late 18th/early 19th century, 7 3/4 in. high. Realized price (including the 10-percent buyer's premium), Christie's East, New York City: **$825**. Gilt bronze figure of a Lama seated on a double-cushion throne engraved with foliage, the right hand raised in vitarka mudra, the left in dhyana mudra (a pose or gesture of meditation and concentration in the attainment of spiritual perfection) and wearing a cap and loose robes with floral incised borders, sealed, Tibetan, 18th century, 6 1/2 in. high. Realized price (including the 10-percent buyer's premium), Christie's East, New York City: **$660**. Gilt bronze figure of seated Vairasaftra seated in dhyanasana with the left hand raised in dharmackra mudra (turning an invisible wheel of the law), the right hand raised holding a vajra and wearing a dhoti with pectoral jewelry and diadem, a double lotus base, Tibetan, late 18th/early 19th century, 6 3/4 in. high. Realized price (including the 10-percent buyer's premium), Christie's East, New York City: **$1,210**

Figure of a seated Benkei wearing a kimono and leggings, holding an oni clutching a basket, gilt details, signed Miyao, Japanese, Meiji period, 14 in. high. **$7,000-$9,000**

Figure of Bodhisattva, gilt, wearing a cowl trailed across the shoulder, flowing robes, Sino-Tibetan, 18th century, 3 1/2 in. high. **$1,000-$1,200**

Figure of Bodhisattva Amitayus seated in dhyanasana (meditation pose with hands in lap) on a draped throne with foliate support corners, Chinese, late 18th century, 7 in. high. **$650-$950**

Figure of Buddha standing on a tiered octagonal throne wearing shoes with pointed toes and a long robe with elaborate flammiform (form of a flame used for decorated effect) decoration in relief, both hands held forward in abhaya mudra, the face with a downcast expression, the tiered crown with double conical finial flanked by flammiform (form of a flame used for decorated effect) ear lappets, Thai, 19th century, 22 in. high. **$800-$1,000**

Figure of Buddha on a bronze base, Chinese, figure possibly 17th century, base probably 19th century, overall 23 in. by 13 in. $4,500

Figure of Buddha (Mon-D'varavati style), encrusted green patina, Thai, 20th century, 18 1/2 in. high. **$750-$1,000**

Figure of Buddha, gilt, hands joined and upturned over crossed legs, necklace at the chest, Chinese, 17th century, 7 in. high. **$950-$1,600**

Figure of Buddha, gilt, robes over one shoulder, seated (with legs crossed) upon a double lotus base, one hand upturned, the base with impressed vajara, Chinese, 18th century, 10 in. high. **$2,000-$2,750**

Figure of Buddha, gilt, seated in dhyanasana (meditation pose) on a stepped lotus base, the base reduced, Tang Dynasty, Chinese, 3 3/4 in. high. **$1,500-$2,000**

Figure of Buddha seated in dhyanasana on double lotus base, Sino-Tibetan, 19th century, 6 in. high. **$400-$600**

Figure of Buddha seated in dhyanasana on a tiered, waisted throne and wearing a sanghati decorated with linear incisions, his right hand in bhumisparsa mudra, his left hand in dhyana mudra (a pose or gesture of meditation and concentration in the attainment of spiritual perfection) (a pose or gesture of meditation and concentration in the attainment of spiritual perfection), his face downcast, the tightly curled hair with a pointed finial, Burmese, 18th century, 9 3/4 in. high. **$700-$850**

Figure of Buddha seated in dhyanasana, hands raised in mudra, the interior of the oval base with a cylindrical tube, encrustations, minor damage, Tang Dynasty, 5 1/4 in. high. **$1,250-$1,875**

Figure of Buddha seated on a double lotus base, robes open, gilt traces overall, minor damage to three fingers, Ming Dynasty, Chinese, 13 in. high. **$2,500-$3,500**

Figure of Buddha seated in dhyanasana on double lotus base, hands in dhyana mudra (a pose or gesture of meditation and concentration in the attainment of spiritual perfection), holding a pearl, Chinese, 17th century, 11 1/2 in. high. **$1,800-$2,400**

Figure of Buddha seated in a lotus position on a lotus plinth, Korean, Yi Dynasty, 7 in. high. **$500-$700**

Figure of a standing Buddha, right hand in varada mudra (hand gesture formed by an open right palm and extended fingers), mandorla (symbol in the form of two circles coming together, overlapping one another to form an almond shape in the middle) missing, Korean, Koryo Dynasty. **$1,000-$1,500**

Figure of a dragon with tama, Japanese, early Meiji period, 12 in. long. **$600-$800**

Figure of a carp, naturalistic, gilt eyes, signed Seizan, Japanese, late Meiji period, 12 3/4 in. long. **$1,600-$2,200**

Figure of a cock, his feathers in shibuichi, shakudo, and sentoku, comb painted red, gilt eyes, Japanese, Taisho period, 14 1/4 in. high. **$700-$1,000**

Figure of crabs on rocks with some gilt highlights, cast bronze, dating to the 20th century. The bronze measures 12 1/4 in. in length and 6 1/2 in. tall. **$500**

Figure of a crane on a shaped base standing before a plum branch, in need of resoldering, Japanese, circa 1900, 14 in. high. **$150-$250**

Figure of a crayfish, naturalistic, articulated body, Japanese, circa 1930, 4 1/2 in. long. **$550-$750**

Figure of Dakini Vajravarahi, dancing on a prostrated figure on a lotus throne wearing a long billowing scarf, a garland of severed human heads and a five-leaf crown, a flammiform (form of a flame used for decorated effect) aureole with skulls and vajras (thunderbolts) in relief behind, Nepalese, 19th century, 19 in. high. **$800-$1,200**

Figure of Dharmapala Mahakala (a protector of religious law) in yab-yum (father-mother union symbolizing the uniting of wisdom and compassion) with his Sakti (goddess of suffering), seated in dhyanasana (meditation pose with hands in lap) on a double lotus throne, three ferocious heads, each with a third eye, wearing skull crowns, flaming red pigmented hair behind, the primary right hand holding the triratna (the three components of the Buddhist and Jain [a religion based on cosmic principles] creeds), his remaining five hands in karana mudra (a ritualized hand gesture), his upper left hand holding a mirror, his sakti with her arms around his neck, Sino-Tibetan, 18th century, 4 1/2 in. high. **$2,500-$3,500**

Figure of a kame (turtle) with vase upon the top of its shell, the vase realistically designed with cranes and pine, plum, and bamboo (Three Friends motif) in relief, Japanese, early Meiji period, 7 in. high. **$800-$1,200**

Figure of Khmer bronze goddess, circa 16th century, with 20 smaller arms issuing from her upper arms and wearing a loincloth, dancing on two prostrate demons, and wearing a two-tiered headdress bearing multiple heads, a mounting tenon on the base, 7 in. tall, rare. **$2,500-$2,750**

Figure of Dharmapala Yama (in Tibetan Buddhism, one of the eight fierce protective deities) standing on the back of a bull lying on a prostrated nude figure on a lotus throne, the figure with both hands raised, the bull wearing a jeweled harness with knob finial on his back, the base plate incised with visvavajra (double thunderbolts), Sino-Tibetan, 18th century, 11 in. high. **$2,500-$3,000**

Figure of Dharmapala Mahakala (a protector of religious law), six arms, his primary right arm missing from the elbow joint, his primary left arm holding a kapala (skull cup), his remaining hands in karana mudra (a ritualized hand gesture) to hold attributes, three heads with three bulging eyes, open mouth with tongue and fangs, skull crowns, necklaces including severed human heads, scroll-incised borders around his waist, Sino-Tibetan, 19th century, 12 in. high. **$600-$800**

Figure of an elephant, realistically modeled, Japanese, circa 1910, 5 in. high. **$250-$375**

Figure of a dignitary, hands clasped at the chest, Korean, Yi Dynasty, 10 1/2 in. high. **$600-$900**

Figure of a female holding a tray, she stands on a circular base, Indian, 19th century, 9 in. high. **$125-$200**

Figure of Ganesha (the elephant-faced god who removes obstacles) cast recumbent on an oval dais, Thai, 19th century, 8 in. long. **$300-$450**

Figure of Ganesha in dancing position, six arms held out on either side, each holding an attribute, the figure adorned with jewelry and a domed crown, Thai, 20th century, 30 in. high. **$1,000-$1,500**

Figure of a grasshopper with articulated joints, signed Yoshi, Japanese, circa 1930, 3 1/2 in. long. **$350-$550**

Figure of Guandi (god of war) seated and wearing flowing robes over his armor, a dragon in relief on his stomach, the base with four bracket feet, traces of gilt, Ming Dynasty, Chinese, 16 in. high. **$3,000-$4,000**

Figure of a guardian, fierce expression, arms raised, hair in top knot, some damages, Tang Dynasty, 4 1/2 in. high. **$1,200-$1,800**

Figure of a guardian, long robes, holding a scroll and standing on a lotus base, gilt decoration, 17th century, Chinese, 14 in. high. **$850-$1,250**

Figure of Laksmi, the consort of Vishnu, standing in tribhanga (a standing posture with the body following an 'S' curve) on an oval double lotus base set on a rectangular plinth, her knopped hair with a lotus medallion backed by small open-work floral disc mandoria, dark brown patina, South Indian, 17th/18th century, 25 in. high. Realized price (including the 10-percent buyer's premium), Christie's East, New York City. **$1,540**

Pair of figures of pigeons with glossy black finish, cast bronze, taller figure is 6 1/2 in. by 7 1/4 in. **$800**

Figure of Mahakala, gilt, on a rectangular lotus base, holding skull cup and chipper, his other four hands with drums and naga (serpent) heads, Tibetan, 6 in. high. **$700-$900**

Figure of Parvati standing in tribhanga (standing posture with the body following an 'S' curve) on a square pedestal, South Indian, 20th century, 18 3/4 in. high. **$200-$300**

Figure of a rabbit, the hair realistically executed, signed Shosai chu, Meiji period, Japanese, 6 1/2 in. long. **$900-$1,200**

Figure of a rat, realistically executed, movable tail, Japanese, circa 1910, 7 in. long. **$300-$400**

Figure of a seated monkey holding a peach, Japanese, early 20th century, 4 1/2 in. high. **$700-$900**

Figure of Shoki, the demon killer, brandishing his sword, Japanese, late 19th century, 10 in. high. **$400-$650**

Figure of a tiger, realistically modeled, upon a carved wood stand, Japanese, circa 1900, 24 in. long. $2,000-$3,000

Figure of Shiva, the multi-armed deity, holding attributes and sitting astride an ox on a rectangular plinth, Thai, 19th century, 11 in. high. **$400-$625**

Figure of Virabhadra standing on a square, tapering base with both hands held out in front of him, his right hand holding a khadga (a sword, a symbol of enlightenment), his left holding a khetaka (shield), he wears a long dhoti and jewelry, Indian, 19th century, 15 in. high. **$450-$660**

Figure of Vairapani (on a lotus base) leaning to the right with a snake under each foot, two snakes over his shoulders, another snake behind his tiara, Sino-Tibetan, 18th century, 7 in. high. **$1,200-$1,850**

Figure of a warrior standing on rock-work, wearing a tunic and holding a weapon, parcel gilt, Chinese, 17th century, 14 in. high. **$750-$1,000**

Flower bowl with floral motif inlaid in silver, Japanese, circa 1910, 7 1/4 in. by 2 1/4 in. **$250-$375**

Group, yab-yum (father-mother union symbolizing the uniting of wisdom and compassion), Vairadhara seated in dhyanasana (meditation pose with hands in lap) on an associated repoussé single lotus throne, his primary hands in Karana mudra, the secondary hands holding a vajra and clutching his Sakti (goddess of suffering, who also holds attributes), Nepalese, 17th century, 4 in. high. **$1,700-$2,500**

Jardiniére, rounded with three stub feet, the body cast with two dragons in low relief, signed Toshitsugu, Meiji period, Japanese, 11 1/2 in. diameter. **$550-$725**

Left: Inkwell in the form of a fishing basket, basket-weave body, the lid with sentoku (yellow metal alloy consisting of copper, zinc, and tin), shakudo (dark pickled alloy, a mixture of copper, gold, and other materials), and gilt fish, glass insert, Japanese, circa 1910, 3 in. high. **$250-$350**. Right: Inkwell in the form of a teapot, applied silver motifs of birds on one side and flowers on the reverse, silver finial and chain, glass insert, Japanese, circa 1915, 4 in. high. **$250-$350**

Mirror cast in low relief with pine and birds, Muromachi period, Japanese, 4 in. diameter. **$350-$575**

Mirror (miniature), gilt, circular, cast on one side with lotus and petals surrounding a plain boss, encrusted, Tang Dynasty. **$1,750-$2,500**

Mirror, raised octofoil (circular design of eight petals) border, a central boss, encrustations, Han Dynasty, 4 1/4 in. diameter. **$1,200-$1,750**

Mirror, silvered with six mythical animals around a central boss, encrusted, Six Dynasties, 5 1/2 in. diameter. **$800-$1,275**

Mirror, TLV with foliate lappets around a central domed boss divided by smaller bosses, dragon scrolls, and TLV motifs, encrustation, Han Dynasty, Chinese, 7 in. diameter. **$600-$850**

Place-card holder in fan shape with gilt flowers, basket, and trim, Japanese, circa 1900, 3 in. wide. **$300-$400**.

Sentoku (yellow metal alloy consisting of copper, zinc, and tin), drum-form box and cover with silver wires and trim, the hinged lid with No masks, Japanese, circa 1900, 4 in. diameter. **$300-$400**

Pricket candlesticks, bands of archaistic motifs, large central pans and bell-shaped bases, Chinese, 17th century, 23 1/2 in. high. **$800-$1,200**

Mirror, Ming Dynasty, 1368-1644, an especially large and heavy example with detailed wave and leaf design, 9 1/4 in. diameter, weight 5 lbs., excellent condition, rare. $1,000-$1,250

Tsuba (sword guard) in the form of a monkey climbing on bamboo rigging, gilt highlights, mounted on a wooden base, size with base, 3 3/8 in. by 3 7/8 in. by 1 3/8 in. $250

Seal, Buddhistic lion finial with collar and bell around its neck, Chinese, 19th century, 2 1/2 in. high. **$100-$150**

Stem bowl cast in Chou style with archaistic U-shaped and E-shaped geometric motifs, a wave pattern on the foot, Chinese, 18th century, 7 in. high. **$900-$1,400**

Tazza (tall footed servers like compotes), their baluster bodies cast with birds on leafy branches, branch-form handles, Japanese, circa 1900, 11 1/2 in. high, pair. **$800-$1,275**

Temple bell, panels of raised studs and suspension hook, Japanese, 18th century, 21 in. high. **$1,000-$1,600**

Pair of Japanese vases, measuring approximately 10 in. in height and 5 in. at their widest, dating to the late 19th or early 20th century. The vases have raised designs of complementary but not identical birds. They have been cast in a six-lobed design. The bases are unmarked. Fine original condition with their original patina. **$400**

Vase with applied shibuichi (gray-green patinated alloy of copper with varying quantities of silver), shakudo (dark pickled alloy, a mixture of copper, gold, and other materials), and sentoku (yellow metal alloy consisting of copper, zinc, and tin) wisteria around the shoulders, Japanese, circa 1890, 8 in. high. **$600-$850**

Vase, beaker form, the body with a dragon in high relief, Japanese, circa 1920, 12 in. high. **$375-$500**

Vase, modified pear shape, the body with two carp, their eyes gilt, Japanese, circa 1900, 7 in. high. **$900-$1,200**

Vase, beaker form, the center with four gilt archaistic zoomorphic heads divided by vertical flanges with key pattern and two gilt bands, early Ch'ing (Qing) Dynasty, Chinese, 7 1/2 in. high. **$625-$975**

Vase, gilt-splashed, high foot and trumpet neck, early Ch'ing (Qing) Dynasty, 6 1/2 in. high. **$750-$1,200**

Vase, modified pear shape with elongated neck and applied dragon, Japanese, circa 1900, 8 in. high. **$500-$700**

Vase, gilt-splashed, flattened ovoid form, four bosses in a band at the shoulder, tapered foot, Hsüan Te (Xuande) mark, but 19th century, Chinese, 14 in. high. **$1,800-$2,500**

Vase inlaid in silver with a bamboo grove, Japanese, circa 1900, 13 1/2 in. high. **$2,000-$3,000**

Vase, pear-shaped, cast with three t'ao t'ieh (mythical Chinese creature called the beat of gluttony) and loose ring handles, key-pattern bands and cicada lappets, Chinese, 19th century, 21 in. high. **$3,000-$4,000**

Vases, pear-shaped, elongated necks, inlaid with flowers, the details in silver and gilt, Japanese, circa 1910, 12 1/2 in. high, pair. **$2,000-$3,000**

Vase, yen-yen shape, dragon loop handles on the flaring neck, globular body with three dragon-and-cloud scrolls above and below lappet bands, overall gilt splashes, Chinese, early 18th century, 20 in. high. **$3,500-$4,500**

Water dropper, Shishi form, Japanese, circa 1900. **$175-$225**

Yatate (portable writing set that was attached to the obi, or sash), dragon form, Japanese, Showa period, 6 3/4 in. long. $100-$200

Vase decorated with five-towed dragons, inscribed with symbols and flowers in a landscape, early 20th century, 16 1/4 in. by 8 1/4 in. $400

Yatate (portable writing set that was attached to the obi, or sash), open-work handle, dragon on bowl, Japanese, Showa period, 9 in. long. **$125-$225**

Copper

Figure of Bodhisattva Avalokitesvara Padmapani seated in rajalilasana (pose called the king's posture, which expresses ease and relaxed confidence) on a double lotus throne, his right hand resting over his knee, his left on the edge of the throne and holding the stem of a padma (lotus) flowering at his shoulder, wearing a dhoti, long scarf, and jewelry, his knotted chignon with traces of blue pigment, the limbs with traces of gold, Tibetan, 18th century, 4 1/8 in. high. **$600- $900**

Figure of a dragonfly, articulated joints, Japanese, circa 1935, 2 1/4 in. long. **$275-$475**

Figure of Gautama Buddha wearing monastic robe, right shoulder and arm bare, face and limbs gilded, curled hair with blue pigment, Tibetan, 19th century, 6 1/2 in. high. **$350-$550**

Figure of the Surya (sun god) seated in sattvasana (meditation pose) on a double lotus base, hands raised in front and holding flowering stems, wearing armlets, anklets, and a five-pointed crown set with garnets and other stones, gilt traces overall, Nepalese, 18th century, 6 in. high. **$900-$1,200**

Figure of a Lama seated in dhyanasana (meditation pose with hands in lap) on a double lotus throne, right hand raised in nitaraka mudra (kind of pose), left hand in dhyana mudra (a pose or gesture of meditation and concentration in the attainment of spiritual perfection) , elaborate robes, hair with traces of black paint, the base with an incised medallion, Tibetan, 16th/17th century, 6 3/4 high. **$2,000-$3,000**

Figure of Yidam Samvara in yab-yum (father-mother union symbolizing the uniting of wisdom and compassion) with his Sakti (goddess of suffering) standing in alidhasana (right leg bent at the knee and the left leg straight, this pose is taken from classical Indian dance) on two prostrated four-armed deities holding attributes, Nepalese, 18th century, 6 in. high. **$1,200-$1,500**

Plate, oval with a basket-weave motif, the center with two sentoku (yellow metal alloy consisting of copper, zinc, and tin) women holding fans, Japanese, circa 1900, 9 in. long. **$175-$250**

Teapot, squat globular form, domed cover, zoomorphic handle, curved spout, the sides with repoussé medallions, Tibetan, late 19th century, 11 1/2 in. high. **$400-$625**

Tray, basket-work border, the center with a seated Rakan, Japanese, circa 1910, 11 1/2 in. wide. **$500-$700**

Vase, basket form, waisted neck, globular body, the shoulders with applied crustaceans, Japanese, Taisho period, 4 in. high. **$300-$500**

Vase, hammered and enameled with sea shells and crustaceans, signed Ando, Japanese, circa 1910, 7 in. high. **$3,000-$4,000**

Vase hammered and enameled with flowering plum branches, signed Ando, Japanese, circa 1910, 7 in. high. **$3,000-$4,000**

Copper and Silver

Amulet box: pointed arch form, repoussé decoration depicting triratna above (the three components of the Buddhist and Jain [a religion based on cosmic principles] creeds), mukha (a pose, face downward) below, eight emblems between, contents include bone rosary, brass Syamatara, and brass Buddha, Tibetan, 19th century, 4 in. high. **$300-$400**

Water jar (mizusashi), silver body with applied copper fan shapes filled with various flowers in low relief, the lid with loop handle, Japanese, circa 1890, 6 1/2 in. high. **$900-$1,200**

Teapot, silver with applied copper fan-shaped panels filled with foliage, silver lining, bail handle, silver and copper open-work finial, Japanese, circa 1895, 5 in. high. **$550-$750**

Iron

Model of a crayfish, fully articulated, Japanese, early 19th century, 10 in. long. **$1,200-$1,800**

Model of a dragon, Japanese, circa 1910, 10 in. long. **$100-$150**

Model of a dragon standing on all four legs, Japanese, circa 1925, 9 in. long. **$125-$200**

Model of an elephant, trunk raised, Japanese, circa 1930, 6 in. high. **$100-$150**

Teapot, cranes in relief on each side, bronze lid and bail handle, Japanese, late 19th century, 7 in. high. **$150-$250**

Teapot, ishi (stone) finish, bail handle, Japanese, late Edo period, 8 in. high. **$400-$600**

Valra, slender, either end with four arched ribs and four-sided pointed projections, brass finials, Tibetan, 17th century, 7 in. high. **$200-$300**

Plaque, rectangular, repoussé and carved with Benten holding a biwa (stringed instrument similar to a lute or guitar), signed Miochin, late Edo period, Japanese, 13 in. by 11 1/2 in. **$1,400-$2,200**

Komai

Box with inlaid gold and silver scenic motif, grape-and-leaf border, Japanese, Meiji period, 2 1/8 in. diameter. **$2,000-$3,000**
COURTESY OF THE EDSON COLLECTION

Box and cover, fan shape with motifs of bamboo, signed Komai, Japanese, circa 1900, 6 3/4 in. wide. **$2,500-$3,500**

Cabinet, two doors open to reveal six drawers, scenic motifs overall, Japanese, circa 1900, 5 1/2 in. high. **$2,850-$3,800**

Cabinet in the form of a shrine, two doors open to reveal three small drawers, decorated overall with birds, flowers, and landscapes, signed Komai, Japanese, circa 1910, 4 in. high. **$3,200-$4,500**

Chest, hinged lid and two drawers, the motifs including various landscapes, buildings, and Mt. Fuji capped in silver, Japanese, circa 1900, 2 1/2 in. by 3 in. by 2 1/8 in. **$3,000-$4,000**

Dish, circular, decorated with alternating phoenix and dragon pattern around a central circular panel of quail and grasses, Japanese, circa 1910, 6 1/2 in. diameter. **$1,500-$1,80**

Vase, beaker form, two shaped panels of huts and pine, grape-and-leaf ground and borders, marked Komai, Meiji period, Japanese, 4 3/4 in. high. **$2,500-$3,500**

Vase, Komai style, pear-shaped with trumpet neck, decorated with shaped panels of pavilions, rocks, trees, sailing boats, and so on, Japanese, circa 1915, 5 in. high. **$200-$300**

Left: Box and cover with inlaid silver and gold scenic motifs, the interior with an incised gilt liner, Japanese, circa 1925, 5 in. by 3 3/4 in. **$1,200-$1,800**. Right: Box and cover, the motifs inlaid in gold and silver, the interior of the lid with a silver wire inscription that dates this piece 1951, Japanese, 5 in. by 3 1/2 in. **$900-$1,200**

Cabinet with three drawers, each side and each drawer with inlaid gold and silver motifs, Japanese, Meiji period, 2 1/2 in. by 2 1/2 in. **$3,500-$5,000**

Compact, inlaid gold and silver scenic view with Mt. Fuji in the background capped in silver, Japanese, circa 1920. **$100-$150**

Match safe with inlaid gilt designs and a grape-and-leaf border around the reserves, Japanese, circa 1900. **$1,500-$1,850**

Flask-form vase with circular panels featuring scenic motifs, silver and gold inlay with grape-and-leaf borders, Japanese, Meiji period, 6 in. high. **$3,000-$5,000**
COURTESY OF THE EDSON COLLECTION

Pewter

Boxes and covers, circular, the covers decorated with vines, leaves, and fruit inlaid with oval agates, Chinese, early 20th century, 7 in. diameter, pair. **$300-$500**

Cosmetic box with a central Shou character, Chinese, circa 1900, 4 in. long. **$100-$175**

Candlesticks, square, the drip pans with scrolls, the stems with Shou characters, Chinese, circa 1920, 28 in. high, pair. **$350-$500**

Tea caddy, high, rounded shoulders, low, cylindrical neck, knop finial, undecorated, Chinese, late 19th century, 9 in. high. **$100-$150**

Vase, hexagonal with a motif of standing figures, Chinese, circa 1900, 11 in. high. **$125-$175**

Pair of spelter or pot metal foo lions on decorated bases, late 19th century, with some broken details, 7 in. by 3 1/2 in. by 7 1/2 in. **$450/pair**

Sentoku

Bottle/vase inlaid with gold, silver, and bronze motifs of birds and marsh grasses, Japanese, circa 1920, 7 in. high. **$600-$800**

Vase, nanako ground with floral motifs in low relief, Japanese, circa 1910, 8 3/4 high. **$350-$475**

Shakudo

Model of a standing crane, the feathers with some silver inlay, Japanese, circa 1905, 11 1/8 in. high. **$350-$550**

Model of a dragon, hinged legs and jaw, some whiskers missing, Japanese, first half of the 19th century, 14 1/2 in. long. **$1,800-$2,500**

Vase, baluster form, decorated in iroe hira zogan (precious metal paint and inlay, which is polished flush with the surface) with five red-capped Manchurian cranes and bamboo, Japanese, early 20th century, 6 1/8 in. high. **$700-$900**

Vase inlaid with two quails, their bodies decorated with gilt, shibuichi (gray-green patinated alloy of copper with varying quantities of silver), silver, and sentoku (yellow metal alloy consisting of copper, zinc, and tin), Japanese, circa 1880, 3 in. high. **$500-$750**

Silver

Bottle, globular with writhing dragon applied around the rim and forming two handles, the body with repoussé motifs of dragons and flaming pearl, handles resoldered, marked Luen-wo, Shanghai, Chinese, 19th century, 6 in. high. **$375-$500**

Bowl, hexagonal, each panel chased and embossed with fruiting and flowering trees, gilt traces on interior, marked HC, Chinese, circa 1900, 8 in. diameter. **$600-$900**

Bowl, rounded, decorated with painted foliate arches and swirls of foliage below a scroll border, Thai, 20th century, 10 in. diameter. **$250-$400**

Bowl, circular, two dragons in relief, Chinese, late 19th century, 5 in. diameter. **$600-$800**

Bowl, scrolled feet cut as dragons, hexagonal panels embossed and chased with fruit and foliage, Chinese, late 19th century, 6 in. diameter. **$475-$675**

Bowl and cover with underplate decorated with the 12 zodiac signs and petal motifs, bird finial, Burmese, 19th century, 6 in. diameter. **$300-$500**

Box and cover, round with repoussé irises, the ground hammered by hand, minor dent, Japanese, circa 1918, 3 3/4 in. diameter. **$650-$900**

Box and cover, circular, the lid with enameled floral rounders, some losses, Japanese, late Meiji period, 4 in. diameter. **$800-$1,200**

Censer and cover enameled with flowers and foliage in relief on a stippled ground, squat form with three bracket feet, Japanese, late Meiji period, 4 in. high. **$5,000-$7,000**

Left: Basket with tall bail handle, four legs, woven silver, Japanese, circa 1900, 4 in. high (to top of handle). $600-$800. Right: Silver censer with applied gilt mon, Japanese, late Edo/early Meiji period, 3 in. high. **$500-$700**

Censer, parcel gilt, domed foot with ropework border, either side with a figure of Samvara in yab-yum (father-mother union symbolizing the uniting of wisdom and compassion) with his Sakti, foliage ground, three arched dragon handles, a plaited silver chain for suspension, Tibetan, 19th century, 9 in. high. **$400-$600**

Censer with applied panels worked in silver wire and enamels in motifs of phoenix and flowers, Japanese, late 19th century, 4 1/2 in. high. **$2,500-$3,500**

Centerpiece with seven removable fluted flower holders, Chinese, circa 1910, 25 in. long, 10 in. high. **$750-$1,000**

Cigarette box with inlaid shibuichi (graygreen patinated alloy of copper with varying quantities of silver), the lid with Daikoku sitting and leaning on a sack, Japanese, circa 1940, 3 in. wide, 8 1/2 in. long. **$300-$400**

Left: Box and cover with kiku (chrysanthemum) mon on lid, incised motif of flowers and birds, four legs, Japanese, early Meiji period, 3 1/2 in. diameter. **$500-$700**. Right: Box and cover, six legs, the lid decorated with mon and foliage, Japanese, early Meiji period, 3 in. wide. **$450-$650**

Cigarette case with an embossed dragon, gold wash on interior, holds ten regular-sized cigarettes, Chinese, circa 1925. **$200-$300**

Cocktail shaker and six tumblers with tray, the tray with glass center, tumblers with silver sleeves, overall dragon motif in very low relief, marked .950, Japanese, circa 1930. **$950-$1,500**

Cosmetic box and hinged cover, undecorated, encrustations, Chinese, Sung (Song) Dynasty, 2 in. diameter. **$1,200-$1,850**

Fruit basket, six overlapping shell shapes forming the basket, the handles in the form of a twisted leaf, Japanese, circa 1900. **$500-$700**

Goblets, plain bowl, entwined dragons on the stems, Chinese, circa 1925, 5 in. high, **pair. $200-$300**

Card case, filigree, with dragon and flaming pearl motif, Chinese, last half of the 19th century. **$700-$900**

Kettle, the body embossed with studs, plain cover and spout, bail handle, stamped jun gin (silver), Japanese, circa 1885, 12 in. high. **$3,500-$4,500**

Loving cup, plain bowl, bamboo-form stem, mounted on a black wood base, Chinese, circa 1900, 6 3/4 in. high. **$1,000-$1,500**

Commemorative silver medals, Japanese, set number 168 of a series of 250 commemorative medal sets issued in Japan in 1991 to recognize 2,600 years of emperors in Japan. Each medal measures 2 in. in diameter and is made of solid silver weighing 50 grams. There are 36 medals in the set. Each medal is decorated in relief on both the front and back with pictures of all the Japanese emperors from the first up to the last (Hirohito). The set comes in a two-tiered, blue velvet-lined display case along with a certificate of authenticity. **$2,000**

Model of an elephant standing on an oval base and wearing a foliate blanket, the mahoot (elephant servant-one who leads or tends an elephant) in front, the howdah (a seat or covered pavilion on the back of an elephant or camel) with two figures, Indian, 19th century, 10 in. high. **$600-$850**

Model of a junk, three lateen sails, four flags at the stern, seven cannons on the deck, three Chinese sailors, Chinese, 10th century, 9 in. long. **$400-$550**

Model of a rickshaw, Chinese, circa 1920, 3 in. high. **$100-$125**

Mug, flared cylindrical form, molded rim and foot, applied loop handle, Chinese, late 19th century, 4 in. high. **$500-$750**

Pendant of a horse, silver and turquoise, measuring 1 1/2 in. by 1 1/4 in., and 3 in. with the chain, Chinese, dating to the late 19th or early 20th century. This piece may have served as part of a chatelaine or simply as a decorative ornament. **$75**

Photograph frame, the border pierced and enameled in colors with a motif of heron and wisteria, some enamel missing, some dents, Japanese, circa 1890, 9 1/2 in. high. **$1,200-$1,500**

Cigar case with compartments for three cigars, the whole decorated with sea creatures on the front, a carp in a flower and bamboo edged pool on the reverse, all done in repoussé work, the clasp with hand-formed spring, Japanese, circa late 19th or early 20th century, 2 3/4 in. by 5 1/4 in. **$2,200-$2,500**

Clock, opium, the lid with T-pattern openwork, hallmarked, Chinese, late 19th century, 4 1/2 in. square. **$400-$650**

Mallet (Daikoku's mallet) with gold incised motifs, Japanese, Meiji period, 19th century, 7 in. long. **$1,500-$2,200**

Photograph frame, bamboo design in low relief, Japanese, circa 1912, 3 1/2 in. by 4 in. **$400-$600**

Plaque, repoussé, depicting Kali, her principal hands holding a kapala (skull cap), secondary hands holding shield and sword, Tibetan, 19th century, 11 in. high. **$400-$600**

Plate, parcel gilt, circular with a raised center medallion and petal-shaped flutes, each with a pointed terminal, Indian, 19th century, 12 in. diameter. **$700-$900**

Chinese pagoda executed in fine and meticulous detail, standing 6 1/2 in. tall and dating to the early 20th century. It bears the Chinese character for silver. It is missing a few of its bells, but this does not detract from the overall effect. **$75**

Punch bowl with two dragons in high relief, silver liner, marked Yokohomma Sterling, .950, Japanese, circa 1915, 14 in. diameter. **$5,000-$7,000**

Rose-water sprinklers, bulbous body, raised foot, elongated neck, a layer of scrolling filigree, Indian, 19th century, 12 1/2 in. high. **$500-$750**

Salts, boat-shaped with concave rims, oval feet, Chinese, late 19th century, 1 in. wide. **$350-$500**

Salt and pepper in the form of lanterns, marked jun gin, .950, Japanese, circa 1930, 2 3/4 in. high. **$275-$400**

Sherbet cups (eight to the set), each with dragons in high relief, plain stems, Chinese, circa 1925, 4 3/8 in. high, each. **$150-$175**

Stem cup, U-shaped bowl engraved with songbirds perched on bamboo branches, bamboo-form stem, signed WH (Wang Hing), Chinese, circa 1900, 10 in. high. **$1,000-$1,500**

Left to right: Salt and pepper shakers in the form of stone lanterns, Japanese, early Showa period, 4 in. high. **$200-$300**. Salt and pepper set in the form of a kettle and brazier, loose ring handles and spoon, Japanese, early Showa period, 4 1/2 in. high. **$250-$350**

Teapot on bamboo-form stand, covered sugar and open creamer, the covers formed as lotus leaves with twig finials, each piece with relief lotus buds and leaves around the body, marked Hung Chong, Shanghai, Chinese, late 19th century. **$2,000-$3,000**

Teapot, the body in the form of a section of bamboo, the sides with bamboo leaves in green and ochre enamels, loop handle forming the finial, Japanese, circa 1905. **$1,000-$1,500**

Tea service: teapot, covered sugar, and open creamer, decorated with repoussé birds and bamboo, bamboo finials, marked WH 90 (Wang Hing); Chinese, circa 1900. **$1,800-$2,400**

Thermos bottle decorated with the Three Friends motif (pine, plum, and bamboo), marked .950, Japanese, circa 1910. **$400-$625**

Water jar (mizusashi) hammered and overlaid with designs rendered in copper, Japanese, late 19th century, 6 1/2 in. high. **$2,000-$3,000**

Whiskey bottle, cornered and punched form, overall design of dragons, corked stopper inserted into silver knop finial, Chinese, circa 1930. **$375-$500**

Wine cup, the bowl with dragons in low relief, the stem entwined with dragons, Chinese, circa 1925, 3 1/2 in. high. **$125-$175**

Silver salts in the form of planters with gilt interiors, Chinese, circa 1890, 3 in. diameter, pair. $250-$350. Salt and pepper set in the form of rickshaw, marked .950, Japanese, early Showa period, 3 in. high. **$250-$350**

Tongs with dragon-and-cloud pattern in high relief, Japanese, circa 1885. **$500-$750**

Vase, silver and enamel, motif of enameled irises and foliage in high relief accompanied by motif of waterfowl, stippled ground, Japanese, Meiji period, 19th century, 6 in. high. **$1,800-$2,400**
COURTESY OF THE EDSON COLLECTION

Miscellaneous

Japanese mixed-metal pill box, circa late 19th or early 20th century, silver case engraved with chrysanthemums and signed Toshimasu, the top with a mixed-metal relief of a Samurai carrying an Oni (demon) on his back, the full moon over a stream before him, the relief of bronze with gold and silver inlay, 1 in. by 1 7/8 in. **$2,200-$2,500**

Wine ewer with lacquer stand and wood box, Japanese, early Meiji period, 7 in. high. **$1,800-$2,500**

18th century hollow metal painted Buddha, measuring 9 in. by 6 1/2 in. The piece is done in the Ming Dynasty style with orange and blue paint. There are paint losses but the overall richness of the painted garments is still very evident. **$275**

Japanese copper-based mixed metals pouch clasp in the shape of a butterfly, measuring approximately 2 cm across, dating to the late 19th or early 20th century. **$75**

Japanese metal plaque or tray, measuring 9 in. square, dating to the second half of the 20th century. The plaque has a cast design of two crawfish among leaves. The front has a rich patina that may have been applied or may reflect the copper alloy metal used in the manufacture. It is signed by the artist in a seal on the front that reads as: KOH. Mint original condition. **$100**

Japanese mixed-metal brush holder or sleeve vase, measuring 9 1/2 in. high and 3 1/2 in. across. The body is made of a copper alloy that has been treated to give it a mossy green patina. The artist has used raised and flat silver and copper alloy metals to create a bird and chrysanthemum design. Portions of the design are gold-chased. It is unsigned and in fine original condition, mid-20th century. **$150**

Japanese copper alloy plate, with four medallions of Japanese figures and scenes, measuring approximately 7 in. in diameter, dating to the early to mid- 20th century. The relief carving in the plate is exceptionally well done and has been enhanced by an ornate border and silver to highlight some areas. The plate is signed in an inlaid cartouche on the reverse. **$150**

Japanese metalwork letter opener, finely worked scene of a fisherman and carp, circa 19th century, 12 in. long. **$150-$250**

Paintings

CHINESE ARTISTS

The following list of artists and dates may prove helpful. It includes a number of artists not mentioned in the price guide, which follows.

Bian Sho	circa 1730-1750	Jin Nong	1687-1764
Cai Jia	circa 1730-1782	Ju Cao	1811-1865
Chen Banding	1878-1970	Ju Lian	1828-1904
Chen Fang	1896-?	Kang Yuwei	1850-1927
Chen Fushan	b. 1905	Lain Jian	1747-1799
Chen Hongshou	1598-1652	Li Keran	b. 1907
Cheng Po	20th century	Li Xiongcai	b. 1910
Chen Shun	1483-1544	Li Yihong	b. 1941
Chen Zi	circa 1650-1697	Lin Fengzi	1886-1959
Cheng Shifa	b. 1921	Ni Tian	1855-1919
Cheng Suson	18th century	Pan Tianshou	1898-1971
Dai Jin	1388-1462	Peng Yulin	1816-1890
Dai Xi	1801-1860	Pu Ru	1896-1963
Dao Chao	active in the early to mid 17th century	Qi Baishi	1863-1957
		Ren Yi	1840-1895
Deng Fen	1892-1964	Ren Yu	1853-1901
Deng Shiru	1743-1805	Shi Lu	1918-1982
Ding Jing	1695-1775	Sun Xingyan	1752-1824
Ding Yanyong	1902-1978	Wang Chong	1494-1533
Du Qizhang	20th century	Wang Su	1794-1802
Fang Zeng	b. 1938	Wang Zhen	1866-1938
Fei Danxu	1801-1850	Wang Zuetao	1903-1984
Fu Baoshi	1904-1965	Weng Tonghe	1830-1904
Fu Shan	1605-1690	Wu Changshuo	1844-1927
Gao Dai	17th century	Wu Shixian	b. circa 1916
Gao Jianfu	1879-1951	Xie Zhiguang	1900-1976
Gu Yun	1855-1896	Xu Beihong	1895-1953
Guan Liang	b. 1900	Xu Gu	1824-1896
Guan Shangue	b. 1912	Yang Shanshen	b. 1913
Hong Yi	1880-1942	Yang Yisun	1812-1881
Hu Xigui	1839-1883	Yu Yue	1821-1906
Hua Yan	1682-1756	Zhang Daqian	1899-1933
Huang Junbi	b. 1898	Zhang Shuqi	20th century
Huang Shaoqiang	1901-1942	Zhang Yehu	Southern Sung
Huang Yi	1744-1841	Zhu Oizhan	b. 1891
Huang Zhou	b. 1925		

CHINESE PAINTINGS

Ancestral portrait, shoulder length, an elderly woman, ink and color on silk, matted and framed, late 19th century, framed size, 12 in. by 19 in. **$400-$600**

Ancestral portrait, a family, colors on paper, three noblemen in blue robes, three women in red robes and hair ornaments, the robes with mandarin badge of a phoenix, each seated on draped thrones, 19th century, 55 in. by 90 in. **$2,500-$3,500**

Ancestral portraits, a mandarin couple, ink and color on silk, early 19th century, unframed, each measuring 38 1/2 in. by 73 1/2 in., pair. **$2,000-$3,000**

Oil on canvas, American merchantman at Whampoa, wood frame, late half of the 19th century, framed size 16 1/2 in. by 22 in. **$2,800-$3,800**

Oil on canvas, a British merchant ship in Hong Kong Harbor, circa 1850, 17 1/2 in. by 23 in. **$3,500-$5,500**

Oil on canvas, portrait of a beautiful Chinese lady, seated, wearing a red robe, her hand resting on a table, her hair adorned with ornaments, gilt frame, 19th century, framed size 18 in. by 24 in. **$5,500-$7,500**

Oil on canvas, a Chinese beauty smoking a pipe, seated on a bed, surrounded by female attendants, wood frame, 19th century, framed size 18 in. by 22 in. **$1,500-$2,500**

Oil on canvas, elegantly attired figures in a pavilion and water garden, hardwood frame, Chinese school, early 19th century, framed size 17 in. by 24 in. **$2,000-$3,000**

Oil on canvas, a river landscape, Chinese school, mid-19th century, framed size 13 in. by 19 in. **$650-$900**

Painted leaves, album, ink and color, each leaf painted with a Lohan and attribute, 19th century, 5 in. by 7 in., set of 10. **$1,000-$1,500**

One of a pair of ancestral portraits, the patriarch dressed in a dark blue robe with embroidered green cuffs, bright colors on pith paper, trimmed and framed, Chinese, late Ch'ing Dynasty, framed size 23 in. by 45 1/2 in., **pair. $1,500-$2,200**

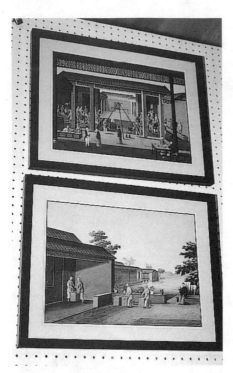

Painting on silk of Buddha sitting beside stacks of books, measuring 7 1/2 in. by 9 1/2 in., dating to the mid-20th century. The painting is mounted on a paper as a scroll, which measures overall 9 in. by 15 in. Fine original condition with vibrant colors and no damage. **$150**

Portrait of an official seated on a throne chair, his robe red with a phoenix mandarin badge, framed, 19th century, framed size, 38 in. by 60 in. **$800-$1,200**

Watercolor on pith paper, an album of insect specimens, 20 paintings in all, 19th century, 16 in. by 12 3/4 in. **$1,200-$1,600**

Watercolor on pith paper, from Methods of Torture and Punishment, framed, some foxing and stain, 19th century, framed size 11 in. by 11 1/4 in. **$100-$150**

Chinese export paintings, gouache on paper, circa 1850, one showing basket weavers, the other showing a market scene, overall frame size each, 18 1/2 in. by 23 1/2 in., sight size 13 1/2 in. by 17 3/4 in., **pair. $2,650**

Two from a series of four paintings-watercolor and gouache on pith paper-depicting various river barges, junks, and sampans plying the shallow waters, Canton School, Chinese, 19th century, 16 in. by 12 in. image size, framed and glazed. Realized price (including the 10-percent buyer's premium), Christie's East, New York City. **$1,980**

Traditional

Fan painting, ink on paper, Plum Blossoms, accompanied by a poem, dated 1760, 20 3/4 in. by 6 3/4 in. **$3,500-$4,500**

Fan painting, ink and color on gold-dusted silk, River Landscape, signed Zou Zhe, dated 1652, 20 in. by 7 1/2 in. **$1,800-$2,500**

Fan painting, ink and color on paper, landscape, signed Zheng Wuchang, one artist's seal, 21 3/4 in. by 7 3/4 in. **$400-$700**

Fan painting (mounted as an album leaf), ink and color on paper, Lotus, accompanied by a two-line poem, signed Gongshou, one artist's seal, one collector's seal. **$1,200-$1,500**

Fan painting, ink and color on gold-dusted paper, Peach Blossoms, inscribed with a poem, signed Ju Cao, dated 1857, two artists' seals. **$625-$900**

Hanging scroll, ink on paper, Lotus, signed Pu Ru, signed, four seals, one collector's seal, 12 3/4 in. by 42 in. **$1,500-$2,500**

Hanging scroll, ink on paper, Old Tree, Rock, and Bamboo, signed Lo Mu, two artists' seals, one collector's seal, 17 in. by 59 in. **$1,000-$1,500**

Hanging scroll, ink and color on paper, Parrot on Branch, by Ding Yanyong, signed and sealed twice, dated summer of 1978, 26 1/2 in. by 53 1/2 in. **$2,500-$3,500**

Hanging scroll, ink and color on paper, Peonies and Rock, by Lu Lian, two artists' seals, dated 1882, 19 3/4 in. by 38 7/8 in. **$1,200-$1,600**

Painting on paper of a Chinese nobleman holding a scepter, in elaborate hat and flowing robes, 17th century, 43 1/2 in. by 22 in. $4,000

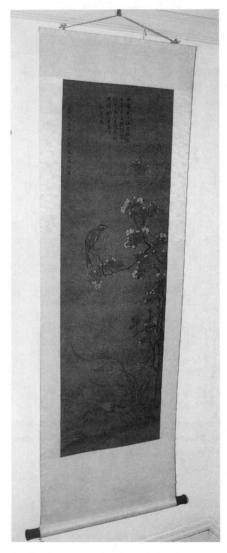

One of a set of four paintings, colors on pith paper, black lacquer frames, Chinese, late 19th century, frame size 10 in. by 15 1/2 in. **$100-$150 each**

Scroll painting of bird on branch of a blossoming cherry or plum tree, attributed to Lu Chih (also spelled Lu Zhi), 1496-1576, an artist known for landscapes who also produced bird and flower paintings, Chinese, 48 in. by 18 in., with attribution. **$600,000**

Hanging scroll, ink and color on light paper, White Robed Kuan Yin, by Zang Daqian, two artists' seals, dated 1946, 16 3/4 in. by 33 in. **$3,500-$4,500**

Hanging scroll, ink and color on paper, Sparrows (perched on leafy branches), signed Yang Shashen, one artist's seal, dated 1983, 18 in. by 25 1/8 in. **$1,000- $1,500**

Hanging scroll, ink and color on silk, Wild Ducks, in the style of Bian Jingzhao (with his seal), 19th century, 21 1/2 in. by 155 in. **$1,000-$1,500**

Hanging scroll, ink and color on paper, Flowering Prunus, by Shi Lu, signed twice, two painted seals, 26 1/4 in. by 54 1/2 in. **$5,000-$7,000**

Scroll painting showing horseman with one black horse and one white horse, with multiple red stamps and calligraphy, Chinese, overall size 58 in. by 27 1/2 in., image 17 in. by 24 in., early 20th century. **$400-$600**

Scroll painting of four sages, with multiple red stamps and calligraphy, Chinese, overall size 58 in. by 27 1/2 in., image 17 in. by 24 in., early 20th century. **$400-$600**

Hanging scroll, ink and color on paper, Shepherdess, by Cheng Shifa, two artists' seals, 1961, 17 1/8 in. by 23 3/4 in. **$650-$900**

Hanging scroll, ink and color on paper, Landscape, by Li Huasheng, two artists' seals, 18 in. by 27 3/4 in. **$600-$800**

Hanging scroll, ink on paper, Calligraphy in Zing Shu (running script), by Wu Changshuo, one artist's seal, dated 1926, 19 1/4 in. by 46 in. **$1,000-$1,500**

Scroll painting showing mountainous landscape with pine trees, Chinese, 78 in. by 23 in., image 38 in. by 20 in., mid to late 20th century. **$80-$120**

Scroll painting showing a woman on horseback and three attendants, Chinese, 68 in. by 25 1/2 in., image 26 in. by 22 in., early 20th century. **$300-$450**

Hanging scroll, ink and color on paper, Camellias and Birds, by Yu Fei'an, three artists' seals, 20 1/4 in. by 35 3/4 in. **$800-$1,200**

Hanging scroll, ink and color on paper, Camellia and Two Birds, Huang Binhong, two artists' seals, 13 1/4 in. by 23 3/4 in. **$1,500-$1,875**

Scroll painting of eagle on rock with pine branches, dated 1951, probably a copy of a painting by Chinese painter Qi Baishi (1863-1957), 62 in. by 18 in. **$850**

Scroll painting showing large red flowers (peonies?), 71 in. by 16 in., Chinese, images 53 in. by 13 in., late 20th century. **$50-$80**

Japanese Paintings

Two calligraphic panels, mid-20th century, both inscribed with poetry written in grass style calligraphy, one filled with additional classical style calligraphy on the reverse, 7 in. by 8 1/2 in., **pair. $200-$250**

Fan painting, sumi on paper, mounted as a hanging scroll (kakemono), Sugawara no Michizane riding an ox, Kano school, early Edo period, 19 1/2 in. by 9 1/2 in. **$1,500-$2,200**

Fan painting, colors and gofun on gold paper, red camellias with a thick trunk, painted in the Rimpa manner, early 20th century, 7 1/2 in. by 12 1/2 in. **$600-$800**

Fan painting, sumi and colors on a mica ground, a branch of maple leaves, old repairs, framed, 19th century, framed size 18 in. by 10 in. **$500-$650**

Hand scroll, ink, colors, and gofun on gold pigment paper, a landscape and townscape with temples and shops, Sumiyoshi school, 19th century, 15 1/2 in. by 24 1/2 in. **$5,000-$7,000**

Hanging scroll, ink and colors on silk, Warrior in Full Armor, by Eigaku Kano (1785-1863), 16 in. by 45 in. **$900-$1,200**

Hanging scroll, ink and colors on silk, Stalking Tiger, by Suido Yamada (1892-1969), 16 1/2 in. by 50 in. **$700-$950**

Hanging scroll, ink and colors on paper, Cat and Kitten, by Takeuchi Seiho (1864-1932), 11 3/4 in. by 18 1/2 in. **$700-$950**

Hanging scroll, ink and colors on silk, a flock of geese among water grasses and reeds under a full moon, signed Seiko Shai, dated Meiji 16 (1883), 32 3/4 in. by 74 in. **$1,000-$1,500**

Set of four fusuma sliding doors depicting Tales of the Genji, colors on gold paper, Japanese, Tosa-Sumitoshi School, 17th century, each panel 28 1/2 in. by 68 1/2 in., some damages. Realized price (including the 10-percent buyer's premium), Christie's East, New York City. **$6,600**

Hanging scroll, sumi and colors on silk, a puppy among dandelions and grasses, late Edo period, 8 3/4 in. by 14 1/2 in. **$700-$850**

Hanging scroll, a tiger appearing through bamboo, creased and damaged, 19th century, 12 in. by 15 1/2 in. **$400-$600**

Hanging scroll, colored lacquer on paper, gourd on a vine, signed Zeshin, 7 1/2 in. by 11 1/2 in. **$6,000-$8,000**

Hanging scroll, ink and colors on silk, Hanna tsuki (Messenger of Flowers), a lady and two servants, one of whom is carrying a floral bouquet, in the style of Zeshin (with his signature), 14 in. by 23 1/4 in. **$575-$700**

Hanging scroll, sumi on paper, Jurojin and a gnarled staff by a large pine tree, signed Minamoto Gyokuton, Taisho period, 15 1/2 in. by 40 in. **$375-$600**

Hanging scroll, ink, colors, and gofun on silk, mandarin duck and aquatic plants, signed Seiko sho, dated Meiji 16 (1883), 32 3/4 in. by 74 in. **$900-$1,200**

Hanging scroll, sumi and colors on paper, a pair of monkeys and their young, Sosen school, dated 1896, 20 1/4 in. by 39 in. **$900-$1,200**

Hanging scroll, sumi and colors on silk, rabbits among autumn grasses, signed Chokusui, late 19th century, 16 1/2 in. by 34 1/2 in. **$550-$775**

Hanging scroll, ink, colors, and gofun on silk, Sparrows and Peonies, signed Anko Shoshi, 20th century, 16 1/2 in. by 50 1/4 in. **$400-$600**

Sumi-e painting, mid-20th century, brush painting of people climbing from a mountain to the moon, calligraphy on both sides, sealed and signed in Japanese and also English on reverse, 9 1/2 in. by 10 1/2 in. $60-$75

Hanging scroll, sumi and colors on silk, two sparrows on a spray of millet, creased, old damages, 19th century, 11 3/4 in. by 15 3/4 in. **$300-$450**

Hanging scroll, sumi on silk, wooded mountainous landscape with buildings, Kano school, 19th century, 14 1/2 in. by 23 1/2 in. **$650-$900**

Painting, sumi and colors on paper, a boy with a falcon on his arm, framed, 19th century, framed size, 9 in. by 23 in. **$300-$500**

Painting, sumi and colors on silk, a monkey eating a peach, Hokusai style, framed, 19th century, framed size 10 1/4 in. by 17 in. **$900-$1,200**

Screen, two-leaf, sumi, colors, and gofun on paper, Hotei playing with four karako in a lakeside scene, old damages, early Meiji period, leaf size 33 1/2 in. by 63 in. **$1,200-$1,600**

Screen, two-leaf, sumi and colors on gold paper, flowering peony, Kano school, 19th century, leaf size 31 in. by 80 in. **$1,000-$1,500**

Screen, two-leaf, sumi and colors on gold-sprinkled paper, an eagle perched on a branch, stained, old repairs, 19th century, leaf size 29 in. by 59 in. **$1,000-$1,500**

Screen, two-leaf, sumi and colors on paper, a group of three cranes standing beneath a large pine, signed Ichigyoun hitsu, some old damages, 19th century, leaf size, 36 3/4 in. by 66 1/2 in. **$3,000-$5,000**

Screen, two-leaf, sumi, colors, and gofun on paper, flowers in a stream, late 19th century, leaf size 23 in. by 41 in. **$500-$700**

Screen, four-leaf, sumi, colors, and gofun on silver-ground paper, autumn leaves scattered amongst rock-work below a full moon, 19th century, leaf size 25 in. by 51 1/2 in. **$2,000-$3,000**

Screen, six-leaf, sumi, colors, and gofun on silver-ground paper; a stag and deer with autumnal flowers, signed Koasai, stained and damaged, Meiji period, leaf size 18 1/2 in. by 43 in. **$750-$1,200**

Screen, six-leaf, sumi, colors, and gofun on gold paper, flowers above boldly breaking waves, 19th century, leaf size 24 in. by 62 1/2 in. **$4,000-$6,000**

Screen, six-leaf, sumi, colors, and gofun on silk; Mt. Fuji, pine, and flowering cherry trees, old repairs, late 18th century, leaf size 24 in. by 60 in. **$1,800-$2,500**

Tibetan Thangka or Buddhist religious painting on cloth, measuring 26 in. by 19 in., 40 in. by 30 in. exterior dimensions, dating to the early 20th century. The Thangka is hand-painted with gold leaf and pigment on silk, then attached to a heavier canvas. "Thangka" is a transliteration from the Tibetan language. The word is used generally to represent various kinds of paintings of Buddha figures and themes. Thangkas were used as part of the worship service in Tibetan Buddhist monasteries. The main parts of Thangka are based on the images and stories of Buddha. They may also contain some historical legends. The drawing style of a Thangka is unique with striking and contrasting colors. **$150**

Watercolor on paper, women gathering kelp at the seashore, Hiroshi Yoshida, dated 1902, 8 1/2 in. by 18 1/2 in. **$1,000-$1,500**

Watercolor on paper, three carp and water reeds, late 19th century, framed size 12 1/2 in. by 18 in. **$400-$600**

Rugs

POINTS FOR THE RUG BUYER

Although the focus of this book is primarily on the antiques and art of China, Japan, Korea, the Pacific Rim, and Southeast Asia, the term "oriental rugs" has traditionally included the weavers of Asia Minor and the Middle East.

In order for the buyer to be knowledgeable enough to distinguish the quality or grade of a rug, he or she must study all types of rugs, especially Persian, focusing on a number of features. For instance, a good rug, whether finely or coarsely knotted, will have a firm, compact body. The thinner the lengthwise warp threads-and the woof (or weft) threads that cross them at right angles-the more compact the weave will be. These threads can be observed on the back of a rug or in the "selvage" (the edge on either side of a woven or flat-knitted fabric so finished as to prevent raveling) and fringe.

Single-knot rugs are the most closely woven rugs. The Ghiordes, or double knot, is found in rugs such as those from the Bijar district (western Iran).

The best Persian rugs have cotton, linen, or silk, rather than wool, for the warp and woof. Moreover, a good rug will have carefully finished edges and will not be unduly crooked. It should have a distinct design and clear colors, as well.

MARKS OF DISTINCTION

As a rule, Kashan (central Iran) and Kerman (southeastern Iran) rugs show the finest knotting and closest weave. Kashan rugs are knotted with silk, but either silk or wool is acceptable. Similarly, Fereghan (northeast Iran) and Sarouk (central Iran) rugs are distinguished by their fine weaving, but it is not as fine as that of the Kermans or Kashans.

Bijars, though coarsely knotted, are firmly woven, usually with a double woof, which makes the rugs very heavy. Tabriz (the capital of East Azerbaijan in northwestern Iran) rugs are, as a rule, more finely woven than Bijars, but are not as fine as Sehnas, which are single-knot rugs. (The "Sehna" knot is named for the city in central Iran.)

The rugs of the nomad weavers, including Kurdish (the northern border of modern Iran and Iraq), Shiraz, and Bakhtiari (both southwestern Iran) are generally coarsely knotted. Tekke Turkoman rugs (primarily modern Afghanistan), which are more finely woven than other nomad rugs and are equal in quality to Tabriz rugs, are the exception. The others have wool for warp and woof. Of this group the common characteristics include a wide, striped selvage ending in a long fringe.

Note: Carpets are generally larger and rugs are generally smaller than 10 feet.

Bakhtiari rug, dark green millefleur ground with oversized stepped pendant medallion (ivory), smaller dark blue floral scalloped medallion, dark blue floral spandrels, red primary border of floral sprays, two pairs of narrow guard borders, 6 ft. 7 in. by 4 ft. 11 in. **$5,000-$5,500**

Bijar rug, red ground, gold petal-form center medallion with blue pendant palmettes and gold floral spandrels, navy blue primary border, a pair of ivory floral guard borders, selvage break, very worn, late 19th century, 12 ft. 5 in. by 5 ft. 5 in. **$7,000-$8,000**

Chinese carpet, Peking type, circa 1890, open gold field with center medallion composed of floral motifs, medallion surrounded by ring of flowers, flowers with vines in corners of field, major border of royal blue, minor inner border of light blue, outer minor border of navy blue, wear mostly even, 8 feet by 10 feet 2 in. **$2,400-$3,000**

Chinese rug, Peking type, circa 1900, beige field, small center medallion, stylized trees, good condition, 27 in. by 52 in. **$500-$600**

Chinese rug, circa 1925, beige field with floral and bird motifs, beige border, even wear, 5 feet 1 in. by 8 feet 6 in. **$850-$950**

Chinese rug, circa 1925, claret field with lattice work design, floral motifs on beige border, good condition, 25 in. by 36 in. **$350-$450**

Chinese carpet, circa 1950, cinnabar field, without border, sculpted bird motifs, very good condition, minor stains, 5 feet by 8 feet 6 in. **$750-$800**

Chinese rug, Peking type, circa 1910, navy blue field with two floral sprigs, major border in rose-pink, minor border in beige, guard rails in both light and dark blue, floral and vine motifs on each end, even wear, 24 in. by 48 in. **$200-$250**

Chinese carpet, blue ground with overall pattern of stylized clouds, scattered cranes, central crane medallion, pale orange key-fret border, narrow guard stripes, worn, early 20th century, 17 ft. 6 in. by 10 ft. 4 in. **$1,500-$2,000**

Chinese carpet (Peking), ivory ground covered with trees, mountains, and the Eight Horses of Mu Wang, blue primary border with floral medallions, three pair of guard borders, worn, losses, animal stains, late 19th century, 1 ft. 4 in. by 6 ft. 3 in. **$6,500-$8,500**

Chinese carpet (Nichols), deep blue with scattered floral sprays and butterflies, gray primary border with prunus blossoms, three guard borders, 17 ft. 7 in. by 11 ft. 5 in. **$6,000-$8,000**

Chinese carpet, cream field with central blue floral-spray medallion, smaller floral medallions at corners, narrow blue guard borders, 11 ft. 9 in. by 9 ft. **$2,000-$3,000**

Chinese carpet, cream field with blue and magenta floral sprays at the corners, narrow blue guard border, circa 1925, 11 ft. 6 in. by 8 ft. 10 in. **$2,000-$3,000**

Chinese rug, ivory field with colored floral sprays in geometric style, outerguard border with Shou characters in deep blue, circa 1925, 11 ft. 8 in. by 9 ft. **$1,500-$2,550**

Chinese carpet, deep blue field with flowering vases and meandering scroll on deeper blue guard border, circa 1910, 7 ft. 6 in. by 4 ft. 2 in. **$2,000-$3,000**

Chinese rug, indigo field with flaming pearls and clouds surrounding five dragons, wave-pattern guard border in colors, late 19th century, 7 in. by 4 ft. **$3,500-$5,000**

Chinese rug, blue field with royal blue clouds, cream guard border with magenta flowers, outer guard border with dragons, damage, moth deterioration, animal stains, circa 1925, 9 ft. 5 in. by 7 ft. 2 in. **$1,000-$1,500**

Chinese rug, pale orange ground with blue and white dragons, deep blue guard border, 4 in. by 7 ft. **$1,200-$1,600**

Chinese rug, black ground with Shou Lao surrounded by Immortals in colors, damaged, 6 in. by 6 ft. 2 in. **$900-$1,200**

Japanese rug, circa 1920, very open design on beige-gold field, asymmetrical design with flowering branches in vase and scholar's table, very good condition, 28 in. by 52 in. **$450-$500**

Kashan carpet, ivory ground with allover pattern of scrolling vines, rosettes, and palmettes, five guard borders, 8 ft. 11 in. by 6 ft. 1 in. **$5,000-$7,000**

Kashan carpet, red ground with three concentric petal-form medallions in blue, blue and green floral sprays, navy blue floral spandrels, navy blue border of palmettes, three pair of guard borders, worn, refringed, 12 ft. 2 in. by 8 ft. 10 in. **$5,000-$6,000**

Kerman carpet, navy blue with floral medallion in cream, burgundy, and green, elaborate floral border, worn, 14 ft. 3 in. by 10 ft. 4 in. **$2,200-$3,600**

Kurdish rug, deep blue ground covered by three vertical rows of flower heads, zigzag inner designs and spandrels, deep blue meandering vine primary border, one pair of narrow claret floral guard borders, worn, losses to guard borders, 6 ft. 11 in. by 4 ft. 2 in. **$700-$900**

Kurdish runner, red with five blue medallions, brown floral spandrels, three guard borders, worn and losses, 12 ft. 11 in. by 3 ft. 5 in. **$1,100-$1,800**

Kurdish runner, navy blue ground, diagonal rows of pentagonal devices, inner trefoil guard border surrounded by an ivory plant leaf and T-device border, repaired and worn, 3 ft. 10 in. by 10 ft. 7 in. **$900-$1,200**

Sarouk Fereghan mat, cream with pattern of meandering vines and botehs, deep blue primary border, one pair of guard borders, worn and unraveling, 1 ft. 8 in. by 1 ft. 6 in. **$500-$650**

Sarouk Fereghan rug, red with blue floral pendant medallion and floral sprays with beige floral spandrels, deep blue primary border with floral arrangements, one pair of red guard borders, badly worn and reduced, late 19th century, 4 ft. 8 in. by 3 ft. 5 in. **$800-$1,200**

Sarouk runner, claret ground with allover pattern of floral bouquets and sprays, deep blue primary border of flowering vines, two pairs of guard borders, repaired and worn, 15 ft. 5 in. by 2 ft. 9 in. $2,000-$3,000

Shiraz rug, midnight blue ground, rust stepped medallion enclosing a smaller blue platform medallion, elaborate vines and rosettes with cream platform medallions in each corner, deep blue border of stylized vines and rosettes, three pair of guard borders, some wear and repair, 6 ft. 10 in. by 4 ft. 5 in. **$1,500-$2,500**

Tabriz rug, melon ground with oval center medallion, overall millefleur with burgundy spandrels, ivory primary border with vines and palmettes, three pairs of guard borders, 7 ft. 7 in. by 4 ft. 8 in. **$4,000-$6,000**

Tekke Turkoman carpet, red-brown ground, four rows of gulls, 12 per row, red-brown border with sunburst design, one pair of guard borders with serrated leaf skirts, refringed, 11 in. by 7 ft. **$3,500-$4,500**

Tekke Turkoman rug, red ground covered with two rows of octagonal cloverleaf gulls (six per row) and star devices, a deep blue primary border with interconnecting leaves, two guard borders with striped kilims, 5 ft. 3 in. by 3 ft. 10 in. **$900-$1,100**

Tekke Turkoman runner, red ground, two rows of gulls, 22 per row, alternating diamond-shaped devices, ivory primary border with palmettes, six narrow guard borders, kilim stripes at each end, 16 in. by 2 ft. 11 in. **$2,000-$2,500**

Snuff Bottles

During the 17th century, the taking of snuff became a popular Chinese practice. Although it was not acceptable for the Chinese to smoke tobacco, snuff was considered medicinal. Accordingly, the snuff bottle, developed in the latter part of the century, was based on the concepts for the Chinese medicine bottles (yao ping).

In the late 19th century, the snuff bottle became a cabinet bottle, purchased for collecting purposes. Many of these cabinet bottles were not well hollowed. At the same time, motifs were more flamboyant.

Today, snuff bottles (antique and contemporary) are highly prized and collected worldwide.

Note: Bottles are not always available with the original cap and spoon. These are interchangeable and, for the most part, do not affect values.

Agate, flattened form, a broad white band around the center, early 19th century. **$400-$600**

Agate, striated, ovoid, smoky gray with brown stippling, 19th century. **$200-$300**

Agate/moss, honey-colored with spinach green masslike tendrils, well hollowed, 19th century. **$400-$600**

Agate/moss, ovoid with mask and ring handles on the shoulders, red, gray, and gold, 19th century. **$800-$1,200**

Carved stone (moss agate?) snuff bottle in the form of a fly on a larger bug, with bone stopper, 3 1/4 in. by 2 in. by 1 5/8 in. $500

Agate/moss, rectangular, honey with blue-green inclusions, 19th century. **$300-$400**

Agate/shadow, ovoid flattened form with a carved bird and flowers, late 19th century. **$700-$900**

Agate/shadow carved to depict a bird and fruit beneath a tree (the design incorporating the natural inclusions in the stone), 19th century. **$800-$1,200**

Agate/shadow, carved, two men seated under a pine, late Ch'ing (Qing) Dynasty. **$1,500-$2,000**

Agate/shadow, carved, an elder, rockwork, and pines, an inscription on the reverse. **$2,500-$3,500**

Amber carved in low relief with bats on one side, the reverse with a pavilion and pine, late 19th century. **$600-$900**

Amber, small size, relief carving of fruiting vines overall, late Ch'ing (Qing) Dynasty. **$200-$300**

Amethyst, eggplant form with carved leaves. **$1,000-$1,500**

Amethyst, mask and ring handles on the shoulders, the stone a pale purple, late Ch'ing (Qing) Dynasty. **$1,000-$1,500**

Amethyst, baluster form, carved with pine, peony, and deer, late Ch'ing (Qing) Dynasty. **$1,000-$1,500**

Bamboo carved in the form of three seed pods, leaves in relief, 19th century. **$225-$325**

Agate, tiger eye, with golden agate stopper, excellent condition, 3 in. by 1 3/8 in. by 5/8 in. **$300**

Carved amethyst snuff bottle in the form of a fish, no stopper, 3 1/8 in. by 1 3/4 in. by 1 1/4 in. **$1,300**

Canton enamel, ovoid, yellow ground painted with phoenix and waterfowl in a landscape, early 18th century. **$5,000-$7,000**

Canton enamel painted with a continuous scene of children at play and a young woman holding flowers, ruyi band on the foot and shoulders, restored, four-character Ch'ien Lung (Qianlong) mark (and of the period), 18th century. **$6,000-$8,000**

Canton enamel, ovoid form, mandarin ducks and aquatic plants beneath tree peony, the reverse with a bird perched on a branch, famille rose, restoration on shoulder and neck, early 18th century. **$6,000-$8,000**

Canton enamel, a continuous landscape with figures, pavilions, and mountains, blue and white, minor fusion flake on shoulder, 18th century. **$3,000-$4,000**

Canton enamel, yellow ground with a dragon-and-cloud pattern, 19th century. **$600-$800**

Canton enamel, turquoise ground with yellow and blue dragon and clouds, early 19th century. **$1,000-$1,500**

Chalcedony, Tzu chou-style carving with figures and rock-work. **$400-$600**

Chalcedony carving of a sage, the reverse with pine and riverscape, blue, late 19th century. **$700-$900**

Left to right: Enamel-on-copper snuff bottle, dragon and flaming pearl, late 19th century. **$500-$600**. Opal snuff bottle with carp and waves, 20th century. **$900-$1,200**. Lac burgauté bottle inlaid with gold and silver foil and mother-of-pearl, late 18th /early 19th century. **$1,000-$1,500**

Chalcedony, ovoid with reddish brown areas on a gray field, 19th century. **$300-$500**

Cloisonné, baluster form, lotus and scrolls on each side, Ming style, late 19th century. **$300-$500**

Cloisonné, double-gourd form, blue ground with lotus and scrolls, late 19th century. **$300-$400**

Cloisonne with overall vine and flowers design, Chinese, dating to the late 19th or early 20th century. It measures 3 1/4 in. high and is slightly under 1 in. at the base. The spoon is ivory. This is made of high-quality yellow cloisonné done in great detail on brass in a floral design. **$250**

Cloisonne, flattened ovoid form, butterflies and flowers in white, yellow, and pink on a turquoise ground, late Ch'ing (Qing) Dynasty. **$250-$350**

Carved glass, with transfer decoration of flowers and leaves, cranberry overlay, the stopper appears to be tourmaline, 1 3/4 in. by 2 1/2 in. by 1 in. **$125**

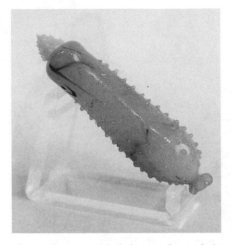

Glass, pale green with darker streaks, made in the form of a cucumber, with yellow glass stopper, 3 1/2 in. by 1 in. **$80**

Carved glass snuff bottle, muddy beige in color, with geometric crosshatched decoration, 1 3/4 in. by 2 1/8 in. by 1/2 in. **$110**

Glass, white and deep green, in the form of a leek, with yellow glass stopper, 3 in. by 1 1/8 in. **$80**

The first Peking glass factory was built in the Forbidden City within the Palace walls in 1696. It was overseen by a German priest, who brought many Western techniques of glass and enamel work to the Chinese. The first Peking glass items produced were made with single-colored or clear glass that was either carved or faceted. Overlay glass was developed later, which involved dipping a glass item into a vat of molten glass of a contrasting color. After cooling, the second color was carved away to reveal the color underneath. As this technique developed, more colors and multiple layers were used. Peking glass items are still being produced today.

Glass snuff bottle with a mountainous landscape overlaid with clear glass, stopper is carved stone, signed, 1 7/8 in. by 3 1/4 in. by 1 in. **$125**

Carved glass overlay in white and salmon red with radiating design that includes yin-yang, tiger eye agate stopper, 2 in. by 2 1/2 in. by 1 1/4 in. **$200**

Coral in the form of a carp leaping through waves and spitting a pearl (which forms the stopper). **$750-$950**

Glass with glass overlay of transfer decoration: three men and woman on one side, and two men (one armed with sword) crossing a bridge on the other side, stone stopper, 1 3/4 in. by 3 7/8 in. by 5/8 in. **$120**

Coral carved overall with tree peonies. **$1,500-$2,000**

Coral, rectangular form, carved in relief with phoenix and foliage on one side, a dragon and clouds on the reverse. **$800-$1,200**

Cloisonné, open-work with a pattern of phoenix and flowering scrolls in colors and gilt, early 20th century. **$600-$900**

Amber Peking glass, measuring 2 3/4 in. by 1 1/4 in., Chinese, dating to the late 19th or early 20th century. The bottle has a stone top that may be jade. Rich overall patina. **$225**

Cloisonné, turquoise ground with a pattern of butterflies and foliate sprigs overall in red, white, blue, and black, late 19th century. **$300-$400**

Peking glass, carved as a monkey, measuring 2 5/8 in. tall and 1 1/2 in. wide, dating to the 19th century. Fine original condition. **$300**

Green and white Peking glass, floral design, measuring 4 1/2 in. high, dating to the late 19th or early 20th century. The cap, with attached spoon, is made of carved ivory. Excellent and original condition with no chips, cracks, or repairs. **$400**

Glass, double-gourd form, black with gold speckling, early 19th century. **$350-$500**

Glass, egg yolk yellow, carved with a band of stiff leaves around the shoulders, 19th century. **$900-$1,200**

Glass, flattened form, an oval panel on each side, deep blue, Ch'ien Lung (Qianiong) mark, but 19th century. **$300-$500**

Glass, octagonal and faceted, deep ruby red, early 20th century. **$200-$300**

Glass, pale green with red circlets of varying sizes. **$150-$275**

Inside-painted glass decorated with a boy riding a water buffalo, signed Ma Shoo Xuan, dated 1905. **$1,000-$1,500**

Inside-painted glass decorated with butter-flies and kittens on both sides, 20th century. **$150-$225**

Inside-painted glass decorated with a con-tinuous scene of carp, pike, catfish, and aquatic plants, signed Zhou Leyuan. **$1,000-$1,600**

Inside-painted glass with a continuous scene of standing ladies and rock-work exe-cuted in vivid colors, signed Ye Zhong San, dated 1908. **$800-$1,100**

Carved glass, hand painted showing birds in a leafy and floral landscape, jade stopper, 3 5/8 in. by 1 in. $100

Ivory carved in the form of the Emperor (?) holding bird and Empress (?) holding fan, hand painted, minor wear, 3 in. by 3/4 in. each. **$3,250/pair**

Inside-painted glass with a continuous scene of figures within a landscape. **$160-$200**

Inside-painted glass decorated with two ladies amongst flowering branches on one side, the reverse with a scholar and his attendant in a landscape, pear-shaped. **$300-$400**

Inside-painted glass, large size, decorated with equestrians against a mountainscape, the reverse with ladies and attendants, early 20th century. **$300-$400**

Inside-painted glass, double bottle, rectangular form, decorated with four landscapes, late 19th century. **$500-$700**

Ivory scrimshaw decorated with a bird on a branch, stylized floral border, 3 1/4 in. by 1 5/8 in. **$900**

Inside-painted glass, rectangular, decorated with birds and squirrels, early 20th century. **$300-$400**

Inside-painted glass, rectangular, decorated with flowers and vases, circa 1925. **$100-$150**

Carved jade snuff bottle in the form of a scarab or cicada, no stopper, 2 1/2 in. by 1 3/4 in. by 3/4 in. **$200**

Inside-painted glass, man on a donkey in a landscape scene wrapping around the bottle, Chinese, signed with a variant of Yeh Chung San and the seal: Yin, measuring 3 in. with glass top and spoon. Yeh Chung San was a famous snuff bottle artist who worked from 1892-1912. His sons and followers continued to produce high-quality bottles signed with his name until the 1950s. Probably a later example done by his followers. **$700**

Overlay glass, five-color, the white ground decorated with a floral spray on each side, early 19th century. **$1,000-$1,500**

Overlay glass, five-color on a milk white ground, carved with bats and Buddhist emblems, 19th century. **$1,000-$1,500**

Overlay glass, five-color on milk glass, double-gourd form with a motif of Buddhist emblems. **$600-$800**

Overlay glass, blue glass carved through to the white glass with a low-relief motif of a horse and pine. **$600-$800**

Overlay glass, blue on milk glass, bats and cranes, late Ch'ing (Qing) Dynasty. **$400-$550**

Overlay glass carved in red with chih lung and scrolls, last half of the 18th century. **$900-$1,200**

Overlay glass, red overlay on bubble-suffused glass, carved with carp and aquatic plants, waves around the base, 18th century. **$2,000-$2,500**

Overlay glass, bubble glass with red overlay, carved with flowering sprays on each side, 19th century. **$600-$900**

Overlay glass, red overlay on clear glass, birds and pavilions above crested waves. **$1,500-$2,000**

Overlay glass, pear-shaped, carved with a red overlay in a continuous scene of pavilions and pines, late 18th century. **$1,200-$1,800**

Overlay glass, red overlay carved through to a yellow ground with five bats encircling a Shou character, 19th century. **$500-$700**

Overlay, snowflake glass with red bats overall, 19th century. **$350-$550**

Hair crystal. **$250-$350**

Hair crystal, ovoid form, thick clouds of black tourmaline needles, early 19th century. **$600-$800**

Hair crystal, flattened ovoid form, tourmaline needles enclosed by iridescence, 19th century. **$1,000-$1,500**

Porcelain, blue and white, showing two figures (master and student?) in a landscape, with red painted ceramic stopper, signed on the bottom, 2 1/8 in. by 2 5/8 in. by 1 in. $220

Hair crystal, flattened form, clear stone with fine black tourmaline needles, well hollowed, early 19th century. **$800-$1,200**

Hornbill carved with two figures under a pine. **$700-$900**

Hornbill carved with figures in landscapes. **$600-$750**

Ivory carved as a dragon on waves. **$400-$600**

Ivory carved as a writhing dragon. **$300-$400**

Ivory, with front and back designs in relief and multicolor scrimshaw of people and bird on branch, in flat, baluster vase shape, measuring 3 in., with ivory top and spoon, Chinese, dating to the late 19th or early 20th century. **$200**

Ivory, cylindrical, carved in deep relief, a court scene, late 19th century. **$700-$1,000**

Ivory, oviform, carved with a hen and chicks, late Ch'ing (Qing) Dynasty. **$700-$900**

Ivory, polychrome double bottle of Emperor and Empress, heads as stoppers. **$400-$600**

Jade, black, carved in relief, a monkey seated on a rock passing a peach to another monkey, the reverse with Lui Hai holding a string of cash before a toad, 19th century. **$2,500-$3,500**

Jade, celadon pebble bottle with russet areas. **$225-$375**

Jade, white, carved in low relief on each side with a large peony. **$700-$900**

Jade, white, carved as a finger citron, last half of the 19th century. **$500-$750**

Jade, white, low relief carving of a pavilion and pine with an elder, mid-19th century. **$600-$900**

Jade, white with overall carved wickerwork pattern, early 19th century. **$900-$1,200**

Jadeite, apple green, mottled, rectangular form, first half of the 19th century. **$2,000-$3,000**

Jadeite, lavender with concave foot rim. **$1,500-$1,800**

Jadeite, lavender, ovoid form, an overall lattice design, 19th century. **$900-$1,200**

Jadeite, pale green with emerald flecks and black splashes, 19th century. **$600-$900**

Jasper carved with branches on a blue-gray ground. **$250-$350**

Ku Yüeh Hsüan (enameling on opaque white glass), milk glass painted with birds perched on branches, Ch'ien Lung (Qianlong) mark, but early 19th century. **$1,200-$1,600**

Ku Yüeh Hsüan (enameling on opaque white glass), milk glass painted with lotus, peony, and leaf scrolls, leaf band on collar and foot, famille rose, Ch'ien Lung (Qianlong) four-character mark (and of the period). **$4,000-$6,000**

Ku Yüeh Hsüan (enameling on opaque white glass), milk glass painted with a continuous motif of flowering branches, famille rose, 19th century. **$900-$1,200**

Lac burgauté, two brown panels, one inlaid in mother-of-pearl with a long-tailed bird perched on a flowering branch, the reverse with peony clusters. **$1,600-$2,200**

Lac burgauté, butterfly form with red-orange panels on each side, Shibayama inlay in a floral motif, 20th century. **$700-$950**

Porcelain, blue and white, showing a court scene (?), with a tourmaline stopper, 3 in. by 1 1/8 in. **$130**

Porcelain, decorated with a seated woman, a holy man (?) with a staff, and a third man (servant?), glazed in blue and red, no stopper, 1 1/4 in. by 3 3/8 in. **$200**

Ceramic snuff bottle in the form of a lohan (?) holding a staff and carrying a gourd on his back, yellow with black decoration, 1 1/8 in. by 3 5/8 in. by 1 1/2 in. **$125**

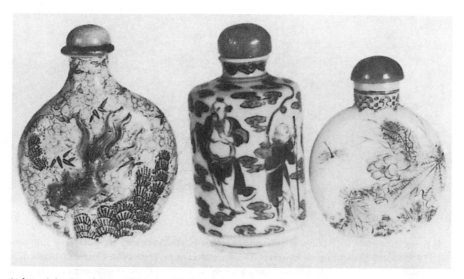

Left to right: Porcelain snuff bottle with fish and aquatic plants in relief, falls rose, Tao Kuang period. **$700-$900**. Porcelain snuff bottle, underglaze blue, copper red, and white decorated with the Eight Immortals, early 19th century. **$350-$550** Ku Yüén Hsüan (enameling on opaque white glass) snuff bottle, famille rose, motif of flowers avid foliage with insects, 19th century. **$1,200-$1,500**

Lac burgauté, octagonal with diapers around a central flower head, 19th century. **$800-$1,000**

Lac burgauté, rectangular and squat, a shaped panel on each side with a landscape motif. **$400-$600**

Lacquer, intricately carved with cinnabar lacquer surface and brass fittings. The bottle is decorated with landscape scenes in relief carving. The spoon is intact. Chinese. The bottle has a false Qianlong (1736-95) reign mark stamped in the brass on the bottom, 3 1/4 in. tall. **$100**

Lacquer, red (cinnabar), carved in deep relief with ladies on a balcony, Ch'ien Lung (Qianlong) mark, but early 20th century. **$150-$225**

Lacquer, cinnabar, carved in high relief with figures and a pavilion, late Ch'ing (Qing) Dynasty. **$400-$600**

Lapis carved with warriors. **$275-$400**

Malachite, flattened ovoid form with a circular panel on each side, late 19th century. **$900-$1,200**

Mongolian silver, cylindrical, inset with turquoise and coral forming small flower heads, late Ch'ing (Qing) Dynasty. **$200-$300**

Mongolian silver inlaid with coral and turquoise on each side, forming large flower heads, late Ch'ing (Qing) Dynasty. **$500-$700**

Mongolian silver, reticulated filigree centered with turquoise on each side, 19th century. **$700-$900**

Left to right: Porcelain snuff bottle, famille rose, 18 Lohan in relief, each with attribute, early 19th century. **$900-$1,200.** Malachite gourd-form snuff bottle, 20th century. **$700-$900.** Glass snuff bottle, milk glass with red overlay motif, late 18th century. $700-$950. Ivory snuff bottle with archaic motifs, late 18th century. **$1,000-$1,500**

Mother-of-pearl, double gourd shape with engraved figures and side rings, measuring 2 1/4 in. by 1 in., Chinese, dating to the late 19th or early 20th century. The tip of the spoon is broken. The bottle has side rings to permit suspension from a chatelaine. **$250**

Mother-of-pearl carved in relief with five bats around a Shou character, the reverse with a dragon. **$500-$700**

Opal carved with a dragon on one side and a phoenix on the reverse. **$500-$600**

Opal in the form of a carp on waves spitting out a pearl (which forms the stopper). **$700-$900**

Opal, rectangular, two children carved in relief. **$400-$600**

Porcelain, blue and white, double, decorated in underglaze blue in a "scholars in the landscape" design typical of late Ming-early Ching Dynasty, Chinese, measuring 2 1/4 in. by 2 1/2 in., with a green stone, possibly jade, top and spoon, dating to the late 18th/early 19th century. **$400**

Porcelain, a motif of two puppies on each side, early 20th century. **$200-$300**

Porcelain, a green grasshopper on each side, last half of the 19th century. **$400-$600**

Porcelain, a green grasshopper on each side, early 20th century. **$175-$225**

Porcelain, a green and orange four-toed dragon and flaming pearl on each side, early 20th century. **$100-$125**

Porcelain, a red dragon writhing around the bottle, late 19th century. **$400-$600**

Carved stone in the form of a mythical lion creature, wood stopper, 2 3/8 in. by 3 3/8 in. by 1 1/8 in. $200

Porcelain in the form of a recumbent elephant supporting a vase on its saddle, famille rose, late 19th century. **$350-$475**

Porcelain, 1000 Flowers pattern, famille rose on a black ground, circa 1925. **$100-$175**

Porcelain molded in relief, a writhing dragon, reticulated ground, famille rose, Ch'ien Lung (Qianlong) mark, but from the Tao Kuang (Daoguang) period. **$800-$1,200**

Porcelain molded in relief, children playing, famille rose, Tao Kuang (Daoguang) period. **$800-$1,200**

Porcelain, with an overall large red, sang de boeuf (ox blood) crackle monochrome glaze, in Meiping shape, measuring 3 in. by 1 1/4 in., with no top or spoon, Chinese, dating to the late 18th or early 19th century. **$350**

Porcelain, Chinese, late Ching Dynasty or late 19th century, and measures approximately 2 1/4 in. high. It is made in an unusual double, or two-bottle, design with underglaze blue landscape decoration. Decoration such as this was introduced in the late Ming period and gradually faded out in popularity until the 19th century. The tops are made of stone—possibly jade—and the spoons are intact. There is a small, old foot rim chip. **$400**

Porcelain, monochrome, deep olive-green glaze typical of the late 18th or early 19th century. The foot is characteristic of the period. The top is made of stone and metal and has an intact spoon, which is probably a replacement. Chinese. It stands 2 1/2 in. high. **$350**

Porcelain, large crackle glaze and a faint red monochrome overglaze, measuring 2 1/2 in. tall, Chinese, dating to the late 19th century. The bottle has an ivory spoon and a stone—possibly lavender jade—top. The Meiping shape, fine glaze effect, and circular finished base all show the hand of a master. Fine original condition. **$400**

Porcelain, with an overall feathery red, fine crackle monochrome glaze, in tapered-shoulder shape, measuring 3 in. by 1 1/4 in., Chinese, dating to the late 18th or early 19th century. The bottle has a red stone top and spoon. Fine original condition. **$400**

Carved stone, ivory color, showing two figures standing next to a pine tree, with animal heads on the shoulders of the bottle, the stopper is carved in the form of a flower, 2 in. by 4 in. by 5/8 in. **$300**

Porcelain, moon flask shape, decorated in underglaze red with foo dogs, Chinese, measuring 4 in. by 3 in. by 1/2 in. The bottle bears a false Chien Lung reign mark on the base and dates to the late 19th or early 20th century. It has a hard stone top and ivory spoon. **$350**

Porcelain molded in the form of a recumbent Buddhistic lion, famille rose, early 19th century. **$600-$900**

Porcelain, moon-flask form with a Rose Mandarin pattern, early 19th century. **$500-$700**

Porcelain reticulated and molded in relief with dragons and clouds, glazed blue, circa 1900. **$400-$600**

Porcelain, Rose Medallion, baluster form, circa 1880. **$300-$400**

Porcelain, white glaze, molded in high relief with 18 Lohan, circa 1800. **$1,000-$1,500**

Porcelain, yellow glaze, writhing dragon molded in relief, mid-19th century. **$700-$900**

Porcelain, blue and white, motif of a standing lady and her attendant, early 19th century. **$300-$500**

Porcelain, underglaze blue and copper red with a lotus motif, early 19th century. **$200-$300**

Porcelain, a seated Lohan and pine tree on each side, famille rose, early 19th century. **$500-$700**

Porcelain, each side with red-orange Buddhistic lions and clouds, early 20th century. **$125-$175**

Porcelain, blue and white, a continuous landscape, Ch'ien Lung (Qianlong) mark, but late 19th century. **$150-$225**

Porcelain, blue and white, riverscape with boats in relief, Ch'eng Hua (Chenghua) mark, but late 19th century. **$400-$600**

Porcelain, underglaze blue and copper red, cylindrical with continuous motif of warriors and horses, 19th century. **$175-$225**

Porcelain, underglaze blue and copper red, cylindrical with the 12 animals of the zodiac, late 18th century. **$700-$900**

Porcelain, underglaze blue and copper red with scholars and attendants in a landscape, early 19th century. **$300-$400**

Porcelain/soft paste, blue and white with a motif of 100 Children. **$900-$1,200**

Porcelain/soft paste, blue and white with camels and attendants, Yung Cheng lyongzheng) mark, but late 18th century. **$500-$700**

Porcelain/soft paste, cylindrical form with the Eight Horses of Mu Wang, late 18th//early 19th century. **$500-$700**

Porcelain, cylindrical, Rooster Pattern, famille rose, Kuang Hsü (Guangxu) mark (and of the period). **$700-$900**

Porcelain, cylindrical, figures in a landscape, famille rose, early 19th century. **$400-$600**

Porcelain, each side decorated with ducks and spring flowers, blue mask and ring handles on shoulders, Tao Kuang (Daoguang) mark (and of the period). **$800-$1,200**

Porcelain, flattened ovoid form covered with a blue glaze, Kuang HsO (Guangxu) mark (and of the period). **$300-$425**

Rock crystal carving of an immortal. **$150-$250**

Rock crystal, faceted hexagonal form, first half of the 19th century. **$400-$600**

Rock crystal painted on the inside with fan-tailed fish and aquatic plants, signed Ye Zhong San and dated 1911. **$1,000-$1,500**

Rock crystal painted on the inside with 18 Lohan and their attributes, signed Ye Zhong San and dated 1919. **$2,000-$3,000**

Rock crystal painted on the inside with a continuous landscape and mountainscape with a sage and attendant, signed Zhou Leyuan. **$1,000-$1,500**

Rock crystal, rectangular, carved with pine trees, last half of the 19th century. **$200-$300**

Rose quartz carved in relief on one side with two cranes and pine and a deer and pine on the reverse. **$350-$450**

Soapstone, gray, low relief carving of prunus and rock-work, the shoulders with mask and ring handles. **$300-$400**

Tiger's eye carved with a bird perched on a flowering branch. **$225-$350**

Tourmaline, green, flattened ovoid form carved with a standing lady on one side and a pine on the reverse, circa 1900. **$600-$800**

Tourmaline, pink, modified peach form with carvings of fruit. **$500-$700**

Turquoise, carved, with bird finial, decorated with birds, leaves, and vines, 1 1/2 in. by 2 1/8 in. by 1/2 in. **$125**

Turquoise, carved with a fish design, measuring 2 in., with a turquoise top and ivory spoon, Chinese dating to the late 19th/early 20th century. **$150**

Turquoise carved with birds in high relief, late Ch'ing (Qing) Dynasty. **$500-$700**

Turquoise carved with flowers and vines in high relief. **$275-$400**

Turquoise, flattened rounded form, the dark stone with light patches, early 19th century. **$1,500-$2,000**

I Hsing (Yixing), blue glaze with an oval scenic panel on each side, 19th century. **$700-$1,000**

I Hsing, two oval panels with landscapes executed in the famille rose palette, first half of the 19th century. **$900-$1,200**

I Hsing, ovoid, melon, ribbed. **$1,200-$1,600**

Southeast Asian Ceramics

Southeast Asian ceramics generally refer to low-fired earthenware and more highly fired stoneware and porcelains, principally from the countries now known as Cambodia, Thailand, and Vietnam. Craftsmen from Burma, Laos, Indonesia, and other Southeast Asian countries also produced ceramic wares for millennia, but Cambodia, Thailand, and Vietnam produced the bulk of surviving ceramics-most of which were exported along trade routes.

Annamese (parts of modern-day Vietnam and Laos) jar and cover, the footed jar painted with four iron brown flower-head panels within pale olive surrounds, pooling to a deeper shade in the areas of low relief, crack in cover, 11th/12th century, 10 in. high. **$3,000-$5,000**

Sawankhalok (a city in what is now Thailand) box and cover, ribbed and decorated with iron brown foliage, 15th century, 5 1/2 in. diameter. **$200-$300**

Sawankhalok bowl and cover incised and painted with scrolling foliage panels, 15th century, 6 1/2 in. diameter. **$300-$500**

Sawankhalok flask painted iron brown with foliage, body with ribs, neck restored, 15th century, 5 1/2 in. high. **$100-$200**

Sawankhalok, group, an elephant surmounted by two figures and painted iron brown under a white slip, restored, 14th century, 5 in. high. **$300-$400**

Lidded vessel, finely made with two small handles and recessed lid with knob, Early Thai, circa 1st millennium AD, 4 1/2 in. by 5 1/2 in., rim chip to lid. **$250-$450**

Sawankhalok lidded cosmetics jar in the form of a persimmon with applied iron brown designs, Thailand, circa 14th century, 2 1/8 in. by 2 1/2 in., excellent condition. **$500-$650**

Sawankhalok lidded dish with blue and white and straw glaze, a small bird forming the knob, early Thai, circa 13th century, 4 1/2 in. tall, rare. **$450-$650**

Sawankhalok kendi painted iron brown with foliage panels, mammiform spout, restored flange and neck, 15th century, 6 1/2 in. high. **$200-$300**

Sawankhalok jar, two handles at rim, ribbed body, celadon glaze, 14th/15th century, 5 in. high. **$200-$300**

Sawankhalok vase, gourd-shaped, two loop handles, lotus bud neck, horizontal ribbing, glazed brown, 16th century, 7 in. high. **$75-$100**

Sawankhalok vase, pear-shaped, celadon glaze over a ribbed body, wide rim, restored, 14th/15th century, 5 1/2 in. high. **$185-$275**

Sawankhalok roof tile, a dragon with pierced mane, its scaly body picked out in brown, 19 1/2 in. high. **$700-$900**

Weapons

SWORDS AND SWORD FURNITURE

Han Dynasty bronze sword, 207 BC-220 AD, with central reinforcing ridge on the blade, and trident design where blade meets handle, the handle with raised scale-like pattern, 17 1/4 in. long. **$1,100-$1,500**

Han Dynasty bronze sword hilt, 207 BC-220 AD, heavy ornate hilt with detailed molded grip and projecting points, 3 in. by 6 in., still attached to remains of iron blade, on custom stand. **$450-$850**

Edo Period tsuba (sword hand guard) made of sentoku (a yellow metal alloy consisting of copper, zinc, and tin) in "takabori," or fine, high relief carving with "takazogan," or incrustation technique in gold and silver, measuring 2 1/2 in. by 2 3/4 in. The tsuba shows a landscape scene and a poet holding a brush. The tsuba is unsigned but has characteristics of both the Mito and Nara schools of smiths. For similar examples, see the catalog of the Peabody Collection published in 1975. This tsuba bears a collection number in India ink. **$800**

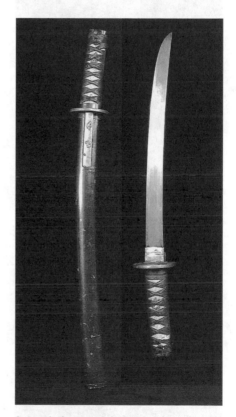

Samurai short sword, circa 19th century or before, the tsuba with twin lotus leaves, its retainer silver, the scabbard lacquered wood, signed on the blade, the brass handle with mixed metal scene of two children watching a butterfly in copper and gold, the handle wrapped with sharkskin, the ornaments within the wraps foo lions of bronze and gold, 20 1/2 in. long, one wrap strand torn, otherwise very good condition, rare. **$2,500-$2,750**

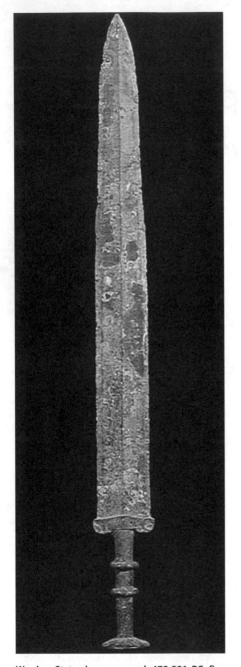

The sword guard known as the tsuba is being widely reproduced in vintage styles. The new tsubas have a slightly oily finish, and are available on many Internet sites for about $100.

Bronze tsuba (sword guard) in the form of a monkey climbing on bamboo rigging, gilt highlights, mounted on a wooden base, size with base, 3 3/8 in. by 3 7/8 in. by 1 3/8 in. **$250**

Warring States bronze sword, 475-221 BC, fine manufacture, blade slightly out of true, 19 in. long (larger example), guaranteed genuine (most on the market, especially those with inscriptions, are not). **$1,500-$2,500**

Left: Iron tsuba (sword guard) with inlaid motifs of a fisherman and pole, fish, grasses, and bird, silver and gold,19th century. **$500-$700**. Right: Shibuichi tsuba (sword guard) with inlaid motif of a boy playing a flute while riding a water buffalo, 19th century. **$1,500-$1,800**

Iron and gilt tsuba, measuring 3 in. by 2 3/4 in., done in pierced relief work with a lotus leaf design with gilt tendrils, dating to the Edo period. The tsuba is signed Echizen Ju Kinai Saku, or made by Kinai in Echizen. The Kinai school of metalsmiths confined their work to tsuba, making pierced relief sword guards of hard iron. This tsuba would appear to date from the 19th century. **$800**

Edo period tsuba (sword hand guard) made of sentoku (a yellow metal alloy consisting of copper, zinc, and tin) in "takabori," or fine, high relief carving with "takazogan," or incrustation technique in gold and silver, measuring 2 1/2 in. by 2 3/4 in. The tsuba shows a landscape scene and a poet holding a brush. The tsuba is unsigned but has characteristics of both the Mito and Nara schools of smiths. For similar examples, see the catalog of the Peabody Collection published in 1975. This tsuba bears a collection number in India ink. **$800**

Other Weaponry and Accoutrements

Bow, bamboo and lacquer, signed Masayoshi, 88 in. long. **$800-$1,200**

Matchlock gun, octagonal barrel, garlic muzzle, sahari hirazogan motif of warriors, signed Senshu ju Tsutsuzemon Shokichi saku, wood stock, brass engraved with cloud motifs, 17th century, barrel length 96 in. **$1,500-$2,000**

Matchlock pistol, iron barrel decorated with dragons in silver nunome-zogan (also called Damascene, an inlay process in which precious metal is hammered into a background field in a free pattern), signed Tamba no komi (for decoration), signed Ashu Todatatsu no Suke saku (for barrel), oak stock, ramrod, brass match holder, pan cover, and lock plate, 17th century, 15 in. long. **$2,500-$3,500**

Powder flask, lacquer on leather, copper mouth with gilt circular motif, 19th century, 6 in. high. **$250-$350**

Powder flask, keyaki wood, circular with bone stopper, 19th century, 7 1/2 in. high. **$400-$600**

Powder flask, bamboo, staghorn stopper, 19th century, 6 in. high. **$200-$300**

Powder horn, wood and staghorn, eggplant shape with wood and metal kagamibuta netsuke (special netsuke that consists of a bowl and a metal lid), mid-19th century, 6 in. long. **$600-$700**

Stirrups (abumi), iron inlaid with silver and brass motifs of Shishi, first half of the 19th century. **$700-$900**

Sword stand for daisho swords (pair of swords, one long and one short), gilt and black lacquer, scenic motif, 20 in. long. **$600-$800**

Wood-Block Prints

Wood-block prints, ukiyo-e, are also referred to as "prints of the floating world." This art form was developed in the last half of the 17th century, with artists and skilled engravers initially creating prints to satisfy the Japanese domestic market.

Design of the wood-block print began with the artist painting a picture or design on thin paper. The engraver then pasted this paper, face down, on a cherry wood block, and transferred the outline onto the wood with the use of gouges and other tools. Both sides of the block were used, and a block was needed for each color.

The result of the engraver's work was a negative in high relief. The painter, following the artist's instructions, painted the colors on each block with brushes. Finally, dampened papers were aligned and laid, in turn, on each block, then hand-rubbed with a pad, producing the color prints. The blocks were recharged after each impression.

Among the various subjects that are of interest to dealers and collectors in today's market are sumo-e (wrestler prints), bonsai (botanical prints), bijinga (prints of beautiful women), shunga (erotic prints), shibai-e (prints depicting actors), nagasaki and yokohama (prints depicting foreigners), uchiwa-e (fan prints), and landscapes.

Size-related terms used to describe wood-block prints include chuban (usually 7 1/2 in. by 10 in.), hashira-e (usually 4 3/4 in. by 28 3/4 in.), hosoban (usually 5 5/8 in. by 13 in.), and oban (usually 10 in. by 15 in.). Oban tate-e is a print that is large in width, while aiban yoko-e is a print that is large in length.

THE ARTISTS

Following are brief descriptions of some artists.

Eisen	(1790-1848): Painter, print maker, and illustrator.
Goyo Hashiguichi	(1880-1921): Print maker.
Harunobu	(1724-1770): Important, influential painter and print maker.
Kawasee Hasul	(1883-1957): Painter and print maker.
Hiroshige	(1797-1858): Painter and print maker. His first published work was in the field of illustrated books. He is among the most important Edo period artists.
Hiroshige II	(1826-1869): Print maker and adopted son of Hiroshige. He also used the name Shigenobu (was known as Hiroshige II from 1858 until 1865).
Hiroshige III after Hiroshige II	(1843-1894): Print maker. Pupil of Hiroshige, who adopted the name Hiroshige III retired, circa 1865.
Hokkei	(1780-1850): Print maker and painter; a student of Hokusai.
Hokusai	(1760-1849): Major painter and print maker who worked in many styles.
Paul Jacoulet	(1902-1960): French artist who lived and worked in Japan.
Kobayakawa Kiyoshi	(1897-1948): Painter and print maker; pupil of Kiyokata.
Kotondo	(1900-?): Theatrical designer and print maker.
Kunichika	(1835-1900): Print maker and pupil of Kunisada.
Kunisada	(1786-1864): Painter and print maker. For the most part, his prints are signed Kunisada until 1844, when he took the name Toyokuni III.
Kunisada II	(1823-1880): Son-in-law of Kunisada I.
Kuniyoshi	(1797-1861): Painter and print maker; pupil of Toyokuni. His works are often sealed with the marks on the right.
Shinsui	(1896-1972): Painter and print artist; pupil of Kiyokata. Ito Shinsui was a specialist in highly stylized paintings of women. His prints do not date earlier than 1916.
Shunsho	(1726-1792): Painter and print maker. Among his pupils were Shucho and Hokusai.
Toyokuni I	(1769-1825): Painter and print maker; student of Toyoharu.
Toyokuni II	(1777-1835): Student and son-in-law of Toyokuni I. Signed his works Toyokuni II after his father-in-law died; then went back to his earlier name, Toyoshige.
Utamaro I	(1754-1806): Major painter and print maker.
Yoshida, Hiroshi	(1876-1950): Western-style painter and print maker who signed his name in English.
Yoshitoshi Talso	(1839-1892): Illustrator and print maker; student of Kuniyoshi.

Japanese woodblock print by Konan Tanagami (1879-1928) of petunias, from his Western Flower Book, Summer Vol. I, published by Yamada Joichi, this series printed in January 1979. The print is in horizontal oban format with a centerfold from the book. Excellent condition. **$95**

Japanese woodblock print by Ito Nisaburo, an early 20th century artist, in vertical oban format of the Kunashiki area of Kyoto (?), published by Uchida. Ito is listed as an artist who studied at the Kyoto City Specialist School of Painting and produced prints of flowers and scenes of Kyoto for Uchida starting in 1910. Excellent condition. **$150**

Japanese woodblock print by Konan Tanagami (1879-1928) of verbena and coleus, from his Western Flower Book, Summer Vol. I, published by Yamada Joichi, this series printed in January 1979. The print is in horizontal oban format with a center fold from the book. Excellent condition. **$95**

Japanese woodblock print by the ukiyo-e artist Hokusai, circa 1830. This print is from one of his ehon (woodblock printed book) of manga, or cartoons. Each of the attached panels of the diptych measures approximately 5 in. by 9 in. The overall print size is approximately 9 in. by 10 in. The impression is excellent condition with a small hole in upper right margin corner and some paper reinforcements of old attachments on the reverse. **$85**

Utamaro, oban tate-e, an okubi-e portrait of a beauty holding a sake cup, signed Utamaro hitsu, publisher's seal unidentified, good impression, color slightly faded, spurious mica ground, slightly soiled. Realized price (including the 10-percent buyer's premium), Christie's, New York City. **$4,950**

Japanese woodblock print of flowers and birds, in chuban size (about 7 1/2 in. by 10 in.), from a kacho-ga series (prints showing birds and/or flowers) by various artists dating to the early 20th century. This print is signed Matsutani Shoun, aka Yamamoto Shoun (1870-1965), an illustrator who worked in this genre. The print has vibrant colors and excellent registration. The paper is quite thin with some mild overall browning. There are minor folds on the back that are not visible from the front. There is some old tape residue on the left margin from previous mounting that has thinned the paper. **$45**

Folio of ikebana flower arrangements titled "Modern Japanese Art of Flower Arrangements," published by Hanano-Shiori-Sha from Kohata, the suburbs of Kyoto, in 1950. This is Volume V of a series in English from the same publisher. The arrangements were painted by Etsujin Kawahara and were printed by Seizaburo Nishikawa. The book contains 23 full-color prints (not woodblock) on heavy paper measuring 10 in. by 14 in. with a description of the arrangement by noted experts of the day accompanying each print. There are also 13 introductory pages of text; all the pages are loose. Both front and back boards are present as are the purple ribbon ties. A few of the prints have very minimal light spots of foxing. The text pages have browned, and there is some foxing and browning on the reverse of the prints. Each print has binding holes on the left margin. Overall very good condition. **$300**

Japanese woodblock print of flowers and birds, in chuban size (about 7 1/2 in. by 10 in.) from a kacho-ga series (prints showing birds and/or flowers) by various artists dating to the early 20th century. This print is signed Imao Keinen (1845-1924), a renowned artist who also worked in this genre. The print has vibrant colors and excellent registration. The paper is quite thin with some mild overall browning. There are minor folds on the back that are not visible from the front. **$45**

Japanese woodblock print of flowers and birds, in chuban size (about 7 1/2 in. by 10 in.), from a kacho-ga series (prints showing birds and/or flowers) by various artists dating to the early 20th century. This print is signed Kinsei-ro or Chika (?). The print has vibrant colors and excellent registration. The paper is quite thin with some mild overall browning. There are minor folds on the back that are not visible from the front. There is some old tape residue on the sides from previous mounting. This does not show through to the front. **$45**

Japanese woodblock print of flowers and birds, in chuban size (about 7 1/2 in. by 10 in.), from a kacho-ga series (prints showing birds and/or flowers) by various artists dating to the early 20th century. This print is signed Bairei (1844-95) a renowned painter who also worked in this genre. This is probably a posthumous print, given the date of Bairei's death. The print has vibrant colors and excellent registration. The paper is quite thin with some mild overall browning. There are minor folds on the back that are not visible from the front. There is some old tape residue on the sides from previous mounting. This does not show through to the front. **$45**

Japanese woodblock print by Hiroshige III (circa 1843-1894) from the book series "Dai Nippon Bussan Zue" or "The Production of Greater Japan," illustrated. As the title says, each print of this series illustrates a scene showing the activities of Japan. The image size is 8 7/8 in. by 6 3/8 in., and the paper size is 9 1/4 in. by 7 in. The color is excellent and uses the aniline dyes typical of Meji-era Japanese prints. The impression is very good. The print has a center folding line and tape stains in the upper and lower margins. **$45**

Hiroshige, oban tate-e, "Sudden Shower at Atake" from the series "One Hundred Views of Famous Places in Edo," signed Hiroshige ga, good impression, color faded. **$2,000-$3,000**

Postwar Japanese woodblock print of Kagoshima in Kyushu Island, in horizontal oban format measuring 16 1/2 in. by 11 in., by the artist Tomikichiro Tokuriki. The print is published by Uchida of Kyoto as part of a series titled "Eight Views of Japan." It is hinged at the top to washi paper (produced from the bark fibers of three shrubs) and is surrounded by a thin paper mat in its original slipcase. The print has been stored in its original hard paper case and is in mint original condition. **$75**

Page from Hiroshige's manga, or notebooks, of bridge structures and boats, dating to the early 1800s. The page is done in black, blue, and red typical of this type of work. It measures approximately 8 in. by 5 in. The paper is quite thin with minimal soiling. The colors are vibrant and the registration is clear. **$75**

Japanese, Edo period, woodblock print by the great master Katsushika Hokusai, from his manga series (or "Scenes from Life"), of a variety of boats, done in black, gray, and red on two pages measuring 10 in. by 7 in., dating to the 1830s. The paper is quite thin. There are symmetrical, small wormholes on the upper inner margins of each print and small, brown circles or foxing in the margins from previous binding. The colors are vibrant and the registration is clear. The print has never been backed. **$100**

Japanese woodblock print titled "The Farmer's House of Shirabawa," done in Sosaku hanga style in predominantly brown and green colors, circa 1969. It is signed and sealed in the block by the publisher, Mikumo Ishihara, and the artist, Inagaki Minakawa. It is also pencil-signed in English and is numbered 273 of 300. The print is in vertical double oban format, measuring 19 1/2 in. by 16 1/2 in. Mint condition. **$75**

Japanese, Edo period, woodblock print by the great master Katsushika Hokusai, from his manga series (or "Scenes from Life"), of a tiger and samurai, done in black, gray, and red on two pages measuring 10 in. by 7 in., professionally mounted and matted on archival paper, dating to the 1830s. **$110**

Japanese, Edo period, woodblock print by the great master Katsushika Hokusai, from his manga (or "scenes from Life") series Vol. ? of a Lohan (an individual who has attained enlightenment by own effort) and men, done in black, gray, and red on one page measuring 5 in. by 7 in., dating to 1816. There are a few, small wormholes in the print. It is neither backed nor mounted. **$50**

Hiroshige, oban tate-e, "Komagata Temple, Azuma Bridge (Komagata-do, Azumabasahi)," from the series "One Hundred Famous Views of Edo"; signed Hiroshige ga and published by Uoya Eikichi, very good impression, color, and condition. Realized price (including the 10-percent buyer's premium), Christie's, New York City. **$638**

Japanese, Edo period, woodblock print by the great master Katsushika Hokusai, from his manga series (or "Scenes from Life"), of poets and scholars, done in black, gray, and red on two pages measuring 10 in. by 7 in., dating to the 1830s. The prints are neither mounted nor backed. **$100**

Sosaku hanga is a 20th century Japanese printmaking movement that was influenced by Western methods of printmaking. Sosaku hanga stressed the involvement of the artist in all aspects of printmaking.

Chromolithograph of geisha carrying umbrellas, published by the French Bibliotheque Didot for the Parisian market, which craved any and all things Japanese, in the late 1800s. The overall dimensions are 11 in. by 15 in. Chromolithography, which used a combination of finely etched and colored stone printing blocks, was very popular in this time. The left edge is slightly irregular, showing that this print was cut from a folio. **$75**

Chromolithograph of Japanese men in various forms of dress, published by the French Bibliotheque Didot for the Parisian market in the late 1800s. The printed area measures approximately 8 1/2 in. by 12 in. The overall dimensions are 11 in. by 15 in. Chromolithography, which used a combination of finely etched and colored stone printing blocks, was very popular in this time. The left edge is slightly irregular, showing that this print was cut from a folio. **$75**

Japanese chromolithograph of geisha and men in a variety of activities and dress, including depictions of transportation of a lady and a child, published by the French Bibliotheque Didot for the Parisian market in the late 1800s. The printed area measures approximately 8 1/2 in. by 12 in. The overall dimensions are 11 in. by 15 in. The left edge is slightly irregular, showing that this print was cut from a folio. **$75**

Postwar Japanese woodblock print of an evening street scene by the publisher Uchida of Kyoto. The print measures 10 1/2 in. by 11 1/2 in. Mint original condition. **$100**

Chromolithograph of geisha and samurai in a variety of activities and dress, including depictions of transportation, published by the French Bibliotheque Didot for the Parisian market in the late 1800s. The printed area measures approximately 8 1/2 in. by 12 in. The overall dimensions are 11 in. by 15 in. Chromolithograpy, which used a combination of finely etched and colored stone printing blocks, was very popular in this time period. This piece shows the exquisite and fine detail that could be attained with this process. The left edge is slightly irregular, showing that this print was cut from a folio. A superb addition to the collection of those who seek Japanese art or for the collector of Orientalia. **$75**

Hokusai, oban yoko-e, "Fuji from Kanaya on the Tokaido" (Tokaido Kanaya no Fuji), from the series "Thirty-Six Views of Mt. Fuji," signed Zen Hokusai Iitsu hitsu and published by Eijudo, good impression (black outline), slight center-fold and slightly faded. Realized price (including the 10-percent buyer's premium), Christie's, New York City. **$3,520**

Japanese woodblock print in deluxe chuban format by the artist, Kunikazu, measuring 7 in. by 10 in., dating to the 1860s. The print shows an actor in a luxurious blue and green kimono with kanji character in green from a kabuki play. The print is highlighted with extra pigment typical of this series of prints by the Osaka artist, Kunikazu. Although it is unsigned, it meets all the criteria of a Kunikazu deluxe print. Fine original condition. **$125**

Postwar Japanese woodblock print of the Great Buddha Daibutsu of Kamakura in Kanagawa prefecture, in horizontal oban format, by the artist Tomikichiro Tokuriki. Published by Uchida of Kyoto as part of a series of scenes of Japan. It is enclosed in a mica-enhanced, washi paper mat. Mint original condition. **$100**

Jacoulet, dai oban tate-e, "Femme de Falalap et Coquillages" from the "Série Mollusque," signed Paul Jacoulet (in pencil), Mandarin Duck seal, numbered 92/150, good impression, color, and condition. Realized price (including the 10-percent buyer's premium), Christie's, New York City. **$2,200**

Japanese woodblock print by Jokata Kaiseki, circa 1929, from a series of 12 prints of Mt. Fuji. This print shows a village with people preparing for a festival. This series of prints was produced from blocks carved by Kawatsura Yoshio. The print is in horizontal oban format, measuring 14 in. by 10 in. Minor wrinkles on the upper edges. **$125**

Japanese woodblock print of flowers and birds, in chuban size, from a kacho-ga series by various artists dating to the early 20th century. This print is signed Kinsei-ro or Chika(?).It has vibrant colors and excellent registration. The paper is quite thin with some mild overall browning. There are minor folds on the back that are not visible from the front. There is some old tape residue on the sides from previous mounting. This does not show through to the front. **$45**

Japanese woodblock print in dyptych format, measuring 14 in. by 10 in., dating to the late 19th or early 20th century. The print shows two actors in kimonos from a kabuki play. The prints bear the signature of Yoshitaki, one of the most prolific artists of the Osaka school in the 1880-'90s. Fine original condition. **$250**

Japanese engraving of a temple, circa 1890, measuring 12 1/2 in. by 17 in. overall. The printed image measures 9 1/4 in. by 6 1/4 in. Fine original condition. **$50**

Japanese woodblock tryptych of a scene from the SinoJapanese War, bearing the signature in the block of the artist, Yoshitoshi, dating to the late 19th century. (Yoshitoshi died in 1892, and the First SinoJapanese War for control of Korea was fought in 1894-95. This is not an original print by Yoshitoshi. The date of the print appears to be Meiji 27, or 1895, so it fits with the timeframe for the war. This may have been one of Yoshitoshi's pupils, or the printer may simply have continued to use his seal in the blocks.) The print shows Chinese and Japanese soldiers in hand-to-hand combat. Each print is in vertical oban format. They are joined at the edges to form the tryptych. The registration and colors of the print are excellent. There is foxing of the upper and left borders. **$200**

Japanese woodblock print of parrots and pomegranates, by Imao Keinen (1845-1924), dating to the Meiji Era. Keinen, born in Kyoto, studied both painting and ukiyo-e, and opened his studio in 1868 at the beginning of the Meiji restoration. He was a frequent exhibitor and prizewinner in both Japan and Paris and was commissioned in 1904 to do paintings for the Imperial household. He specialized in kachoga, a style known for its elaborate rendition of subjects in realistic detail. His prints were primarily of birds and flowers, both of which he uses here. This print originally came from a folio, as evidenced by the number at the top and the holes from the bookmaker's needle on the right margin. Excellent original condition except for the holes. **$80**

Japanese, Edo period, woodblock print by the great master Katsushika Hokusai, from his manga series (or "Scenes from Life"), of a man and animals, including a fox, done in black, gray, and red on two pages measuring 10 in. by 7 in., dating to the 1830s. The prints are neither mounted nor backed. There are some wormholes, but most are in the inner margins. **$100**

Japanese woodblock print of hand-to-hand combat on the ramparts over Port Arthur, titled "The Fall of Port Arthur," dating to the late 1890s. This print shows the Japanese attack on the Russian Port Arthur marking the beginning of Japanese aggression in Asia that ended in their defeat in 1945. It was created by Gekko, a woodblock print artist of the period known also for his family scenes. Prints such as these were published as propaganda to align the people with the controlling government powers and the military aspirations of Tojo. Fine original condition in three sections with no backing. **$250**

Japanese woodblock print of an image by Hiroshige I (1797-1858) from the Tokaido Gojusan-Tsugi No Uchi, or 53 Stations of the Tokaido, first printed in 1833-34 by Hoeido and Senkakudo, in a horizontal oban format. This print is of Station #10, a view of Odawara with a daimyo (member of a Japanese ruling family) being carried across the Sakawa River. There are four versions of this print known, and this appears to be the last, with four figures on the near bank—two coolies and two travelers—green fields, a yellow/orange mist over the village, a small, round-top blue mountain on the right, a red mountain in the distance, a crimson fading to purple sky, and a red Hoeido seal below the signature. The print is done on thin paper that has some wrinkles and mild staining. There are initials in pencil in the bottom left margin, probably from a previous owner. The registration is good except for the line in the blue foreground on the left, and the colors are the typical subdued shades found in earlier Hiroshiges. This is not an original Hiroshige, but probably an early printing done during the Meiji Era. **$250**

Japanese woodblock print from the Osaka school of an actor, in chuban format, measuring 7 1/2 in. by 10 in., dating to the Meiji Era (1868-1912). The print shows an actor in kimono that has an elaborate lobster design on the back. The bowtie obi is very unusual. The kimono is accented with gold lacquer and mica, a technique used only in the finest prints. Mint original condition. It is signed in the block by the artist. **$125**

Early woodblock print by Kunisada of three actors in kimonos, dating to the mid-19th century. The print is done in the early style of black, blue, and red colors that date it to the mid-1800s. It is framed with a patterned wood mat that appears to be from some time in the 1950s. Appears to be in excellent condition. **$200**

Japanese sumi, or ink, painting of a bridge, enhanced with gold lacquer and mica, dating to the Showa-Taisho Eras. The painting appears to have been done on a fabric background, probably raw silk. It is signed with the artist's seal. The painting measures 10 in. by 11 in.; with the mat, the dimensions are 16 in. by 19 in. It is in excellent condition with no evidence of damage. Double mount of cloth and paper. **$120**

Japanese woodblock print by Konan Tanagami (1879-1928) of asters, from his Western Flower Book, Summer Vol. I, published by Yamada Joichi, this series printed in January 1979. The print is in horizontal oban format with a centerfold from the book. It is in excellent condition. **$100**

Engraving of a Japanese merchant's shop, circa 1900, measuring 12 1/2 in. by 17 in. overall. The printed image measures 9 1/4 in. by 6 1/4 in. Fine original condition. **$50**

Japanese woodblock print titled "The Full Moon Viewed on the Seta Karahashi Bridge" from the series "The Scenes of Shiga, Nara and Kyoto" by Eichii Kotozuka, dating from the early to mid-20th century. The print measures 8 1/4 in. by 11 in. It is fixed to the back by one small hinge at the center top. The margins are intact, the impression and colors excellent. The print is matted using crepe, off-white and silver Japanese paper. The mat measures 10 in. by 13 1/2 in. Eichii Kotozuka was born in Osaka in 1906. He was a member of the Nihon Hanga Kiyokai. He did several series of scenes of Kyoto that were published by Uchida, as was this print. **$80**

Shinsui, large oban tate-e; a beauty at the mirror, signed Shinsui ga, Ito seal, published by Watanabe, dated Showa 2 (1927), numbered 12/300, good impression, color, and condition. Realized price (including the 10-percent buyer's premium), Christie's, New York City. **$1,100**

Japanese woodblock print from the master, Ando Hiroshige, titled, "Seki Zokyakuya Oiwake" from the series "Gojusan-Tsugi Meisho-Zue (The Fifty-Three Famous Views)" published by Tsuta-Ya in 1855. The print is in good condition with some mild staining. It has been framed professionally with acid-free technique. **$500**

Japanese woodblock print by Torii Tadamasa (1904-1970). Born Ueno Katsumi, Tadamasa was given the honor of using the Torii name in 1949. He published several series of prints of Kabuki actors for Watanabe through the 1940s and 1950s. This print shows the Kabuki dancer/actor at the culmination of the play, "Dojoji," when he poses atop the great temple bell. The play tells the story of the Buddhist monk, Anchin, and a beautiful young women, Kiyohime. Kiyohime fell in love with Anchin, but he rejected her advances because he had taken a vow of celibacy. When she pursued him, he ran to the Dojoji Temple where he hid under the giant bell. Kiyohime, turning into a serpent/demon, coils around the bell, spitting fire that consumes both Anchin and the bell. In the Kabuki play, the priests purchase a new bell. A temple dancer, Hanako, appears at the temple gates, and pleads for admittance to honor the new bell. The priests let Hanako in to dance around the bell. She does nine dances, each one stranger (each one with a costume change!), and finishes by posing on top of the bell. Only then do the priests realize that she is the demon, Kiyohime, who has returned to injure the bell. In this print version, Kiyohime is posing in triumph on the bell. In others, she is crushed by the bell. Mint condition with excellent colors, registration, and no damage. **$150**

Hokusai manga, or sketchbook, woodblock print, probably from Book VIII, circa 1817. It is a drawing of a priest and a peasant in a landscape setting and covers two pages of the sketchbook, which have been joined together professionally before framing. The print is in its original pink, black, and gray colors. It measures 10 in. by 8 in. unframed and 14 1/2 in. by 12 1/2 in. framed. The framing is done with acid-free, archival papers and mats. **$175**

Chromolithograph with seven separate views of geisha in a variety of activities and dress, including depictions of the young ladies in various stages of preparation for their nightly activities and entertaining their guests both with music and in the bedroom; published late 1800s by the French Bibliotheque Didot for the Parisian market. The printed area measures approximately 8 1/2 in. by 12 in. The overall dimensions are 11 in. by 15 in. The lithographer's name—Urabietta—is shown on the lithograph. Chromolithography, which used a combination of finely etched and colored stone printing blocks, was very popular in this time period. The left edge is slightly irregular, showing that this print was cut from a folio. **$85**

Japanese woodblock print by Hiroshige I (1797-1858) from the Tokaido Gojusan-Tsugi No Uchi, or 53 Stations of the Tokaido, in a horizontal oban format. This print is of Station #31, Maisaka Imagirishuku, or a view of Imaki Point with a white Mt. Fuji in the background in a yellow sky. Hiroshige was commissioned by the Tokugawa Shogun to go to Kyoto from Edo to paint the ceremony of the presenting of the horses, a gift sent by the shogun to the Emperor. Hiroshige was impressed with the scenery along the way and created his first Tokaido series, published by Hoeido and Senkakudo in 1833-'34. This is not from the original Hiroshige series, but probably printed during his lifetime. The horizontal Tokaido was reprinted many times in both individual print and album format during Hiroshige's lifetime. His publishers prevailed upon him to use richer colors in later editions to make them more appealing to the public and to increase sales. This print is from one of these series. It is done on heavier paper, measuring 16 3/4 in. by 11 in., with excellent colors and registration and no noticeable damage. **$250**

Munakata, dai oban tate-e, a sumizurie with hand-applied color titled "Yamazakura no tana," from the series "Shokeisho," signed Shiko Munakata and sealed, dated 3 December 1951, good impression, paper slightly toned, framed and glazed. Realized price (including the 10-percent buyer's premium), Christie's, New York City. **$7,150**

Japanese woodblock print in triptych format by the 19th century master Utagawa Toyokuni III or Kunisada. The print shows a procession of courtesans viewing cherry blossoms in the spring. It has Kunisada's signature in the block in the left lower corner as well as censor's and publisher's seals that date the print to circa 1859-'71. The three prints are in vertical oban format measuring approximately 14 in. by 10 in. The print colors and registration are excellent. There is some wrinkling of the print in the left corner. **$600**

Date and Censor Seals

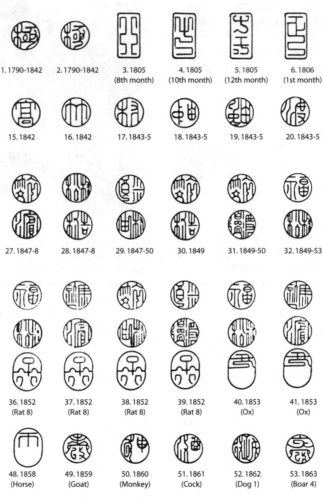

1. 1790-1842 2. 1790-1842 3. 1805 (8th month) 4. 1805 (10th month) 5. 1805 (12th month) 6. 1806 (1st month)

15. 1842 16. 1842 17. 1843-5 18. 1843-5 19. 1843-5 20. 1843-5

27. 1847-8 28. 1847-8 29. 1847-50 30. 1849 31. 1849-50 32. 1849-53

36. 1852 (Rat 8) 37. 1852 (Rat 8) 38. 1852 (Rat 8) 39. 1852 (Rat 8) 40. 1853 (Ox) 41. 1853 (Ox)

48. 1858 (Horse) 49. 1859 (Goat) 50. 1860 (Monkey) 51. 1861 (Cock) 52. 1862 (Dog 1) 53. 1863 (Boar 4)

60. 1870 (Horse) 61. 1871 (Goat) 62. 1872 (Monkey) 63. 1873 (Cock) 64. 1874 (Dog) 65. 1875 (Boar)

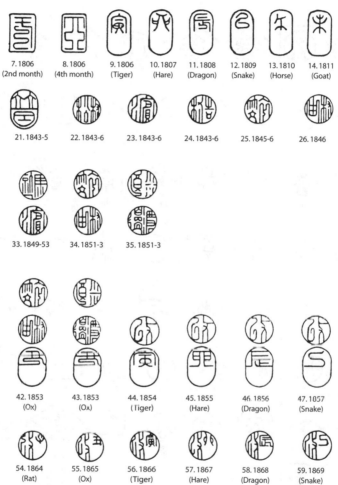

7. 1806 (2nd month)

8. 1806 (4th month)

9. 1806 (Tiger)

10. 1807 (Hare)

11. 1808 (Dragon)

12. 1809 (Snake)

13. 1810 (Horse)

14. 1811 (Goat)

21. 1843-5

22. 1843-6

23. 1843-6

24. 1843-6

25. 1845-6

26. 1846

33. 1849-53

34. 1851-3

35. 1851-3

42. 1853 (Ox)

43. 1853 (Ox)

44. 1854 (Tiger)

45. 1855 (Hare)

46. 1856 (Dragon)

47. 1857 (Snake)

54. 1864 (Rat)

55. 1865 (Ox)

56. 1866 (Tiger)

57. 1867 (Hare)

58. 1868 (Dragon)

59. 1869 (Snake)

66. 1868-1912 Meiji

67. 1912-26 Taisho

68. 1926 onwards Showa

Publishers' Marks

1. Katoya
2. Ezakiya Kichibei
3. Mikawaya Kihei
4. Maruya Kusaemon
5. Mikawaya Rihei
6. Sugiya Kihei
7. Tsuruya Kiemon
8. Tsuruya Kiemon
9. Tsuruya Kiemon
10. Tsuruya Kinsuke
11. Tsutaya Kichizo
12. Tsutaya Juzaburo
13. Maruya Kiyojiro
14. Yamadaya Shojiro
15. Fujiokaya Hikotaro
16. Echigoya Keisuke
17. Iseya Sanjiro
18. Nishimuraya Yohachi
19. Iwatoya Kisaburo
20. Takatsuya Isuke
21. Ningyoya Takichi
22. Kagaya Yasubei
23. Enshuya Hikobei
24. Soshuya Yohei
25. Enshuya Matabei
26. Kagaya Yoshibei
27. Murataya Jirobei
28. Kawachiya Chozo
29. Eirakuya Bunsuke
30. Izumiya Ichibei
31. Kikuya Kozaburo
32. Emiya Kichiemon
33. Izuymiya Ichibei
34. Iwatoya Genpachi
35. Ebiya Rinnosuke
36. Kikuya Ichibei
37. Soneya Ginjiro
38. Kazusaya
39. Ezakiya Tatsuzo
40. Nishimuraya Yohachi
41. Urokogataya
42. Tsujiokaya Bunsuke
43. Nishimuraya Yohachi
44. Moriya Jihei
45. Iseya Magobei
46. Sanoya Kihei
47. Yamamotoya Heikichi
48. Shimizuya
49. Maruya Jinpachi
50. Takeuchi Magohachi
51. Etsuke
52. Itoya Yohei
53. Iseya Tetsukiro
54. Iseya Chubei
55. Ibaya Sensaburo
56. Gusokuya Kahei
57. Daikokuya
58. Wakabayashiya Kiyobei
59. Okuroya Kinnosuke
60. Hiranoya Heisuke
61. Ogawa Heisuke
62. Sumiyoshiya Masagoro
63. Wakasaya Yoichi
64. Moritaya Hanzo
65. Joshuya Shigezo
66. Yamaguchiya Tobei
67. Kawaguchiya Uhei
68. Kagiya Hanjiro
69. Aito
70. Enshuya Yasubei
71. Owariya Kiyoshichi
72. Tamaya Sosuke
73. Mokuya Sojiro
74. Tsujiya Yasubei
75. Uwoya Eikichi
76. Sagamiya
77. Hirookaya Kosuke
78. Tenki
79. Minatoya Kohei
80. Morimoto Junzaburo

Wood Carvings, Bamboo, and Basketry

Basket, ikebana, woven bamboo, Japanese, measuring 11 in. across and 9 in. high, dating to the first half of the 20th century. The basket is made in a moon design for hanging on the wall or to set on a table. Fine original condition. **$200**

Basket, ikebana, handled, measuring approximately 7 1/4 in. square and 9 in. high, Japanese, dating to the mid-1900s. The basket shows fine quality workmanship with accents on the handle and an excellent patina. Fine original condition. **$125**

Basket, ikebana, three-handled, measuring 12 in. across by 9 1/2 in. high, Japanese, dating to the mid-1900s. The basket has three handles that join above the square base. The basket shows excellent workmanship, color, and patina. Fine original condition. **$150**

Basket made for ikebana and display of flowers during the tea ceremony, Japanese, dating to the Meiji period (1868-1912). Woven in an upright fashion of rich, red-brown bamboo that has been exposed to the elements, known in Japan as susutake—bamboo taken from an old, thatched roof where it was exposed to smoke. It is woven in two layers with the first done in a twill-plaited style and the second in a six-mesh, or hexagonal plait (mutsume-ami). The front of the basket is decorated with inserts representing bamboo leaves. The basket has a woven handle and stands on four feet, 15 in. high, 8 1/2 in. across the top. **$325**

Basket made for display of fruit during the tea ceremony, Japanese, dating to the Meiji period (1868-1912). This basket is woven in old, susutake bamboo in a six-mesh, or hexagonal plait (mutsume-ami). Flat baskets such as this are known as morikago and were used to display fruit during the sncha, or green leaf tea, ceremony. It stands on three peg feet and measures 14 in. across by 4 1/2 in. high. **$250**

Basket, bamboo, double-gourd form, woven with intricate designs, used for flower arranging (it lies on its side), Japanese, circa 1900, 9 1/2 in. long. **$600-$800**

Basket, splint bamboo with entwined bail handle, Japanese, early 20th century, 12 1/2 in. high. **$50-$100**

Basket, splint bamboo, pitcher shape with bail handle, Japanese, early 20th century, 6 1/2 in. high. **$100-$150**

Basket, root and wicker, double-gourd form, Japanese, late Meiji period, 12 in. long. **$175-$250**

Left: Bamboo cylindrical container, Chinese, circa 1920, 10 in. high. **$100-$150**. Right: Woven three-tiered basket with incised bamboo handle, brass mounts, Chinese, early 20th century, 9 1/2 in. by 13 1/2 in. **$275-$375**

Fish basket, bamboo and wicker, Japanese, Meiji period, 15 1/2 in. high. **$150-$225**

Brush pot, Chinese, cylindrical bamboo section with joint at bottom forming the base, the dark stained exterior carved with classic scene of mountain pavilions and streams, also three rows of engraved Chinese characters, circa late 19th or early 20th century, 2 1/2 in. by 5 in., age cracks and half-inch hole in bottom. **$150-$350**

Dish, wood, with hard-stone motif of a seated Pu Tai, Chinese, circa 1900, 8 1/2 in. diameter. **$200-$325**

Picnic baskets, woven bamboo, each finely pierced with a bracket foot and trimmed in gilt, the three sections having diapers and woven decorations, pierced handle, Chinese, early 20th century, 8 in. high, pair. **$275-$400**

Box, three-tiered, rectangular handle on rectangular base, Chinese, late 19th century, 6 in. by 8 in. **$400-$600**

Box, carved wood, joined at one corner, the sides and top inset with carved panels of flowers, the base on short bracket feet, Chinese, circa 1900, 14 in. long. **$500-$650**

Brush pot, cylindrical, the patina a honey-brown, the base with a Ch'ien Lung mark (and of the period), Chinese, 18th century, 6 1/4 in. high. **$1,000-$1,500**

Brush pot, bamboo, cylindrical, a scene of pine trees and figures, Chinese, early 19th century, 6 1/2 in. high. **$900-$1,200**

Brush pot, bamboo, carved with a scholar on a terrace in a landscape, Chinese, 19th century, 6 in. high. **$250-$375**

Brush rest, bamboo, carved with a mountainscape, Chinese, late 19th century, 5 in. long. **$150-$225**

Brush holder, scholar's, bamboo, measuring 7 5/8 in. high and 5 1/8 in. in diameter, Chinese, dating to the 19th century. It is carved on a big bamboo joint. The carving depicts a wise man or scholar and a woman on the front. The man holds a branch of wood in hand, and the lady is sitting on the floor with her breast uncovered. An old lady is calling them from behind. There are old pine trees and bamboo in their private garden. The carving is intricate and detailed. **$300**

Cosmetic box, mirrored, hinged door, three drawers, Japanese, Meiji period, 12 in. by 8 1/2 in. by 9 1/2 in. **$225-$375**

Cricket cage made of gourd, sandalwood, and ivory in a floral design, measuring 1 in. by 4 in., Chinese, dating to the early 19th century. Fine original condition. **$300**

Cricket cage carved from a gourd and fitted with a fenestrated wooden top, measuring 3 in. by 3 1/2 in. It is decorated with floral designs and has air holes for the cricket. Chinese. $60

Hibachi, black lacquer-over-pottery, measuring 10 in. high and 7 in. across the opening, Japanese, dating to the mid-20th century. The hibachi is covered in overall black lacquer and has a landscape design done in gold, red, and white lacquer. There are some small dings as well as general wear and scratches in the black lacquer, plus one repaired 1/2 in. defect on the reverse. **$100**

Miniature house (the interior added by the author's husband) with movable doors, floors, and so on, the roof on both sides lifting off as well, movable trees and shrubs, Japanese, late Meiji/early Taisho period, 17 in. wide, 11 in. high. **$700-$950**

Hibachi, keyaki wood, five drawers, copper-lined burner, Japanese, early 20th century, 12 in. by 26 in. by 16 in. **$500-$700**

Hibachi, kiri wood, the body decorated with bamboo and birds in gold lacquer, copper liner, Japanese, late 19th century, 8 1/2 in. high. **$200-$300**

Hibachi, kiri wood, gold lacquer and mother-of-pearl flowers, Japanese, Taisho period, 9 in. high, 14 in. wide. **$300-$425**

Hibachi, root wood with copper liner, Japanese, Meiji period, 34 in. diameter. **$900-$1,200**

Hibachi, wood with gold and red lacquer flowers, copper liner, Japanese, late Meiji period, 12 3/4 in. diameter. **$200-$300**

Jewel case, keyaki and kiri wood, three drawers, Japanese, circa 1910, 10 in. high, 8 in. wide. **$225-$325**

Needle case, bamboo with ivory caps, carved in relief of a procession of nobles, measuring 4 1/2 in. by 3/4 in., Chinese, dating to the late 19th century. The brown silk ball at the end is missing several strands of silk. **$400**

No mask, an old man, chipped, signed Tetsuya, Japanese, late 19th century. **$200-$400**

Panel, carved and pierced wood with motif of birds and flowering prunus, repainted red and gold, Chinese, circa 1900, 12 in. by 15 in. **$50-$85**

Panel, carved wood with Mandarins in a scenic motif, much open work, repainted red and gold, Chinese, early 20th century, 8 1/4 in. by 24 1/2 in. **$75-$125**

Panel depicting a female figure standing on a lotus throne supported by two lions and flanked by female attendants amid openwork, she holds a bow and arrow and is wearing elaborate jewelry (and a quiver on her back), South Indian, 20th century, 76 in. **$1,800-$2,600**

Panel carved and pierced with birds and leafy branches, gilt intact, mounted in a black frame, Japanese, late 19th century, 35 in. by 72 in. **$1,650-$2,400**

Panel carved with flower heads surrounded by scrolling foliage, traces of red paint, Indian, late 19th/early 20th century, 56 in. high. **$500-$650**

Panels (probably removed from a pavilion) carved with peony and leaves, traces of red and gilt, Chinese, late 19th/early 20th century, 11 in. square, **pair. $100-$125**

Root carving of a dragon, Chinese, late 19th century, 9 in. high. **$600-$900**

Root carving of an Immortal seated upon a tree stump, Chinese, 19th century, 10 1/2 in. high. **$300-$500**

Shop sign in the form of a badger holding a sake bottle, Japanese, early Showa period, 18 1/2 in. high. **$600-$800**

Shop sign (doll maker's), two dolls seated under a tree, Japanese, early 20th century, 9 1/2 in. long. **$125-$225**

Shop sign (fan maker's), fan form with calligraphy, Japanese, late 19th century, 24 in. long. **$300-$500**

Panel, carved wood (probably taken from a door–now framed for hanging), Chinese, circa 1900, frame size 23 1/2 in. long. **$600-$800**

Shop sign (pawnbroker's) in the shape of a bat, red and gilt lacquer on wood, iron suspension hook, Chinese, 19th century, 78 in. high. **$1,000-$1,500**

Shrine, miniature, kiri wood, Torii gate, Japanese, early Showa period. $300-$400

Shrine, miniature, kiri wood, Torii gate, Japanese, late Meiji period, 4 in. high. **$300-$400**

Panel, carved wood, depicting bakemono (the one in the center is called Hitosume Kozo), Japanese, Meiji period, 20 in. by 13 1/4 in. **$1,500-$2,000**

Smoker's box, rosewood, two drawers and copper liner, Japanese, early 20th century, 9 in. long. **$100-$175**

Table for playing Go, hardwood, Japanese, 20th century, 9 in. by 16 in. by 17 in. **$75-$125**

Vase, bamboo, carved mountainscape, Chinese, late 18th/early 19th century, 9 1/4 in. long. **$1,200-$1,600**

Vases, bamboo, carved with birds in relief amidst pine trees, signed Seko, Japanese, late 19th century, 13 1/2 in. high, **pair. $500-$800**

Wood carving of Amida wearing loose vestments and raising his hand, his hair in rahotsu style (in Buddhist imagery, hair coiled in tight spirals), old wear and damages, wood worm, replacement of hands, possibly late 16th/early 17th century, Japanese. **$2,500-$3,500**

Traveling shrine, lacquer over wood with gilt interior, figure of Buddha probably not original, Japanese, mid-19th century, size open 18 in. by 22 1/2 in. by 9 1/2 in. **$2,000**

Table decoration, centerpiece, elaborately carved and lacquered with gilt details, showing court scenes, with six legs in the form of foo lions, one finial missing, possibly made for export, circa late 19th century, 14 in. by 6 in. by 9 3/4 in. **$800**

Wood carving of a bearded elder seated upon rock-work, inlaid ivory eyes and teeth, marked China, circa 1925, 9 in. high. **$65-$95**

Wood carving of Bodiharma wearing a cowled robe, Chinese, late 19th century, 9 in. high. **$450-$600**

Wood carving of Buddha seated on a waisted throne, his hands in Bhumisparsa (meditation posture of witness, also known as "touching the earth" or "calling the earth to witness") and dhyana mudra (pose or gesture of meditation and concentration in the attainment of spiritual perfection), traces of gilt on the figure, Burmese, 20th century, 24 in. high. **$700-$900**

Wood carving of Daikoku, a sack over one shoulder, a mallet over the other, one leg raised, some damage, Japanese, circa 1900, 6 1/2 in. high. **$600-$800**

Wood box for stamps, with pierced ceramic floral decoration on top, applied soapstone medallions on sides, and a small ceramic scene of four men carrying a palanquin (conveyance, usually for one person, that consists of an enclosed litter borne on the shoulders of men by means of poles, used especially in eastern Asia), interior has three curved compartments for stamps, excellent condition, 5 in. by 1 5/8 in. by 1 3/8 in. **$250**

Wood carving of an elder wearing a large, round hat, inlaid ivory eyes and teeth, marked China, circa 1925, 7 in. high. **$50-$75**

Wood carving of a falcon perched on a gnarled tree stump, Japanese, late 19th century, 14 in. high. **$300-$500**

Wood carving of Gama Sennin standing on a rock-work base and holding a basket of flowers, toads clambering about, Japanese, late 19th century, 7 1/2 in. high. **$600-$800**

Wood carvings of gong bearers, each standing with articulated arms poised on a mound base, elaborate robes carved with zigzag motifs, Burmese, 19th century, 28 1/2 in. high, pair. **$800-$1,200**

Wood scenes, carved gilt and polychrome on custom-made bases, probably fragments from furniture, showing noblemen on horseback with servants, 6 in. by 3 3/4 in. by 1 3/4 in., **pair. $175**

Wood carving of Hotei, treasure bag over his shoulder, slight damage, signed Masanao, Japanese, late 19th century, 5 in. high. **$600-$750**

Wood carving of smiling Hotei with inlaid-ivory teeth and eyes, accompanied by children, marked China, early 20th century, 10 in. high. **$125-$150**

Wood carving of Kuan Yin, the patina a yellowish brown, Chinese, late 19th century, 7 in. high. **$400-$600**

Wood carvings of Kuan Yin, each seated on a rocky base, each having traces of gilt, Chinese, late 19th century, 18 in. high, pair. **$2,500-$3,500**

Wood carvings of Lohan, each having inlaid-ivory eyes, the ivory teeth missing from one, marked China, circa 1920, 7 1/2 in. high, **pair. $100-$125**

Bamboo carving of a phoenix upon an open-work base, Chinese, late Ch'ing Dynasty, 11 in. high. $900-$1,200

Wood carving of two bakemono masks, each grotesque face inlaid with ivory teeth and horn eyes, Japanese, circa 1900, 4 in. diameter. **$900-$1,200**

Wood-carved mask of a demon with fanged teeth and sunken eyes, some gilt remaining, Japanese, 19th century, 30 in. high. **$700-$900**

Wood carving of a No performer holding a sceptre, the kimono painted in colors, Japanese, late 19th century, 11 in. high. **$800-$900**

Wood carving of a priest (in sitting position) holding a lotus pod surmounted by a sacred pearl, glass-inlaid eyes, some gilt remaining, old wear and damages, Japanese, 18th century. **$3,000-$4,000**

Wood carving of a recumbent water buffalo looking to the right, signed Kiromitsu, Japanese, 19th century. **$500-$600**

Wood carving of Sennin Kiku Jido upon a mountain overlooking a stream, chrysanthemums covering the entire sculpture, Japanese, late Edo period, 18 in. diameter. **$3,500-$4,500**

Wood carving of Shoki and Oni, the demon killer struggling to hold Oni, some damage, signed Kogetsu, Japanese, circa 1900, 7 in. high. **$750-$950**

Wood carving of a seated tiger looking to the right, ittobori style, Japanese, circa 1900, 9 in. long. **$400-$600**

Wood carving of a warrior riding on a rampant horse supported by a kneeling attendant, Indian, 20th century, 29 in. high. **$300-$600**

Wood carving of a water buffalo, inlaid ivory eyes, marked China, early 20th century, 5 1/2 in. long. **$50-$65**

Wood carving of a woman holding a basket of fruit, signed Kogetsu, Japanese, early 20th century, 6 in. high. **$400-$600**

Wood carvings of the Eight Immortals, each with attribute, some damage, Chinese, early 20th century, 8 in. high. **$1,800-$2,400**

Wood sake container, kiri wood, well-bucket form, the exterior with three bamboo bands, Japanese, early 20th century, 13 1/2 in. diameter. **$175-$300**

Wood carving of Daikoku with mallet and sack, "Mingei" (folk art), Japanese, Meiji period, 23 in. high.
$1,000-$1,500

Wood carving of a Japanese Stellar's eagle, early to mid-19th century, weathered painted surface, possibly a house decoration, 18 1/2 in. by 16 in. by 7 in. **$4,500**

Wood carving, rosewood figure of Shou Lao, the God of Longevity, leaning on his staff, with a crane, Chinese, late 19th or early 20th century, probably a tourist item, on a rosewood base, 13 3/8 in. by 4 1/2 in. by 4 in. **$225**

Wood carving (gilt wood) of Quan Yin (also spelled Kuan Yin), one of the deities of Chinese Buddhism, mid-19th century, 11 1/2 in. by 7 3/4 in. by 5 1/2 in. **$850**

Carved figure of a Chinese nobleman in elaborate robes, with lacquered and gilt decoration, late 19th century, 9 1/2 in. by 4 in. by 3 1/2 in. **$175**

Left: Wood carving of Kuan Yin, Chinese, circa 1930, 4 in. high. **$50-$75**. Right: Wood carving of the Disappointed Rat Catcher, Japanese, late 19th century. **$500-$700**

Wood carving of a duck tomb figure, Han Dynasty (207 BC-220 AD), traces of original paint, part of bill missing, 13 1/2 in. by 10 1/2 in. by 8 in. **$475**

Wood carved dolphin, probably 13th to 15th century AD, also probably from a tomb, worn and crusty surface, 12 1/2 in. by 16 3/4 in. by 4 1/2 in. **$285**

Wood-carved theatrical mask, Japanese Meiji period (1868-1912), 7 in. by 6 1/2 in. **$300**

Wood figure of a Lohan (an individual who has attained enlightenment by his own effort) holding fruit, measuring 6 in. by 1 1/2 in., marked CHINA, dating to the late 19th or early 20th century. There is one partial age crack in the hand. Lustrous, light patina. **$50**

Wrist rest, bamboo carved with a riverscape, Chinese, early 20th century, 9 in. long. **$200-$275**

Wood carving, group of three Immortals depicted as hermits in tattered clothing, one standing with a gnarled staff, another seated with a fly whisk, their female companion holding a branch of lingzhi (Chinese herb promoting spiritual potency), crack, Chinese, Ch'ing Dynasty, 10 in. high. Realized price (including the 10-percent buyer's premium), Christie's East, New York City. **$1,540**

Wrist or hand rest, Imperial bamboo, with carved Chinese characters, commissioned by the Dowager Empress Cixi in the late Qing Dynasty. It measures about 4 in. wide by 10 1/2 in. long. This piece, like most wrist rests, is made of high quality bamboo. Bamboo, being evergreen, is a symbol of longevity. Because it grows straight but bends with the wind, it is also a sign of an honest and adaptable official. The rest has embossed characters and a seal. In the middle, the larger Chinese characters translate as: the sky/cloud flies over the stars, which can be interpreted to be good wishes or a subtle expression of the Dowager Empress' control over the Emperor Guangxu. The left panel has the date of manufacture as being the 16th year during the reign of the Emperor GuangXu, or 1891, on the 16th day of the 18th month of the Chinese lunar calendar. On the bottom left-hand corner is a large Imperial seal stamp/chop mark of the Empress Dowager Cixi. There is a phoenix carving on the top. The phoenix signifies goodness and benevolence because it is the bird that can fly closest to heaven, and is also a symbol of high achievement. The phoenix is traditionally associated with the Empress. On the bottom right-hand side, there is a dragon carving. The dragon is a benevolent creature and an emblem of Imperial authority, and was reserved for the emperor. Dowager Empress Cixi was the concubine/wife of the Xian-Feng Emperor (1851-1861), and the mother of the Tong-Zhi Emperor (1862-1874). She took control of the Heavenly Kingdom (China) during the mid to late Qing Dynasty when she placed her five-year-old son, Aisin-Gioro Zai-Chun, on the dragon throne to become the Tong-Zhi Emperor. She ruled China during a period of great upheaval that included the Taiping Rebellion, the Boxer Rebellion, and the sacking of the palace in Beijing. This wrist rest with the imperial seal is in excellent condition with rich patina. **$350**

Wood carving of Shoki (slayer of demons), his robes with phoenix mon in red and black lacquer, Japanese, late Edo/early Meiji period, 9 in. high. **$600-$900**

Rosewood carved figure of a woman with a bird, Chinese, late 19th or early 20th century, probably a tourist item, on a rosewood base, 14 1/2 in. by 6 in. by 4 in. **$185**

Carved wood scepter with cloisonné panels, a symbol of power and influence, significant damage to wood, 22 1/4 in. by 6 1/4 in. by 3 1/8 in. **$450**

Wood carved figure of an "oni" (demon) with black and red lacquer finish, possibly 18th century, 11 1/2 in. by 7 in. by 5 in. **$2,200**

Wood figure of a dancer(?),Thai painted, with stand, 38 in. by 15 1/2 in. by 9 in. **$800**

The Tongue-Cut Sparrow

The Japanese folktale of the tongue-cut sparrow has been told for centuries with many variations. Here is one version:

An old man and his wife lived in a little house in an old village in Japan. One morning when the old woman slid open the screens on the side of their house, she saw a little sparrow, near death from the cold. She picked him up and fed him. Then she held him in the morning sunshine until the dew was dried from his wings. Afterward, she let him go, so that he might fly home to his nest, but he stayed with her to thank her with his songs.

Each morning, the sparrow perched on the roof of the house and sang out his joy. The old man and woman thanked the sparrow for this, for they liked to be up early and at work. But near them lived a cross old woman who did not like to be awakened so early. At last she became so angry that she caught the sparrow and cut his tongue. Then the poor little sparrow flew away to his home. But he never could sing again.

When the kind woman discovered what had happened to her pet, she was very sad. She said to her husband, "Let us go and find our poor little sparrow." So they started together, and asked of each bird by the wayside, "Do you know where the tongue-cut sparrow lives?"

Soon they came to a bridge and two roads. They did not know which way to turn, and at first could see no one to ask. At last they saw a bat, hanging head downward, taking a nap. They asked, "Friend Bat, do you know where the tongue-cut sparrow went?"

"Yes. Over the bridge and up the mountain," said the bat.

They went over the bridge and up the mountain, but again they found two roads and did not know which one to take. A little field mouse peeped through the leaves and grass, so they asked him, "Do you know where the tongue-cut sparrow went?"

"Yes. Down the mountain and through the woods," said the field mouse.

Down the mountain and through the woods they went, and at last came to the home of their little friend. When he saw them coming, the poor little sparrow was very happy indeed. He and his wife and children all came and bowed their heads down to the ground to show their respect. Then the sparrow rose and led the old man and the old woman into the house while his wife and children hastened to bring them boiled rice, fish, and lettuce.

When the sun began to sink, the old man and woman started home. The sparrow brought out two baskets. "I would like to give you one of these," he said. "Which will you take?" One basket was large and looked very full, while the other one seemed very small and light. The old people thought they would not take the large basket, for that might have all the sparrow's treasure in it, so they said, "The journey home is long, so please let us take the smaller one."

They took it and walked home over the mountain and across the bridge, happy and contented. When they reached their own home, they decided to open the basket to see what the sparrow had given them. Inside they found many rolls of silk and piles of gold, enough to make them rich, so they were more grateful than ever to the sparrow.

The cross old woman who had cut the sparrow's tongue was spying through the screen when they opened their basket. She saw the rolls of silk and piles of gold, and wondered how she might get some for herself. The next morning she went to the kind woman and said, "I am so sorry that I cut the tongue of your sparrow. Please tell me the way to his home so that I may go to him and tell him I am sorry."

The kind woman told her the way and the cross woman set out. She went across the bridge, over the mountains, and through the woods. At last she came to the home of the little sparrow. He was not so glad to see her, yet he was very kind to her and did everything to make her feel very welcome. The family made a feast for her, and when she started home the sparrow brought out two baskets as before. Of course the cross old woman chose the large basket, for she thought that would have even more wealth than the other one.

The basket was very heavy and caught on the trees as she was going through the wood. She could hardly pull it up the mountain with her, and she was all out of breath when she reached the top. She did not get to the bridge until it was dark.

When at last she reached home she was tired out, but she pulled the screens tightly closed so that no one could look in, and opened her basket. A whole swarm of horrible creatures burst out! They stung her and bit her, and she could not escape them. Finally, they all swooped down upon her, picked her up, and flew away with her. She was never seen again.

Guidelines for Care of Oriental Antiques and Art

Ceramics

Under no circumstances should you use the dishwasher to clean ceramic objects. Fine antiques and collectibles are not dishwasher-safe; in fact, pottery and terracotta objects should not even be immersed in water. Instead, pottery should be cleaned with a damp cloth, and terracotta should be cleaned with a minimal amount of water and dried immediately. Gentle dusting may be the best way to keep terracotta clean.

Porcelain, on the other hand, is safely cleaned with mild soap and tepid water. Always be sure, though, to place a thick towel in the bottom of the sink or wash area to prevent damaging the object by bringing it into direct contact with the surface of the wash area.

Never hang cups from cup hooks. Handles are not strong and can easily break.

Furniture

Never use liquid wax on Oriental furniture. To clean kiri wood and other blonde woods, first mix a solution that is one-third turpentine, one-third vinegar, and one-third warm water, and test it on an inconspicuous part of the object. If the solution cleans that portion safely, apply it overall. Then use the finest grade of steel wool to take off old wax and dirt. Hard wax or shoe polish, the same color as the finish, may be used after cleaning-approximately 12 to 15 layers for a hard surface. Buff the last layer with a soft cloth for the perfect finish.

Always check the interior of a tansu: Its condition should be as good as that of the exterior. Sometimes, however, you'll find that fine-quality wood has been used on the doors and/or drawers, and that cheaper, thinner, or otherwise inferior wood has been used on the interior. Beware of objects in this category, as the inferior wood may crack from the weight of the objects in the drawers.

Also check the back panel, which is often cracked. If damaged, it should be replaced. The replacement will not diminish value.

Ivory

A brush is the best tool to use for cleaning ivory, although you can use mild soap and tepid water to remove surface dirt, provided the object is in excellent condition. Ivory should be dried immediately in order to prevent warping and cracking.

Jade

Jade can also be washed with mild soap and tepid water, but be sure to rinse it thoroughly, and use a soft cloth for drying the object.

Lacquer

Clean lacquer wares by wiping them with a lint-free cloth. Applying a very small amount of lemon with the cloth is permissible, but never use wax or strong detergents on lacquered objects.

Any room in which lacquered furniture is stored should contain a humidifier. In addition, lacquered objects should be rotated, especially in the winter, when they are generally subjected to a great deal of dry heat.

Finally, lacquer should be kept out of direct sunlight.

Metalwares

Silver should be cleaned with a fine quality polish according to the directions on the label of the polish container. Never clean other metalwares. Their natural patina (finish), which changes over the years, is highly prized by collectors. Metalwares that have been cleaned either with polishes or abrasive cleansers are less valuable.

Paintings, Screens, and Scrolls

Silk or paper paintings, screens, and hanging scrolls should be displayed for only short periods of time. Remember to avoid displaying them in direct sunlight, which will cause fading.

Otherwise, store paintings, screens, and scrolls away from heat, light, and dampness, with tissue layers between panels. Periodically unroll scrolls (every three to six months) to allow them to "breathe." Keep the atmosphere in which they are displayed or stored temperate by using a humidifier in the winter and air conditioning in the summer.

Always check the backs of screens for mildew.

Prints

A print should be sharp and clear, and made from the first or original strike. Trimming, fading, holes, dirt, and foxing (brown spots) will reduce its value, so it is wise to protect the print from these problems by framing it. If you prefer not to frame a print, store it between sheets of paper (or of cardboard with rag content). Chemically treated paper will damage a print.

Like scrolls, prints should never be hung in direct sunlight. Occasionally rotate the prints you wish to display prominently with those that have been put in darker places.

Marks

For the most part, collectors cannot rely solely upon marks as a gauge for authenticity. The McKinley Tariff Act of 1891-requiring that all articles of foreign manufacture be plainly marked, stamped, branded, or labeled in legible English words so as to indicate the country of origin-was instituted in order to provide consumers with a more complete knowledge of what they were buying. Still, many wares that are unmarked, or which are marked in Japanese or Chinese characters without the country of origin written in English, are not necessarily objects produced prior to 1891.

From 1891 to March 21, 1921, the word Nippon was acceptable as proper marking of country of origin for goods manufactured in Japan and exported to the United States. Later, Treasury Decision #26989 used the words gummed label and rubber stamp for the first time in defining identification requirements, and many collectors have assumed that the use of an affixed sticker on Japanese export wares (and on Chinese exports, to a lesser degree) was not initiated until this 1917 decision. However, the word labeled in the McKinley Tariff Act also indicated an affixed sticker, whereby the use of labels to indicate country of origin has been acceptable since March 1, 1891.

Chinese Marks

Chinese six-character reign marks are written in three vertical rows. Other Chinese marks include hallmarks, maker's marks, place marks, commendation marks, and symbols. Some of these take the form of six characters written in two horizontal rows.

Written in standard script, Chinese marks were most often done in underglaze blue. However, marks can be found in pink, red, gold, orange, and so on. Seal marks were written with a brush and seldom were stamped. Incised and stamped marks are most commonly found on monochromatic wares.

The periods whose reign marks were most often copied in later periods include Yung Lo, 1402-1423; Hsüan Te, 1426-1435; Cheng Hua, 1465-1487; Wan Li, 1573-1619; K'ang Hsi, 1662-1723; Yung Cheng, 1723-1736; and Ch'ien Lung, 1736-1796. Some of these periods became significant because of their shortness (and the resulting rarity of objects produced during those periods), and some were important because of the innovations that occurred within them.

Authentic period pieces, of course, have always brought the highest prices. Pieces with Imperial marks are also especially valuable.

Japanese Marks

Japanese marks and seals include makers' names, date marks, and place marks. Like their Chinese counterparts, significant Japanese marks were copied, forged, and bartered: One potter in awe of another had no difficulty copying the other's mark or seal. To further complicate matters, Chinese reign marks were copied and are frequently found on Japanese Imari (Arita). If the Japanese characters for Dai Ni Hon (or Dai Nippon) appear in a mark, the object was produced no earlier than 1868.

Assessing Quality

The quality of any object should correspond to the quality of the mark. The surest way to obtain quality pieces, however, is to buy from reputable sources. In addition, take every opportunity to acquaint yourself thoroughly with the kinds of objects that interest you most: Handle them, ask questions about them, and read as much as you can about them, subscribing to relevant periodicals and building your own reference library. If courses or seminars dealing with the topic are offered locally, enroll in them. It is better to buy one piece of high quality than to buy several pieces of lesser quality.

North American Museums with Permanent Exhibitions of Orientalia

ALBRIGHT-KNOX ART GALLERY
1285 Elmwood Ave.
Buffalo, NY 14202

THE ART GALLERY OF GREATER VICTORIA
1040 Moss St.
Victoria, British Columbia
Canada V8V4P1

THE ART INSTITUTE OF CHICAGO
Michigan Ave. and Adams St.
Chicago, IL 60603

THE BOSTON MUSEUM OF FINE ARTS
465 Hunt Ave.
Boston, MA 02115

THE BROOKLYN MUSEUM
188 Eastern Pkwy.
Brooklyn, NY 11238

THE CINCINNATI ART MUSEUM
Eden Park
Cincinnati, OH 45202

THE CITY ART MUSEUM OF ST. LOUIS
St. Louis, MO 63110

CLEVELAND MUSEUM OF ART
11150 East Blvd.
Cleveland, OH 44106

E. B. CROCKER ART GALLERY
216 O St.
Sacramento, CA 95814

THE DENVER ART MUSEUM
100 W. 14 Pkwy.
Denver, CO 80204

THE DETROIT INSTITUTE OF ARTS
Detroit, MI 48202

THE M. H. DE YOUNG MEMORIAL MUSEUM
Golden Gate Park
San Francisco, CA 94118

THE FREER GALLERY OF ART
Washington, D.C.

THE J. PAUL GETTY MUSEUM
1200 Getty Center Drive
Los Angeles, CA 90049-1687

HERRON MUSEUM OF ART
Purdue University
Indianapolis, IN 46205

HONOLULU ACADEMY OF ARTS
900 S. Beretania St.
Honolulu, HI 98614

LOS ANGELES COUNTY MUSEUM OF ART
5905 Wilshire Blvd.
Los Angeles, CA 90036

THE JACQUES MARCHAIS CENTER OF
TIBETAN ART
338 Lighthouse Ave.
Staten Island, NY 10306

THE METROPOLITAN MUSEUM OF ART
5th Ave. and 82nd St.
New York, NY 10028

THE MINNEAPOLIS INSTITUTE OF ARTS
2400 3rd Ave. South
Minneapolis, MN 55404

THE MONTCLAIR ART MUSEUM
Montclair, NJ 07042

MUSEUM OF ART
Providence, RI

WILLIAM ROCKHILL NELSON GALLERY OF ART
MARY ATKINS MUSEUM OF FINE ART
4525 Oak St.
Kansas City, MO 64111

THE NEWARK MUSEUM
Newark, NJ 07101

THE PORTLAND ART MUSEUM
Portland, OR

THE RINGLING MUSEUM OF ART
Sarasota, FL 33580

RIVERSIDE MUSEUM
Riverside, CA 94305

ROYAL ONTARIO MUSEUM
100 Queen's Park

Toronto, Ontario
Canada M5S2C6

SEATTLE ART MUSEUM
Volunteer Park
Seattle, WA 98112

THE STANFORD UNIVERSITY MUSEUM
Stanford, CA 94305

THE TOLEDO MUSEUM OF ART
Toledo, OH 43697

THE UNIVERSITY MUSEUM
Philadelphia, PA 19104

THE WADSWORTH ATHENEUM
600 Main St.
Hartford, CT 06103

WALKER ART CENTER
Vineland Pl.
Minneapolis, MN 55403

THE WALTERS ART GALLERY
222 State St.
Springfield, MA 01103

WORCESTER ART MUSEUM
55 Salisbury St.
Worcester, MA 01608

YALE UNIVERSITY ART GALLERY
New Haven, CT 06520

Appraisers

AMERICAN SOCIETY OF APPRAISERS
555 Herndon Pkwy., Ste. 125
Herndon, VA 20170
(703) 478-2228
Fax (703) 742-8471
http://www.appraisers.org/
asainfo@appraisers.org

INTERNATIONAL SOCIETY OF APPRAISERS
Riverview Plaza Office Park
16040 Christensen Rd., Ste. 102
Seattle, WA 98188-2929
(206) 241-0359
Fax (206) 241-0436
http://www.isa-appraisers.org/
isahq@isa-appraisers.org

THE APPRAISERS ASSOCIATION OF AMERICA
386 Park Avenue South, Ste. 2000
New York, NY 10016
(212) 889-5404
Fax (212) 889-5503
www.appraisersassoc.org
aaa1@rcn.com

Resources

ANTIQUE MANOR
Highway 63 North
Stewartville, MN 55976
(507) 533-9300

ANTIQUES RIVERWALK
Period antique furniture and fine art accessories
and collectibles in the Historic Warehouse District
of Minneapolis
210 3rd Ave. N.
Minneapolis MN 55401
(612) 339-9352
http://www.antiquesriverwalk.com
info@antiquesriverwalk.com

JAMES E. BILLINGS, APPRAISER AND CONSULTING
EDITOR
817 Columbia Pkwy.
Minneapolis, MN 55418
(612) 788-7890
billi010@tcu.umn.edu

JONATHAN BRUNING
Period antiques and works of art
PO Box 22272
Minneapolis, MN 55422-0272
(612) 529-0622

THE CHINA COAST GALLERY
PO Box 610
Austin, Texas 78767
(512) 288-3043
Fax (512) 327-0332
http://www.chinacoastgallery.com/
E-mail: info@chinacoastaustin.com

CHUCK HUDGINS
(612) 789-5949

SARAH C. RANDOL
210 Third Ave. N.
Minneapolis, MN 55401
(612) 339-9352

CLAIRE STEYAERT
Antiquaire Expert
(612) 339-7396
(612) 799-2350

CIRCLE OF THE MOON ANTIQUES
219P Berlin Rd., Ste. 160
Cherry Hill, NJ 08034
(856) 428-8325
Fax (856) 428-9282
http://www.antiquearts.com/stores/circle/
E-mail: Info@circleofthemoon.com

EDGAR L. OWEN, LTD.
Antiquities, ancient coins, and world art
PO Box 714
Lake Hopatcong, NJ 07849
(973) 398-9557
Fax (973) 398-8082
http://www.EdgarLOwen.com/
E-mail: EdgarOwen@att.net

THE IRIDESCENT HOUSE
227 First Ave, S.W.
Rochester, MN 55902
(507) 288-0320

KIMIKO MOLASKY
1045 Van Slyke Ave.
St. Paul, MN 55103
(651) 487-3779
mkmolasky@aol.com

R&D ANTIQUES AND ORIENTAL ART
PO Box 112507
Carrollton, TX 75011-2507
http://www.randdorientalart.com/
E-mail: info@randdorientalart.com

Glossary

100 Antiques: A design used in old Chinese embroideries, costumes, and woodblock prints

Ainu: indigenous people of Japan

akirti mukha: pose, face downward

alidhasana: right leg bent at the knee and the left leg straight, taken from classical Indian dance

Amida Nyorai: Buddha of the Western Paradise

Ando: name of the artist or studio

aogai: abalone shell inlay

ardhapanyankasana: seating posture

ashinga: grotesque figure of a man with long legs

Avalokitesvara: one of the Buddhist deities, "avalokita" means "observes the sounds of the world" and "esvara" means "lord." The full name has been variously interpreted as "the lord who hears/looks in every direction" and "the lord of hearing the deepest."

awabi: abalone

awaji ware: coarse stoneware made in Awaji Province, Japan

bakemono: goblin or monster; also a spirit with evil powers or a witch

banko: style of Japanese pottery that originated in the early 18th century

battledore: rectangular wooden paddles, some highly decorated, used with a shuttlecock in a New Year's game for girls (called "oibane" or "hanetsuki"), also called "hagoita"

Benares brocade: from the city where this fabric originated, also called Varanasi

Benkei: in Japanese legend, a fierce warrior with enormous strength

Benten: one of the seven lucky gods of Japan, and the only female, patron of writers, musicians, painters, and sculptors

bhumisparsa: meditation posture of witness, also known as "touching the earth" or "calling the earth to witness"

bidri: inlaying of gold or silver on a steel or copper base

biwa: stringed instrument similar to a lute or guitar

Bodiharma: Indian priest (448-529 AD) who brought Dyana Buddhism from India to China's Shaolin Temples

bodhisattva: enlightened being; god or goddess

bosses: raised ornamentation

boteh: leaf-shape design, like a paisley

cabochon: gem or bead cut in convex form and highly polished but not faceted; also this style of cutting

celadon: pale green in color

cha wan: also spelled chawan, a bowl used in the tea ceremony

Chen Wu: in Chinese mythology, Lord of the Night Sky

Ch'eng Hua: emperor who ruled China from 1465-1487

Chia Ching: Chinese emperor who ruled from 1522-1566

Chia Ch'ing: also spelled Jiaqing, the emperor who ruled China from 1796-1820

Ch'ien Lung: also called Qianlong, the Chinese Emperor who ruled from1736 to 1796

Ch'in Dynasty: also called Qin, in Chinese history dates vary, but usually set at 221-206 BC

Ching (or Ch'ing) Dynasty: see Manchu

chih lung: also called Li, or Li-Lung, these are hornless Chinese dragons. They may symbolize the scholar.

Chokaro Sennin: in Japanese mythology, an immortal mountain hermit who had a magic pumpkin. When he blew on the pumpkin, a horse came out for him to ride. Chokaro is always shown with a pumpkin out of which a horse may be peeking.

Chou Dynasty: also spelled Zhou, 1134-256 BC

chun yao: style of pottery made in northern China, the body of Chun ware is thick and covered with an impure glaze

Ch'ung Cheng: in Chinese history, the period from 1644-1912

cizhou: see tz'u chou

coromandel: Chinese lacquered screen, often folding

Daikoku: Japanese god of wealth and farmers

caisho: pair of swords, one long and one short

Dakini Vajravarahi: powerful Buddhist diety

Daoguang: see Tao Kuang

Daruma: also known as Bodhidharma, the founder of Chan Buddhism in China (known as Zen Buddhism in Japan). He is said to have lost the use of his arms and legs after meditating in front of a wall for nine years.

dhoti: skirt worn by some Indian men and boys

dhyana mudra: pose or gesture of meditation and concentration in the attainment of spiritual perfection

dhyanasana: meditation pose with hands in lap

doucai: see tou ts'ai

Ebisu: Japanese god of fishermen and good fortune

Edo Period: in Japanese history, the years from about 1600 to 1868; Edo is the original name of Tokyo

famille jaune: yellow family

famille: French for family, used when referring to a design or color group

flammiform: form of a flame used for decorated effect

foo: usually referring to mythical Chinese dogs or lions

Fukusuke: in Japanese mythology, a dwarf believed to bring happiness

fundame: matte finish of gold lacquer

Fuku: see Fukurokuju

Fukurokuju: in Japanese mythology, god of happiness, wealth, and longevity

Gama Sennin: benign Japanese sage who is always accompanied by a toad and can assume the shape of a snake, or change his skin and become young again; he possesses the secret of immortality

Gansu Yangshao: often applied to pottery, referring to the ancient Chinese province of its origin

Gautama Buddha: also Prince Siddhartha Gautama, the historic Buddha, born in southern Nepal about 566 BC

Gentoku: from a story based on an episode in the life of the Chinese emperor Chao Lieh Ti (also romanticized as Zhao Lie Di, founder of the Shu Han Dynasty/Kingdom of Shu, 160-223, reigned 221-223 AD). He is also known by the names Huan Te (Japanese: Gentoku) and Liu Pei (Japanese: Ryubi), one of the figures in the Chinese novel The Romance of the Three Kingdoms. When invited to a feast to celebrate his marriage, his brother-in-law Sun K'uan besieged the castle. The only place not surrounded was the steep western battlement at the foot of which the river Huang Ho (or Dankei, according to another source) ran through a gorge. When one of his retainers showed him this dangerous means of escape, Gentoku quickly mounted his horse and jumped over 30 feet to safety.

ginbari: silver foil wrapped around a metal body, applied with translucent or transparent enamel

go: an analytical board game that probably originated in China in the first millennium BC

gofun: a white powder pigment produced from shells and used on Japanese prints to create a desired effect

gosai: glazing of generally not more than five colors

Guangxu: see Kuang Hsu

Guanyin: See Kuan Yin

guri: carved lacquer

gyobu nashiji: large nashiji flakes placed individually with a bamboo or steel needle

hagoita: see battledore

hako netsuke: in the form of a tiny box and cover

haori: short silk jacket

heidatsu: gold foil covered in lacquer, which is afterwards polished so that the gold is visible

Hirado: an island off the northwest coast of Kyushu, Japan, that has been famous for porcelain manufacture since the mid-18th century

hiramakie: known as low relief, this technique was introduced in the Kamakura period (sources differ: either 1186 or 1192 to 1333). A single layer of lacquer is applied to the ground, sprinkled with gold or silver powders, and allowed to dry. A coat of thin lacquer is then applied to fix the particles and then given a final polish.

hirame: large, irregular flakes of gold roughly sprinkled on a black lacquer ground, also fat gold flakes used in lacquer decoration (named for their resemblance to a flounder)

Hoho Erxian twins: also spelled Hehe Erxian twins, deities of peace and harmony

Hong Zhi: see Hung Chih

horagi: conch

Hotei: see Pu Tai

howdah: seat or covered pavilion on the back of an elephant or camel

Hsien Feng: Chinese emperor who ruled from 1851-1861

Hsuan Te: also spelled Xuande, the Chinese emperor who ruled from 1426-1435

Hsuan T'ung: the name taken in 1908 by Henry P'u Yi when he became last emperor of China; he renounced the throne in 1912

Hung Chih: also spelled Hong Zhi, the Chinese emperor who ruled from 1488-1505

hung-mu: a kind of redwood

iga ware: heavy type of Japanese pottery that originated in the 7th or 8th centuries

I-Hsing ware: also called Yixing ware, refers to the brown stoneware, mainly teapots, made in China's Yixing county on the western shore of the Great Lake, between Shanghai and Nanking.

ikebana: Japanese flower arranging

Inaba: Inaba Cloisonné Co., established 1887

iroe hira zogan: precious metal (gold or silver) paint and inlay, which is polished flush with the surface

ittobori style: carving with a single knife

joss-stick: incense stick

Jurojin: Japanese god of longevity

kagamibuta: special netsuke that consists of a bowl and a metal lid

kakihan: written seal, signature

kakiemon a pottery style synonymous with the line of potters who worked at the Nangawa kiln, near Arita, Japan

Kali: a Hindu goddess, her name is derived from the Hindu word that means "time"; also means "black"

kame: "turtle" in Japanese

kanamono: various small metal plates that decorate and hold armor together, the various rivets, and the ornaments

K'ang Hsi (also Kangxi): of or relating to the second emperor of the Ch'ing Dynasty of China, who lived from 1654-1722, and whose reign began in 1662

kanji: Chinese characters first imported to Japan in the 5th century via Korea. Kanji are ideograms, i.e., every character has a meaning and corresponds to a word.

kapala: skull cup

kappa: supernatural creatures that live both on land and in water; they have a beak-like snout, and fins on their hands and feet; they also have a shell on their back, and a water-filled dish on their head. As long as the dish is full of water, kappa keep their supernatural powers. They love sumo wrestling and cucumbers, and that is why cucumber sushi rolls are called kappa maki.

katakiribori: chiseling that imitates a paintbrush's stroke

kati mudra: hand on hip

kebori: fine hairline engraving

kendi: smoking device

Kenzan style: named after a famous Kyoto ceramist and his school of work

kesho-mawashi: ceremonial apron worn by sumo wrestlers during their "dohyo-iri" or ring-entering ceremony

kesi: tapestry weaving

khadga: sword, symbol of enlightenment

khetaka: shield

Khmer: the center of the ancient Khmer Civilization is at the Angkor Wat area, situated on the plain of present-day Siemreap Province north of the Great Lake of Tonle Sap, Cambodia

Kiku mon: Chrysanthemum family crest

kiku: chrysanthemum

Kiki Jido: from the Noh play, "Chrysanthemum Child"

Kinko: from the Chinese Legend of Kinko (also spelled Qin Gao). Kinko was a recluse living near a stream where he spent most of his life (200 years) painting pictures of fish. One day the king of the fish came to offer Kinko his services as a guide through the world of the river. Kinko returned after a month, riding on the back of a carp, and was welcomed back home by his disciples who had been meditating during his absence. After leaving a message to his followers never to kill any fish, he dove into the water and never came back again.

kinji: brilliant gold lacquer

kiri: type of fast-growing tree, also called paulownia

kirigane: lacquer technique used for details, with gold and silver particles

kirin: mythical creature

komai: named for the family that originated a form of damascene (the ornamentation with wavy patterns like those of watered silk, or with inlaid work of precious metals) used to decorate swords, guns, and various types of sword furniture

Koryo Dynasty: in Korean history, about 936-1392

koshin: rearward or backward looking

kozuka: small knife accompanying a short sword

Kuang Hsu: also spelled Guangxu; the Chinese emperor who ruled from 1875 to 1908

Kuan Yin: Chinese goddess of compassion; variously spelled Quan Yin (or Quan Shi Yin), Kwan Yin, Guan Yin, and Guanyin

Kunichika: Japanese artist Toyohara Kunichika (1835-1900)

Kutani: pottery, also, the late Edo period name of the area where it was originally produced

kylin: mythical creature

Kyogen: the classical comic theater that balances the more serious Noh dramas; while Noh is musical in nature, Kyogen emphasizes dialogue

lappet: a fold or flap on a garment or headdress

laque burgauté: technique of decorating lacquer ware with inlaid designs employing shaped pieces of iridescent blue-green shell

lingzhi: Chinese herb promoting spiritual potency

Lishui: from the name of the town of this style's origin in Guangdong province, China

Lohan: in Chinese, a follower of Buddha who has achieved enlightenment

Lung Ch'uan: Chinese pottery named for the county in Chekiang province where the kilns were located

Mah Jongg: a game played with tiles; similar games are believed to have originated in China in the first millennium AD

mahoot: elephant servant, one who leads or tends an elephant

Mahakala: one of the Eight Guardians of the Law, whose duty is to protect Buddhism against its enemies

makara: a mythical sea creature with an elephant head

mammiform: having the form of a breast

Manchu Dynasty: The Ching (Qing) Manchu Dynasty invaded China in 1644 and deposed the former Ming Dynasty. The last Manchu emperor was deposed in favor of a republic in 1911.

mandala: a Hindu or Buddhist graphic symbol of the universe; specifically, a circle enclosing a square with a deity on each side; also, a graphic and often symbolic pattern usually in the form

of a circle divided into four separate
sections or bearing a multiple projection of an image

Mandarin: a public official in the Chinese
Empire of any of nine superior grades;
also, a form of spoken Chinese used
by the court and the official classes of
the Empire

mandorla: symbol in the form of two circles coming together, overlapping one
another to form an almond shape in
the middle

Manju: kind of netsuke named for its
resemblance to the Japanese rice cakes
of the same shape (round)

Masanao: the school of Masanao carvers
of Ise, Japan, were famous for their
netsuke carving

mei ping: lobes and floral scrolls carved
and incised under the glaze

Meiji period: in Japanese history, 1868-
1912

Ming Dynasty: in Chinese history, 1368-
1644

Minogame: kind of tortoise

mishima: stoneware made of gray clay to
which white slip is applied using a
variety of decorative techniques

mizutsugi: small water kettle used to
replenish the mizusashi (water container) with cold water at the end of a
temae (tea ceremony)

Momoyama period: in Japanese history,
1490-1573

Mon: family crest

Mon D'varavati: referring to the independ-
ent state and people of Dvaravati,
which flourished from the 7th to 11th
centuries in much of present-day
Thailand

moriage: special type of raised decoration

used on some Japanese pottery

mugwort: plant (Artemisia vulgaris) also
called by other names, including
chrysanthemum weed

Mukozuke: a small serving dish

muranashiji: lacquer with small gold flakes
in irregular clusters

Muromachi period: in Japanese history,
1338-1573

Mu Wang: Mu Wang (circa 985 to 907
BC) was an emperor of the Chou
Dynasty who traveled around his
kingdom in a chariot drawn by eight
horses. He visited the goddess Hsi
Wang Mu in her western garden,
where the tree that bore the Peach of
Immortality grew. The eight horses
occur in painted decoration, especially
relaxing from their day's labors.

naga: serpent, snake

nashiji: irregularly shaped flakes of gold
suspended in clear or yellowish lacquer; also called "pear ground," gold,
silver, or gold-silver alloys of reddish-
yellow coloration used on lacquer,
principally as a ground

natsume: a Japanese lacquered tea caddy

Nichols carpet: named for Walter Abner
Burns Nichols, American
adventurer/entrepreneur, who popu-
larized the "Chinese deco" rugs manufactured in Tientsin in the 1920s and
1930s

nishiki brocade: multicolor brocade prints
originated by Suzuki Harunobu
(1725-1770)

nitaraka mudra: pose

Noh: also spelled No, a classical Japanese
performance form that combines elements of dance, drama, music, and
poetry

nunome-zogan: also called Damascene, an inlay process in which precious metal is hammered into a background field in a free pattern

obihasami: form of netsuke used with the lower part to be displayed from under the obi (sash) that it clasps

octofoil: design, usually circular, of eight petals

Okame: Japanese goddess of luck

Okatomo style: named for one of the early great netsuke carvers, famous for his animal subjects (active before 1781)

okina: character, usually an old man, found in the traditional Japanese Noh dramas

oni: devil or demon

Ono no Tofu: noted 10th century Japanese calligrapher; he had tried seven times to win promotion at court and was about to leave in despair when he saw a frog trying over and over to climb a willow branch, only succeeding on the eighth attempt; he took courage, persevered, and subsequently rose to high rank

otobide: a mask used in Noh dramas; meaning a startled expression, it features big eyes and a wide open mouth

padma: lotus

Padmapani: in the Buddhist pantheon, the lotus holder, creator of the world and all animate beings

palanquin: conveyance, usually for one person, that consists of an enclosed litter borne on the shoulders of men by means of poles, used especially in eastern Asia

Parvati: also known as the Hindu goddess Durga or Lalitha, the wife (consort) of Lord Shiva; she exists in various divine forms (both friendly and fearful)

paulownia: see kiri

Peking knots: An embroidery technique also called French knots

pliqué-à-jour: style of enameling in which usually transparent enamels are fused into the openings of a metal filigree to produce a stained-glass effect

prunus: the botanical name for a large group of deciduous and evergreen trees and shrubs

Pu Tai: called "the laughing Buddha," known in Japan as Hotei

Qianlong or Qian Long: see Ch'ien Lung

Qing Dynasty: see Manchu

rahotsu: in Buddhist imagery, hair coiled in tight spirals

rajalilasana: pose called the king's posture, which expresses ease and relaxed confidence

rakan: Japanese term for the "arhats" or Buddhist saints who have already become perfect in this life. It refers particularly to the 500 immediate disciples of Gautama, the historic Buddha.

rimpa: painting style originated by Ogata Korin (1658-1716), known for its flamboyant approach, which transformed subjects from nature into abstract, random, and flat patterns

Ritsuo: signature for Ogawa Haritsu, a famous lacquer artist of the early 18th century. His designs were often embellished with inlays of porcelain or pewter.

roiro: black lacquer used for the ground

roironuri: a waxy black or mirror-black finish; a brilliant and highly reflective black lacquer

ruyi: scepter

Sakti: goddess of suffering

sampan: a flat-bottomed Chinese skiff usually propelled by two short oars

sang de boeuf: ox blood, usually referring to a glaze

sansai: also spelled sancai and san t'sai, meaning three-color wares, usually green, amber, and cream

satsuma: form of Japanese ceramics in which faience (pottery) is covered with a glaze that produces a network of crackles and is itself ornamented with polychrome enamels

sattvasana: meditation pose

sentoku: yellow metal alloy consisting of copper, zinc, and tin

Seto porcelain: a high-fired ware made in the Seto (Aichi Prefecture) and Mino (Gifu Prefecture) areas of Japan since the 14th century

shakudo: dark pickled metal alloy; a mixture of copper, gold, and other materials

Shekwan ware: a kind of mud figure, named for the town in Kwangtung province, southern China, where they have been made for centuries

Shan States: The Shans dominated most of Burma (now Myanmar) from the 13th to the 16th centuries

shibayama: carved inlays of mother of pearl and other materials

shibuichi: gray-green patinated alloy of copper with varying quantities of silver

Shigaraki: the former capital of Japan where pottery production was established in the late 12th century

shishi: imaginary lion-like dog, placed in pairs right and left of temple entrances; the Japanaese equivalent of the Chinese foo (or fu) dog.

shishiaibori: low relief carving below the level of the (tsuba) surface

shishimai: the lion dance, performed as a prayer for a good harvest and household safety for the year; the dance is performed by a red lion on the first and second days of the New Year, and by a pair of male and female lions, red and white, on the third day.

Silla Dynasty: also spelled Shilla, in Korean history, Old Silla Dynasty was 57 BC-668 AD; the Unified Silla Dynasty was 668–935 AD

shogun: one of the military rulers of Japan

shogunal: of or referring to one of a line of military governors ruling Japan until the revolution of 1867-'68

shojo: characters from Japanese mythology; they are adolescents with red hair living on the bottom of the ocean; they brew an alcoholic beverage and like to drink

shoki: in Chinese mythology, a slayer of demons

Shou Lao: Chinese god of longevity; also Shou marks, a sign of longevity

Showa Period: in Japanese history, 1926-1989

sneezer: the Japanese believe one sneeze means someone is speaking highly of you and two indicate someone speaking ill of you

somada: technique of inlaying shell fragments of blue, green, and violet in a lacquer ground

Song or Sung Dynasty: in Chinese history, 960-1280 AD

so school: style of netsuke carving famous for it intricacy and attention to detail

Sugawara no Michizane: influential Japanese scholar and politician who lived from 845-903 AD

Sui Dynasty: in Chinese history, 581-618 AD

sumi: also spelled sumi-e, Japanese ink painting

Swatow: pottery named for the south China port, a type of Chinese provincial ware decorated in white slip on a blue ground

TLV: motifs in the form of the letters T, L, and V

t'ao t'ieh: mythical Chinese creature called the beast of gluttony

tabako-bon: smoking implements

tai fish: the red sea bream, a sign of good luck in Japan

Taisho Period: In Japanese history, 1912-1926

takamakie heidatsu: high relief lacquer decoration with silver inlay

takamakie: high relief; this technique involves building up a design using two or more layers of lacquer or lacquer compounds. The final surface is usually decorated.

tama: jewel

Tang Dynasty: in Chinese history, 618-907 AD

tansu: Japanese chest of drawers

Tao Kuang: also spelled Daoguang, the Chinese emperor who ruled from 1821-1851

tazza: shallow cup or vase on a pedestal

temmoku: iron-rich pottery glaze, also called "tenmuko," which refers to a mountain between China's Zhejiang and Anhui provinces, and is the Japanese pronunciation of Mt. Tienmu; the original name for wares

with this glaze in Chinese was "jianzhan."

tenaga: grotesque figure of a man with long arms

T'ien Chi: the Chinese emperor who ruled from 1620-1627

Ting wares: pottery named for the Chinese city where the kilns were first located, Tingchow, during the first millennium AD

Tobosaku: the witty adviser to Wu Ti, a Han emperor, represented as a smiling old man carrying a peach, sometimes accompanied by a deer

togidashi: polished or rubbed lacquer, the design flush with the ground

Tokugawa: referring to the Tokugawa shogunate (1603-1868)

Tomotada: for Izumiya Tomotada, a famous netsuke carver

Tongue-Cut Sparrow: see story on page 500

tonkotsu: tobacco box

tou ts'ai: also spelled doucai, meaning joined color or contrasting color

tribhanga: meaning "three bends," a standing posture with the body following an "S" curve

trigrams: the eight possible combinations of three whole or broken lines used especially in Chinese divination

triratna: three components of the Buddhist and Jain (a religion based on cosmic principles) creeds

tsuba: sword guard

tsubo: a narrow mouthed jar for storage of seed

tsuishu: a Japanese carved lacquer technique

Tung Chih: Also spelled T'ung-Chih, the Chinese emperor who ruled from 1862-1873

tz'u chou: also spelled cizhou, pottery with designs, often floral, that are bold and striking and involve the use of sgraffito

uchiwa: rigid, as opposed to folding, fan

Vairapani: attendant of Amoghasiddhi, a Buddha associated with worthy accomplishment and infallible success

vajradhara: essence of the historical Buddha's realization of enlightenment

vajras: thunderbolts

varada mudra: hand gesture, formed by an open right palm and extended fingers

vina: stringed instrument

Virabhadra: in Hindu myth, a monster created by Shiva

Wan Li: also called Shen Zong, the emperor who ruled China from 1573-1619

Wei Dynasty: in Chinese history, 386-534 AD

wu ts'ai: also spelled wucai, pottery with five colors, typically red, yellow, blue, green, and purple

yab-yum: father-mother union, symbolizing the uniting of wisdom and compassion

yaozhou: named for the centuries-old kiln located in Huangpu Tongchuan, northern China

yatate: portable writing set that was attached to the obi (sash)

yen-yen: a shape, commonly associated with a vase, also referred to as a phoenix tail (feng wei zun); the splayed foot is said to resemble the tail of the mythological phoenix bird, the emblem of the empress.

Yidam Samvara: the presiding diety in the Buddhist pantheon

Ying Ching: glazes associated with this kiln in northern China

Yongzheng: also spelled Yung Cheng, the Chinese emperor who ruled from 1723-1735

Yuan Dynasty: in Chinese history, 1279-1368, when China was ruled by the Mongols

Yi Dynasty: in Korean history, 1392-1910

yu-musen: combination of wired and wireless motifs

Yung Cheng: see Yongzheng

Yung Lo: Chinese emperor from 1403-1424

Zeshin: Shibata Zeshin was a Japanese painter, printmaker, and lacquerer who lived from 1807 to 1891

Zhuanshu (also zhuan shu): a seal-style of Chinese calligraphy

About the Authors

Mark F. Moran is an antiques dealer and author who resides in Rochester, Minnesota. He has written extensively on American folk art, paintings, etchings, clocks, metalwares, sterling silver, and other antique collecting areas for *Antique Trader*, *Maine Antique Digest*, and *Antique Review*. He has worked in dealer development and vetting for antiques shows in the Midwest, and has reported on antique auctions from sales across the country. He has also lectured on folk art and conducted appraisals.

With over a 30-year career in daily newspapers, he has worked as a reporter, columnist, editor, and photographer. He has twice been honored with Associated Press Page One Awards.

Susan Andacht is the program coordinator of the Art and Antiques Institute at C.W. Post Campus/ Long Island University, Brookville, NY, She is a faculty member of both the Art and Antiques Institute and the Appraisal Studies Programs at George Washington University, Washington, D.C. Andacht is a former faculty member of the Appraisal Studies Program at Yeshiva University, New York City.

Her articles have been published in *Orientalia Journal*, *Antique Trader Weekly*, the *Ukyio-e Society Newsletter*, *Interior Design Magazine*, *Andon*, *Arts of Asia*, and the New England Appraisers Association Newsletter, among others.

An experienced lecturer at the university and professional levels, Andacht serves as a consultant for corporations, insurance companies and individuals, as well as other appraisers (both generalists and specialists). A member of the Long Island Antiques Professional Antiques Dealers Association, Andacht has performed curatorial duties in her specialty for three major museum exhibits and has written a number of books.

Index